The Magnolia Plantation

Experience Victorian Romance With Southern Hospitality

CIRCA 1885

Joe and Cindy Montalto, Proprietors

Gainesville, Florida

The information contained in this publication is prepared as accurately as possible from material provided by the innkeepers for the most part and is subject to change. Therefore, it is necessary to contact each property listed to confirm all of the information before making a reservation. All references to ratings or approvals of the properties by any agency is based upon information provided by the innkeeper and is not guaranteed by the author and publisher.

The responsibility for making a reservation rests solely between the guest or agent and innkeeper in terms agreeable to all parties regardless of any and all representations made in this publication. We declare and disclaim any liability for errors or omissions and our liability for any loss or damage to any party that might occur through the use of this publication.

Ninth Edition, 1995
Published 1987, 1988, 1989, 1990, 1991, 1992, 1993, 1994

Published by:

BED & BREAKFAST Guest Houses & Inns of America®

PO Box 38929 Memphis Tennessee   38183-0929   Tel 901-755-9613

ISSN: 1056-8069   ISBN: 0-9629885-1-0 9.95   SAN: 279-4436

$9.95

New England Edition

CONTENTS

PREFACE

Bed & Breakfast accommodations are thriving in the United States more than ever .... as American travelers discover the excitement of European-style Bed and Breakfast, Guest Houses and Country Inns, right in their own backyard!! Long the **accommodation of choice** for Europeans, Bed and Breakfast accommodations are experiencing a phenomenal growth in the United States - beginning in the late 1980's and continuing today - offering travelers exciting lodging choices at every stop.

If you're unfamiliar with Bed & Breakfast accommodations - you have a whole new experience awaiting you by selecting a different inn for each trip if you like, whether your trip is business, a family vacation or a nearby weekend get-away or for a *special occasion!* B&Bs are smaller and more intimate compared to commercial hotels. Guests feel like they're staying at a friend's or relative's home -rather than a motel. The typical property listed in this publication has five to seven guest rooms which means you truly become a family member - from the moment you arrive until you return. You'll meet all of the guests and the innkeepers, who jealously see to your every comfort. After-all, they are truly people who enjoy meeting each guest, swapping tales, exchanging stories and trading ideas. They are well-travelled too and understand the meaning of comfort while traveling. So a Bed & Breakfast is not just the warmth of a cozy evening fireplace in a friend's home or a complimentary sherry upon arrival ... but a feel of being home at every stop during your trip.

And what a variety of homes, castles, tepees and entire private islands from which to choose!! Bed and Breakfasts are generally a home with one or two "extra" bedrooms located anywhere from traditional suburban neighborhoods to rural farms. Guest Houses would be similar to "tourist homes" offering five to nine guest rooms and generally more extensively furnished and decorated, including more guest amenities, while a Country Inn, for our purposes, provides more personalized service in an intimate setting with fewer than thirty guest rooms. Just as each family is unique - so it each Bed and Breakfast - which is looked after with the loving attention of the owner/innkeeper - insuring each guest feels at home. Each innkeepers' interests are reflected in their Bed & Breakfast and you might meet a former olympic skier, politician, artists, dancers, sailing enthusiasts, antique buffs who will lead you to the "best buys", authors, writers, well-known photographers, museum curators ... along with doctors, lawyers and indian chiefs .... and even Clint Eastwood, if he's in, at his *Eastwood Ranch* in Carmel California is a Bed & Breakfast.

Each Bed & Breakfast represents a new adventure - as close as around the corner. Travelers choose from an endless array of accommodations - allowing your imagination to run rampant. Spend a night in a tepee on a true Indian Reservation (offering a honeymoon special), all of San Francisco's night lights are outside your windows in a Francisco Bay lighthouse or choose the bedroom where celebrities such as Clark Gable and Carole Lombard and Jack and Jackie Kennedy honeymooned. Choose a luxury 100 foot yacht for a night or your own island off the Georgia Coast! For the adventuresome, a frontier cabin in Alaska without running water, phone or electricity - to the world's only underwater lodge off Key West Florida offering four guest rooms twenty fathoms below the sea - are ready for guests! Today you can stay in the family estates of famous families such as Bigelow, Palmolive, Stanley (Stanley steamer auto fame), William Wrigley and Barnum of the famous Barnum and Bailey Circus fame. If you're looking for a romantic oceanfront with candlelight dining - there are many along with TV and movie sets of leading programs and/or movies such as *On Golden Pond* (Holderness, New Hampshire listings), Alan Alda's *Four Seasons* (Edson Hill Manor, Stowe, Vermont), *Matlock* (Tranquil House, Maneto, North Carolina), *Knotts Landing* (The Cotten House in California) - or a great adventure for an exciting family vacation, new adventures await within this ninth edition.

The Mansions (Barbara Streisand's a frequent guest) in San Francisco offers it's own certified ghost, a night of magic before dining and a five million dollar art and sculpture collection - to an Inn in Santa Fe, New Mexico called *Lightening Fields*, where guests spend the night in the center of a desert field surrounded with steel rods, designed to attract lightening strikes - providing an enlightening experience! For **"kids of all ages"**, *The Hugging Bear Bed & Breakfast* offers over four thousand teddy bears throughout the Inn. You'll find over 10,000 choices and innkeepers anxious to greet you .... providing years of enjoyable memories and adventures to share with friends.

One of the B's in Bed and Breakfast represents the guest rooms where innkeepers make every effort to see to your comfort. Canopy beds abound, four posters, brilliant brass, wicker and gorgeous antique heirlooms appear almost everywhere - while fitted with a handmade quilt or down comforters. In addition, many inns offer jacuzzi, evening turn-down service, complimentary evening sherry at bedside and a late night chocolate upon your pillow.

The second B in Bed and Breakfast is important to travelers too - and that represents breakfast, normally included in your room rate. Breakfast ranges from a continental or light breakfast to a sumptuous gourmet, four course meal featuring local specialties of grits in the South, fresh-picked strawberries or blue berries for your cereal or maple syrup you made the day before. You can frequently choose to have "breakfast in bed", before a winter's fire or on the veranda in spring and summer - often overlooking a flowering patio garden or a lush rolling meadow. And if you find a particular recipe to your liking -- your innkeeper will be thrilled to share it.

You'll find **best-selling cookbook author** Julee Rosso-Miller (*The Silver Palate, The Silver Palate Good Times Cookbook*) selecting and perhaps preparing your breakfast at the *Wickwood Country Inn* in Saugatuck, Michigan while in the beautiful Northwestern Montana mountains at *Huckleberry Hanna's Montana Bed and Breakfast*, you'll find famous cookbook author Deanna Hansen-Doying busily preparing breakfast in between her next book for her *Huckleberry Hanna Series* of cookbooks.

Why are Bed and Breakfast's increasing in popularity? Because they are economical - an important factor to every traveler today. As commercial hotel room rates soar, travelers are learning B&Bs offer the **best value today**. Business travelers save the most because Bed and Breakfast's offer weekday discounts -- just when business travelers need the savings. Weekday rates at B&B's offer the best values - many offering up to 50% discounts!

Who should consider a Bed and Breakfast for their lodging needs? Easily everyone who travels! More than fifty percent of all Europeans stay only at Bed and Breakfasts for a good reason. Business travelers tired of the **same old hotel room** and suffering with the *same old hotel blues*. Even the *Wall Street Journal* in 1989 reported the trend of business travelers changing to Bed and Breakfast accommodations. Family vacationers can choose a waterfront, mountain top wooded log cabin or a farm with all the animals where their children can feed the chickens, geese and other animals while gathering fresh eggs for their breakfast; women traveling alone love the security and comfort B&Bs offer; honeymooners, family relocations, retirees, antique collectors, the parents of college-bound children .... just about every traveler will find a lodging to meet their needs in this directory.

Once you've decided to try a Bed and Breakfast ... you face the most difficult portion of the trip ... that of finding "just the right one". Since B&Bs have small advertising budgets they are not easily found and frequently their names are *highly guarded secrets passed on only to the best of acquaintances.* Therefore, guidebooks have developed into the leading source of information on B&Bs and probably offer the only means of maintaining your sanity during your search. Your choice of guidebooks is not easy since there are literally thousands of choices. Since you chose this directory, we'll be the first to let you know you have the most comprehensive, complete and accurate directory available. We can easily say that because our primary subscribers for years have been travel agents. Published since 1987, our directory has earned the reputation as the **most complete reference available"** from subscribers and book reviewers alike. This means you have the largest reference available of Bed and Breakfasts - with over 10,000 listings in the Index Section, compared to other national guides with two hundred to a several thousands listings. Secondly, you will find more extensive descriptions .... **so you'll know all of the details even before contacting the Bed and Breakfast** to make your reservation. Phone numbers change, fax numbers are added, 800 numbers become available --- continuous changes you need to have to make finding *just the right Bed & Breakfast* and enjoyable part of your trip ... or job if you're a travel agent.

This ninth edition includes changes to help you enjoy your Bed and Breakfast experiences even more. More photographs and line drawings are included. This edition introduces a new feature - regional groupings rather than one large national listing. We've divided the United States into four regions, with Canada as the fifth region making it easier to use. This edition introduces innkeepers to readers. Innkeepers across the USA have contributed articles about their town, state or area which appear at the beginning of each region. Their articles offer ideas, suggestions and points of interest. Just as each Bed and Breakfast and town is different .... you'll find thousands innkeepers with a common thread of hospitality, goodwill and a sincere interest in welcoming travelers to their communities. We know you will enjoy their articles and we hope you will stop and personally meet them.

One comment pertaining to a travel industry issue regarding descriptive information on properties appearing in Bed and Breakfast publications such as this one. Member-innkeepers prepare their own listing descriptions for a number of reasons. Due to the large number of properties, it's impossible to visit and review each property and still publish a national publication.

Secondly, innkeepers know their Bed & Breakfast, nearby activities and sights and their town better than anyone else - therefore, they have the best knowledge. How objective are they going to be? We have found them to be very objective - after all, unlike a reviewer or rating organization, they face each guest upon arrival and have to justify their glowing description if it is not deserved. Even professional travel writers and reviewers are subject to over and/or under statement - but they depart the following day and don't face arriving guests to justify a review to the guest. This publication is a directory and not a guidebook (we do not review Bed & Breakfasts) containing a listing of accommodations following traditional European Bed & Breakfast style of properties across the United States and Canada. This information, we feel, benefits travelers by learning about the thousands of wonderful and beautiful Bed & Breakfasts overlooked by many guidebooks.

Thank you for using this directory as a reference source for your many new adventures, acquaintances and friendships that develop during your travels. If you are pleased with the book, we would appreciate your telling friends and innkeepers you visit about us. It helps innkeepers to know which books are used by guests and travel agents. More importantly, it helps you too because more Bed and Breakfasts will include descriptions in future editions providing a wider choice of lodgings for your next trip. If you know of a Bed & Breakfast, Guest House or Country Inn that is not included in our directory, we would appreciate your letting us know about them or letting the innkeeper know. Perhaps you'll find your favorite Bed and Breakfast listed in future editions, allowing other travelers to experience the same enjoyment they'll treasure in the years to come and share with others.

INTRODUCTION

The purpose of this directory is to provide travelers with the most comprehensive, single reference source of current, accurate and complete information on Bed and Breakfast-type of accommodations throughout the United States and Canada and to promote Bed and Breakfast accommodations to the traveling public. The properties listed meet our criteria of the traditional European B&Bs, limited to a maximum of thirty guest rooms; are host-owner operated in the daily operation of the inn and provide period, unique, antique, unusual or non-commercial decor and furnishings. This directory had been prepared exclusively for travel agents for the past eight years and the content has been designed to provide complete booking information about the properties listed before calling. Because this material has been prepared for professionals, important information is included you won't find in other books; information such as *toll-free 800 numbers, discount periods, money-saving packages, airport distances* and much more. Published annually, the information is accurate and complete compared to books published every two years.

Making a reservation at a Bed and Breakfast is the same as any hotel, the difference is that **each property is different**, so a full understanding and description of the property is essential for a pleasant and enjoyable trip. Reputable innkeepers are just as interested as the guest in making sure there aren't any misunderstandings and that the Bed and Breakfast will exceed the guests' expectations. For the sake of clarity and a common understanding, the terms utilized are listed below.

BED & BREAKFAST RESERVATIONS

It just takes a few minutes to find *"just the right B&B"* anywhere in the USA by following a few steps. Since each Bed & Breakfast is unique, a complete description and understanding of the property is essential and time permitting when you call to make your reservation, we suggest your requesting the innkeeper to provide you with brochures for you to review before arriving. The brochures are beautifully prepared and the innkeepers are pleased to send one to you.

1. First, look into the **Index Section** which is an alphabetical list by state, city and Bed & Breakfast names.

2. If the B&B's name is **bolded**, look in the **Descriptive Section** for the Bed & Breakfast's name. This section is arranged alphabetically by state, city and Bed & Breakfast name.

3. Call the Bed and Breakfast you select to confirm the information listed and to make your reservation. Request that a brochure and reservation confirmation is sent to you.

4. You will find some listings without descriptions and the notation *"Refer to the same listing name under_____ city for a complete description."* **Cross-City Listings** indicate B&Bs in nearby towns.

One last note about reservations .... ***MAKE THEM EARLY!*** You've taken an excellent step in preparing yourself for your Bed and Breakfast adventures by purchasing a directory. Don't miss an opportunity to stay at your favorite Bed and Breakfast or in a favorite room. Innkeepers are booked weeks, months and even years in advance for traditional holidays, weekends, vacation periods. Weekday periods are less hectic and you'll find better availability on shorter notice. But ... that may not be the case. Since you've taken the first step in planning your trip - don't forget to call early.

INTERPRETING THE DESCRIPTIVE LISTINGS

RES TIME This is the best time to call for making a reservation. When a time is not listed you can't go wrong calling between 8am and 8 pm.

SEASONAL This indicates any period when the B&B is closed to guests. If NO is listed, this usually means guests are accepted year round. Some listings indicate RATES VARY which means the room rates vary by season and it is necessary to obtain more information from the innkeeper regarding their seasonal period rates.

ROOMS The number of private and shared bath guest rooms are listed here. Listed beneath each category are the Single and Double occupancy rates for that room type. Usually a range of rates are quoted and the type of room and the appropriate rate needs to be confirmed with the innkeeper. The room rate will depend upon the amenities, size, decor and location of the room. So if you're looking for a pool side or ocean front room with a canopy bed, jacuzzi and fire place and so forth, the room will be priced accordingly.

PHONES/FAX Phone numbers are listed (including 800's when available) along with fax numbers

PAYMENT *Cash, check, travelers check* and specific credit cards accepted; confirm what credit cards are accepted since this frequently changes.

MEALS The second "B" in B&B is breakfast which is usually (but not always) included in your room rate. Information concerning breakfast is included in the descriptive information. This information should be confirmed as well since innkeepers change the type and style of breakfast served. The definition of the various meals are understood to be:

Breakfast

★ Continental: Juice, hot beverage and pastry or breads
★ Continental Plus: The same as above but also includes choices of several breads, pastries and cold cereals

★ Full: The same as above plus eggs, meats, pancakes, waffles or other main entree
★ Gourmet: An unusual or different means of preparing a food dish, often a specialty of the innkeeper

EP   European Plan indicates **NO** meals are included
MAP Modified European Plan includes breakfast and dinner
AP   American Plan includes all three meals
FAM Family Style Dining Service pertains to how meals are served

DESCRIPTIVE SECTION

The listings in this section have been prepared by the innkeeper to describe their property, furnishings, decor, proximity to points of interest, local activities, their background, complimentary breakfast description and is intended to provide you with a flavor of the Bed and Breakfast. All B&Bs are not museums filled with antique furnishings and not all travelers are interested in staying in museums. Hopefully the descriptions will convey the uniqueness of each Bed & Breakfast.

*/** Notation At The B&B's Name
This notation is published for professional travel agents and indicates the innkeepers are agreeable to paying a 10% commission fee for their reservation services. This amount is not added to the guest's rate but rather paid by innkeeper. A single * indicates the property normally pays commissions; a double ** indicates we guarantee the commission payment to the travel agent. To be eligible to participate in the guaranteed commission program, travel agents must purchase their publications directly from the publisher.

Permitted Children, pets, smoking and drinking have been listed **when they are permitted** by your hosts. When one of the categories is not listed, it means the hosts do not permit that activity. Staying at a Bed and Breakfast is like staying at a friend's home .... so you should always ask the host if they permit the particular activity if you're not sure.

Reservations Check the reservation requirements before calling and confirm them with the innkeeper when calling because they are subject to change. Ask for a **written confirmation from the innkeeper** to eliminate possible errors.

Airport The name and distance/s to nearby airports is listed for guest's convenience.

Packages Types of packages available are listed when available and provide excellent savings for travelers.

Discounts Since each Bed and Breakfast has their own discount policies, check when calling.

Brochure Each innkeeper has brochures, write-ups, news articles, maps and other material they gladly provide guests. Request this information when making your reservation.

New England

New England

Spring Peaceful fields with a haze of dew in early morning and a deer or two standing still; Tiny buds emerging on branches covering sleepy valleys with pale greens; Fresh mountain air and flowers everywhere; hiking through woods and wondering at the breathtaking views from the mountain tops.

Summer Cool mornings and warm afternoons; white, sandy beaches; babbling brooks; blue lakes; majestic mountains; art shows; antiques, auctions; summer country fairs; swimming, boating, fishing.

Fall Glorious colors everywhere as the green leaves turn to gold, red, yellow; pumpkins, hot cider, fall festivals; biking along winding roads and discovering the beauty and simplicity of a timeless world.

Winter Blankets of snow covering sleeping villages, still lakes, silent brooks, shining mountains; alpine and cross-country skiing, snowmobiling, sleigh rides, ice skating; warm fireplaces at day end.

- Marie A Kauk, Innkeeper **Hilltop Acres** Wentworth New Hampshire

Marblehead Massachusetts

Marblehead, an historic sea coast village on Boston's North Shore, has much to offer. Explore it's patriotic past as reflected in period architecture and historic sites. Enjoy the natural beauty of a rocky coastline studded with beaches and parks overlooking picturesque Marblehead harbor. Watch lobstermen pulling their traps, elegant yachts setting sail and small boats rounding race buoys. Walk charming old footpaths past lovely homes and gardens of traditional New England character. Browse the antique shops, art galleries and boutiques which offer treasures special to Marblehead. Relax over a bowl of New England clam chowder, feast on a boiled lobster or enjoy a gourmet dinner at local restaurants, offering both casual and elegant dining.

At *Abbot Hall*, the famous painting *The Spirit of '76* can be viewed. The *Jeremiah Lee Mansion* is an example of Georgian architecture with period furnishings. The *King Hooper Mansion*, an early 18th century mansion with slave quarters and a ballroom, now serves as an art gallery sponsored by the Marblehead Arts Association. Summer concerts are held at *Crocker Park*, overlooking the harbor and Marblehead Neck. *Fort Sewall* was built in the 1600's to ward-off pirates. Experience the unique character of Marblehead by staying in one of its many charming Bed and Breakfast homes.

Susan finds time to handle all the chores of operating her bed and breakfast while maintaining a schedule of activities ranging from dressmaking to competitive swimming - and everything in between. She admits to being "***a domestic person. I love my home and everything that goes along with making it a welcoming place to be, including baking, decorating and arranging flowers***". Rising early to greet guests and prepare breakfast isn't a problem - because she will have already been jogging or biking. Most days she can be found in a local pool training for Master's swim meets. She is a top-ten ranked national swimmer in over eight events and holds many New England records. Today, Susan is enthusiastic about her home, Marblehead and welcoming new guests to experience the adventure of visiting New England.

- Susan Livingston, Innkeeper ***Harborside House***
  Marblehead, Massachusetts

Boothbay Harbor Maine

The rock-bound coast of Maine and Boothbay Harbor is a popular destination for visitors yearning for fresh sea air, scenic lighthouses, lobsters and boating adventures. Popular since the turn-of-the-century, the Boothbay Region combines the economies of a working fishing village and a resort area.

In Spring, Summer and Fall, boat trips on big boats, little boats, sail boats, fishing boats - or your own rented boat, will transport you to offshore islands for hiking and picnicking or seal and puffin watching.

Others will cruise along the rocky and spruce-treed coast to see light-houses and off-shore for deep sea fishing. Golf, swimming, tennis, bird-watching, art galleries, antique shops, maritime museums add to the many activities in the Region. Within an hour's drive are white sandy beaches and shopping outlets including the famous LL Bean. In summer, yachts and windjammers visit the Harbor adding color and excitement for boat watchers. In winter, a quieter atmosphere prevails. The local country club is a great place to cross country ski, and West Harbor Pond finds ice skaters enjoying the crisp, clean air.

Boothbay Harbor is a working lobster fishing village. The lobstermen bring in the daily catch to local wharves where as you watch the sun set over the Harbor, you can relish the tender morsels dipped in butter. These activities can be seen from the shore near the Fisherman's Memorial or at many of the accommodations which are located right on the shore. You'll love Boothbay Harbor.

- Diane Campbell, Innkeeper **Anchor Watch Bed & Breakfast**
  Boothbay Harbor Maine

Newport Rhode Island

To the visitor Newport offers the perspective of an island, the excite-ment of a port, world-class, wealth, and a blend of contemporary and past delights. The town represents two eras in American history - downtown reflects the original 17th Century community and the man-sions on Bellevue Avenue show the extravagance and spectacle of the Gilded Age.

Newport has more Colonial-era buildings than any city in the United States. Washington Square was the center of Colonial Newport. One end of the square is the Brick Market (1762), currently being restored as a museum. The other end of the square is the Old Colony House (1739). It was from the balcony of the Colony House that Rhode Is-land issued its own Declaration of Independence on May 4, 1776. Next to the Colony House on Broadway is the Wanton-Lyman-Hazard House, Newport's oldest house built in the 1690's. About a block up the hill from there is the Touro Synagogue built in 1759 and the old-est continuously operating synagogue in the U.S. Over on the Point, another historic area, is the Hunter House which served as headquar-ters for the French naval forces in 1780. Visit The Hunter House to see it priceless collection of Townsend-Goddard furniture.

Strung along Bellevue Avenue are the famous Gilded Age Mansions.

These are the magnificent summer *cottages* built by people like the Vanderbilts and the Astors. When visiting the Mansions, it is worth strolling along the Cliff Walk, a 3-1/2 mile footpath, which runs behind the Mansions and overlooks the ocean. Ocean Drive, a 10 mile drive around the south end of the island, has beautiful picturesque ocean. Stop for a picnic at Brenton Point Park.

If all this sightseeing has tired you out, you can take a relaxing boat ride on the Bay or visit one of several sandy beaches. Newport has something to offer everyone regardless of age, interests or time of year.

- Sam & Rita Roger, Innkeepers **The Melville House**
Newport Rhode Island

Sandwich, Massachusetts

The town of Sandwich was founded in 1637, the first town on Cape Cod, and one of the oldest communities in America. It is picturesquely situated along historic Route 6A, the King's Highway, on the north shore of Cape Cod, at the eastern end of Cape Cod Canal.

A tour of the town might begin at the Village green and Town Hall Square, where you will find the Sandwich Glass Museum, First Church, with its *"Christopher Wren"* steeple, the Dexter Grist Mill, Thornton Burgess Museum, Hoxie House, oldest house on the Cape, Town Hall, itself of historical interest, and, a block away, the Doll Museum.

Heritage Plantation, nearby, maintains more than a thousand varieties of trees, shrubs and flowers on the grounds where Charles Dexter developed the internationally recognized Dexter rhododendrums. The plantation is also known for its three museums of Americana. The Antique Car Museum, in a Shaker round barn replica, houses forty antique and classic cars, including a stunning 1930 Dusenburg Tourester, once owned by Gary Cooper, and President William Howard Taft's White Steamer, the first official White House automobile. The Art and Military Museums display vintage treasures, including a restored and running 1912 carousel. The beach and Cape Cod Canal are within a mile of the Village.

- Elaine Dickson, Innkeeper, **Capt. Ezra Nye House Bed &
Breakfast,** Sandwich, Massachusetts

Connecticut

---

*Eastover Farm B&B   **Bethlehem CT**
Mr Mrs Erik Hawvermale   Rt 132 Guilds Hollow Rd 06751
203-266-5740

Rates:	**Pvt Bath** 7	**Shared Bath** 4	**Payment Terms:**
Single	$ 70.00	$ 155.00	Check
Double	$ 80.00	$ 186.00	MC/V

Gracious colonial c1773 on 70 acres of manicured lawns with farm animals, close to White Flower Farm, nature preserves, and plenty of New England hospitality from these lovely hosts. Continental breakfast included. **BROCHURE:** Yes **PERMITTED:** Children **SEASONAL:** No [C11ACCT-921]

---

*Jared Cone House   **Bolton CT**
Mrs Cinde Smith   25 Hebron Rd 06043
203-643-8538

Rates:	**Pvt Bath** 3	**Payment Terms:**
Single	$ 55.00	Check
Double	$ 65.00	

Right off the Village Green is this colonial residence c1790's with spectacular views, fireplaces, and plenty of hospitality for relaxing in the traditional New England style. Full breakfast included in rate. Close to plenty of fine shopping, antiquing, fine dining, and tennis, golf, and swimming. **RESERVATIONS:** One night's deposit required at res time, refund if canceled 10 days prior to arrival date **SEASONAL:** No **BROCHURE:** Yes **PERMITTED:** Children, smoking [C03ACCT-922]

---

*Sanford Pond House   **Bridgewater CT**
George & Charlotte Pond   PO Box 306 06752
203-355-4677   **Res Times** 8am-5pm

Rates:	**Pvt Bath** 5	**Payment Terms:**

Single	$ 80-100.00	Check
Double	$ 80-100.00	

A Litchfield County setting for this elegant 1845 Greek Revival mansion completely restored, unique room decor in that includes king or queen size canopy beds, fireplace, veranda and sitting areas. Guest rooms overlook the lovely formal gardens and fountains. Continental plus breakfast included. Close to all attractions, dining and local wineries. **RESERVATIONS:** Deposit to hold room, 7 day cancel policy **SEASONAL:** No **BROCHURE:** Yes **PERMITTED:** Children 12-up [C11ACCT-923]

Four Roses Guest Inn	**Bristol CT**
Wilma Flint	34 Summer Place 06011
203-572-0211	

Rates:	**Pvt Bath** 6	**Payment Terms:**
Single	$ 65.00	Check
Double	$ 85.00	MC/V

Perfect country setting for this New England farmhouse c1755 with original stone walls, fireplaces in every room, wood floors, with Early American furnishings. Your chance to really taste the frontier life! Wonderful homemade breakfast with original recipes handed down through generations of Americans. Close to outdoor activities including boating, canoeing, fishing, golf on championship courses, and all winter sports within 30 minutes. Full breakfast included. **RESERVATIONS:** 50% deposit required in 5 days, 10 day cancellation notice for refund **SEASONAL:** No **BROCHURE:** Yes **PERMITTED:** Children, limited pets, smoking [G02BFCT-6585]

---

*Riverwind Inn	**Deep River CT**
Barbara Barlow	209 Main St 06417
203-526-2014	**Res Times** 8am-8pm

Rates:	**Pvt Bath** 4	**Payment Terms:**
Single	$ 80.00	Check
Double	$ 90.00	MC/V

Delightful setting for a restored 1850 Inn furnished with antique pieces, family heirlooms, and handicrafts in country theme.

Fireplace in dining room, full New England breakfast includes Smithfield ham and other specialties of the hostess. **SEASONAL:** No **BROCHURE:** Yes **PERMITTED:** Smoking, social drinking [C11ACCT-929]

Homestead Inn	Greenwich CT
*Lessie Davison/Nancy Smith	420 Field Point Rd 06830
203-869-7500	**Res Times** 8am-10pm
	Fax 203-869-7500
Rates: **Pvt Bath** 23	**Payment Terms:**
Single $ 90.00	AE/DC/MC/V
Double $ 105-165.00	

Nestled on three acres of ancient maples and oaks is this unique c1799 homestead Colonial and Victorian with cupola and wrap-around porch features, just a stroll from Long Island Sound waters. Completely restored and featured in articles in *Fortune*, 10/81, *Colonial Homes* 10/86 and *Interior Design* 4/80, are three charming buildings offering decor that includes antiques mostly with whimsical flair!! Nothing has been overlooked, eg., beds have two pillows, one hard and one soft. Award-winning French dining on the premises by Chef Jacques Thiebeult offering extraordinary soups, diverse entrees, and an array of pure French Delight!! Close to Island Beach for short boat trips or antique shopping, guests are sure to find many points of interest. Inn is available for weddings and includes a honeymoon suite! **RESERVATIONS:** Credit card to hold room, 24 hour cancellation for full refund **SEASONAL:** No **PERMITTED:** Limited children, smoking, drinking. Continental breakfast included. **CONFERENCES:** Perfect setting for relaxing and exquisite business and social meetings **LANGUAGES:** German, French, Spanish [A05ACCT-936]

Shore Inne		Groton Long Point CT
Helen Ellison		52 E Shore Rd 06340
203-536-1180		**Res Time** 8am-8pm
Rates: **Pvt Bath** 3	**Shared Bath** 4	**Payment Terms:**
Single $ 58.00	$ 52.00	Check
Double $ 62.00	$ 57.00	MC/V

Spectacular view of the coastal waters from this gracious Inn located on the water's edge. Relax all day long by visiting the local attractions, Mystic Seaport (3 miles), Marine Life Aquarium, Fort

Griswold, or stroll along the beaches, fish, play tennis, golf. Or you can relax in the TV room, library, or sun room. Continental breakfast included. **SEASONAL:** Open: Apr-Oct **BROCHURE:** Yes **PERMITTED:** Children, smoking, drinking [C11ACCT-939]

Old Mill Inn   Hartford CT
Phyllis & Ralph Lumb
203-763-1473   **Res Times** 7am-10pm

Rates:	**Pvt Bath** 3	**Shared Bath** 2	**Payment Terms:**
Single	$ 60.00	$ 50.00	Check
Double	$ 60.00	$ 50.00	

Refer to same listing name under Somersville CT from complete description. [M01DPCT-6549]

Tollgate Hill Inn   Litchfield CT
Frederick Zivic   Rt 202 & Tollgate Rd 06759
203-482-6116   **Res Times** 8am-7pm
       Fax 203-567-8379

Rates:	**Pvt Bath** 10	**Payment Terms:**
Single	$ 85-95.00	Check
Double	$ 85-95.00	

Listed on the *National Register of Historic Places* is this completely restored Inn, formerly the Capt Bull Tavern, c1745. Relive 1700's with pine paneled walls, dutch door fireplace, and a former historic schoolhouse next door that contains four of the guest rooms. Continental breakfast included. **RESERVATIONS:** Deposit requested at reservation time with refund if canceled & prior notice given **SEASONAL:** No **BROCHURE:** Yes **PERMITTED:** Children, pets, drinking [C11ACCT-949]

Tucker Hill Inn   Middlebury CT
Susan Cebelenski   96 Tucker Hill Rd 06762
203-758-8334

Rates:	**Pvt Bath** 2	**Shared Bath** 2	**Payment Terms:**
Single	$ 75.00	$ 65.00	Check
Double			

Just off the village green is this classic center hall colonial serving guests for over forty years as a restaurant and guest house. Guest rooms are individually furnished in antiques including comfortable wing back chairs and balconies in some rooms. Full breakfast is served and includes a specialty of the hostess. Close to antiques, museums, and all outdoor sporting activities. **SEASONAL:** No **BROCHURE:** Yes **PERMITTED:** Limited children, smoking and drinking. **CONFERENCES:** Yes, up to 10 persons with facilities for dining with gourmet entrees [C11ACCT-952]

Harbour Inne & Cottage	**Mystic CT**
Charles Lecoures, Jr	15 Edgemont St 06335
203-572-9253	**Res Times** 24 Hrs

Rates:	**Pvt Bath** 7	**Payment Terms:**
Single	$ 65-105.00	Check
Double	$ 65-200.00	Tylers Ck

In the heart of historic Mystic, *Harbour Inne & Cottage* is just two blocks from the railroad depot and offers completely remodeled facilities as the very last home on the left of Edgemont Street. Guests are within an easy walk to shops, restaurants and the Mystic Seaport Marine Museum. A cottage and four separate rooms are finished in cedar, offering a comfortable rustic feeling. There are double beds and TV's in each room, and a dining area and kitchen where guests prepare their own breakfast. The Inne overlooks water and offers slips for people to motor in with their boats. Charlie, your host, has traveled the world and enjoys being close to the water and has several boats - to enjoy his favorite sport - fishing. Amenities include beautiful views of Mystic River and Fishers Island Sound, harbor front picnic tables, canoes and rowing boats available for fishing, cable TV and air conditioning. **RESERVATIONS:** Payment in full before arrival, 2 week cancel policy for refund less $25.00 service fee **SEASONAL:** Rates vary **PERMITTED:** Children, pets, drinking, smoking **BROCHURE:** Yes **AIRPORT:** Groton/New London-20 mi **DISCOUNTS:** Off-season [R08GPCT2-956]

Red Brook Inn	**Mystic CT**
Ruth Keyes	PO Box 237 06372
203-572-0349	**Res Times** 9am-11pm

Rates:	Pvt Bath 10	Payment Terms:
Single	$ 85-169.00	Check
Double	$ 85-169.00	MC/V

Relive the days of early Americana in an authentic c1740 tavern and stage coach stop which has been totally rebuilt and furnished with authentic antiques. Your host/owner, in love with colonial history all of her life, saved the Haley Tavern by disassembling and rebuilding every stone and timber when the Connecticut Dept of Transportation required land for a highway project. After year's of painstaking restoration, Ruth shares her beautifully appointed Inn with guests today. Each guest room is a showcase of antiques with color coordinated accessories and working fireplaces in some rooms. Ruth's extensive and fascinating collection of hand-blown glass, pewter & brass and old lamps can be enjoyed by everyone. A long harvest table in the Keeping Room offers guests a family style full breakfast featuring baked eggs, sourdough or apple pancakes or Ruth's favorite, walnut waffles all served with fresh fruit, juice, sausage links and fresh brewed coffee or tea. Cooler months bring a crackling fire in the huge open hearth fireplace. American history buffs will want to visit the many museums (Mystic Seaport Museum) Old Mystic Village and sights at nearby Newport, Rhode Island or Boston as a day trip. **AIRPORT:** Warwick RI-45 mins **PACKAGES:** *Thanksgiving, Christmas Colonial Dinner* weekends **RESERVATIONS:** Full payment in advance, one week cancellation policy for refund, check-in noon-8 pm **SEASONAL:** No **BROCHURE:** Yes **PERMITTED:** Children, limited drinking **CONFERENCES:** Yes, groups to 25 persons [Z05FPCT2-980]

Maples Inn			New Canaan CT

Joan Louleau
203-966-2927

179 Oenoke Ridge 06840
Res Times 8am-8pm

Rates:	Pvt Bath 22	Shared Bath 2	Payment Terms:
Single	$ 90.00-up	$ 80-Up	Check
Double	$ 100.00-up	$ 90-Up	AE/MC/V

New England setting for this Country Inn with turn-of-the-century charm including country antique furnishings and family heirlooms and all modern amenities. Convenient location with Nature Center and town square within walking distances. Continental breakfast included. **SEASONAL:** No **BROCHURE:** Yes **PERMITTED:** Children 10-up, smoking, drinking [C11ACCT960]

Greenwoods Gate   Norfolk CT

Ms Deanne P Raymond   105 Greenwoods Rd East 06058
203-542-5439

Rates:	Pvt Bath 3		Payment Terms:
Single	$ 68-80.00		Check
Double	$ 130-160.00		MC/V

Exciting 1797 colonial residence offering warmth and country elegance by a hostess who offers full hospitality to all guests. Guests rooms are furnished in period antiques, with deluxe suites and modern amenities. Homemade breakfasts awaken you while they are being prepared from family recipes. **SEASONAL:** No **BROCHURE:** Yes **PERMITTED:** Limited children, limited smoking [C11ACCT-970]

Manor House   Norfolk CT

Diane & Hank Tremblay   Maple Ave 06058
800-488-5690 203-542-5690

Rates:	Pvt Bath 4	Shared Bath 2	Payment Terms:
Single	$ 75.00	$ 65.00	Check
Double	$ 90-130.00	$ 75-95.00	MC/V

Fantastic baronial mansion c1898 rich in taste and design that still offers guests a glorious retreat on five acres, genuine Victorian antique furnishings fireplaces, many Tiffany & leaded glass windows, private elevator, balconies, & sleigh and carriage rides during the year. Full breakfast might include blueberry pancakes, homemade muffins or biscuits, orange-spiced waffles, or another specialty of the hosts. **SEASONAL:** No **BROCHURE:** Yes **PERMITTED:** Children 12-up, limited smoking, limited drinking **CONFERENCES:** Yes, including evening dining [C11ACCT-971]

Harbor House Inn   Old Greenwich CT

Dolly Stuttig/Dawn Browne   165 Shore Rd 06850
203-637-0145

Rates:	Pvt Bath 17	Shared Bath 6	Payment Terms:
Single	$ 70.00	$ 50.00	Check
Double	$ 85.00	$ 60.00	MC/V

Harbor House Inn - **"Your Home Away From Home".** We are a lovely Bed and Breakfast located in an exclusive area by the water. A short walk to a charming New England town and train. Shops and fine restaurants are close by while the beach is just a ten minute walk. The lobby is filled with "old world charm". A fully equipped kitchen and laundry are available for guests. A continental breakfast is include in your room rate. Antiques - this area is bountiful along with theaters, parks and lovely country roads for exciting New England sightseeing. New York City is just 45 mins away. Daily maid service is provided. **RESERVATIONS:** Credit card or check for 50% of length of stay; 48 hr cancel notice policy for refund **SEASONAL:** No **PERMITTED:** Children, drinking **BROCHURE:** Yes **DISCOUNTS:** Inquire at res time **AIRPORT:** Laguardia NYC-40 mins [R10EPCT2-976]

Old Lyme Inn	Old Lyme CT
Diana Atwood	85 Lyme St 06371
203-434-2600	

Rates:	Pvt Bath 13	Payment Terms:
Single	$ 95.00	Check
Double	$ 130.00	AE/MC/V/DC

Elegant restored empire mansion home to famous impressionist painters and filled with paintings, period antiques, and perfect spot for seeing sights near Mystic, Gillettes Castle, Essex. Continental breakfast included. **SEASONAL:** No **BROCHURE:** Yes **PERMITTED:** Children limited, smoking, and drinking. [C11ACCT-978]

Epenetus Howe House	Ridgefield CT
Diane & John Armato	91 N Salem Rd 06877
203-438-HOWE	**Res Times** 8am-10pm

Rates:	Shared Bath 4	Payment Terms:
Single	$ 65-85.00	Check
Double	$ 75-95.00	MC/V

Step back in time to unwind and relax just 1-1/2 hours from NYC in a charming and carefully preserved 1725 home nestled in a New England countryside. The Historic *Epenetus Howe House* is one of Ridgefield's oldest homes and a rare example of Dutch Hudson River influence in the area. Many original features include wide plank chestnut floors, plastered walls and ceilings, doors, trim, and hardware are all remarkably preserved. You're within walking distance to the charming Main Street lined with fascinating boutiques, quaint antique shops, historic sites and museums. A host of recreational and cultural activities available. Dining is unexcelled with a number of fine four-star restaurants to choose from during your stay. Relaxing is easy here from a cozy fireplace to a heated spa or complimentary bikes for pleasant countryside touring. Continental breakfast is included "in-bed" or in the beautiful dining room. **RESERVATIONS:** One night's deposit or credit card to hold room, cancel notice one week prior to res date for refund, 3:00pm check-in **SEASONAL:** No **BROCHURE:** Yes **PERMITTED:** Children, limited pets, limited drinking, limited smoking [A10APCT-985]

**Old Mill Inn			**Somersville CT**
Ralph & Phyllis Lumb			63 Maple St 06072
203-763-1473			**Res Times** 7am-10pm

Rates:	**Pvt Bath** 3	**Shared Bath** 2	**Payment Terms:**
Single	$ 60.00	$ 50.00	Check
Double	$ 60.00	$ 50.00	

Relax in a gracious old New England home located in a friendly north central Connecticut village setting, where comfort and hospitality are paramount. Twin beds or full double beds in well-appointed, air conditioned rooms. Upstairs sitting room has cable TV, phone and refrigerator. Downstairs living room has a stereo, fireplace and books everywhere. A beautiful dining room with hand-painted walls and a glass wall overlooks a vista of green lawn surrounded by gardens, flowering trees and shrubs. You're convenient to shopping and restaurants, Bradley Intl Airport, Trolley, Air and Indian Museums, golf and other attractions. Breakfast includes juice, fruit, pastries, cereals and hot beverages **RESERVATIONS:** One night's deposit to guarantee, 7 day cancel policy. Check-in 4pm, late check-in with prior arrangement **SEASONAL:** No **BROCHURE:** Yes **PERMITTED:** Children over 5, drinking **CONFERENCES:** Can comfortably accommodate up to 20 persons [Z01DPCT-5905]

Captain Parkers Inn At Quinebaug   **Thompson CT**

David Parker/Cynthia Miller   32 Walker Rd (Quinebaug) 06262
800-707-7303   203-935-5219   **Res Times** 24 Hrs

Rates:	Pvt Bath 4	Shared Bath 2	Payment Terms:
Single	$ 95.00	$ 55.00	Check
Double	$ 95.00	$ 55.00	MC/V

Captain Parker's Inn is located in a quiet, rural neighborhood in the most northeastern corner of Connecticut. Built by Captain Parker, it features beautiful varied hardwoods throughout. Although it is situated about an hour from the ocean, the decor portrays a nautical theme with a Victorian flair and an elegant atmosphere. The Inn lends itself to romantic getaways and small weddings. Each guestroom features a different hardwood flooring and trim and most have a bath ensuite. The more-than-ample common areas include a library with a wood stove, a large foyer with a baby grand piano, a relaxing entertainment room, formal dining room with a cozy fireplace and a hospitable kitchen. The private, manicured acre and a half of grounds can be enjoyed from a long screened-in front porch or from the rear deck with a built-in hot tub. The Captain takes breakfast seriously - starting with flavored coffee, juice, fresh bread and a choice of entrees that includes eggs, omelette, pancakes, hot cereal or a delicious healthy (low-fat) meal. The New England countryside can be enjoyed with the complimentary bikes provided guests who can enjoy the miles of striking green farmland or the sights such as nearby Sturbridge Village, wine-tasting at Mellea Winery, antiquing and the beautiful fall foliage. Activities include hiking, fishing, golf, apple-picking, hayrides, sleigh rides and x-country skiing. Picnic lunches in a basket with beverages and a blanket are available at a reasonable rate. **RESERVATIONS:** 50% deposit to guarantee reservation, 14 day cancel notice for refund **PERMITTED:** Children 13-up, limited smoking **BROCHURE:** Yes **CONFERENCES:** Yes, for groups to twenty **AIRPORT:** TF Green-30 mins **PACKAGES:** *Bicycling, Horseback Riding (trails & lessons), Gourmet Cuisine Weekend* [I08GPCT2-20080]

Captain Stannard House   **Westbrook CT**

138 S Main St 06498
203-399-4634   **Res Times** 8am-8pm

Rates:	**Pvt Bath** 7	**Payment Terms:**
Single	$ 70.00	Check
Double	$ 85.00	AE/MC/V

Lovely seacoast town Inn, complete with New England traditional antique furnishings and family heirlooms dating from 1889 and fully restored. You can relax directly upon the river bank or stroll to the beach nearby. The Inn is close to some of the most interesting attractions in Connecticut. **BROCHURE:** Yes **PERMITTED:** Children, smoking, drinking [C11ACCT-1002]

Captain Parkers Inn At Quinebaug   **Woodstock CT**

David Parker/Cynthia Miller
800-707-7303 203-935-5219   **Res Times** 24 Hrs

Rates:	**Pvt Bath** 4	**Shared Bath** 2	**Payment Terms:**
Single	$ 95.00	$ 55.00	Check
Double	$ 95.00	$ 55.00	MC/V

Refer to the same listing name under Thompson, Connecticut for a complete description. [M08GPCT2]

Ashford
HENRIETTA HOUSE
203-429-0031

Baltic
WINDSWEPT FARM
401-364-6292

Bantam
ROCKWOOD FARM

Bethlehem
*EASTOVER FARM
203-266-5740

Bolton
*JARED CONE
HOUSE
203-643-8538

Bridgewater
*SANFORD POND
HOUSE
203-355-4677

CHIMNEY CREST
MANOR
203-582-4219

FOUR ROSES INN
203-572-0211

Brooklyn
TANNERBROOK
203-774-4822

Chester
CHESTER VILLAGE
203-526-9770

INN AT CHESTER
800-949-STAY

Clinton

CAPTAIN DIBBELL
HOUSE
203-669-1646

Colchester
HAYWARD HOUSE
203-537-5772

Cornwall Bridge
CORNWALL INN &
RESTAURANT
800-786-6884

Cos Cob
HARBOR HOUSE
INN
203-661-5845

Coventry
MAPLE HILL FARM
203-742-0635

MILL BROOK FARM
203-742-5761

Deep River
*RIVERWIND INN
203-526-2014

SELDEN HOUSE
B&B
203-526-9195

Durham
DANIEL MERWIN
HOUSE B&B
203-349-8415

DURHAM B&B
203-349-3513

East Haddam
BISHOPS GATE
203-783-1677

STONECROFT INN
203-873-1754

East Hartford
TOWN HALL INN

East Killingly
HOLLAND HOUSE

Essex
GRISWOLD INN
203-767-1776

Glastonbury
BUTTERNUT FARM
203-633-7197

Greenwich
*HOMESTEAD INN
203-869-7500

STANTON HOUSE
INN
203-869-2110

Groton Long Point
*SHORE INNE
203-536-1180

Hartford
**OLD MILL INN
203-763-1473

Ivoryton
COPPER BEECH
INN
203-767-0330

IVORYTON INN
203-767-0422

Kent
1741 SALTBOX INN
203-927-4376

CONSTITUTION
OAK FARM
203-354-6495

FLANDERS ARMS
203-927-3040

Lakeville
WAKE ROBIN INN
203-435-2515

Ledyard
APPLEWOOD
FARMS
203-536-2022

Litchfield
LITCHFIELD INN
203-567-4503

ON THE GREEN
203-567-9151

***TOLLGATE HILL
INN**
203-482-6116

Madison
DOLLY MADISON
INN
203-245-7377

MADISON BEACH
203-245-1404

STEVENS INN AT
CAFE LAFAYETTE

Manchester
DUCK HARBOR
203-783-3495

Middlebury
*TUCKER HILL INN

203-758-8334

Middletown
BUCKLEYS B&B
203-346-8479

Moodus
FOWLER HOUSE
203-873-8906

Mystic
ADAMS HOUSE
800-321-0433

BRIGADOON
203-536-3033

COMOLLI HOUSE
203-536-8723

**HARBOUR INNE &
COTTAGE**
203-572-9253

INN AT MYSTIC
800-237-2415

RED BROOK INN
203-572-0349

STEAMBOAT INN
203-536-8300

WHALERS INNE
203-536-1506

New Canaan
*MAPLES INN
203-966-2927

ROGER SHERMAN
INN
203-955-4541

New Hartford
HIGHLAND FARM
203-379-6029

New Haven
INN AT CHAPEL
HILL 203-777-1201

QUEEN ANNE &
ANTIQUES
800-347-8818

New Milford
HOMESTEAD INN
203-354-4080

New Preston
BIRCHES INN
203-868-0229

BOULDERS INN
203-868-0541

HOPKINS INN
203-868-7295

INN ON LAKE
WARAMAUG
800-LAKE-INN

Newton
HAWLEY MANOR
INN
203-426-4456

Noank
PALMER INN
203-572-9000

Norfolk
BLACKBERRY
RIVER
203-542-5100

*GREENWOODS GATE
203-542-5439

*MANOR HOUSE
800-488-5690

MOUNTAIN VIEW INN
203-542-5595

WEAVERS HOUSE
203-542-5108

North Stonington
ANTIQUES & ACCOMMODA-
TIONS
203-535-1736

RANDALLS ORDINARY
203-599-4540

Norwalk
SILVERMINE TAVERN
203-847-4558

Norwich
NORWICH INN & SPA
800-892-5692

Old Greenwich
**HARBOR HOUSE
203-637-0145

Old Lyme
BEE & THISTLE INN
203-434-1667

JANSE B&B
203-434-7269

*OLD LYME INN
203-434-2600

Old Mystic
OLD MYSTIC INN B&B
203-572-9422

Old Saybrook
SANDPIPER INN
203-399-7973

Plainfield
FRENCH RENAISSANCE HOUSE
203-564-3277

Pomfret
CLARK COTTAGE AT WINTERGREEN
203-928-5741

COBBSCROFT
203-928-5560

Portland
CROFT
203-342-1856

Putnam
FELSHAW TAVERN
203-982-3467

KINGS INN
203-928-7961

THURBER HOUSE
203-928-6776

Quinebaug
CAPTAIN PARKERS INN AT QUINEBAUG

800-707-7808

Ridgefield
ELMS INN
203-438-2541

**EPENETUS HOWE HOUSE
203-438-HOWE

FARVIEW MANOR
203-438-4753

HORSE SHOE FARM
MARLEY B&B
203-438-9486

STONEHENGE
203-438-6511

WEST LANE INN
203-438-7323

WINDOVER ESTATE
203-438-2594

Riverton
*OLD RIVERTON INN
203-379-8678

Salisbury
RAGAMONT INN
203-435-2372

UNDERMOUNTAIN INN
203-435-0242

WHITE HART INN
203-435-2511

YESTERDAY'S
YANKEE
203-435-9539

Sherman
BARNES HILLS
203-354-4404

Simsburg
SIMSBURY HOUSE
800-TRY-1820

Somersville
**OLD MILL INN
203-763-1473

South Woodstock
INN AT
WOODSTOCK HILL
203-928-0528

Stamford
INN AT MILL RIVER

Stonington
FARNAN HOUSE
203-535-0634

Stonington Village
LASBURYS B&B
203-535-2681

Storrs
ALTAVEIGH INN
203-429-4490

FARMHOUSE ON
THE HILL
203-429-1400

Thompson
CORTISS INN
203-935-5652

**CAPTAIN PARKERS
INN AT
QUINEBAUG**
800-707-7808

SAMUEL WATSON
HOUSE
203-399-7565

Tolland
OLD BABCOCK
TAVERN
203-875-1239

TOLLAND INN
203-872-0800

Torrington
YANKEE PEDLAR
INN
203-489-9226

Uncasville
1851 GUEST
HOUSE
203-848-3849

Waterbury
HOUSE ON THE
HILL
203-757-9901

West Hartford
YANKEE B&B
203-561-1006

West Mystic
BAKERS RIVER
LODGE
203-536-7296

LEVENTHAL B&B

West Woodstock

EBENEZER
STODDARD HOUSE
203-974-2552

Westbrook
***CAPT STANNARD
HOUSE**
203-399-4634

TALCOTT HOUSE
203-399-5020

Westport
ANTIQUE HOUSE
203-454-2727

COTSWOLD INN
203-226-3766

INN AT
LONGSHORE
203-226-3316

Wethersfield
*CHESTER
BUCKLEY HOUSE
203-563-4236

Winsted
PROVINCIAL
HOUSE
203-379-1631

Woodbury
CURTIS HOUSE
203-263-2101

Woodstock
**CAPTAIN
PARKERS INN AT
QUINEBAUG**
800-707-7808

Maine

---

*Bayview Inn & Hotel   **Bar Harbor ME**
John Davis   111 Eden St Rt # 3 04609
207-288-3173   **Res Times** 8am-8pm

Rates:	**Pvt Bath** 32	**Payment Terms:**
Single	$ 95-up	Check
Double	$ 105.00-up	AE/DC/MC/V

This gracious waterfront estate serves as an elegant and intimate Inn where former guests includes many world-leaders. Townhouses are available too. A continental breakfast is included. There's swimming, tennis and complete dining facilities available. **SEASONAL:** No **BROCHURE:** Yes **PERMITTED:** Children, smoking, drinking **CONFERENCES:** Yes including full facilities **LANGUAGES:** French, Spanish [E11ACME-3457]

---

*Holbrook House   **Bar Harbor ME**
Dorothy & Mike Chester   74 Mount Desert St 04609
800-695-1120 813-924-7847

Rates:	**Pvt Bath** 10	**Shared Bath** 2	**Payment Terms:**
Single			Check
Double	$ 90-up	$ 80-Up	AE/MC/V

Beautiful 1876 Victorian summer cottage within Bar Harbor and close to Acadia National Park. Furnished with period antiques and oriental rugs, guests can relax and enjoy the New England hospitality. Continental breakfast is served in a sunlit solarium. Tennis & swimming are available. **RESERVATIONS:** Deposit at res time to guarantee room reservation **SEASONAL:** No **DISCOUNTS:** 10%-Senior Citizens **BROCHURE:** Yes **PERMITTED:** Children 9-up, limited smoking, limited drinking [E11ACME-3464]

---

*Maples   **Bar Harbor ME**
Richard & Michele Suydam   16 Roberts Ave 04609
207-288-3443   **Res Times** 9am-9pm

Rates:	Pvt Bath 3	Shared Bath 2	Payment Terms:
Single	$ 65-80.00	$ 55.00	Check
Double	$ 65-80.00	$ 70.00	MC/V

Beautiful Victorian residence just a short stroll to the ocean allows guests to unwind and relax in this great New England setting. If you're interested in the many sights, you can choose from Acadia National Park and the Nova Scotia Ferry for your pleasure. All the sporting activities are here; tennis, golf, swimming along with plenty of antiquing and interesting shops. **RESERVATIONS:** One night's deposit at res time with 10 day cancel policy **SEASONAL:** No **BROCHURE:** Yes **PERMITTED:** Limited drinking [E11ACME-3467]

**Mira Monte Inn			**Bar Harbor ME**
Marian Burns			69 Mt Desert St 04609
800-553-5109 207-288-4263			**Res Times** 8am-9pm
			Fax 207-288-3115
Rates:	**Pvt Bath** 12	**Suites** 3	**Payment Terms:**
Single	$ 115-145.00	$ 180.00	Check
Double	$ 115-145.00	$ 180.00	AE/DISC/MC/V

Treat yourself to the simple elegance in this turn-of-the-century retreat that entertained those who could afford the luxury of summering in Bar Harbor. This 1864 structure is graced with wrap-around porches, balconies and bay windows and is nestled on grounds of beautiful sweeping lawns, paved terraces and lovely gardens. Guest rooms befit the lifestyle of the period with antique and period furnishings, wallpapers, private baths and lace curtains - without sacrificing the cleanliness, comfort and convenience of today. All rooms have a/c and phones. Guests can dream alongside one of the many fireplaces or spend a serene afternoon on the grounds, where the smell of salt air and flowers blend fragrances - long remembered! Morning brings a full country breakfasts buffet served on an elegant 1810 Federal Period server. Guests can choose a private patio, porch, balcony or a family-style table for breakfast. Just a five minute walk brings you to Bar Harbor's finest shops, restaurants and waterfront. The Acadia National Park offers 33,000 acres (just a five minute drive) for mountains, seashore, lakes, meadows, forests and a full schedule of Ranger guided activities from June to early October. Enjoy climbing, hiking, boating, fishing, whale-watching, windsurfing, tennis, and golf. **PACKAGES:** *Fly & Drive* **RESERVATIONS:** Two night minimum (in season) with two night deposit; 7 day cancel policy for refund less $10 service fee **DISCOUNTS:** Off-season discounts are available (10-18 to 6-14)   **SEASONAL:** *Closed 10/128-5/1 **BROCHURE:** Yes **PERMITTED:** Children, drinking, limited smoking **CONFERENCES:** Yes, in a separate building on the grounds [Z07GPME2-3468]

Stratford House Inn			**Bar Harbor ME**
Barb & Norm Moulton		45 Mount Desert St 04609	
207-288-5189			

Rates:	**Pvt Bath** 8	**Shared Bath** 2	**Payment Terms:**
Single	$ 75..00-Up	$ 65.00-Up	Check
Double	$ 85-110.00	$ 75-95.00	AE/MC/V

Former home of *Little Women* publisher, this tudor-style residence is close to any woodland and water activity which might interest guests. Continental breakfast is included. Library and sitting room are for guests use. **RESERVATIONS:** Deposit to guarantee room with 10 day cancel policy for refund less $10 service fee **SEASONAL:** No **BROCHURE:** Yes **PERMITTED:** Children, limited pets, limited smoking [E11ACME-3472]

Granes Fairhaven Inn			**Bath ME**
Jane Wyllie		N Bath Rd 04530	
207-443-4391		**Res Times** 8am-8pm	

Rates:	**Pvt Bath** 1	**Shared Bath** 2	**Payment Terms:**
Single	$ 50.00 EP	$ 40.00 EP	Check
Double	$ 50.00 EP	$ 40.00 EP	

Lovely Country Inn for swimming, golfing and hiking if you like with all the country furnishings and plenty of home comfort and atmosphere with antique furnishings, handmade quilts and great New England hospitality. Continental breakfast is included with other meals available on the premises with prior notice. **RESERVATIONS:** 50% of stay required as deposit **SEASONAL:** No **BROCHURE:** Yes **PERMITTED:** Children, smoking [E11ACME-3479]

** *Hiram Alden Inn*	**Belfast ME**
Jim & Jackie Lovejoy	19 Church St 04915

207-338-2151   **Res Times** 24 Hrs

Rates:	**Shared Bath** 8	**Payment Terms:**
Single	$ 40.00	Check
Double	$ 55-60.00	

Enjoy New England in a stately 1840 Greek Revival home situated on an acre in Belfast's historical residential area and just minutes to the restored downtown commercial and waterfront district. The first in-town B&B in Belfast, it reflects the original owner's appreciation for quality craftsmanship and discerning eye for architectural style and beauty. Charming features include imported marble fireplace mantels, ornate tin ceilings, a "walk-in" butler's pantry, handcarved cherry wood staircase with a curved "pocket door". Your charming host's motto is *"Accommodating you is not a hobby . . . but our full time occupation".* The formal dining room offers guests a full breakfast including house specialties of blueberry nut pancakes, ham on french toast, scrambled eggs, bacon/sausage, fresh fruit, juices and muffins with all the warm beverages prepared just to each guest's taste. Summer adds fresh-picked berries to the menu! The town setting offers a panoramic view of Penobscot Bay, home to over 200 sailboats, lobster and working tugs. Must-sees are the historic home tour, a variety of galleries, arts & craft shops and a summer theater group. Don't miss a cruise on the 110-ft ship Mount Katahdin for sightseeing the islands. **RESERVATIONS:** One night's deposit with 7 day cancel policy, arrival after 6pm with notice **SEASONAL:** No **BROCHURE:** Yes **PERMITTED:** Children, drinking, limited pets, limited smoking **CONFERENCES:** Yes for groups to 15 persons [R02BCME-3480]

**Anchor Watch	**Boothbay Harbor ME**
Diane Campbell	3 Eames Rd 04538
207-633-7565	**Res Times** 10am-8pm

Rates:	**Pvt Bath** 4	**Payment Terms:**
Single	$ 75-95.00	Check
Double	$ 80-100.00	MC/V

Lighthouse beacons, lobster boats and islands with fir trees provide the setting for our cozy Bed & Breakfast on the prettiest shore of the Harbor. Country quilts, stencilling set the style inside. Breakfast features a baked cheese omelet or perhaps a baked orange French toast or blueberry blintz. Enjoy an intimate table for two or sit with other guests from all over the world at an ocean-view window. The lawn slopes down to the water ending with a pier and float. Within a five minute walk are shops, boat trips, Monhegan ferry and many fine restaurants. Within an hour's drive are white sandy beaches, maritime museums and the famous LL Bean and Freeport shopping outlets. Your host, Captain Bob, operates the Maranbo II and Balmy Days II excursion boats taking sightseeing and dinner cruises from Pier 8. Guests receive a *special fare* discount on the Harbor Tour. When Diane isn't at the B&B, she'll be found sailing in the Harbor or at the boat trip ticket booth at Pier #8. Bob and Diane live in the house next door to the *Anchor Watch* and in summer, Diane's dad stays at the B&B. Therefore, during the off-season, the *Anchor Watch* kitchen is available for guests to use for snacks or even cooking lobster. *This charming seaside Captain's house offers a warm welcome to travelers from afar.* **RESERVATIONS:** One night's deposit, one week cancel policy for refund or if less, only if room is rebooked **SEASONAL:** No **PERMITTED:** Drinking **BROCHURE:** Yes **PACKAGES:** *Spring Boat Trip* (one hour cruise) [Z07GPME2-6984]

Hilltop Guest House			**Boothbay Harbor ME**
Mrs Cora Mahr			44 McKnown Hill 04538
207-633-2914			**Res Times** 9am-7pm

Rates:	**Pvt Bath** 1	**Shared Bath** 5	**Payment Terms:**
Single	$ 45.00	$ 38.00	Check
Double		$ 38.00	

Family oriented farmhouse lodging overlooking Boothbay Harbor and town with a relaxed setting. Large comfortable rooms and even a tree swing in the yard. **RESERVATIONS:** Deposit required at res time **SEASONAL:** No **BROCHURE:** Yes **PERMITTED:** Children, limited smoking, limited drinking [E11ACME-3506]

L Ermitage		**Bucksport ME**
Virginia & James Conklin		219 Main St 04416
207-469-3361		**Res Times** 9am-10pm

Rates:	**Shared Bath** 3	**Payment Terms:**
Single	$ 45.00	Check
Double	$ 50.00	DC/MC/V

Patterned after traditional European inns, this turn-of-the-century white colonial from the 1830s comforts guests with antique furnishings, oriental carpets and many collectibles your hosts enjoy sharing with guests. Full breakfast included. On Penobscot Bay near Fort Knox. **BROCHURE:** Yes **PERMITTED:** Limited smoking, limited drinking **LANGUAGES:** French **SEASONAL:** No [E11ACME--3527]

Goodspeeds Guest House	**Camden ME**
Al Matos	Rt 52 60 Mountain St 04843
207-236-8077	**Res Times** 7am-9pm

Rates:	Pvt Bath	1	Shared Bath	7	Payment Terms:
Single			$ 49.00		Check
Double	$ 75.00		$ 65.00		

This 1879 Federal-style farmhouse has been restored and offers a great location for visiting the attractions in the quaint town of Camden. Interior detail includes stained-glass windows, wide pine planked floors, delightfully colored wallpapers with touches of antiques and heirloom furnishings. The guest rooms are furnished with a variety of wicker, canopy and cannon ball beds with several offering wonderful views of the nearby mountains. The host/owners collection of antique clocks and other collectibles create the warmth and feeling of old world charm. A continental breakfast is included and can be enjoyed outdoors in the wonderful Maine sunshine. Excellent restaurants, shops, sailing, hiking, swimming, picnicking, cycling, antiquing, county fairs and Shakespearean performances. One of Camden's original grave yards next door makes for an interesting glimpse into Camden's history. Fall brings brilliant color and unforgettable memories of New England. A quiet location-just five blocks from the harbor. **RESERVATIONS:** One night's deposit (if longer 50% of length of stay) plus 7% tax, required, 7 day cancel policy for full refund **SEASONAL:** Open 6/1-10/15 **BROCHURE:** Yes **PERMITTED:** Drinking, children 12-up, limited smoking **LANGUAGES:** French [Z11CPME-3536]

Hawthorn Inn	**Camden ME**
Pauline & Bradford Staub	9 High St 04842
207-236-8842	**Res Times** 9am-9pm
	Fax 207-236-6181
Rates: **Pvt Bath** 10	**Payment Terms:**

Single	$ 70-140.00	Check
Double	$ 75-145.00	MC/V

Relive the Queen Victorian period in this gracious mansion with turrets dating from 1894, created by a prosperous coal merchant as his estate. Since then, this home has only had four occupants and has recently been listed on the *National Register of Historic Places.* Inside, two large parlour rooms invite you to linger, perhaps over tea or lemonade,  served each afternoon by your English hostess, Pauline and her husband Brad. There are four bright and airy rooms off the second floor which overlook Camden Harbor or Mount Battie and two snug garden rooms (one with clawfoot tub) downstairs. Beautiful spiral staircase and dining room that removes the morning chill during breakfast complete the downstairs. A beautifully furnished carriage house with two luxury townhouse apartments offering fully equipped kitchens, private deck and whirlpool Jacuzzi. A full breakfast is included with muffins hot from the oven, fresh fruit and artful egg dishes. On sunny days, you'll enjoy dining on the deck that offers a great harbor view. Your English hostess hasn't overlooked anything in pleasing her guests! Nearby, and next to the grounds is the Bok Amphitheater for summer concerts and Shakespearean plays; with the town center just a five minute walk - to schooners, shops, restaurants and Mt Battie. The *Hawthorn Inn* is a very special place . . . and all of our guests are very special people. **RESERVATIONS:** Advanced 2 night payment as deposit, two week cancel policy for refund **BROCHURE:** Yes **PERMITTED:** Limited children, drinking permitted. Check-in 2-7pm, prior notice required if later, check-out 10:30 am; no smoking please **CONFERENCES:** Perfect setting for memorable weddings, social engagements and small seminars. [I03GPME2-8645]

**Norumbega Inn	**Camden ME**
Murry Keatings	Rt 1 40843
207-236-4646	**Res Times** 9am-7pm

Rates:	**Pvt Bath** 13	**Payment Terms:**
Single	$ 175-Up	Check

Double $ 175-Up   AE/MC/V

This romantic Victorian "castle by the sea", is fashioned of heroic proportions from local stone and overlooks Penobscot Bay and islands. Listed on the *National Register of Historic Places*, guests enjoy the delightful mythical city of Norumbega created by Joseph Sterns, a prosperous inventor who built his castle in 1866. Mr. Sterns furnished his mansion with the best of what he experienced in the manor houses of England and castles along the Rhine. Renovated by the Keatings in 1987 as a luxury Inn, it stands today as a tribute to the fine craftsmanship and antique period furnishings of the nineteenth century. From the ornate fireplaces in the downstairs parlors to the handsome library with wrap-around balcony and glass windows - the dramatically wood paneled public rooms, reminiscent of an English manor house, and the balconies and porches with their spectacular views - each guest feels at home in "their own castle". Thirteen country-guest rooms include king-size beds, sitting areas, private bath with some rooms offering private balconies, fireplaces and picture-window views. An exciting penthouse suite sits above the treetops and is furnished in modern color and style with bold floral wallcoverings, subtle mint carpeting and a regal bath with ebony jacuzzi and shower. Morning brings a delicious royal fare of a variety of teas, coffee, juices, seasonal fruit, home-baked breads and muffins, egg dishes, meats and other culinary delights all served outdoors on the stone terrace or in the main dining room. Afternoon brings tea, beverages and hors d'oeuvres for guests to enjoy while planning their evening dining at one of Camden's excellent restaurants. A friendly helpful staff is ready to assist you . . . and to make sure your bed is turned-down before retiring . . . chill your favorite beverage . . . arrange your dinner reservations. We want your visit to be a special and memorable experience - a castle to call home. **AIRPORT** Bangor-60 mi; Portland Jetport-80 mi **PACKAGES:** *Weekend, Mid-Week, Holiday, Mystery* **RESERVATIONS:** Deposit required to confirm res, 10 day cancel policy less $20 service fee **SEASONAL:** No **BROCHURE:** Yes **PERMITTED:** Children 7-up, smoking, social drinking **CONFERENCES:** Excellent facilities for intimate business or social meetings including sumptuous meals prepared to order [I03EPME-3543]

Wooden Goose Inn   **Cape Neddick ME**

K Rippetow & A Sienicki
207-363-5673

Rt 1   03902
Res Times 9am-8pm

Rates: **Pvt Bath** 6   **Payment Terms:**
Single $ 75-85.00   Check
Double $ 85-up

A 19th Century farmhouse, former home of a sea captain, has been restored and furnished with crystal, oriental carpeting with plenty of nostalgia. Three course full breakfast begins each day and includes choices of eggs Benedict, omelette or Florentine with homemade breads. Close to Portsmouth and Ogunquit. Airport pickups with advance notice. **RESERVATIONS:** One night's deposit required **SEASONAL:** No **BROCHURE:** Yes **PERMITTED:** Children, smoking, drinking [E11ACME-3551]

Ocean Reefs On Long Cove   **Chamberlain ME**

John J Hahler
207-677-2386

Rt 32   04541-8605

Rates: **Pvt Bath** 4   **Payment Terms:**
Single $ 44.00   Check
Double $ 55.00

Ocean views abound here of lobster fisherman unloading their catch or of waves breaking over the reefs. Salt breezes everywhere! Continental breakfast included. **SEASONAL:** No **BROCHURE:** Yes **PERMITTED:** Children 13-up [E11ACME-3559]

Craignair Inn*   **Clark Island ME

Norman & Terry Smith
207-594-7644

Clark Island Rd 04859
Res Times 9am-9pm

Rates: **Pvt Bath** 8   **Shared Bath** 14   **Payment Terms:**
Single $ 76.00 $ 42.00   Check
Double $ 86.00 $ 62.00   AE/MC/V

This quaint Maine village offers guests a year-round opportunity to enjoy New England hospitality at the *Craignair Inn* nestled on four acres of shore front coastline. Originally a boarding house for workers at nearby quarries, it was converted into an Inn in 1940

---

offering cheery rooms overlooking the picturesque water setting and gardens. Guest rooms are simple and comfortable offering quilt covered beds, colorful wall coverings, hooked rugs on the floors and antique furnishings. A perfect locale for artists, writers and naturalists seeking a change of pace enjoying the sailboats, lobster fishermen, clammers, shore birds and the abundant wildlife on the islands, tidal pools, meadows and woodlands. Winter brings x-country skiing, ice skating, downhill at the Camden Snow Bowl (just a short drive) and a crackling fire in the large library which provides refuge from the silent fog that slowly rolls onto land in the evening. A full breakfast is included with dinner available in the dining room on the premises which specializes in local seafood, meats, homemade sauces, breads, pastas and pastries. There's plenty to see with antiquing, galleries, golf, miles of hiking, riding, tennis, sailing, concerts, museums and numerous country fairs and a special granite quarry of deep saltwater for a warm swim in the afternoon before dinner. **AIRPORT:** Portland Jetport-80 mi **RESERVATIONS:** One night's deposit by check in mail, one week cancel policy for refund **BROCHURE:** Yes **SEASONAL:** Clo February **PERMITTED:** Children, pets, drinking, smoking **CONFERENCES:** Yes, small conferences [Z07GPME2-3562]

**Brannon Bunker Inn		**Damariscotta ME**	
Jeanne & Joseph Hovance		HCR 64 Box 045M 04543	
207-563-5941		**Res Times** 9am-9pm	

Rates:	**Pvt Bath** 5	**Shared Bath** 2	**Payment Terms:**
Single	$ 60.00	$ 50.00	Check
Double	$ 65.00	$ 55.00	AE/MC/V

The Inn in Winter

Brannon-Bunker Inn is an intimate, relaxed country B&B, rurally situated in Maine's mid-coast region, just five miles off Rt 1 south of Damariscotta on Rt 129. The original Cape cottage portion (c1820) has been home to many generations of Mainers. The 1920's owners turned the barn into a dance hall, "La Hacienda". Over the intervening years, the barn and carriage house were converted into comfortable sleeping rooms with private and shared baths. Today, eight sleeping rooms are furnished in themes reflecting the charm of yesterday with the comforts of today, with a selection of queen, double and twin beds. The quiet beauty of stenciled walls, quaint wallpapers, homemade quilts, dried flowers and country crafts sets off the warmth and solid comfort of the carefully selected antique furnishings. One of the sitting areas reflects Joe's interest in World War I military collectibles. A complimentary Continental-plus breakfast features juices, cold cereals, fresh fruit in season, hot beverages and great homemade muffins - with time for conversation and mapping out the days' activities. You're just ten mins to the lighthouse, historic fort, sandy beaches, golf, Audubon Center, boating trips, canoe rentals, antique shop right at the Inn, fine dining and beautiful New England scenery. **RESERVATIONS:** 50% of stay as deposit at res time to confirm res with 7 day cancel policy for refund **SEASONAL:** Closed Christmas **BROCHURE:** Yes **PERMITTED:** Children, drinking, limited smoking [O04FPME1-3566]

Artists Retreat	Eastport ME
Joyce Webster	29 Washington St 04631
207-853-4239	

Rates:	Shared Bath 5	Payment Terms:
Single	$ 50.00	Check
Double	$ 60.00	MC/V

Step back to 1846 in this Victorian home, just two blocks from Eastport's waterfront, that is a Victorian buff's delight with touches of ornately carved and marble-topped furnishings. There are many special examples of Victorian Renaissance, like the bedsteads with high carved backs brought back following trips South after the Civil War! The guest rooms are on the second & third floors with a small library, sitting area with an Artist's Retreat on the fourth floor. Well-lit with skylights, guest artists are welcomed to use it! Enjoy this tranquil village setting that once vied with New York as the busiest port in the 19th Century. While the tall ships are gone now, the harbor is a hub of activity, especially with fishing boats and their fresh *New England Catch* ready for dinner at one of the many local restaurants.   Boat excursions for nature-trips and bird-watching (also whales & seals) **RESERVATIONS:** 25% deposit of entire stay at res time, 7 day cancel policy, less $10 service fee **SEASONAL:** No **BROCHURE:** Yes **PERMITTED:** Children, drinking, limited smoking **CONFERENCES:** Large living room for groups to forty [R02BCME-3574]

Atlantic Seal B&B   Freeport ME
Captain Thomas & Gaila Ring
207-865-6112   **Res Times** 7:30-9pm

Rates:	Pvt Bath 2	Shared Bath 2	Payment Terms:
Single	$ 90.00	$ 55.00	Check
Double	$ 100-125.00	$ 65-85.00	

Refer to the same listing name under South Freeport, Maine for a complete description [M10CPME-11610]

Bagley House   Freeport ME
Susan Backhouse/Suzanne O'Connor
800-765-1772 207-865-6566   1290 Royalsborough Rd 04032
                                         Res Times 8am-10pm

Rates:	Pvt Bath 5	Payment Terms:
Single	$ 70-85.00	Check
Double	$ 85-100.00	AE/DISC/MC/V

Six acres of lovely fields and woods surround this magnificent 1772 country home offering guests a peaceful stopping place to recall another era.   Featured in the *Los Angeles Times*, Nov 1988, guests are welcomed with fresh flowers, hand-made quilts, antique furnishings and wide pine floors.   One guest room boasts its own fireplace for cozy winter evenings.   The kitchen's huge fireplace and beehive oven inspires mouth-watering breakfast each morning. Just minutes from downtown Freeport, Bowdoin & Bates Colleges, nature lovers will enjoy hiking, berry-picking and great x-country skiing.   LL Bean and more than 100 upscale shops and outlets are in Freeport for treasure-hunters and bargain-seekers!   Four state parks, several museums, island cruising, summer music theater, music festivals, country fairs, small-town bean suppers, auctions and antiquing keep guests busy.   Just 35 mins from Portland Intl Jetport or a 2-1/2 hr drive to scenic Boston, *The Bagley House* offers guests a convenient setting for enjoying traditional New England hospitality. **RESERVATIONS:** One night's deposit or credit card, 7 day cancel policy for full refund **DISCOUNTS:** 5% AARP **BROCHURE:** Yes **AIRPORT:** Portland Jetport-25 min **PERMITTED:** Children, drinking **CONFERENCES:** Ideal for small retreat for to 7-10 persons **SEASONAL:** No *Dinner Weekend* [Z07GPME27406]

**Bayberry B&B	**Freeport ME**
Frank Family	8 Maple Ave 04032
207-865-1868 207-865-6021	

Rates:	**Pvt Bath** 5	**Payment Terms:**
Single	$ 69-95.00	Check
Double	$ 69-95.00	MC/V

Welcome to the *Bayberry Bed & Breakfast*, built in 1853, located in the village district, two blocks north of LL Bean and all the fine shops and restaurants. The *Bayberry Bed & Breakfast* has recently been restored and the early charm of the old Federal House has been preserved with its oak, walnut, maple and wide pine floors. All of the rooms have private baths and are tastefully decorated. Guests may choose between king, queen, double or twin beds. Guests may also enjoy the bright and sunny sitting room with cable TV, VCR, books, games and also perfect for conversing. Relax in our colorful garden with blooming shrubs and flowers. Enjoy a leisurely afternoon in a lounge chair under a hundred year old blue spruce. A delicious full breakfast (prepared with fresh local produce) is served daily in the dining room. Start your morning with a hot cup of coffee or tea, fresh fruit, chilled juice, homemade bread, muffins, biscuits, pancakes, waffles, crepes or french toast and omelette. Freeport has a beautiful coastline with spectacular views, harbor cruises, sailing, fishing, golf, biking and hiking. Restaurants and their outdoor tables line Main Street in summer. Freeport has more than one hundred outlets, factory stores, craft shops and boutiques for pottery, porcelain, leather, silver, antiques and the world famous LL Bean, opened 24 hours every day. The mellow atmosphere, the warmth, the charm, the touch and the total experience will stay with you for a long time. Spend a memorable week, weekend or midweek in our delightful and cozy Inn. We look forward to welcoming you to Freeport and the *Bayberry Bed & Breakfast*. **RESERVATIONS:** 50% deposit **PERMITTED:** Children, no pets **BROCHURE:** Yes **SEASONAL:** Rates vary **DISCOUNTS:** College students **AIRPORT:** Portland Jetport-20 mi **PACKAGES:** Yes [R07GPME2-19569]

**Capt Josiah Mitchell House	**Freeport ME**
Alan & Loretta Bradley	188 Main St 04032
207-865-3289	**Res Times** 9am-9pm

Rates:	**Pvt Bath** 7	**Payment Terms:**
Single	$ 65-Up	Check
Double	$ 75-Up	MC/V

In-town Freeport, you're just a five minute walk to LL Bean Co along tree-shaded sidewalks that border beautiful old sea captains' homes. From the moment you arrive, you'll know you've discovered a very special place. This lovely former captain's residence is furnished with period antiques, four-poster beds, Victorian period satins and velvets, beautiful oil paintings and an exquisite collection of Oriental rugs covering the original floors. A gracious and grand dining room with a magnificent chandelier is the setting for breakfast. After shopping in the quaint shops, spend time relaxing on the large veranda furnished with antique wicker and a *remember-when porch swing*! Plenty of shopping, hiking trails, golfing and dining spots (offering great lobster). The summer theater & Bowdoin College is nearby and you're just two hours from terrific skiing. Year-round sights include the wonderful Maine beaches, just 30 mins by car. Your gracious host will be most helpful to tell you the history of the famous Capt Mitchell, whose diary was used for writing *Mutiny of the Bounty*. For a treat, try the Mark Twin Room! **RESERVATIONS:** Full payment in advance, arrive by 8 pm **DISCOUNTS:** Winter rates lower **BROCHURE:** Yes **AIRPORT:** Portland ME-20 mi **SEASONAL:** Rates vary **PERMITTED:** Limited children, drinking **LANGUAGES:** Czech [Z07GPMA2-6119]

---

*Isaac Randall House	**Freeport ME**
Glyn & Jim Friedlander	5 Independence Dr 04032
207-865-9295	**Res Times** 7am-10pm

Rates:	**Pvt Bath** 8	**Payment Terms:**
Single	$ 65-95.00	Check
Double	$ 75-105.00	MC/V

The *Isaac Randall House* is a lovely Federal-style farmhouse built

171 years ago as a wedding present for Isaac, Jr and his bride, Betsy Cummings. Later, the home became a stop on the underground railway helping slaves escape into Canada. In years past, the property has been a dairy farm, a prohibition and depression-era dance hall and a tourist court. Today, restored as a Country Inn, its friendly ambience welcomes guests year-round. This historic farmhouse is located just off Rte 1, on six acres of land with a spring-fed pond. All of the guest rooms are charmingly appointed with antiques, oriental rugs and quilts. Guests are within walking distance to the famous LL Bean and many other luxury factory outlet stores. Guests can relax outdoors and enjoy the beautiful New England weather, walk among the wildflowers along the path to the pond, broil a steak on our barbecue, make a snack in the fully-appointed guest service-kitchen or just sit back and enjoy games or conversation in the common room. Open year-round, nearby are beaches, golf, summer theatre, mountain parks and seashore preserves. Excellent dining is just a stroll away! **DISCOUNTS:** Seniors and stays of 4 nights and longer. **AIRPORT:** Portland's Jetport-13 miles **RESERVATIONS:** Encouraged, preferred rates off-season for travel agents **SEASONAL:** Rates vary **BROCHURE:** Yes **PERMITTED:** Children, pets in certain rooms. No smoking **LANGUAGES:** French, Spanish [I08GPME2-3589]

Dark Harbor House Inn	Islesboro ME
Matt Skinner	PO Box 185 04848
207-734-6669	

Rates:	Pvt Bath 4	Shared Bath 3	Payment Terms:
Single	$ 70.00	$ 65.00	Check
Double	$ 85.00	$ 75.00	

An elegant example of a summer Georgian Revival Mansion off the Maine coast on it's own island for a quiet and peaceful setting. Continental breakfast is included. Complimentary bikes and wine. **SEASONAL:** No **BROCHURE:** Yes **PERMITTED:** Limited smoking, limited drinking [E11ACME-3601]

Alewife House   **Kennebunk ME**

Maryellen & Tom Foley   1917 Alewive Rd Rt 35 04043
207-985-2118   **Res Times** 7am-11pm

Rates:	**Pvt Bath** 2	**Shared Bath** 1	**Payment Terms:**
Single	$ 75.00	$ 75.00	Check
Double	$ 75.00	$ 75.00	MC/V

Step back in time in this 1756 farmhouse nestled on six acres of rolling hills, gardens including a babbling brook -- between area lakes and the ocean. Our B&B has enchanted guests for the past five seasons. Antique furnishings, pumpkin pine floors, stenciled walls and six fireplaces offer comfort and charm to guests from California to England, Russia and Sweden. Each guestroom accommodates two adults. Our accommodations have been selected by *Yankee Magazine* and Bernice Chessler's *B&B Guide* as a favored place to visit. A waterfall, small country church, old barns and stone fences are a few of the rural delights within walking distance. We are located about ten minutes by car from area beaches of Kennebunk and Kennebunkport. The *Alewife House* environment is a treasure all four seasons and guests are always made to feel special. A continental plus breakfast with fresh fruit and perked coffee is served on our sun porch each morning. Visit The Ashes of Roses Antiques Shop on our grounds. *Alewife House* is conveniently located 90 miles north of Boston, 45 mins south of LL Bean (Freeport ME) and 30 mins south of Portland. **AIRPORT** Portland-20 mi **RESERVATIONS:** Deposit of entire stay required at res time, 14 day refund policy, if less than 14 day notice, 90% refund if re-rented; check-in 5pm, check-out 11am **SEASONAL:** No **BROCHURE:** Yes **PERMITTED:** Children 13-up, drinking, smoke-free environment, no pets [G05FPME1-3605]

Lake Brook Guest House   **Kennebunk ME**

Carolyn McAdams   57 Western Ave 04043
207-967-4069

Rates:	**Pvt Bath** 2	**Shared Bath** 2	**Payment Terms:**
Single	$ 75.00	$ 65.00	Check
Double	$ 85.00	$ 75.00	

A great location, just one mile from Kennebunk Beach, bikes available & picnic lunches (nominal charge). Enjoy all the activities such as boating, fishing, canoeing. A full breakfast is included. **RESERVATIONS:** Deposit to hold room **BROCHURE:** Yes **PERMITTED:** Children, [C11ACME-1390]

**1802 House B&B Inn	**Kennebunkport ME**
Ron & Carol Perry	PO Box 646-A 04046-1646
800-932-5632 207-967-5632	**Res Times** 8am-10pm

Rates:	**Pvt Bath** 6	**Payment Terms:**
Single	$ 55-105.00	Check
Double	$ 65-125.00	AE/MC/V

1802 House - is informal, secluded, delightfully quiet and completely smoke-free.   The Inn, bounded by the Cape Arundel Golf Club on two sides (nonmembers may play), is a ten minute walk from Dock Square. A morning choir of songbirds greets guests from the dewy fairways that roll past the breakfast room. The fresh ocean breezes and clear maine sunshine bath the Inns' decks and gardens. Each of the six recently remodelled, updated and cheerful guest rooms includes a private bathroom. Some rooms have fireplaces with queen size beds, others have four poster queen size beds and some rooms have two beds. The Inn and all guest rooms are furnished with antiques; each room offers the privacy and amenities that make the *1802 House* a "Down-East" home away from home. A full country breakfast awaits our guests each morning and consists of juices, coffee, tea and hot chocolate; a fresh fruit course; a main dish that might be Bavarian Apple Pancake with bacon or Baked Eggs Florentine gratinee with ham; each served with freshly baked muffins and breads. Popular local activities include sightseeing along the coastline, including President Bush's seaside home, swimming, boating, fishing, antiquing, shopping and delicious dining. Please inquire about our off-season dinner packages. **RESERVATIONS:** Full deposit for stays to 2 days, 50% for 3 day or longer stays, 14 day cancel policy for refund **BROCHURE:** Yes **PERMITTED:** Children 12-up, drinking **CONFERENCES:** Limited **AIRPORT:** Portland Jetport-25 mi **LANGUAGES:** Some French, German **PACKAGES:** *Off-Season Dinner* [I03GPME2-5934]

Alewife House   **Kennebunkport ME

Maryellen & Tom Foley
207-985-2118   **Res Times** 7am-11pm

Rates:	Pvt Bath 2	Shared Bath 1	Payment Terms:
Single	$ 75.00	$ 75.00	Check
Double	$ 75.00	$ 75.00	MC/V

Refer to the same listing name under Kennebunk, Maine for a complete description. [M05FPME2-16893]

---

*Captain Lord Mansion   **Kennebunkport ME**

Bev Davis/Rich Litchfield   PO Box 800 04046
800-522-3141 207-967-3141   **Res Times** 9am-7pm
                                                    Fax 207-967-3171

Rates:	Pvt Bath 16	Payment Terms:
Single	$ 89-130.00	Check
Double	$ 89-130.00	AE/MC/V

Luxurious 1812 mansion richly appointed with genuine antiques and period wallcoverings and fabrics.   Octagonal cupola and four-story spiral staircase -just some of the interesting highlights. Working fireplaces in most guest rooms. **RESERVATIONS:** Credit card number to guarantee, 7 day cancel policy **SEASONAL:** No [C11ACME-1380]

Captain Fairfield House   **Kennebunkport ME

Bonnie & Dennis Tallagnon   PO Box 1308 04046
800-322-1928 207-967-4454   **Res Times** 9am-8pm

Rates:	Pvt Bath 9	Payment Terms:
Single	$ 70-145.00	Check
Double	$ 75-149.00	AE/MC/V

This gracious 1813 Federal Mansion is in Kennebunkport's placid historic district. Conveniently located and only steps to the Village & Harbour, guests are a few minutes walk to Dock Square Marinas, shops, area restaurants and beaches. This Inn is ideal for those who wish to be near activities, yet seek a peaceful and quiet retreat. Graceful and elegant, the Inn's common rooms and bedrooms are individually and beautifully decorated with Period furnishings and wicker, which lend an atmosphere of tranquility and charm.

Fireplaces are available in some rooms with comp firewood (except July & August) for cozy evenings. Guests may relax in our living-room, browse in the library, or enjoy the tree-shaded grounds and gardens, following an active day on the Maine Coast. Guests awaken to birdsong from the gardens, the smell of fresh sea air and the aroma of gourmet  coffee brewing in the kitchen. A full complimentary breakfast is always a treat - fresh fruits and juices, homemade breads, muffins and preserves; omelettes, crepes, pancakes, waffles and other specialties begin your day. The guest refrigerator is stocked with iced tea, chilled spring water and ice. Truly - home away from home! Exceptional and unique restaurants and shops abound. After a visit to this historic seaport one appreciates why former President Bush chose Kennebunkport as his summer retreat. **DISCOUNTS:** 10% for week stays and midweek off-season, 5% students and seniors **AIRPORT:** Portland Intl-30 mins driving **RESERVATIONS:** One night's deposit within 7 days of booking, 10 day cancel policy for refund less $10 service fee, two day min weekends July and August and holidays, arrival 2-8pm, later by prior arrangement **SEASONAL:** No **BROCHURE:** Yes **PERMITTED:** Alcoholic beverages, children 7-up, limited smoking **LANGUAGES:** French [I05FPME2-3610]

Inn at Harbor Head	Kennebunkport ME
Joan & Dave Sutter	RR 2 Box 1180 Pier Rd 04046
207-967-5564	**Res Times** 9:30-9:30

Rates:	**Pvt Bath** 4	**Payment Terms:**
Single	$ 85-150.00	Check
Double	$ 85-150.00	MC/V

The nostalgia of a bygone era lingers in this picturesque fishing village, inviting guests to relax and savor the feeling of "letting go", so essential for a good vacation or important getaway. Your charming artist/innkeeper has beautifully decorated and furnished the Inn with original sculpture, family portraits, marine paintings, Oriental carpets, antique furniture and hand-painted murals on guestroom walls. The ocean & harbor are in view from the windows and a stroll down the yard will put you at the water's edge. The guest rooms are furnished with queen or king size beds, one with a raised whirlpool tub surrounded by hand-painted ceramic tiles. A perfect location for exploring the White Mountains, Boothbay Harbor, or Ogunquit's Marginal Way. Fresh coffee begins the day at 7:30 with a gourmet's delight at 9:00, set with china and silver, to befit a typical offering of fresh squeezed orange juice, broiled grapefruit or bananas and a main course of stuffed french toast covered with fresh fruit or freshly made roast-beef hash with poached egg and salsa - guests come back just for breakfast! Full service includes nightly turndown service, Godiva Chocolates, a champagne split for special occasions. Parking passes for Goose Rocks Beach (comp chairs & towels) area maps and a basketful of menus to sample the freshest fish and best lobster in the world! **RESERVATIONS:** Strongly recommended; one night's deposit within 10 days, 10 day cancel policy, 2 night min, 3-7pm check-in; 11am check-out **SEASONAL:** Closed Christmas **BROCHURE:** Yes **PERMITTED:** Drinking [R02CPME-1387]

**_Inn On South Street_	**Kennebunkport ME**
Jacques & Eva Downs	PO Box 478A 04046
207-967-5151	**Res Times** 9am-9:30pm

Rates:	**Pvt Bath** 4	**Payment Terms:**
Single		Check
Double	$ 85-185.00	MC/V

Combine charm and romance in this 19th Century Greek Revival home fully restored and listed on the *National Register of Historic Places* in a picture-perfect setting. The interior decor reflects the area's connection with a maritime past and offers three uniquely furnished guest rooms with queen-sized beds, antique and period furnishings in each room. Also one luxurious 3-room suite-apartment with fireplace, whirlpool tub, queen-sized four-poster bed. Featured in *Country Inns Bed & Breakfast*, Fall '87 & Summer 1990 issue of *Discerning Traveller*. Early risers find steaming coffee at 7:00 am. A full homemade breakfast later includes Jack's homebaked breads, pancakes or other Down's family specialties. You'll enjoy breakfast in the country kitchen with a lovely ocean and river view or if you're in the honeymoon suite, you'll have a private breakfast overlooking the herb gardens. Each guest room is complete with fresh flowers, fluffy comforters, pillows & towels. *Complimentary:* Afternoon tea, wine or lemonade. Convenient, a quiet location within easy walking distance of shops, restaurants, beaches and the historic village areas. *Rated A+* by *ABBA* **DISCOUNTS:** Yes, for week long stays. **AIRPORT** Portland ME-30 mi; Boston Logan-80 mi **RESERVATIONS:** 50% deposit or one night's rate (whichever is greater) or credit card to hold room, 14 day cancel policy for refund. Two night min on weekends, holidays and in-season (6/1-10/1). **SEASONAL:** Closed Christmas and March **BROCHURE:** Yes **PERMITTED:** Children, pets with prior approval **LANGUAGES:** German, Spanish, Russian [I07GPME2-1388]

**Kennebunkport Inn	**Kennebunkport ME**
Rick & Martha Griffin	One Dock Square 04046
800-248-2621 207-967-2621	**Res Times** 24 Hrs
	Fax 207-867-3705

Rates:	**Pvt Bath** 34	**Payment Terms:**
Single	$ 62.50-125.00	Check
Double	$ 79.50-179.00	AE/MC/V

Set in centre square is this elegant Nineteenth-Century Mansion offering fine New England hospitality, elegant accommodations and wonderful dining. The Inn was built by a wealthy tea and coffee merchant, Burleigh S Thompson. It boasts four hundred feet of river frontage, a private float, large stable and was furnished without regard to expense.  Set along the banks of the Kennebunk River, today guests enjoy the picturesque New England seaport town setting. Each of the charming rooms and apartments are attractively furnished, many according to the period. The River House, built in the 1930's, offers twin and double-bedded rooms, individually decorated. All rooms offer private baths and color TV and the more recent rooms are more deluxe and include 4-poster beds. A continental breakfast is available Nov to April. A full breakfast is available from May to Oct. Candlelight dining with classical background music is featured in two intimate dining rooms featuring Laura Ashley wallpaper, stenciling, hurricane lamps and create a light and festive feeling. Gourmet choices range from grilled duck breast with a superb raspberry sauce to mustard ginger rack of lamb and all of the New England seafood specialties. Daytime activities include shopping at the numerous shops at your doorstep featuring antiques, arts & crafts and clothing. You can choose swimming in the pool or nearby beaches, golf, tennis, boating, horseback riding, bicycling, theaters or sightseeing along the rocky coast and country roads. **DISCOUNTS:** 10% *AARP, AAA* **AIRPORT:** Logan-80 mi; Portland-30 mi **PACKAGES:** Two, Three and Four night packages **SEASONAL:** No **RESERVATIONS:** One night's deposit, 14 day cancel policy less $10 service fee, 3-day min stay on Summer & holiday weekends; 2-day min stay on Spring and Fall weekends **CONFERENCES:** Nov-April, 20 persons **BROCHURE:** Yes **PERMITTED:** Children, drinking, limited smoking **LANGUAGES:** French [I07GPME2-3611]

**Kilburn House	**Kennebunkport ME**
Samuel Minier/Muriel Friend	6 Chestnut St 04046
207-967-4762	**Res Times** 8am-10pm

Rates:	Pvt Bath	2	Shared Bath	2	Payment Terms:
Single	$ 75.00		$ 45-60.00		Check
Double	$ 75.00		$ 60.00		AE/MC/V

Centrally located just outside of Dock Square in town, the *Kilburn House* was the home of artists Margaret Kilburn-Fisher and William Fisher. Margaret was skilled in etching, stained glass and various arts and crafts while William is noted for his American scenes in oil and water colors. Today their works along with other works from their favorite artists are displayed through-out the house and the B&B is proudly run by William Fisher's immediate family. There are four guest rooms on the second floor and a delightful and airy suite encompassing the entire third floor with views in all directions. A warm, fresh full breakfast is served each morning and is included in the room rate. A short walk from the *Kilburn House* are many exquisite shops and restaurants while a short drive takes you to the fishing village of Cape Porpoise, Goose Rocks, Kennebunk Beaches and to Portland, Freeport (home of LL Bean) and Ogunquit. **DISCOUNTS:** Yes **AIRPORT:** Portland ME-25 mi **RESERVATIONS:** One night's deposit **SEASONAL:** Open

5/15-10/12, Closed 10/13-5/14 **BROCHURE:** Yes **PERMITTED:** Children, drinking [R11EPMA2-1389]

Maine Stay Inn & Cottages	**Kennebunkport ME**
Carol & Lindsay Copeland	34 Maine St 04046-1800
800-950-2117 207-967-2117	**Res Times** 8am-10pm

Rates:	**Pvt Bath** 17	**Payment Terms:**
Single	$ 75-180.00	Check
Double	$ 75-180.00	AE/MC/V

Beautiful 1860 Victorian Inn with Italianate hip roof, accentuated by Queen Ann period flying staircase, wrap around porch, bay windows and masterful architectural detail. The *Maine Stay* offers a variety of accommodations, from charming rooms and suites in the main house, to delightful one-bedroom cottages, some with fireplaces and separate kitchens. A sumptuous full breakfast plus afternoon tea and desserts are included. Cottage guests can have breakfast basket delivered to their door or enjoy breakfast with the rest of our guests in the dining room. Our living room, which is often filled with the aroma of home baked goodies, is a comfortable place to sit and meet fellow travelers or enjoy a fire on a cold winter day. The Inn is perfectly situated in Kennebunkport's historic district. Our spacious grounds offer a peaceful resting spot amid the gigantic Maine pines. Our location, four blocks from the village, allows guests a leisurely walk to the shops, galleries, restaurants and the harbor. Golf, tennis and beautiful swimming beaches are all within one mile. Scenic Kennebunkport can be viewed via guided trolley car ride or by boat cruise. Other activities include boating, whale watching, antiquing, and walking tours of the historic district. Bicycling, horseback riding, x-country skiing and ice skating are available in the area. **AIRPORT:** Portland Jetport 25 mi, Boston Logan 75 mi **PACKAGES:** *Romance Renewed Package*, includes 2 night's lodging **RESERVATIONS:** 50% deposit or one night's stay within 7 mailing days, 14 day cancel policy for refund less $15 service fee **SEASONAL:** No **BROCHURE:** Yes **PERMITTED:** Children, drinking, limited smoking **CONFERENCES:** Yes, for small groups in dining room, living room and fireplace suite [J11DPME-1391]

Olde Garrison House	Kennebunkport ME
Louise & Lyman Huff	Cape Porpoise 04014
207-967-3522	**Res Times** 8am-8pm

Rates:	Pvt Bath 3	Shared Bath 2	Payment Terms:
Single	$ 62.00	$ 50.00	Check
Double	$ 68.00	$ 58.00	

Relaxed New England atmosphere in this Cape Cod-style cottage overlooking a cove with plenty of salty air, gulls and lobster. The owners are lobster fishermen and you're at the right place if you're a lobster lover! Your hosts will lead you to the best ones around! Cottage is private and fully furnished including a complete kitchen and bath. **RESERVATIONS:** Full payment in advance of date, 15 day cancel notice for full refund less $20 service fee **SEASONAL:** Open 5/15-10/15 **BROCHURE:** Yes **PERMITTED:** Children 12-up, drinking, smoking [E11ACME-1394]

Port Gallery Inn	Kennebunkport ME
Lucy Murphy	Corner Spring & Maine 04046
207-967-3728	

Rates:	Pvt Bath 7	Payment Terms:
Single	$105-165.00	Check
Double	$175.00	AE/MC/V

Recapture the era and spirit in one of the few remaining Victorian homes in town and a residence since 1890. Surrounded by its white picket fence this picture-perfect B&B fits everyone's dreams! High ceilings, moldings, woodwork and decor are reminiscent of the turn-of-the-century. Enjoy the Marine Art Gallery with oils and watercolors by Lawrence E. Donnison that recreating New England seafaring history. Guest rooms are spacious with comfortable and elegant period reproduction furniture with modern amenities such as color TVs hidden in Queen Anne cabinets! Guests are within easy walking distance of fine New England cuisine and shoppes. Nearby are beautiful rocky beachfronts with miles of sand just perfect for ship and whale watching. There's golfing, tennis, canoeing, biking and sightseeing. Boston-1-1/2 hrs; Portland-27 mi; Freeport-40 mi; for visiting, A continental breakfast is included. **RESERVATIONS:** Deposit at res time with 10 day cancel policy, 25% service fee; Rain-check if less than 10 days; Check-in 4pm **BROCHURE:** Yes **PERMITTED:** Smoking, limited children [E06BCME-2962]

White Barn Inn	Kennebunkport ME
Laurie Cameron	PO Box 560C 04046
207-967-2321	

Rates:	**Pvt Bath** 24	**Payment Terms:**
Single	$ 90.00 EP	Check
Double	$ 110.00 EP	AE/MC/V

A restored and renovated barn offers a casual yet elegant atmosphere. Dining is excellent; winner of *1983 Silver Spoon Award*! Continental off-season. **RESERVATIONS:** One night's deposit at res time **SEASONAL:** No **BROCHURE:** Yes **PERMITTED:** Children [C11ACME-1399]

Winters Inn		Kingfield ME
Mike Thom		Winters Hill 04947
207-265-5421		**Res Times** 7am-11pm

Rates:	**Pvt Bath** 9	**Shared Bath** 2	**Payment Terms:**
Single	$ 90.00	$ 75.00	Check
Double	$ 105.00	$ 85.00	AE/MC/V

Originally designed by the Stanley Brothers, developers of the *Stanley Steamer* automobile, this charming Victorian mansion offers New England elegance and atmosphere with modern amenities. Listed on the *National Register of Historic Places*. Meals available on the premises with added cost. **RESERVATIONS:**

Deposit or credit card to hold room, 48 hour cancel policy **SEA-SONAL:** No **BROCHURE:** Yes **PERMITTED:** Children, smoking **LANGUAGES:** French [C11ACME-1403]

Melfair Farm		**Kittery ME**
Claire Cane		365 Wilson Rd 03904
207-439-0320		

Rates:	**Shared Bath** 4	**Payment Terms:**
Single	$ 70.00	Check
Double	$ 75.00	

This 1871 New England traditional farmhouse in rolling pasture provides guests with warmth and hospitality. Close to shopping, beaches and historical Portsmouth. Continental plus breakfast. **RESERVATIONS:** Deposit required at res time **SEASONAL:** No **BROCHURE:** Yes **PERMITTED:** Children 11-up, drinking **LANGUAGES:** French [C11ACME-1404]

Halcyon Days B&B		**Machias ME**
Pat & Donna LaValle		7 Freemont St 04654
207-255-4662		**Res Times** 7am-10pm

Rates:	**Shared Bath** 3	**Payment Terms:**
Single	$ 35.00	Check
Double	$ 50.00	MC/V

Halcyon Days is an ancient Greek expression for peaceful, happy, golden times . . . and what guests can expect when sharing your hosts 1890 Homestead Bed & Breakfast while in Down East Maine. Restored to radiate the charm and serenity of a simpler lifestyle, our neighborhood home features comfortable, tasteful furnishings accented with the romance of florals and lace. This hillside location affords a panoramic view of the Machias River and the town beyond which is enjoyed year round from the heated, enclosed porch. Guests enjoy a hearty homestyle full breakfast served on the enclosed porch or at the family breakfast nook - or perched on a stool alongside the cooking island to chat with the chief cook and bottle washer! The choice is yours. Located just off Rt 1, guests are within walking distance of quaint downtown shops, tennis courts and river fishing. Being just across from Bad Little Falls Park, guests can enjoy watching Harbor Seals frolic with their pups or spot Osprey and Bald Eagles searching the river for their next meal. Other activities include hiking, island hopping to visit the light houses, whale and seal watching tours, white water and canoe expeditions, golf, beach combing, clamming and summer theater and chamber music concerts. Picnic lunches and family-style dinners are available at added cost and with advance notice **DISCOUNTS:** 10% of stays over 4 days **AIRPORT:** Bangor Intl-95 mi **RESERVATIONS:** One night's deposit to confirm res with 24 hr cancel policy for refund (unless re-rented), late arrival (after 9pm) by prior arrangement only **SEASONAL:** No **BROCHURE:** Yes **PERMITTED:** Children 12-up, limited drinking, limited smoking (in parlor only) **CONFERENCES:** Yes, groups to 10 persons [R12DPME-14843]

Penury Hall		**Mount Desert Island ME**
Gretchen & Toby Strong		PO Box 68 04679
207-244-7102		

Rates:	**Shared Bath** 3	**Payment Terms:**
Single	$ 45.00	Check
Double	$ 50.00	

An 1830 frame home furnished in a traditional mixture of antiques, family heirlooms and original art. Friendly and hospitable, your hosts make for an enjoyable visit to this charming town. Full breakfast included. **RESERVATIONS:** Deposit required at res time **SEASONAL:** No **BROCHURE:** Yes **PERMITTED:** Children 17+, drinking [C11ACME-1423]

Songo B&B House		**Naples ME**
Judy & Ben Garron		PO Box 554 04055
207-693-3960		**Res Times** 9am-8pm

Rates:	**Pvt Bath** 2	**Shared Bath** 3	**Payment Terms:**
Single	$ 70.00	$ 65.00	Check
Double	$ 80.00	$ 75.00	

Rustic country setting for this residence offering year-round activities for the entire family. Close to historic Songo Locks, swimming, tennis and golf are available with excellent skiing in winter. Full breakfast included. Just off Rt 302 **SEASONAL:** No **BROCHURE:** Yes **PERMITTED:** Limited children [C11ACME-1429]

Captains House   Newcastle ME

Joe Sullivan/Susan Rizzo   19 River Rd 04553
207-563-1482

Rates:	Shared Bath 5	Payment Terms:
Single	$ 60.00	Check
Double	$ 70.00	

Grand Greek Revival styling in this former sea captain's residence on the Damariscotta River, c1840. Large sunny guest rooms with excellent views. Full country breakfast included. **RESERVATIONS:** 50% deposit required within 7 day of booking **SEASONAL:** No **BROCHURE:** Yes **PERMITTED:** Limited children [C11ACME-1433]

**Newcastle Inn   Newcastle ME

Ted & Chris Sprague   River Rd 04553
800-832-8669 207-563-5685   **Res Times** 10am-6pm

Rates:	Pvt Bath 15	Payment Terms:
Single	$ 70-110.00*	Check
Double	$ 90-135.00*	MC/V

The oldest continuously operating Inn (c1930s) in the area, started as a Cape with a carriage house in the mid-1800s and has been tastefully transformed into a classic New England dormered Federal-Style colonial that is nestled on a picture-perfect bank of the Damariscotta River. Inside, guests find the owner/hosts retained all the fine touches including beautiful stenciled floors, award winning needlework and your hosts extensive rabbit collection, an inviting fireplaced common living room for relaxation and conversation, with a large glassed and screened porch for year-round nature and river viewing. Winter brings hot cider and a fireplace for guests to gather around. Wide, open halls and winding staircases lead to the guest rooms on the second and third floors, several with fascinating views of the town of Darmariscotta, the water and with fireplaces. Year-round activities for everyone include: Boothbay Harbor, Freeport, Pemaquid Regions all within a short drive, swimming, boating, fishing, antiquing, bird-watching (puffins & bald eagles) and picturesque terrain for biking. Relax in the backyard watching the ever-changing scenery. **MEALS:** Multi-course gourmet breakfast is served in the sun-filled dining room and a prix fixe five course candlelight fireside dinner is available *(MAP $105-145 S/$145-190 Double, off season) and hors d'oeuvres (6-7pm). *Food & Wine* magazine calls the *Newcastle Inn* *". . . exactly what a small country inn should be . . . superb."* **RESERVATIONS:** One night's deposit required, 7 day cancel policy less $20 service fee. If room is rerented, deposit may be used for credit within 6 months of canceled stay. **BROCHURE:** Yes **PERMITTED:** Limited drinking, no smoking **CONFERENCES:** Yes, Seasonal from 11/1-5/30 **PACKAGES:** Inquire at res time [Z07GPME2-7443]

---

*Oliver Farm Inn   **Nobleboro ME**
                                                        Old Rt #1   04555
207-563-1527

Rates:	Shared Bath 5	Payment Terms:
Single	$ 55.00	Check
Double	$ 60.00	

Completely restored farmhouse built c1795 and furnished with classic Early American antiques where guests can relax in comfort on this 20 acre setting. Homemade quilts, stenciled walls and many family heirlooms furnish the guest rooms. A full breakfast is included with complimentary evening snacks and beverages. **SEASONAL:** Open 6/15-10/15 **BROCHURE:** Yes **PERMITTED:** Children [C11ACME-1437]

---

*Blue Shutters Inn   **Ogunquit ME**
Jean Dahler   6 Beachmere Place   03907
207-646-2163

Rates:	Pvt Bath 5	Payment Terms:
Single	$ 70.00	Check
Double	$ 75.00	

This tranquil setting offers spectacular views, great New England hospitality and beautiful scenery year-round. Quaint beaches just a short stroll away. **SEASONAL:** No **BROCHURE:** Yes **PERMITTED:** Smoking & drinking [C11ACME-1447]

---

*Hartwell House   **Ogunquit ME**
Trisha & Jim Hartwell   116 Shore Rd   03907
207-646-7210

Rates:	Pvt Bath	9	Payment Terms:
Single	$ 120.00		Check
Double	$ 140.00		MC/V

Elegant residence offers genuine antiques from England and Early Americana. Perfect setting to relax while visiting New England with over two acres of sculptured gardens. Continental breakfast is included. Swimming and tennis available. **BROCHURE:** Yes **PERMITTED:** Limited smoking, limited drinking **SEASONAL:** No **CONFERENCES:** Yes for business or social events including gourmet dining. [C11ACME-1453]

Morning Dove B&B			**Ogunquit ME**

Peter & Eeta Schon   30 Bourne Lane 03907-1940
207-646-3891   **Res Times** 9am-9pm

Rates:	Pvt Bath	4	Shared Bath	2	Payment Terms:
Single	$ 75-105.00		$ 55-80.00		Check
Double	$ 75-105.00		$ 55-80.00		AE/DISC/MC/V

The *Morning Dove* is a tastefully restored 1860's farmhouse formerly owned by the Moses Littlefield family. It has light airy rooms furnished with antiques and European accents. The owner is an ASID interior designer and has designed each room to be totally unique. Antique collectibles such as brass beds, quilts, lace curtains and art by local artists are some of the furnishings. Breakfast is served cafe-style on the Victorian porch or in the elegant dining room. The Inn is conveniently located on a quiet side street and surrounded by spectacular and now famous gardens. Its a short stroll to the beaches, the Marginal Way, Perkins Cove, the Playhouse, shops, galleries and restaurants. The trolley stops on the corner. Candies and welcoming wine are complimentary. Hiking, tennis, outlet shopping and Mount Argamenticus for fall foliage are all nearby. Its an easy drive to Kennebunkport, Portsmouth's Strawberry Banke, Freeport, Kittery and Portland. The Portland Jetport is just 35 minutes and Boston's Logan Airport is and hour and fifteen minutes. **RESERVA-TIONS:** 50% deposit within 7 days of booking to hold room, 10 day cancel policy for refund less $10 service fee; min stay during peak periods (mid-June to Labor Day) discounts for long stays **BRO-CHURE:** Yes **PERMITTED:** Drinking, children 12-up **PACKAGES:** *Champagne Package*, off-season **LANGUAGES:** Conversational French [S04GPME2-6831]

Seafair Inn   Ogunquit ME
Jeff Walker   24 Shore Rd   03907
207-646-2181

Rates:	Pvt Bath	16	Shared Bath	3	Payment Terms:
Single	$ 75.00		$ 60.00		Check
Double	$ 95.00		$ 70.00		MC/V

Beautiful restored Victorian residence and Inn complete with antique furnishings and period pieces. Close to all sights, shops, antiques and fine dining. Beach nearby. Continental breakfast included. Afternoon high tea and pastry. **BROCHURE:** Yes **PERMITTED:** Children, smoking, limited drinking **SEASONAL:** No **LANGUAGES:** French [C11ACME-1461]

Yardarm Village Inn   Ogunquit ME
LC & PC Drury   142 Shore Rd   03907
207-646-7006

Rates:	Pvt Bath	8	Payment Terms:
Single	$ 59.00-Up		Check
Double	$ 59.00-Up		

Yardarm Village Inn - With old New England atmosphere is adjacent to Perkins Cove In Oqunquit and offers comfortable accommodations in this quiet part of Ogunquit, yet guests are just a short walk from the Marginal Way, Perkins Cove and the town beaches. All of the guest rooms include private baths, cable TV, refrigerators and air conditioning. A continental breakfast is included and the breakfast coffee an famous homemade blueberry muffins are a must! *Yardarm Village Inn Wine & Cheese Shop* offers domestic and international wines of distinction with cheeses and crackers to pique the most discriminating tastes. **AIRPORT:** Portland-29 mi **SEASONAL:** No **BROCHURE:** Yes **PERMITTED:** Children, drinking, limited smoking [R10EPME2-1465]

Inn At Parkersburg   Portland ME
Judy & Bob Riley   135 Spring   04101
207-774-1059

Rates:	Pvt Bath	5	Shared Bath	2	Payment Terms:
Single	$ 85.00		$ 75.00		Check

Double $ 100.00 $ 85.00   MC/V

An 1845 circa townhouse in the center of town in a unique three-story design, one of Portland's finest.   Fresh flowers, night-time chocolates and comfy towels are just a few touches this charming hostess provides. Continental breakfast included. **BROCHURE:** Yes **SEASONAL:** No **PERMITTED:** Children 5-up, smoking [C11ACME-1474]

York Harbor Inn   **Portland ME**
Gary Dominquez
800-343-3869 207-363-5119   **Res Times** 8am-11pm
                                    Fax 207-363-3545

Rates:	**Pvt Bath** 29	**Shared Bath** 5	**Payment Terms:**
Single	$ 79.00	$ 69.00	Check
Double	$ 99.00	$ 89.00	AE/DC/MC/V

Refer to the same listing name under York Harbor, Maine for a complete description. [M06FPME1-8252]

Craignair Inn   **Rockland ME**
Norman & Terry Smith
207-594-7644   **Res Times** 9am-9pm

Rates:	**Pvt Bath** 5	**Shared Bath** 16	**Payment Terms:**
Single	$ 75.00	$ 40.00	Check
Double	$ 80.00	$ 65.00	DISC/MC/V

Refer to the same name listed under Clark Island, Maine for a complete description. [M08BCME-8800]

Sign of the Unicorn   **Rockport ME**
Winnie Easton   191 Beauchamp Ave 04865
207-236-8789

Rates:	**Pvt Bath** 2	**Shared Bath** 2	**Payment Terms:**
Single	$ 75.00	$ 75.00	Check
Double	$ 80.00	$ 75.00	

Great location for visiting Rockport. Overlook Rockport Harbor and enjoy sailing, fishing, golf, theater, tennis with fine dining at many excellent seafood restaurants full gourmet breakfast included. Sitting room and piano for guests **BROCHURE:** Yes **PERMITTED:** Children, limited smoking, limited drinking [C11ACME-1484]

**Crown 'N' Anchor Inn	**Saco ME**
John Barclay/Marth Forester	121 North St 04072-0228
207-282-3829	**Res Times** 24 Hrs

Rates:	**Pvt Bath** 6	**Payment Terms:**
Single	$ 50-85.00	Check
Double	$ 50-85.00	MC/V

Dating from 1827-28, this Greek revival two-story home was built by George Thacher, Jr, descendant of the First Congressman from the district of Maine and is a fine example of rich detail and delicate lightness typical of the Federal/Adamesque-style and with a temple front. Listed on the *National Register of Historic Places* in the State of Maine, ornate Victorian furnishings, double parlors with twin mirrors and a bountiful country breakfast provide lasting memories for guests after departing. The *Normandy Suite* on the second floor is a favorite, offering Indian shutters, fireplace and a private adjacent whirlpool bath. All rooms at the *Crown 'N' Anchor Inn* are furnished with period antiques, many collectibles and provide both a homelike atmosphere and luxurious pampered comfort while vacationing or taking time for a special weekend. Located on North Street, the *Crown 'N' Anchor Inn* is at the hub of local attractions. The York Institute Museum, Thornton Academy and the Dyer Library are all a leisurely walk from the center of the lovely tree-lined main street of Saco, a treasure-trove of 18th and 19th Century architecture. A short drive brings guests to the ocean beaches of Saco or Old Orchard Beach. Kennebunkport, Wells, Ogunquit and the shopping malls of Kittery and Freeport are but minutes away. **RESERVATIONS:** One night deposit to guarantee, 10 day cancel policy; less than 10 day cancellation, 50% refund, no refund for non-arrival **SEASONAL:** Rates vary **PERMITTED:** Limited children, limited pets, limited drinking, no smoking **BROCHURE:** Yes **PACKAGES:** Yes, inquire at res time **CONFERENCES:**

Groups to fifty persons **LANGUAGES:** French [I04GPME2-12828]

Homeport	**Searsport ME**
Edith & George Johnson	Rt 1 Box 647 Main St 04972
800-742-5814 207-282-3829	

Rates:	**Pvt Bath** 6	**Payment Terms:**
Single	$ 37.00	Check
Double	$ 60-75.00	AE/DISC/MC/V

This sea captain's residence with widow's walk has been fully restored and is listed on the *National Historic Register*. Your charming hosts operate their inn as a traditional English and Scottish "bed & breakfast" which has been open to the public for sixteen years. *Homeport* continues to offer guests a rare opportunity to enjoy the warm, homey, hospitable atmosphere while visiting New England. The guest rooms are complete with antique furnishings, family heirlooms, canopy beds, crystal chandeliers and lace curtains. Guests can enjoy the family room with its English Pub, *The Mermaid* and the dining room, both on the lower level. A porch or patio setting is offered for breakfast which includes exquisite views of the Bay. A full breakfast is included. Year-round activities include sailing, tennis, golf, cruises on the Bay, pleasant walks along the shore, forest trails and hills with visits to interesting antique and gift shops. October offers brilliant Fall foliage while Winter offers fine x-country skiing. A Victorian oceanside cottage is available for weekly rental at $475.00. **DISCOUNTS:** 10% travel agents; 5% Seniors; 5% weekly stays. **AIRPORT:** Bangor Intl Airport-40 mins **RESERVATIONS:** $25 non-refundable deposit for each night's stay in advance is required **SEASONAL:** No **BROCHURE:** Yes **PERMITTED:** Limited children, smoking, drinking [I07GPME2-1488]

Atlantic Seal B&B	**South Freeport ME**
Captain Thomas & Gaila Ring	25 Main St 04078
207-865-6112	**Res Times** 7:30am-9pm

Rates:	Pvt Bath 2	Shared Bath 2	Payment:
Single	$ 90.00	$ 55.00	Check
Double	$ 100-125.00	$ 65-85.00	

Lovely harbor views await you in each cozy bedroom of our 1850's Cape Cod home, located on the ocean in historic South Freeport Village and furnished with antiques and nautical collections of our seafaring family. "The Glen" has an antique full-size sleigh bed and a shared bath. "The Heart's Desire" has a queen-sized four-poster pineapple bed and a windowseat, and may have a shared or private bath. "The Dash" has a full-size and queen-size bed and private bath, complete with a Jacuzzi whirlpool bath for two and a separate shower. All three guest rooms feature sea breezes, fresh flowers, thick towels, comfortable beds, homemade quilts and down comforters. Enjoy our friendly down-east hospitality, complimentary snacks & beverages by the fireplace in our old-fashioned parlor, hearty sailor's breakfast and cruises of Casco Bay. Just a five minute drive to outlet stores. Resident dog and cat. Open year-round. **RESERVATIONS:** One night's deposit, 14 day cancel notice less $10 service charge, late arrival by prior arrangement **SEASONAL:** Closed Christmas **BROCHURE:** Yes **PERMITTED:** Limited children, smoking outside [R09CPME-10012]

Claremont Southwest Harbor ME

Mr Mrs Allen McCue
207-244-5036

Rates:	Pvt Bath 23	Shared Bath 3	Payment Terms:
Single	$ 110.00	$ 85.00	AE/MC/V
Double	$ 110.00-up	$ 95.00	

An 1844 summer Inn on the Sound Shore offering traditional New England styling and atmosphere and the home for the Annual Croquet Tournament. Full breakfast included. Other meals available with added cost. **BROCHURE:** Yes **PERMITTED:** Children, smoking and drinking [C11ACME-1499]

Broad Bay Inn & Gallery Waldoboro ME

Jim & Libby Hopkins
207-832-6668

Main St 04572
Res Times 8am -8pm

Rates:	Pvt Bath 1	Shared Bath 4	Payment Terms:

Single	$ 70.00	$ 45-65.0	Check
Double	$ 75.00	$ 55-65.00	MC/V

A lovely colonial Inn offering candlelight dinners on the weekends. Sunny guest rooms are filled with Victorian furnishings with canopy beds in some rooms. Close to Maine's coastal sights and points of interest which include artist's workshops, Camden Shakespeare Theatre, summer stock and jazz concerts. Full breakfast included with other meals available at added cost. **COMPLIMENTARY:** Bikes, tea or sherry outdoors in the early evening **RESERVATIONS:** One night's deposit at res time **SEASONAL:** No **BROCHURE:** Yes **PERMITTED:** Children 16-up, limited smoking [E09BCME-1523]

Le Vatout B&B	**Waldoboro ME**
Don Slagel	Rt 32 South 04572
207-832-4552	**Res Times** 8am-10pm

Rates:	Pvt Bath 1	Shared Bath 3	Payment Terms:
Single	$ 75.00	$ 45.00	Check
Double	$ 75.00	$ 55-65.00	MC/V

A rural setting midway between Brunswick and Belfast (perfect stopping place for exploring the scenic peninsulas of mid-coast Maine) is the locale for this restored pre-Civil War home on the village edge. Just a half mile off Rt 1, you'll enjoy the coast and the quiet Maine countryside. Enjoy meeting this interesting host who dabbles in most everything including his landscaped yard and gardens (included in the Annual Garden Tour Event). He also has a musical background and experience as an actor/singer, musician and teacher. Full breakfast included. **RESERVATIONS:** Credit card to hold room, 24 hr cancel policy for refund. Late arrival only if guaranteed with advanced payment **SEASONAL:** No **BROCHURE:** Yes **PERMITTED:** Children, limited drinking, limited smoking **LANGUAGES:** French, German, Spanish [E02BCME-1520]

**Stacked Arms*	**Wiscasset ME**
Dee, Sean, Pat Maguire	Birch Point Rd 04578
207-882-5436	**Res Times** 8am-9pm

Rates:	Shared Bath 5	Payment Terms:
Single	$ 45-50.00	Check

Double	$ 65-80.00	MC/V

A saltbox cabin that was moved to this beautiful hilltop location around the turn-of-the-century and has had three additions. All of the bedrooms are decorated in different styles and colors. Enjoy New England charm year-round and its gorgeous fall foliage and summer flower gardens in this setting just one mile from town. Full breakfast is served in a large sunny dining room which overlooks beautiful flower gardens, terraces and even a pond! You're close to everything here: plenty of shopping for pottery and antiques and museums. Just 20 mins from Boothbay Harbor and coastal New England, LL Bean, swimming & beaches at Reid State Park and great x-country skiing trails nearby with bike and walking trails during the summer months. Experience New England hospitality in this peaceful and serene setting shared with a military family who enjoy sharing their home with new friends. Picnic lunches and dinner available at added cost. **RESERVA-TIONS:** One night's deposit with 48 hr cancel policy; arrival before 9 pm unless prior arrangements have been made **SEASONAL:** No **BROCHURE:** Yes **PERMITTED:** Limited children, limited smoking, limited drinking [A03DPME-3614]

Wild Rose of York			York ME

Fran & Frank Sullivan   78 Long Sands Rd 03909
207-363-2532

Rates:	Pvt Bath 2	Shared Bath 2	Payment Terms:
Single	$ 48.00	$ 38.00	Check
Double	$ 56.00	$ 46.00	

This 1814 residence captures ocean breezes while nestled atop its hillside setting and offers guests cozy guest rooms with antique beds, patchwork quilts and fireplaces. Close to deep sea fishing, golf, hiking and plenty of shops and restaurants for an enjoyable visit in New England. Your host is a biology professor. Continental breakfast is included. **COMPLIMENTARY:** Tea, sherry and cookies in afternoon. **BROCHURE:** Yes **SEASONAL:** No **PERMITTED:** Children, smoking, drinking [E11ACME-3617]

O'Regans Inn	York Beach ME

Ms Maureen O'Regan   49 Main St 03910
207-363-5706

Rates:	**Shared Bath** 5	**Payment Terms:**
Single	$ 60.00	Check
Double	$ 65.00	

A quaint New England Inn close to the ocean offering charm and traditional New England hospitality to all guests and located in the center of town. Walk to all the sights, shops and antique areas. A continental breakfast is included. There's tennis, swimming and plenty of sightseeing. **BROCHURE:** Yes **PERMITTED:** Children, limited smoking **SEASONAL:** No [E11ACME-3621]

**York Harbor Inn		**York Harbor ME**

Gary Dominquez
800-343-3869 207-363-5119
Rt 1A 03911
Res Times 8am-11pm
Fax 207-363-3545

Rates:	**Pvt Bath** 29	**Shared Bath** 6	**Payment Terms:**
Single	$ 79.00	$ 69.00	Check
Double	$ 99.00	$ 89.00	AE/CB/DC/MC/V

For over one hundred years, the historic charm and hospitality of the *York Harbor Inn* have welcomed those seeking distinctive lodging and dining experiences. Nestled in the heart of York Harbor, amid classic oceanfront estates and the sights and sounds of the Atlantic - - the *York Harbor Inn* enjoys a truly auspicious natural setting. A short walk takes you to a peaceful, protected beach. A stroll along Marginal Way reveals hidden coastal scenes and fine properties. Golf, tennis, biking, deep-sea fishing and outlet shopping are all close by. Each of the guest rooms is furnished with fine antiques, some offering Ocean Views and fireplaces. The oceanfront Dining Room offers top-rated cuisine and fine wines; and the downstairs tavern, *The Wine Cellar*, features pub-style comfort and entertainment. **DISCOUNTS:** Senior citizens, off-season rates available **AIRPORT:** Boston Logan Intl-55 mi; Portland Jetport-50 mi; Pease Tradeport-10 mi **PACKAGES:** Yes, inquire at res time for details **RESERVATIONS:** 50% deposit required at res time with 14 day cancel policy for refund; 100% deposit for one night's stay,. late check-in available with prior arrangements **BROCHURE:** Yes **PER-**

MITTED: Children, drinking, limited smoking **CONFERENCES:** Yes, five meeting rooms, 5000 sq ft **LANGUAGES:** Spanish, French [I07GPME2-3625]

Addison
PLEASANT BAY
B&B
207-483-4490

Alfred
OLDE BERRY INN
207-324-0603

Aquia
INN AT COLD
STREAM
207-732-3595

Bailey Island
CLOVERLEAF
COTTAGES B&B

DRIFTWOOD INN

KATIES KETCH

LADY & THE LOON
307-833-6871

Bangor
*PHENIX INN
207-947-3850

Bar Harbor
ATLANTEAN INN
207-288-3270

BASS COTTAGE, IN
THE FIELD

*BAYVIEW INN &
HOTEL
207-288-3173

BLACK FRIAR INN
207-288-5091

BREAKWATER 1904

800-238-6309

CANTERBURY
COTTAGE
207-288-2112

CASTLEMAINE INN
c1865
207-288-4563

CLEFTSTONE
MANOR
800-962-9762

GRAYCOTE INN
800-GRA COTE

HEARTHSIDE INN
207-288-4533

*HOLBROOK
HOUSE
800-695-1120

KAY LODGING
207-288-3531

LEDGELAWN INN
207-288-4596

MANOR HOUSE INN
800-437-0088

*MAPLES
207-288-3443

**MIRA MONTE INN
800-553-5109

PRIMROSE
COTTAGE
207-288-4031

RIDGEWAY MANOR

SHADY MAPLES
207-288-3793

*STRATFORD
HOUSE
207-288-5189

THORNHEDGE INN
207-288-5398

TIDES
207-288-4968

TOWN GUEST
HOUSE
800-458-8644

*ULLIKANA IN THE
FIELD
207-288-9552

Bass Harbor
BARR HARBOR INN
207-244-5157

POINTY HEAD INN
207-244-7261

Bath
1024 WASHINGTON
B&B
207-443-5202

ELIZABETHS B&B
207-443-1146

GLAD II
207-443-1191

*GRANES
FAIRHAVEN
207-443-4391

Belfast

ADALINE PALMER
HOUSE
207-338-5790

FROST HOUSE
207-338-4159

****HIRAM ALDEN
INN**
207-338-2151

HORATIO
JOHNSON HOUSE
207-338-5153

JEWELED TURRET
INN
207-338-2304

NORTHPORT
HOUSE
800-338-1422

PENOBSCOT
MEADOWS
207-338-5320

Bethel
BAKERS B&B
207-824-2088

BETHEL INN &
COURT
207-654-0125

CHAPMAN INN
207-824-2657

DOUGLAS PLACE
207-824-2229

FOUR SEASONS
INN
207-824-2755

HAMMONS HOUSE
207-824-3170

L'AUBERGE INN
207-824-2774

NORSEMAN INN
207-824-2002

POINTED FIR B&B
207-824-2251

SUDBURY INN
207-824-2174

SUNDAY RIVER INN
207-824-2410

TELEMARK INN
207-836-2703

Bieeldfordpool
LODGE
207-284-7148

Bingham
MRS FRANCES
GIBSON
207-672-4034

Blue Hill
ARCADY DOWN
EAST
207-374-5576

BLUE HILL FARM
COUNTRY INN
207-374-5126

BLUE HILL INN
207-374-2844

JOHN PETERS INN
207-374-2116

Boothbay
CAPT SAWYER
PLACE
207-633-2290

COBURN HOUSE
INN

KENNISTON HILL
INN
207-633-2159

LINEKIN BAY
RESORT

SPRUCE PT INN &
LODGES

THISTLE INN
207-633-3541

Boothbay Harbor
ADMIRALS
QUARTERS
207-633-2474

**ANCHOR WATCH
207-633-7565

ATLANTIC ARK INN
207-633-5690

BOOTHBAY
HARBOR INN
207-633-6302

GREEN SHUTTERS
INN
207-633-2646

HARBOUR TOWNE
INN
207-633-4300

*HILLTOP GUEST HOUSE
207-633-2914

HOWARD HOUSE
207-633-3933

JOHNATHANS B&B
207-633-3588

SEAFARER B&B
207-633-4441

TOPSIDE
207-633-5404

WELCH HOUSE
207-633-3431

WESTGATE GUEST HOUSE
207-633-3552

Bridgton
NOBLE HOUSE
207-647-3733

TARRY-A-WHILE RESORT
207-647-2522

Bristol
BRISTOL INN

OLD CAPE OF BRISTOL MILLS B&B
207-563-8848

Brunswick
AARON DUNNING HOUSE
207-729-4486

BRUNSWICK B&B
207-729-4914

CAPT DANIEL STONE INN
207-725-9898

DOVE B&B
207-729-6827

HARBORSGATE B&B
207-725-5894

HARRIET BEECHER STOWE HOUSE
207-725-5543

SAMUEL NEWMAN HOUSE
207-729-6959

Bucksport
*L ERMITAGE
207-469-3361

OLD PARSONAGE INN
207-469-6477

RIVER INN
207-469-3783

Camden
A LITTLE DREAM
207-236-8742

ABIGAILS
207-236-2501

AUBERGINE
207-236-8053

BLACKBERRY INN
207-236-6060

BLUE HARBOR HOUSE
800-248-3196

CAMDEN HARBOUR INN
207-236-4200

CHESTNUT HOUSE
207-236-6137

EDGECOMB-COLES HOUSE
207-236-2336

ELMS
207-236-6250

**GOODSPEEDS GUEST HOUSE
207-236-8077

HARTSTONE INN
207-236-4259

**HAWTHORN INN
207-236-8842

HIGH TIDE INN
207-236-3724

HOSMER HOUSE B&B
207-236-4012

INN AT SUNRISE POINT
800-23-SUNRISE

LORD CAMDEN INN

207-236-4325

MAINE STAY B&B
207-236-9636

NORUMBEGA INN
207-236-4646

OWL AND
THE TURTLE
207-236-4769

WHITEHALL INN
207-236-3391

WINDWARD HOUSE
207-236-9656

Cape Elizabeth
CRESCENT BEACH
INN
207-799-1517

INN BY THE SEA

Cape Neddick
CAPE NEDDICK
HOUSE
207-363-2500

SEA CHIMES B&B
207-646-5378

*****WOODEN GOOSE
INN**
207-363-5673

Cape Newagen
NEWAGEN SEA-
SIDE INN
207-633-5242

Cape Rosier
HIRAM BLAKE

CAMP

**Carrabassett
Valley**
SUGARLOAF INN
207-237-2701

Casco Village
CASCO INN

Castine
CASTINE INN
207-326-4365

HOLIDAY HOUSE
207-326-4335

MANOR INN
207-326-4861

PENTAGOET INN
207-326-8616

Center Lovell
CENTER LOVELL
INN
207-925-1575

WESTWAYS ON
KEZAR LAKE
207-928-2663

Chamberlain
*****OCEAN REEFS ON
LONG COVE**
207-677-2386

Chebeague Island
CHEBEAGUE INN
BY THE SEA
207-846-5155

Cherryfield
BLACK SHUTTER

INN

RICKER HOUSE
207-546-2780

Clark Island
*****CRAIGNAIR INN**
207-594-7644

Copper Mills
CLARYKNOLL
FARM
207-549-5250

Cornish
*CORNISH INN
207-625-8501

**Cumberland
Center**
SUNRISE ACRES
FARM
207-829-5594

Damariscotta
*****BRANNON
BUNKER INN**
207-563-5941

DOWNEASTERS
INN

ELIZABETHS B&B
207-563-1919

Deer Isle
EGGEMOGGIN INN
207-348-2540

PILGRIMS INN
207-348-6615

Deer Isle Village
LAPHROAIG B&B

207-348-6088

Dennysville
LINCOLN HOUSE
COUNTRY INN
207-726-3953

Dexter
BREWSTER INN OF
DEXTER
207-924-3130

Dixfield
VON SIMM'S
VICTORIAN INN
B&B
207-562-4911

Dixmont
BEN-LOCH INN
207-257-4768

Dover-Foxcroft
BIRCHES

CRAWFORD FARM

Eagle Lake
CAMPS OF ACADIA

East Boothbay
FIVE GABLES INN
207-633-4551

LIMEKIN VILLAGE
B&B
207-278-7624

OCEAN POINT INN
207-633-4200

East Broadbay
TREASURE ISLAND

East Machais
EAST RIVER B&B
207-255-8467

East Waterford
WATERFORD INNE
207-583-4037

Eastport
*ARTISTS
RETREAT
207-853-4239

TODD HOUSE
207-853-2328

WESTON HOUSE
207-853-2907

EWENICORN FARM
B&B
207-439-1337

*HIGH MEADOWS
B&B
207-439-0590

Ellsworth
EAGLES LODGE
207-667-3311

VICTORIAS B&B
207-667-5893

Five Islands
COVESIDE

GREY HAVENS INN
207-371-2616

Fort Kent
DAIGLES B&B
207-834-5803

Foxcroft
FOXCROFT B&B
207-564-7720

Freeport
181 MAIN STREET
207-865-1226

**ATLANTIC SEAL
B&B**
207-865-6112

BAGLEY HOUSE
800-765-1772

BAYBERRY B&B
207-865-1868

**CAPT JOSIAH
MITCHELL HOUSE**
207-865-3289

COTTAGE STREET
INN
207-865-0932

COUNTRY AT
HEART
207-865-0512

HARRASEEKET INN
800-342-6423

HOLBROOK INN
B&B
207-865-6693

*ISAAC RANDALL
HOUSE
207-865-9295

LUCERNE INN
800-325-5123

OLD RED FARM
207-865-4550

WHITE CEDAR INN
207-865-9099

Freyburg
ADMIRAL PEARY
HOUSE
800-237-8080

WOOD DOCTORS
COUNTRY INN

FORD HOUSE INN
207-935-3442

Gorham
COUNTRY SQUIRE
B&B
207-839-4855

Gouldsboro
SUNSET HOUSE
207-963-7156

*Grand Lake
Stream*
LEENS LODGE

WEATHERBY
FISHING RESORT

Greenville
CHESUNCOOK
LAKE HOUSE

EVERGREEN
LODGE

GREENVILLE
MANOR
207-695-2206

Guilford
GULIFORD B&B
207-876-3477

TREBOR INN
207-876-0470

Hancock
CROCKER HOUSE
207-433-6806

LE DOMAINE
207-422-3395

Hancock Point
CROCKER HOUSE
COUNTRY INN
207-422-6806

Harrison
TOLMAN HOUSE
INN
207-583-4445

Hartford
GREEN ACRES INN
207-597-2333

Haven
HAVEN
207-646-4194

Hulls Cove
INN AT CANOE
POINT
207-288-9511

Isle Au Haute
KEEPERS HOUSE
207-367-2261

Isleboro
MOSS INN
207-734-6410

Isleford
ISLAND B&B
207-244-9283

Islesboro
*DARK HARBOR
HOUSE INN
207-734-6669

Jonesboro
CHANDLER RIVER
LODGE
207-434-2651

Jonesport
TOOTSIES B&B

Kennebunk
**ALEWIFE HOUSE
207-985-2118

ARUNDEL
MEADOWS INN
207-965-3770

CAPT LITTLEFIELD
207-985-3937

KENNEBUNK INN
1799
207-983-3351

*LAKE BROOK
GUEST HOUSE
207-967-4069

MERRYFIELDS INN

Kennebunkport
**1802 HOUSE
B&B
207-967-5632

**ALEWIFE HOUSE

Maine

207-985-2118

BREAKWATER
207-967-3118

BURRLEHEAD
COVE
207-967-3879

CAPT JEFFERDS
INN
207-967-2311

***CAPT LORD
MANSION**
800-522-3141

****CAPTAIN
FAIRFIELD HOUSE**
800-322-1928

CHETWYND HOUSE
207-967-2235

COLONY

COVE HOUSE
207-967-3704

DOCK SQUARE INN
207-967-5773

ENGLISH
MEADOWS INN
207-967-5766

ENGLISH ROBIN
207-967-3505

FALKEYARD FARM
207-967-5965

*FARM HOUSE B&B
207-967-4169

GREEN HERON INN
207-967-3315

HARBOR INN
207-967-2074

INN AT GOOSE
ROCKS
207-967-5425

***INN AT HARBOR
HEAD**
207-967-5564

****INN ON SOUTH
STREET**
207-967-5151

****KENNEBUNK-
PORT INN**
800-248-2621

**KILBURN HOUSE
207-967-4762

KYLEMERE HOUSE
1818
207-967-2780

****MAINE STAY INN
& COTTAGES**
800-950-2117

NORTH STREET
GUEST HOUSE

OCEAN VIEW
207-967-2750

OLD FORT INN
800-828-3678

***OLDE GARRISON
HOUSE**

207-967-3522

*PORT GALLERY
207-967-3728

PORT GARDENS
207-967-3358

SEASIDE INN
207-967-4461

SHAWMUT INN

SUNDIAL INN
207-967-3850

TIDES INN BY THE
SEA
207-967-3757

VILLAGE COVE INN
207-967-3993

WELBY INN
207-967-4655

*WHITE BARN INN
207-967-2321

Kingfield
HERBERT INN
207-265-2000

INN ON WINTERS
HILL
207-265-5421

ONE STANLEY AVE

THREE STANLEY
AVENUE
207-343-5541

*WITNERS INN

207-265-5421

Kittery
*MELFAIR FARM
207-439-0320

Kittery Point
HARBOUR WATCH
207-439-3242

WHALEBACK INN
B&B
207-439-9570

Lincolnville
CEDARHOLM
COTTAGES
207-236-3886

RED HOUSE
207-236-4621

SIGN OF THE OWL
207-338-4669

YOUNGTOWN INN
207-763-3037

Litchfield
OLD TAVERN INN
207-268-4965

Longville
LONGVILLE
207-235-3785

Lubce
BAYVIEWS
207-733-2181

Lubec
BREAKERS-BY-THE-
BAY
207-733-2487

DUE EAST
BAILEY'S MISTAKE
207-733-2413

HOME PORT INN
207-733-2077

OVERVIEW
207-733-2005

Lubel
HUGEL HAUS B&B
207-733-4965

Machias
CLARK PERRY
HOUSE
207-255-8458

****HALCYON DAYS
B&B**
207-255-4662

Manset
MOORINGS

Millbridge
BAYSIDE INN
207-546-7852

Monhegan
MONHEGAN
HOUSE
207-594-7983

Monhegan Island
ISLAND INN
207-596-0371

SHINING SAILS INC
207-596-0041

TRAILING YES

Mount Desert
COLLIER HOUSE
207-288-3162

Mount Desert Island
*PENURY HALL
207-244-7102

Mount Vernon
FEATHER BED INN
207-293-2020

Naples
*AUGUSTUS BOVE
HOUSE
207-693-6365

CHARMWOODS ON
LONG LAKE
207-693-6798

HAVEN
207-693-6602

INN AT LONG LAKE
207-693-6226

LAMB'S MILL INN
207-693-6253

***SONGO B&B
HOUSE**
207-693-3960

New Harbor
BRADLEY INN
207-677-2105

GOSNOLD ARMS
207-677-3727

New Portland
GILMAN STREAM

B&B
207-628-6257

Newcastle
CAPTAINS HOUSE
207-563-1482

ELFINHILL
207-563-1886

GLIDDEN HOUSE
207-563-1859

MARKERT HOUSE
207-563-1309

MILL POND INN
207-563-8014

****NEWCASTLE INN****
800-832-8669

Newport
LAKE
SEBASTICOOK B&B
207-368-5507

Nobleboro
OLIVER FARM INN
207-563-1527

Norridgewock
NORRIDGEWOCK
COLONIAL INN
207-634-3470

North Edgecomb
CHANNELRIDGE
FARM
207-882-7539

North Haven
PULPIT HARBOR
INN

207-867-2219

North Waterford
OLDE ROWLEY INN

Northeast Harbor
ASTICOU INN

GREY ROCK INN
207-276-9360

HARBORSIDE INN
207-276-3272

Oakland
BEAR SPRING
CAMP

PRESSEY HOUSE -
1850
207-465-3500

Ogunquit
ADMIRALS INN
207-646-7093

ADMIRALS LOFT
207-646-5496

BEAUPORT INN
207-646-8680

BLUE SHUTTERS
207-646-2163

BLUE WATER INN
207-646-5559

CHANNING HALL
207-646-5222

CLIPPER SHIP
GUEST HOUSE
207-646-9735

DUNE ON THE
WATERFRONT

GAZEBO
207-646-3733

***HARTWELL
HOUSE***
207-646-7210

HIGH TOR
207-646-8232

INN AT
FIELDSTONE

JUNIPER HILL INN
207-646-4501

LEISURE INN
207-646-2737

**MORNING DOVE
B&B**
207-646-3891

OGUNQUIT HOUSE
207-646-2967

PUFFIN INN
207-646-5496

SEAFAIR INN
207-646-2181

STRAUSS HAUS
207-646-7756

TERRACE BY THE
SEA
207-646-3232

TRELLIS HOUSE
207-646-7909

YARDARM
VILLAGE INN
207-646-7006

YELLOW MONKEY
INN
207-646-9056

Oquossoc
OQUOSSACS OWN
B&B
207-864-5584

Otisfield
CLAIBERNS B&B
207-539-2352

Peaks Island
KELLERS B&B
207-766-2441

MOONSHELL INN
207-766-2331

Pemaquid Falls
LITTLE RIVER INN
& GALLERY
207-677-2845

Phippsburg
RIVERVIEW

Poland Spring
POLAND SPRING
INN
207-998-4671

Port Clyde
COPPER LIGHT
207-372-8510

OCEAN HOUSE
207-372-6691

Portland
*INN AT
PARKERSPRING
207-774-1059

INN ON CARLETON
207-775-1910

POMEGRANATE INN
207-772-1006

WEST END INN
207-772-1377

**YORK HARBOR
INN**
207-363-5119

Prospect Harbor
OCEANSIDE
MEADOWS INN
207-963-5557

Prouts Noch
BLACK POINT INN

Rangeley
COUNTRY CLUB
INN
207-864-3831

FARMHOUSE INN
207-864-5805

Rangely
RANGELY INN
800-MOMENTS

Raymond
NORTH PINES
HEALTH RESORT
207-655-7624

Robinhood

BENJAMIN RIGGS
HOUSE
207-371-2256

Rockland
CRAIGNAIR INN
207-594-7644

Rockport
BREAD & ROSES
B&B
207-236-6116

ROSEMARY
COTTAGE
207-236-3513

*SIGN OF
THE UNICORN
207-236-8789

Round Pond
BRIAR ROSE B&B
207-529-5478

Saco
**CROWN 'N'
ANCHOR**
207-282-3829

Sanford
ALLENS INN
207-342-2160

Sargentville
OAKLAND HOUSE
207-359-8521

Scarborough
HIGGINS BEACH
207-883-6684

Searsport
BRASS LANTERN

INN
207-548-0150

CARRIAGE HOUSE
INN
207-548-2289

**HOMEPORT
207-548-2259

MCGILVERY
HOUSE
207-548-6289

*THURSTON
HOUSE
207-548-2213

Sebasco Estates
ROCK GARDENS
INN
207-389-1339

Sedgewick
SEDGEWICK B&B

Short Sands Beach
HOMESTEAD INN
B&B
207-363-8952

Skowhegan
BRICK FARM B&B
207-474-3949

South Berwick
ANIC B&B

South Brooksville
BREEZEMERE
FARM INN
207-326-4618

BUCKS HARBOR

INN
207-326-8660

South Casco
MIGIS LODGE
207-655-4524

THOMAS INN
& PLAYHOUSE
207-655-7728

South Freeport
**ATLANTIC SEAL
B&B
207-865-6112

South Gouldsboro
BLUFF HOUSE
207-963-7805

South Harpswell
HARPSWELL
HOUSE
207-833-5509

South Thomaston
*WESKEAG INN
207-596-6676

South Waldoboro
BARN

Southport
ALBONEGON INN
207-633-2521

Southwest Harbor
*CLAREMONT
207-244-5036

HARBOR LIGHTS
HOME
207-244-3835

HARBOUR WOODS
207-244-5388

ISLAND HOUSE
207-244-5180

ISLAND WATCH
B&B
207-244-7229

KINGSLEIGH INN
207-244-5302

LINDENWOOD INN
207-244-5335

TWO SEASONS

Springfield
OLD FARM INN
207-738-2730

Stonington
CAPTAINS
QUARTERS

Stratton
WIDOWS WALK
207-246-6901

Strong
COPPER HORSE
INN
207-684-3300

Sullivan
SULLIVAN HARBOR
FARM
207-422-3591

Sullivan Harbor
ISLAND VIEW INN
207-422-3031

Sunset
*GOOSE COVE
LODGE
207-348-2508

Surry
SURRY INN
207-667-5091

Tenants Harbor
EAST WIND INN &
MEETING HOUSE
207-372-6366

MILL POND HOUSE
207-372-6209

The Forks
CRAB APPLE
ACRES
207-663-2218

Thomaston
BEDSIDE MANOR
INN
207-354-8862

CAP'N FROST'S
B&B
207-354-8217

GRACIES B&B
207-354-2326

*RIVER HOUSE
B&B
207-354-8936

Topsham
CAPT PURINTON
HOUSE

MIDDAUGH B&B
207-725-2562

WALKER WILSON
HOUSE
207-729-0715

Twin Mountain
PARTRIDGE HOUSE

Van Buren
FARRELL-MICHAUD
HOUSE
207-868-5209

Vinalhaven
FOX ISLAND INN
207-686-2122

Waldoboro
BLACKFORD INN
207-832-4714

***BROAD BAY INN &
GALLERY**
207-832-6668

***LE VATOUT B&B**
207-832-4552

LETTENEY FARM
VACATIONS
207-832-5143

MEDOMAK HOUSE
207-832-4971

ROARING LION
207-832-4038

SNOW TURTLE INN
207-832-4423

TIDE WATCH INN
207-832-4987

Walpole
BITTERSWEET INN
207-563-5552

Washington
WINDWARD FARM
207-845-2830

Waterford
KEDARBURN INN
207-583-6182

LAKE HOUSE
207-583-4182

Waterville
LAMPLIGHTER
B&B
207-872-2432

Weld
KAWANHEE INN
207-778-4306

LAKE WEBB
HOUSE B&B
207-585-2479

WELD INN
207-585-2429

Wells
BAYVIEW INN B&B
207-646-9260

GREY GULL INN
207-646-7501

PURPLE
SANDPIPER
GUEST HOUSE
207-646-7990

West Bath

BAKKE B&B
207-442-7185

NEW MEADOWS
INN
207-443-3921

West Bethel
KINGS INN
207-836-3375

**West Boothbay
Harbor**
LAWNMEER INN
207-633-2544

West Gouldsboro
SUNSET HOUSE
207-963-7156

Winter Harbor
MAIN STAY INN
207-963-5561

Wiscasset
SQUIRE TARBOX
INN
207-882-7693

STACKED ARMS
207-882-5436

Yarmount
HOMEWOOD INN
207-846-3351

York
CANTERBURY
HOUSE
207-363-3505

DOCKSIDE GUEST
QUARTERS
207-363-2868

*HANNAHS LOFT
207-363-7244

SCOTLAND BRIDGE
INN
207-363-4432

SUMMER PLACE
207-363-5233

**WILD ROSE OF
YORK**
207-363-2532

York Beach
CANDLESHOP INN
207-363-4087

HOMESTEAD INN
B&B
207-363-8952

LIGHTHOUSE INN
207-363-6023

O'REGANS INN
207-363-5706

York Harbor
BELL BUOY
207-363-7264

EDWARDS
HARBORSIDE
207-363-3037

INN AT HARMON
PARK
207-363-2031

MOORELOWE
207-363-2526

YORK HARBOR

INN
800-343-3869

Massachusetts

Allen House Victorian Inn   **Amherst MA**
Alan & Ann Zieminski   599 Main St 01002
413-253-5000   **Res Times** 24 Hrs

Rates: **Pvt Bath** 5   **Payment Terms:**
Single $ 45-95.00   Check
Double $ 55-105.00   Tvlrs Ck

Featured in the *New York Times* Travel Section (May 8, 1994), *Fodors '94* and *Bon Appetit* (featured Christmas Inn, 1994) - *The Allen House Victorian Inn*, in the heart of Amherst on over three landscaped acres with its many peaked gables, ornately carved Austrian verge board, oriental Chippendale and multiple relief shingles, is one of the finest examples of Queen Anne - Stick-style architecture. The interior was restored with historic precision to every last detail to reflect the Aesthetic Movement, the Victorian subculture that emphasized art in the interior decor. The original handcarved cherry wood fireplace mantels are catalogued by the Metropolitan Museum of Art in New York City. This 1886, eighteen room architectural gem offers five spacious museum-quality guest rooms with private bath and air conditioning. A full formal breakfast, afternoon and evening tea and refreshments are served at guests' convenience. Free pick-up service from the nearby Amtrack Train and bus stations. Free local bus transportation, walk to nearby Emily Dickinson Homestead, Amherst College, the Univ of Massachusetts, fine galleries, museums, theaters, concerts, shops and restaurants. Visit nearby Mount Holyoke, Smith and Hampshire Colleges, Northampton, Historic Deerfield and Old Sturbridge Village. *1991 Historic Preservation Award Winner; AAA ♦ ♦ ♦ ; ABBA Rated Excellent* **RESERVATIONS:** None, call for information **SEASONAL:** No **PERMITTED:** Children 11-up, drinking, smoking on outside verandas **BROCHURE:** Yes **AIRPORT:** Hartford-Springfield-Bradley-45 mins [R08GPMA2-16699]

---

*Ashfield Inn   **Ashfield MA**
Michael & Susan Brakefield   Main St 01330
413-628-4571

Rates:	Pvt Bath	2	Shared Bath	2	Payment Terms:
Single	$ 80.00		$ 80.00		Check
Double	$ 90.00		$ 85.00		AE/MC/V

Elegant Georgian mansion on estate filled with gardens, porches, and seclusion for a perfect romantic setting. Beautiful interior with grand sweeping center hall stairway leading to period furnished guest and common rooms. All the details are here: terry robes, chocolates at night, flowers, and an exciting gourmet full breakfast served in the main dining room. **RESERVATIONS:** 50% deposit of length of stay in advance or credit card for guarantee. Five day notice of cancellation for refund **SEASONAL:** No **BROCHURE:** Yes **PERMITTED:** Children 10-up, limited smoking [E11ACMA-1626]

**Captain Samuel Eddy House Inn	**Auburn MA**
John & Carilyn O'Toole	609 Oxford St S 01501
508-832-5282 508-832-3149	**Res Times** After 4 pm

Rates:	Pvt Bath	5	Payment Terms:
Single	$ 52.00		Check
Double	$ 67-90.00		MC/V

Let us make your expectations in lodging your most memorable Country Inn experience. Step back in time to the warmth and charm of the 18th Century. Soft music enhances the evening for your candlelight dinner in the dining room or private parlors. Our chef will prepare a portion of dinner on the open hearth and breads in the bee hive oven. Breakfast is never ordinary, with favorites of stuffed French toast with berries and cream or ham and egg souffle. The bed chambers offer oak and canopy beds king, queen & twin sizes. Antique furnishings adorn the chambers, that include private baths and sitting areas. You'll find turned-down beds, chocolates, and a gift on your pillow, encouraging champagne dreams. Country walks, ice skating, yard games and a refreshing pool are just a few activities offered for your relaxation. Visit the country store with antiques, crafts, period clothing and herbs. The Inn is located less than 45 mins from Boston, 10 mins from Worcester and 15 mins from Sturbridge, all which have a wide variety of interesting places to explore. Brimfield has an antique flea market (May, July, Sept) which is the largest in New England, with over 4000 dealers. Special events include **Stew & Stories, Murder Weekends**, small weddings and rehearsal dinners. Dinner, MAP, full breakfast & evening tea. **RESERVATIONS:** 50%

deposit, late arrivals must call ahead. **SEASONAL:** No **BROCHURE:** Yes **PERMITTED:** Children welcomed, limited smoking, limited drinking **CONFERENCES:** Yes, including dining [Z06EPMA2-6544]

**Bacon Barn Inn	**Barnstable MA**
Mary Giuffreda	3400 Main St 02630
508-362-5518	**Res Times** 8:30am-6pm

Rates:	**Pvt Bath** 3	**Payment Terms:**
Single	$ 85-95.00	Check
Double	$ 85-95.00	

Come visit a Victorian Country Barn with a unique romantic atmosphere and listed on the *National Register of Historic Places.* Formerly a part of the Daniel Bacon estate, a wealthy captain from Boston, the property later became the home of Ambassador Robert Bacon. The property still maintains much of its original architecture, such as the cupola and pegged beams throughout the Inn. The spaciousness of the fireplaced common area combined with the elegantly decorated rooms make this a special retreat to enjoy while visiting Cape Cod. A homemade country breakfast is served each morning on the enclosed porch filled with wicker on tables set just for two. Off-season guests enjoy their breakfast in front of a warm cozy fire in the dining area. Located in historic Barnstable Village, guests are within walking distance to many fine restaurants, shopping, antiques, Barnstable Harbor, Millway Beach and whale watch cruises. Conveniently located, we are just a short drive to Hyannis where guests can take a ferry to Nantucket or Martha's Vineyard. **RESERVATIONS:** 50% deposit with reservation - 14 day cancel notice for refund, 3 pm check-in, 11 am check-out **SEASONAL:** Rates vary **BROCHURE:** Yes **PERMITTED:** Drinking, children 13-up [R03DPMA-11982]

**Cobbs Cove	**Barnstable MA**
Evelyn Chester/HJ Studley	Rt 6A 02630
508-362-9356	**Res Times** 9am-9pm
	Fax 508-362-9356

Rates:	**Pvt Bath** 6	**Payment Terms:**
Single		Check
Double	$ 149-189.00	AE/MC/V

Wonderful secluded Timbered Colonial Inn, just a delightful

get-away for couples on Cape Cod's historic Northside District. Lovely waterviews everywhere and of Barnstable Village harbor. You can enjoy all the beach activities with just a short walk to the bathing beach, charter fishing facility, or whale watch from the Inn. Fine shopping at the nearby village stores and dining in unique Cape Cod restaurants and delicious seafood!! All accommodations are spacious with whirlpool tubs in all baths with imported bath oils & terry robes. Gratuitous refreshments daily. Large Count Rumford fireplace in Keeping Room for guests. Fabulous library for guest's use. Hearty full Yankee breakfasts served in garden-patio area. Dinner for guests only, upon request **RESERVATIONS:** $100.00 deposit per night seven days prior to arrival **BROCHURE:** Yes **PERMITTED:** Drinking, limited smoking **CONFERENCES:** Yes, small groups **LANGUAGES:** French [A06GPMA2-1632]

****Honeysuckle Hill**   Barnstable MA

Barbara Rosenthal
508-362-8418

Rates:	Pvt Bath	3	Payment Terms:
Single	$ 90-105.00		Check
Double	$ 90-105.00		AE/DC/MC/V

Refer to the same listing name under West Barnstable, Massachusetts for a complete description. [M10EPMA2-16414]

***Belvedere B&B**   Bass River MA

Judy & Dick Fenuccio   167 Main St 02664
617-398-6674   **Res Times** 8am-7pm

Rates:	Pvt Bath	2	Shared Bath	3	Payment Terms:
Single	$ 55.00		$ 45.00		Check
Double	$ 65.00		$ 55.00		

Perfect Federal design colonial 1820 circa, nestled on a country lane owned by a sea captain, Capt Isaiah Baker, that remains much the same as it did then. Furnished with period antiques. Hearty New England breakfast included. **SEASONAL:** No **BROCHURE:** Yes **PERMITTED:** Limited children, limited drinking [C11ACMA-1637]

Captain Isaiah House   Bass River MA

Alden & Marge Fallows   33 Pleasant St   02664
617-394-1739

Rates:	Pvt Bath 6	Shared Bath 2	Payment Terms:
Single	$ 45.00	$ 40.00	Check
Double	$ 55.00	$ 50.00	

Restored sea captain's home in historic district with plenty of ambience for the late 1800's. Fireplaces in all rooms to warm those hearty spirits. Continental breakfast include with homebaked breads & breakfast rolls to start each day. **SEASONAL:** No **BROCHURE:** Yes **PERMITTED:** Children, smoking, drinking [C11ACMA-1638]

1810 House B&B   Boston MA

Susanne & Harold Tuttle
617-659-1810   **Res Times** 8am-9pm

Rates:	Pvt Bath 2	Shared Bath 1	Payment Terms:
Single	$ 55-65.00	$ 55.00	Check
Double	$ 65-75.00	$ 65.00	

Refer to the same listing name under Norwell, Massachusetts for a complete description. [M07FPMA1-17769]

Allen House   Boston MA

Christine Gilmour
617-545-8221   **Res Times** 8am-10:30am

Rates:	Pvt Bath 2	Shared Bath 2	Payment Terms:
Single	$ 89-119.00	$ 79-99.00	Check
Double	$ 89-119.00	$ 79-99.00	AE/MC/V

Refer to the same listing name under Scituate, Massachusetts for a complete description. [M01FPMA2-16688]

Beacon Hill B&B   Boston MA

Susan Butterworth   27 Brimmer St   02180
617-523-7376

Rates:	Pvt Bath 3		Payment Terms:

Single	$ 115-145.00	Check
Double	$ 115-145.00	

Beacon Hill Bed & Breakfast is an 1869 Victorian six-story townhouse overlooking the Charles River. It lies on "the Flat" within the historic district of Beacon Hill, a neighborhood known for its architectural elegance, gas-lit, tree-lined streets, brick sidewalks, window boxes and hidden gardens. The location is **Boston's Best** - a short walk to Boston Common and the Public Garden, *Cheers*, the State House and Freedom Trail connecting historic sites including Qunicy Market, downtown, Filene's Basement and Theater District. Charles Street is lined with antique & flower shops with a public garage and a subway stop connecting you within 15 mins to Harvard, the Museum of Fine Arts, the Isabella Stewart Gardner Museum, Symphony Hall, Kennedy Library, hospitals, universities and Logan Airport. The three guest rooms are very spacious with sitting rooms and fireplaces, eleven to twelve foot ceilings, original doors, moldings & hardware. They are attractively furnished with an eye to comfort. A full complimentary breakfast featuring homemade granola & baked goodies is served in the coral dining-sitting room with a river view, crystal chandelier, oriental rug and family antiques. Your hostess, who has lived here for 26 years, is a caterer and a former French teacher who spent her childhood in Paris. She looks forward to sharing her intimate knowledge of Boston with her guests. **RESERVATIONS:** One night's deposit, 21 day cancel notice for refund less $10, two night minimum weekends, three day minimum holidays **SEASONAL:** No **BROCHURE:** Yes **PERMITTED:** Limited children, limited drinking **LANGUAGES:** French [Z09GPM-A2-12003]

**Cape Cod Sunny Pines Inn	**Boston MA**
Jack & Eileen Connell	
508-432-9628	**Res Times** 9am-9pm

Rates:	**Pvt Bath** 8	**Payment Terms:**
Single	$ 75-95.00	Check
Double	$ 85-100.00	AE/MC/V

Refer to the same listing name under Harwich, Massachusetts for a complete description. [M05FCMA2-11835]

**Harborside House

Boston MA

Susan Livingston
617-631-1032

Res Times 8am-8pm

Rates:	**Shared Bath** 2	**Payment Terms:**
Single	$ 60-65.00	Check
Double	$ 70-75.00	

Refer to the same listing name under Marblehead, Massachusetts for a complete description. [M05FPMA2-14781]

**Land's End Inn

Boston MA

David Schoolman
508-487-0706

Res Times 9am-10pm

Rates:	**Pvt Bath** 16	**Payment Terms:**
Single	$ 98-240.00	Check
Double	$ 98-240.00	

Refer to the same listing name under Provincetown, Massachusetts for a complete description. [M11BCMA-6553]

**Manor On Golden Pond

Boston MA

David & Bambi Arnold
800-545-2141 603-968-3348

Res Times 9am-9pm

Rates:	**Pvt Bath** 27	**Payment Terms:**
Single	$ 110-175 MAP	Check
Double	$ 155-220 MAP	AE/MC/V

Refer to the same listing name under Holderness, New Hampshire for a complete description. [M10EPNH2-16450]

**Oasis Guest House

Boston MA

Joe Haley
617-267-2262

22 Edgerly Rd 02115
Res Times 8am-Midnight
Fax 617-267-1920

Rates:	**Pvt Bath** 11	**Shared Bath** 5	**Payment Terms:**
Single	$ 78.00	$ 50.00	Check
Double	$ 78.00	$ 55.00	AE/MC/V

The *Oasis Guest House* was designed and decorated with a clear understanding of the special needs of the traveler. Comfort, quality, cleanliness and an affordable price. Totally renovated, the *Oasis* is conveniently close to Prudential Center (Hynes Auditorium) in Boston's Back Bay. Our lobby, living room. outdoor decks and accommodations are handsomely appointed with comfortable furnishings blended with modern conveniences. Amenities include all new private and shared baths, central a/c, color Tvs and a computer phone system. A complimentary breakfast is served each morning and includes coffee, juice and danish while complimentary set-ups (BYOB) and hors d'oeuvres are offered each evening. A friendly staff is always available to assist you. Come experience the rewards of staying in an atmosphere that caters to your lifestyle and budget. Like many of the finer hotels in Boston, we are centrally located in the Back Bay - yet unlike the finer hotels, our rates are substantially lower. **RESERVATIONS:** One night deposit required to guarantee reservation, 24 hour check-in **PERMITTED:** Drinking, limited smoking **BROCHURE:** Yes **DISCOUNTS:** Yes, inquire at res time **AIRPORT:** Logan-10 mins [ZO97GMA2-7243]

**York Harbor Inn			**Boston MA**
Garry Dominquez			
207-363-5119		**Res Times** 8am-11pm	

Rates:	Pvt Bath	29	Shared Bath 6	Payment Terms:
Single	$ 79.00		$ 69.00	Check
Double	$ 99.00		$ 89.00	AE/MC/V

Refer to the same listing located under York Harbor ME for a complete description. [M06BCME-8253]

---

*Captain Freeman Inn		**Brewster MA**
Carol Covitz	15 Breakwater Rd RR#4 02631	
508-896-7481		

Rates:	Pvt Bath	7	Shared Bath 3	Payment Terms:
Single	$ 60-70.00		$ 50-Up	Check
Double	$ 70-80.00		$ 60-Up	

Built in 1860 without concern for expense including details such as imported plaster moldings & two-tone inlaid wood floors, you can enjoy the restoration the present owner/hosts are completing.

Ideal for family stays in this Village Green locale; continental breakfast included outdoors around pool, weather permitting **SEASONAL:** No **BROCHURE:** Yes **PERMITTED:** Children 12-up [C11ACMA-1650]

**Isaiah Clark House	**Brewster MA**
Chas & Ida Dicesare	1187 Main St 02631
508-896-2223	

Rates:	**Pvt Bath** 7	**Payment Terms:**
Single	$ 82-100.00	MC/V
Double	$ 82-100.00	

Guests return to the *Isaiah Clark House* time and time again because of the charming Colonial ambiance, the five acres of landscaped grounds and the delicious Full American breakfasts served on the deck or in the 1780 Keeping Room. The seven guest rooms are decorated differently with antiques and canopy beds. Fluffy robes, evening chocolates, Afternoon Tea and complimentary use of bicycles are some of the amenities that have made this Inn so popular. Walk to beautiful Cape Cod Bay or bike the nearby Cape Cod Bike Trail. A sunset at Paine's Creek Beach is unforgettable. The Inn is a great location whether you choose to relax in a hammock or explore the many natural attractions of the Cape. All bedrooms are air conditioned in summer; and three have working fireplaces providing a cozy and romantic getaway Fall and Winter Vacation spot. Honeymooners are offered a special five night package! This historical Inn makes for a great Holiday anytime of the year. Recommended as *Best of the Outer Cape* by *Innsiders Guide to Cape Cod.* **AIRPORT:** Hyannis/Barnstable-15 mins; Boston's Logan-90 mins. **DISCOUNTS:** 10% Seniors (62+) **RESERVATIONS:** Deposit required, 10 day cancel policy for refund **SEASONAL:** No **BROCHURE:** Yes **PERMITTED:** Children 13-up, drinking, limited smoking **CONFERENCES:** Meeting room available **LANGUAGES:** Italian, German, French [R10EPMA2-1652]

---

*Ocean Gold B&B			**Brewster MA**
James & Margaret Geisler			RR #2 02631
617-255-7045			

Rates:	**Pvt Bath** 1	**Shared Bath** 2	**Payment Terms:**
Single	$ 75.00	$ 55.00	Check

Double $ 85.00 $ 65.00

Charming two story contemporary home in a lovely wooded suburban area with whirlpool, fireplace and country fresh eggs and hosts that will make your visit an event. Close to Atlantic and Bay for lobstering. Full breakfast included **SEASONAL:** No **BROCHURE:** Yes **PERMITTED:** Limited drinking. [C11ACMA-1653]

**Old Manse Inn	**Brewster MA**
Sugar & Doug Manchester	1861 Main St 02631
508-896-3149	**Res Times** 8am-10pm

Rates:	**Pvt Bath** 9	**Payment Terms:**
Single	$ 60-90.00	Check
Double	$ 70-100.00	AE/DC/MC/V

Brewster on Cape Cod is called the *"sea captain's town"* for its historical role for world-travelling sea captains of the China-trade era. One such home is the *Old Manse Inn,* built in the early 1800s by Capt Winslow Lewis Knowles - has been renovated by the present owners, providing nine guest rooms and two gracious dining rooms. A warm cozy atmosphere has been created by the antique furnishings, hand-braided and Oriental rugs, patchwork quilts and old-fashioned wallpapers. Each guest room is individually appointed and includes a private bath with fireplaces in some. The common rooms are a favorite gathering area with their early spring and late fall fires, comfortable sofas and original prints and paintings. *Dinner At The Manse* features a gourmet menu and romantic candle-light dining and recommended by *Travel & Leisure, Boston Herald* and the *Los Angeles Times,* **Mobil ★★★**. The *Chef de Cuisine* prepares elegant selections including mussel, fontina, plum tart; ginger marinated breast of chicken served on lemon pasta with apricot sauce and for dessert, a spectacular bittersweet chocolate mousse meringues. (Dining is available Memorial Day to Oct 15). A full complimentary breakfast is provided. Sugar and Doug invite you to share their delightful manse, the fine food and friendly surroundings, the heritage of this famous "sea captain's town" and hope you will return often to renew fond memories of your stay with them. **RESERVATIONS:** One night's deposit or 50% of stay, bal upon arrival, two weeks cancel policy for refund, call for late arrivals (after 9 pm) Commissions only for min of 2 night stay **PERMITTED:** Drinking, limited smoking **SEASONAL:** Yes **BROCHURE:** Yes **DISCOUNTS:** Special midweek rate for three night minimum stay **AIRPORT:** Hyannis-30 min; Boston Logan-2 hrs. [Z08GPMA2-1654]

Beacon Inn			**Brookline MA**
Hy Gloth		1087 & 1750 Beacon St	02146
617-566-0088		**Res Times**	9am-9pm

Rates:	Pvt Bath 8	Shared Bath 16	Payment Terms:
Single	$ 65.00	$ 58.00	Check
Double			

These spacious turn-of-the-century townhouses have been converted into two of Brookline's most charming guest houses. The original woodwork is reminiscent of their 19th Century construction with fireplaces in the lobby extending a friendly welcome to all guests. There are large, comfortable furnished guest rooms that offer bright sunny surroundings at a surprisingly affordable price. The area offers a wide variety of restaurants, shops, museums, theaters, and other attractions. Boston's major hospitals are easily accessible by public or private transportation. Free parking available. No meals available. **RESERVATIONS:** Check for full payment 10 days in advance of arrival; arrival after 8:00 pm subject to $10.00 additional charge **SEASONAL:** No **PERMITTED:** Children, limited smoking, limited drinking [A07ACMA-1656]

Salty Dog Inn			**Cape Cod MA**
Lynn & Jerry Goldstein		Cotuit	02635
508-428-5228		**Res Times**	9am-9pm

Rates:	Pvt Bath 1	Shared Bath 4	Payment Terms:
Single	$ 60-75.00	$ 45-55.00	Check
Double	$ 60-75.00	$ 50-60.00	MC/V

Experience *The Cape* in the town *Yankee Magazine* referred to as *"... one of the most beautiful (settings) in America."* This charming and quaint Inn was owned by a sea captain and eventually converted into a gracious small Inn **RESERVATIONS:** Full payment policy **SEASONAL:** No **BROCHURE:** Yes **PERMITTED:** Children [E02BCMA-1680]

Anderson Wheeler Home   Concord MA

David & Charlotte Anderson   154 Fitchburg Turnpike 01742
508-369-3756

Rates:	**Shared Bath** 5	**Payment Terms:**
Single	$ 65.00	Check
Double	$ 65.00	MC/V

Original *Whipple Tavern* rebuilt after a fire in 1890. Served as a stagecoach stop and continues to offer guests antique furnishings mixed with four poster or canopy beds and with working fireplaces in all rooms. Thoreau's cabin and *Walden's Pond* are just a short distance. Continental plus breakfast included. **SEASONAL:** No **BROCHURE:** Yes **PERMITTED:** Children and social drinking. [E11ACMA-1674]

**Swift River Inn*   Cummington MA

Brenda Burdick   151 South St 01026
800-532-8022 413-634-5751

Fax 413-634-5300

Rates:	**Pvt Bath** 22	**Payment Terms:**
Single	$ 69.00	Check
Double	$ 69.00	AE/DISC/MC/V

The Swift River Inn is a former turn-of-the-century gentleman's dairy farm that was restored for guest lodging, dining and recreation. Our twenty-two suites and guest rooms are uniquely decorated and are named after local artists, attractions and authors. Our restaurant specializes in fresh fish and regional cuisine. Breakfast, lunch and dinner are served, in addition to a bountiful Sunday Brunch. A continental breakfast of fresh home-made pastries is included in our room rates. *The Lodge At Swift River Inn*, added in November 1992, serves as the recreation center. During the winter months, we offer cross-country skiing on six hundred acres with 24km of impeccably groomed trails. In addition, we have snowmaking on 5km and night skiing on 2.5km. Two New England favorites, sleigh rides and ice skating are also available. Summer and fall recreation programs include: tennis, swimming, mountain biking, nature walks, fishing, volley ball, badminton, boccie ball, horseshoes and more! The setting of the *Swift River Inn* is ideal for corporate meetings, executive retreats, weddings and family reunions. The Library is the perfect place for intimate gatherings. The Meadow-brook Room is ideal for small meetings and receptions. The Hayloft Ballroom, with its open-beamed ceiling and the Pinnacle Room of the Lodge are perfect for parties and weddings, accommodating groups to 175 persons. The Trailside Tavern has a casual, relaxed atmosphere and serves food and drinks with entertainment on most weekends. Conferences can be combined with outdoor recreation which are ideal for stress reduction and team building. **RESERVATIONS:** Last night's deposit required; 14 day cancellation policy for refund **SEASONAL:** Rates vary **PERMITTED:** Children, drinking, no smoking **BROCHURE:** Yes **DISCOUNTS:** AARP, AAA, Off-season, midweek, corporate rates available **AIRPORT:** Hartford, CT Bradley-62 mi **PACKAGES:** *Cross-country Skiing, Family, Romance B&B, MAP*, inquire at res time [I07GPMA2-17202]

**Four Chimneys Inn			**Dennis MA**
Russell & Kathy Tomasetti			946 Main St 02638
508-385-6317			**Res Times** 7am-10pm

Rates:	**Pvt Bath** 6	**Shared Bath** 2	**Payment Terms:**
Single	$ 95.00	$ 55.00	Check
Double	$ 95.00	$ 55.00	AE/DC/MC/V

The *Four Chimneys Inn* is a ch-arming Queen Anne Victorian located on Historic Rt 6A in Den-nis. It is located across from Scargo Lake which offers some of the best fresh water fishing on Cape Cod. The bay beaches, Dennis Village, the Cape Play-house, the Cape Art Museum, restaurants and shops are all a short walk away. As you walk  through the antique double front doors, the large entrance foyer with its unique staircase is very inviting. Eleven foot ceilings with medallions, spacious rooms with marble fireplaces and large windows add to the charm of the Inn. The living room has a working fireplace. The library has a TV with VCR and eight foot

French doors leading to the screened porch. Enjoy a continental breakfast in the dining room or on the porch. Guests relax on the patio or under the arbor surrounded by perennial gardens. All bedrooms are located on the second and third floors. Six spacious bedrooms have private showers or tub baths. The two cozier rooms share a hall bath. The bedrooms have a queen bed or a queen and a twin bed. The smaller guest rooms have a double bed. All guest rooms offer garden, wooded or lake views. **AIRPORT:** Boston Logan-90 mi; Cape Cod Airport-10 mi **RESERVATIONS:** Full deposit for up to two days or 3 day weekend; 50% deposit for three days or longer, bal upon arrival, 14 day cancel policy less 10% service fee **SEASONAL:** No **BROCHURE:** Yes **PERMITTED:** Children 7-up, limited drinking, limited smoking **CONFERENCES:** Common rooms accommodate to 50 persons [I07GPMA2-1688]

**Isaiah Hall B&B Inn	**Dennis MA**
Marie Brophy	152 Whig St 02638
800-736-0160 508-385-9928	**Res Times** 8:30am-10pm

Rates:	**Pvt Bath** 10	**Shared Bath** 1	**Payment Terms:**
Single	$ 64-96.00	$ 52-54.00	Check
Double	$ 74-107.00	$ 57-59.00	AE/MC/V

Come share the delight of Cape Cod's past. Sleep on antique white iron and brass beds warmed by quilts. Wake to the sound of birds and the smell of coffee. Breakfast on hearty breads and muffins in a spacious antique-filled dining room evoking a bygone era. Take a leisurely walk past beautiful old homes to our beach or village. These simple country pleasures await you at the *Isaiah Hall Bed & Breakfast Inn*. Tucked away on a quiet historic street, this lovely 1857 farmhouse has had a tradition as an Inn since 1948 with cheerful guestrooms in both the Main House and Carriage House. Today, it continues as a romantic country refuge where you may chose to relax on a porch rocker, in front of a victorian stove in the converted carriage house great room with white wicker furniture and knotty pine walls. The guestrooms are decorated with charming country antiques with most having private baths and queen beds. Three rooms have two beds, four rooms include balconies and one has a fireplace. Non-smoking rooms are available. Air conditioning is available. A walk through the village will provide you with fine restaurants, antiques, crafts and one-of-a-kind shops, as well as the Cape Museum of Fine Arts, and in summer, the Cape Playhouse. Close by you can enjoy bike trails, tennis and golf. Located in the heart of the Cape, Dennis offers a central homebase for day trips to other scenic, recreational and historic points of interest. **DISCOUNTS:** Yes, inquire at res time. **AIRPORT:** Hyannis/Barnstable-8 mi **PACKAGES:** Spring, Sunday to Thursday **RESERVATIONS:** One night's deposit at res time or 50% if longer, 10 day cancel notice for refund; late arrival with advance notice. **SEASONAL:** Closed 10/15-3/31 **BROCHURE:** Yes **PERMITTED:** Children 7-up, drinking, limited smoking **CONFERENCES:** Yes, for small groups [I07GPMA2-1689]

**Rose Petal B&B	**Dennisport MA**
Gayle & Dan Kelly	152 Sea St 02639
508-398-8470	**Res Times** 8am-9pm

Rates:	Pvt Bath	2	Shared Bath	1	Payment Terms:
Single	$ 89.00*		$ 62.00*		Check
Double	$ 89.00		$ 62.00		AE/MC/V

A most picturesque traditional New England home complete with picket fence, guests are invited to share this historic 1872 residence. Built for Almond Wixon, whose family was among the original settlers of the village of Dennisport. He was lost at sea with all on board the *Cross Rip Light Ship* in 1918. Completely restored and decorated in 1986 to  accommodate guests in a delightful seaside resort neighborhood, your hosts (former university administrators) welcome every guest to their lifestyle. The guest rooms offer queen size or twin beds and air conditioning. There's a comfortable parlor to enjoy TV, piano or current magazines. For your convenience, a refrigerator is available. A full homemade breakfast is prepared each morning where Dan, an expert baker and pastry chef tempts your senses with his culinary expertise along with fresh ground coffee, specialty teas, cereals, juice and fresh fruit. The interesting history of Cape Cod is just a short stroll away from century-old houses and cottages and the warm water of the beaches of Nantucket Sound. A short drive takes you to the ferries to Nantucket and Martha's Vineyard and the nearby antique and craft shops and restaurants offering a variety of dining experiences. *Rated ABBA 3 Crown, AAA* ♦♦♦ **RESERVATIONS:** Full deposit in advance for 1-2 nights, 50% for longer stays within 5 days of booking, bal due upon arrival; 14 day cancel policy including partials **SEASONAL:** Rates vary **PERMITTED:** Children, drinking, limited smoking **BROCHURE:** Yes **LANGUAGES:** Some French **DISCOUNTS:** *Off-season rates $45 & 72.00 **AIRPORT:** Boston Logan **PACKAGES:** *Whale Watching, Restaurant Dining* [I07GPMA2-11078]

Parsonage			East Orleans MA
Chris & Lloyd Shand			202 Main St 02643
508-255-8217			

Rates:	Pvt Bath 2	Shared Bath 4	Payment Terms:
Single	$ 55.00	$ 50.00	Check
Double	$ 60-70.00	$ 55.00	MC/V

Lovely tree-lined street with period homes of sea captains and early residents, this Cape Cod home is reminiscent of the 1770's with low ceilings, huge walls, wavy glass windows, antique furnishings and heirlooms. Breakfast included on the patio weather permitting, with cranberry muffins, a homemade delight, and fresh brewed coffee. Minutes to all water activities and sights **SEASONAL:** No [C11ACMA-1695]

**Ship's Knees Inn*			East Orleans MA
			186 Beach Rd 02643
508-255-1312			**Res Times** 8am-9pm
			Fax 508-240-1351

Rates:	Pvt Bath 8	Shared Bath 14	Payment Terms:
Single	$ 70-100.00	$ 45.00	Check
Double	$ 70-100.00	$ 55-80.00	MC/V

Built over 170 years ago, this restored sea captain's home invites guests to an old-style New England lodging surrounded with the charm of yesteryear but with the convenience of today. This intimate setting, just a short stroll to scenic Nauset Beach on Cape

Cod, offers lantern-lit doorways to nineteen rooms, each individually appointed in special colonial colors and authentic antiques. There are beamed ceilings, quilts and old four-poster beds. Several rooms include beautiful ocean views and fireplaces. In-addition, overlooking the Orleans Cove is the Cove House with three rooms and a one-bedroom apartment and two housekeeping cottages providing the total escape. Seclusion and serenity await the less adventuresome vacationer at Nauset Bay, one of the finest in North America. Swimming pool and tennis on the premises and lovely Cape Cod for shopping and fine restaurants. High Season rates are 5/2-10/30, low season rates are approx 25% less. Cottages and apartments are available weekly in-season and daily off-season. **DISCOUNTS:** Yes, inquire at res time **AIRPORT:** Hyannis Regional-20 mi **RESERVATIONS:** One night's deposit at res time (two nights if more than 3 days), bal due upon arrival, 15 day cancel policy for refund. Cove House, cottages and efficiencies available **SEASONAL:** Rates vary **BROCHURE:** Yes **PERMITTED:** Children in Cove House, cottages and efficiencies, drinking, no pets, no smoking at the Inn [J07GPMA2-2978]

**Overlook Inn	**Eastham MA**
Ian & Nan Aitchison	Country Rd Rt 6 02642
800-356-1121 508-255-1886	**Res Times** 9am-9pm

Rates:	**Pvt Bath** 10	**Payment Terms:**
Single	$ 65-110.00	Check
Double	$ 65-110.00	AE/MC/V

The *Overlook Inn* is a finely restored captain's mansion in Eastham, on the beautiful outer cape. Located across from the Cape Cod National Seashore, the Inn has 1-1/2 acres of beautiful treed grounds. The ten bedrooms are furnished with antiques, brass beds, down comforters, terry towel bath robes and all have private baths. On the main floor, there is a parlor where afternoon tea is served each day, a library, a Victorian billiard room and a large dining room overlooking the garden area. Nan enjoys making Scottish dishes for breakfast and her scones, made from her grandmother's recipe, should not be missed at tea time. There are beautiful nature trails and bike trails. **RESERVATIONS:** Full deposit for less than three nights; 50% deposit if longer; 10 day cancellation policy, less 10% service fee **SEASONAL:** No **BROCHURE:** Yes **PERMITTED:** Limited drinking **CONFERENCES:** Yes, for small groups **LANGUAGES:** French Spanish [Z01EPMA-1692]

**Arbor	**Edgartown MA**
Peggy Hall	222 Upper Main St 02539
508-627-8137	**Res Times** 8am-8pm

Rates:	**Pvt Bath** 8	**Shared Bath** 2	**Payment Terms:**
Single	$ 90-135.00	$ 75-95.00	Check
Double	$ 90-135.00	$ 75-95.00	MC/V

Some say it was floated over on a barge from the adjoining island of Chappaquiddick at the turn of the century. Others say it was pulled by oxen on a sled of sorts across the icy narrows of Katama Bay. History abounds at the *Arbor*, but it cannot touch the warmth and hospitality which exists today. Innkeeper, Peggy Hall, is 100% responsible for this and has transformed this once gentle farmhouse into a very lovely friendly Inn. Victorian English Country in decor, Peggy has restored where possible, renovated to keep up with the times and added-on when necessary. Eight of the ten guest rooms each have its own private bath and only two rooms share a bath. You will enjoy a delicious continental breakfast in the fireplaced dining room our outside in the English tea garden. A highlight of your visit could be the social hour in the living room with its balconied library. Just a short stroll to the enchanting village of Edgartown with its chalk white picket fences heralding the gateway to old whaling captain's homes, fine restaurants and the bustling activity of its scenic harbor. If you just want to relax there's a hammock in the rear garden. Peggy will gladly direct you to unspoiled beaches, walking trails, sailing, fishing and all of the delights of this storybook island of Martha's Vineyard. **AIRPORT:** Vineyard Airport-7 mi. **RESERVATIONS:** Full deposit 3 days or less, 50% if longer; 3 day min stay (7/1-8/31) and two day min other times (5/1-6/14 & 9/16-10/31), two week cancel policy, refund less 10% fee **SEASONAL:** Yes **BROCHURE:** Yes **PERMITTED:** Children 13-up, drinking, limited smoking **CONFERENCES:** Yes, the house can be utilized for meetings [I07GPMA2-6832]

**Capt Dexter House	**Edgartown MA**
Rick	PO Box 2798 02539
508-627-7289	**Res Times** 9am-9pm

Rates:	**Pvt Bath** 11	**Payment Terms:**
Single	$ 65-190.00*	Check
Double	$ 65-190.00*	AE/DC/MC/V

Built in 1840 by a seafaring merchant, this historic country colonial Inn on the island of Martha's Vineyard offers a wonderful vacation any time of the year. The home is traditionally New England - from its white clapboard siding and black shutters to its original double-width floor boards. The home is located on a quiet residential street, yet it is only a short stroll to the Harbor, shops and restaurants of town. The rooms have been decorated to provide the feeling of a bygone era, but with today's conveniences. Most bedrooms have canopied four-poster beds, period antiques and working fireplaces. The cutting garden provides fresh flowers to the Inn. The landscaped garden is a haven for relaxing after a day at the beach, bicycling, horseback riding or taking one of the island's numerous nature walks. Guests start each day with a home-baked continental breakfast in the elegant dining room setting. Upon returning to the Inn during the day, guests are offered complimentary aperitif and lemonade. The hospitality and personal service of the live-in innkeepers is nationally known. **AIRPORT:** Martha's Vineyard-2 mi. **DISCOUNTS:** Yes, inquire at res time **PACKAGES:** *Off-season*, inquire at res time **RESERVA-TIONS:** Full deposit for 3 nights or less, 50% for 4+ nights. *High season May-October; off-season rates $65-130.00; 14 day cancel policy for refund, arrival before 10pm **SEASONAL:** 3/1-12/31 **BROCHURE:** Yes **PERMITTED:** Children, drinking, limited smoking **CONFERENCES:** Yes, if booking entire property; facility for groups to twelve [Z07GPMA2-11966]

**Colonial Inn	**Edgartown MA**
Linda Malcouronne	38 N Water St 02539
800-627-4701 508-627-4711	**Res Times** 8am-12am

Rates:	**Pvt Bath** 42	**Payment Terms:**
Single	$ 60-185.00	Check
Double	$ 60-185.00	AE/MC/V

Affordable Luxury .... This delightful and gracious 42 room Inn sits overlooking the harbor in the heart of historic Edgartown. All rooms offer modern day necessities of heat, a/c, color cable TV, private full baths, phone, yet are kept in the style and warmth of a turn-of-the-century Inn. TV's are nestled inside armories. Dust ruffles and comforters snuggle on top of welcoming beds (many of which are brass). Swags at windows offer optimum views, some of Edgartown Harbor and others of gardens or courtyards. The Inn provides eight shops, a restaurant (lunch and dinner) and a beauty shop on premises. A complimentary continental breakfast is served in the greenhouse which opens onto the garden courtyard. Two porches with views overlooking the harbor are available to guests. The rockers on the wrap around front porch offer a favorite perch to *"celebrity watch"*. Swimming, boating, fishing, galleries, golf, tennis, shops and museums are just steps away. The award-winning staff know that "the guest signs our paychecks" and go to great lengths to anticipate guest needs. **RESERVATIONS:** One night's deposit by credit card, 2 week cancel policy for refund **SEASONAL:** Open 4/1-12/31 **PERMITTED:** Children, drinking, smoking **BROCHURE:** Yes **CONFERENCES:** To 25 persons on site, 200 off-site. **DISCOUNTS:** Groups of six or more rooms **AIRPORT:** Martha's Vineyard-8 mi **PACKAGES:** *Home For The Holidays* (11/1-12/9), *Colonial Christmas, Happy Haunting Weekend, Fall In Love, Big Deal On Wheels* (bicycle the Vineyard), *Picture Perfect* (July-August) [Z07GPMA2-1700]

**Point Way Inn	**Edgartown MA**
Linda & Ben Smith	104 Main St 02539
508-627-8633	

Rates:	**Pvt Bath** 15	**Payment Terms:**
Single	$ 120-205.00	Check
Double	$ 120-250.00	AE/MC/V

A charming 150 year-old sea captain's house whose host/owners add a magical touch to each guest's stay in a remodeled Inn and their year-round home. The Inn offers a variety of accommodations including a 2-room suite, French doors and decks, fireplaces in most rooms, period wall coverings, New England antiques with four-poster  canopy beds in some and a decanter of sherry on each night stand. Make yourself at home in the gracious living room with a large fireplace, fridge for ice or your libations and the library with an intriguing 500 pc custom-made wooden jigsaw puzzle. Breakfast is Linda's treat with one of her recipes for breakfast breads, New England popovers, fresh squeezed orange juice and plenty of fresh hot coffee, all served outdoors in the gazebo, a backyard walled garden, before a crackling fireplace or on the front porch swing for avid people watchers! In summer, afternoons bring lemonade and cookies in the gazebo, in winter, a traditional tea in the living room. Plenty to see but leave your car; these hosts offer a car for guests to use on a first come first serve basis so you don't really need one with great hosts who share their town with guests before venturing out. **SEASONAL:** Rates vary *High season rates (6/30-9/7) rates vary down to $65-115.00 (11/3-3/31), with 10% discount for singles. Holiday rates slightly higher. **DISCOUNTS:** Seniors, *AAA* **RESERVATIONS:** Full deposit less than 3 days stay, 50% if 4 days or longer, bal due upon arrival 14 day cancel policy less 10% service fee. Rate does not include Mass Tax **BROCHURE:** Yes **PERMITTED:** Children, drinking, smoking, boarding can be arranged nearby for pets **CONFERENCES:** Yes [I07GPMA2-1709]

**Edgewater B&B	**Fairhaven MA**
Kathy Reed	2 Oxford St 02719
508-997-5512	

Rates:	**Pvt Bath** 5	**Payment Terms:**
Single	$ 60.00	Check

Double $ 80.00   AE/MC/V

Located in the historic Poverty Point section of Fairhaven, *Edgewater Bed & Breakfast* offers unique accommodations for tourists, visiting friends and relatives as well as business people, looking for a friendly, homelike atmosphere. This gracious waterfront home was originally built by Elnathan Eldredge in the 17-60's as his home and store where he supplied the whaleships that were being constructed at the foot of Oxford Street. It is truly on the edge of the water on the very banks of the Acushnet River with the Fairhaven skyline on one side and at night, the glimmering lights of New Bedford on the other. Once inside whether you sit in the dining room on the window seat in front of the curved windows or in the sunken living room complete with a cozy fireplace, you will feel that you are in a boat so near are the gently caressing waves of the river. Beyond the sweeping views, rolling lawns, porches and the quiet serenity, *Edgewater* remains the perfect place for guests to relax in the comfort and privacy of one of five accommodations, each with its own bathroom, period furnishings and waterview; two with working fireplaces. In the morning, guests enjoy a leisurely continental breakfast served in the lovely, formal dining room where home made muffins and Portuguese sweetbread are featured items. *Edgewater* is conveniently located near New Bedford, the historic whaling port, ferries to Cuttyhunk and Martha's Vineyard, Cape Cod, Plymouth, Newport and lots of factory outlets. You will find *Edgewater* the perfect year-round vacation spot.   **AIRPORT:** Providence RI, Green Airport-25 mi; Boston Logan-50 mi **RESERVATIONS:** Deposit required, 72 hr cancel policy for refund **BROCHURE:** Yes **PERMITTED:** Drinking, children 4-up [I07GPMA-2-1711]

Capt Tom Lawrence House	**Falmouth MA**
Barbara Sabo-Feller	75 Locust St 02540
800-266-8139 508-540-1445	**Res Times** AM & PM

Rates:	**Pvt Bath** 6	**Payment Terms:**
Single	$ 65-90.00	Check

Double $ 75-110.00   MC/V

Beautiful 1861 whaling captain's residence is now an intimate Inn for those who appreciate warm hospitality and delicious breakfasts. Close to the beach, bikeway, island ferries, shops, restaurants and bus station. Explore entire Cape Cop, Vineyard and Plymouth by day trips. Elegant spacious corner guest rooms, all with private bath, firm beds (king, queen and twin sizes), some of which include canopies. Laura Ashley and Ralph Lauren linens. The living room includes a Steinway piano, antiques and working fireplace. Our full breakfast will be the highlight of your morning. It includes fresh fruit, homemade granola and a variety of creative entrees such as seafood crepes, eggs florentine or quiche Gisela. We grind our flour from organically grown grain which gives extra freshness to our homebaked breads, muffins, pancakes or Belgian waffles served with a scrumptious warm strawberry sauce and whipped cream. We invite you to stay in our congenial home that blends New England tradition with continental hospitality - a peaceful spot to relax in all seasons. Innkeeper is fluent in German. New fully furnished apartment that sleeps four. Central air conditioning in whole facility. **DISCOUNTS:** Yes, inquire at res time **PACKAGES:** Yes, inquire at res time **AIRPORT:** Boston Logan-65 mi **RESERVATIONS:** One night's deposit or 50% of stay, bal due upon arrival; 14 day cancel policy for refund less $20 service fee. Two night min 5/31 to 10/9; 5% t/a commission with two night min **SEASONAL:** Clo: 1/1-1/31 **BROCHURE:** Yes **PERMITTED:** Children 12-up, drinking **LANGUAGES:** German [I108GMA2-2979]

**Grafton Inn	**Falmouth MA**
Liz & Rudy Cvitan	261 Grand Ave S 02540
800-642-4069 508-540-8688	**Res Times** 8am-10pm
	Fax 508-540-1861

Rates:	**Pvt Bath** 11	**Payment Terms:**
Single	$ *75-135.00	Check
Double	$ *75-135.00	AE/MC/V

Oceanfront - Historic Queen Anne-style Victorian. Miles of

beautiful beach and breathtaking views of Martha's Vineyard. Eleven air conditioned guest rooms are attractively furnished with period antiques and comfortable beds. Each has a private bath. Thoughtful amenities enhance your comfort and relaxation. A sumptuous full breakfast is served at private tables on our sundrenched enclosed porch overlooking Nantucket Sound. Fresh flowers, handmade chocolates, afternoon wine and cheese. We are on the bike path and provide complimentary bicycles, as well as sand chairs and towels for the beach. Peruse the Inn's library of area menus, theaters and attractions. We are happy to make dinner arrangements and reservations. CATV and videos available on the porch and living room. Public phones located in common area. It is steps away to two fine restaurants and a five minute walk to the Island ferry. Shops, year round golf courses, deep sea fishing are a few minutes from the Inn; Falmouth Village is 1/2 mile. Planned daily itineraries to suit your interests. Discount tickets to attractions are available to guests.***AAA & Mobil Rated* AIRPORT:** Boston Logan-70 mi; TF Green-75 mi **RESERVATIONS:** 50% deposit, check-in 2-7pm, after 7 by arrangement, **SEASONAL:** Closed 12/15-1/15 **BROCHURE:** Yes **PERMITTED:** Drinking, children 16-up **CONFERENCES:** Groups to 20 **LANGUAGES:** Croation

**Peacocks Inn On The Sound	**Falmouth MA**
Phyllis & Bud Peacock	313 Grand Ave 02541
508-457-9666	**Res Times** Noon-9pm

Rates:	**Pvt Bath** 10	**Payment Terms:**
Single	$ 75-105.00	Check
Double	$ 95-125.00	AE/DC/MC/V

Oceanfront million dollar view and miles of beaches at your doorstep! Located on a bluff overlooking the Vineyard Sound - guests can choose one of the ten newly renovated guest rooms offering private baths and decorated in Country Comfort decor.
The spacious rooms, most with ocean view, include queen size beds, country decor with dust ruffles, comforters, baskets of flowers, homemade afghans and teddy bears - with fireplaces and

hardwood floors in some. A common room with a massive stone fireplace, color cable TV and seating areas is the perfect gathering place for breath-taking views of the ocean while sipping summer lemonade or snuggled before the winter fire with hot cider and a novel from the library. Morning begins with coffee or tea outdoors, if you like,

taking in the morning sea and salt air, before returning to the cozy country dining room for a gourmet feast where you'll enjoy fresh seasonal fruit, special juice combinations, homemade blueberry and apple muffins, sticky buns, cream cheese coffee cake and a special entree such as Belgian waffles with fruit butter, banana stuffed French toast with blueberry compote or eggs Florentine. After a leisurely breakfast, there are endless opportunities to relax by lounging on the beach, swimming, fishing, sailing, exploring the Falmouth area by bike or by wandering through the many shops in Falmouth Village. Within 90 minutes are numerous day trips while Martha's Vineyard ferry is within walking distance and offers exciting trips to the towns and countryside of this lovely island. *Mobil, ABBA Rated* **RESERVATIONS:** Full deposit to 3 nights, 50% if 4 nights and longer with 2 night minimum; 14 day cancel policy for refund less 10% or $15 minimum **SEASONAL:** Rates vary **PERMITTED:** Drinking, limited children, smoking outdoors only **BROCHURE:** Yes **AIRPORT:** Boston Logan-1-1/2 hr **PACKAGE:** *Honeymoon* [I06FPMA1-12509]

**_Round Hill Non-Smoking B&B_	**Great Barrington MA**
Thomas & Margaret Whitfield	17 Round Hill Rd 01230
413-528-3366	**Res Times** 7am-10pm

Rates:	Pvt Bath 2	Shared Bath 5	Payment Terms:
Single	$ 105-140.00	$ 65-75.00	Check
Double	$ 115-150.00	$ 75-85.00	AE/MC/V

What is it like to stay at *Round Hill Farm*? Our visitors tell us: *"It's like staying with old friends who live in the country in a rambling home with a fantastic view, a wonderful barn and lots of land . . . where you can bring your friends, and the food is great. . ."* A classic New England hilltop working farm,

overlooking 300 spectacular acres, *Round Hill Farm* is on a quiet road only five minutes from the lovely little market center of the Southern Berkshires. It provides a genuine peace and quiet less than three hours from New York or Boston, a delightful home base for Tanglewood, the Norman Rockwell and Hancock Shaker Village museums, just ten minutes from Butternut Basin and Catamount ski areas. *Round Hill* offers two quite different possibilities for guests: the magnificent top-rated 1820's "Uttermost Barn" has two luxurious guest suites (one with gourmet kitchen and deck), cathedral ceilings, a/c, grandeur and privacy. The traditional 1907 Farmhouse has several sunny, immaculate guest rooms, replete with fine linens, antiques and superb libraries. Visitors have a separate entrance and their own elegant parlor. Wraparound porches with wicker rockers overlook a private, rural paradise. All of our guest rooms have privacy locks and terry robes; most have over-size beds; some have in-room telephones. We have walks, wildlife, jogging and bicycle maps, swimming holes in our trout stream, with tennis nearby and cross-country skiing from the door. Generous breakfasts are individually prepared and served in a big sunny kitchen at the time visitors choose; these feature such treats as home-made yogurt with fresh fruit, hot oatmeal, eggs prepared five different ways, sourdough toast and fruited coffee cake. Please call for our brochure. **DISCOUNTS:** Extended stays of 5 days or longer **AIRPORT:** Albany, 55 mi and Bradley, 57 mi **RESERVATIONS:** Advance reservations required, one night deposit weekday, full deposit weekends **SEASONAL:** No **BROCHURE:** Yes **PERMITTED:** Children 16-up and visiting horses welcomed **LANGUAGES:** French [J08DPMA-1728]

---

*Seekonk Pines Inn   **Great Barrington MA**

Linda & Chris Best   142 Seekonk Cross Rd 01230

800-292-4192 413-528-4192   **Res Times** 8am-9pm

Rates:	**Pvt Bath** 6	**Payment Terms:**
Single	$ 50-85.00	Check
Double	$ 70-105.00	MC/V

Seekonk Pines is the life's work of Linda and Chris Best, artist, gardener, musician, electrician and sign craftsman. Since 1978 they have been pouring their many talents into creating a relaxing and unique haven for those visiting the Berkshires. The home consists of a restored 1830 farmhouse with a Dutch Colonial addition. Rooms are lovingly decorated with Lindas' watercolors, quilts made by three generations of women in Linda's family and antiques collected from over the years and refinished in the Inn's picturesque barn. The grounds offer a full-size inground pool, beautiful gardens and picnic tables. Guests may either bring their own bikes or borrow one of the Inn's, to enjoy the lovely back roads. The Inn's four acres are surrounded by 325 acres of a neighboring estate which welcomes hikers and x-country skiers. Breakfast is the social event of the day. A full country breakfast leaning towards a heart-healthy menu is served family-style at one large country table. Linda's heart-healthy blueberry souffle and Chris' multi-grain pancakes are featured. In season, guests may enjoy fresh-picked strawberries, blueberries, blackberries, raspberries and peaches - all grown on the property. Other times, there is a guest pantry and small refrigerator stocked with beverages, hot water dispenser and a huge selection of teas and coffee. Located nearby are New England's prettiest villages, scores of antique shops, three state forests, two downhill ski slopes, Tanglewood Music Center, a wide selection of fine restaurants and all the myriad of cultural events made famous in the Berkshires. **RESERVATIONS:** One night deposit for stays to four nights, 50% deposit for longer stays; 14 day cancel policy for refund less $10 service fee **PERMITTED:** Children, drinking, horse pasture available for guests' horses **BROCHURE:** Yes **LANGUAGES:** German **DISCOUNTS:** Extended stays; 5 nights-up 5%; 7 nights-up 10% **AIRPORT:** Hartford

Bradley or Albany-50 mi [I07GPMA2-1729]

**Miles River Country Inn	**Hamilton MA**
Gretel & Peter Clark	823 Bay Rd Box 149 01936
508-468-7206	

Rates:	Pvt Bath 3	Shared Bath 5	Payment Terms:
Single	$ 55-65.00	$ 50-60.00	Check
Double	$ 60-85.00	$ 60-80.00	MC/V

This 200 year old rambling colonial on 30+ acres adjoins many more of meadows, woodlands and wetlands.   Sweeping lawns are graced with seven gardens and two ponds. The Miles River flows through the property. Set among Boston's fabled North Shore estates, the Inn is a haven for travelers and wildlife alike. One sees or hears Great Blue Heron, countless varieties of duck, great horned and screech owls right from the Inns' windows.   There are shaded garden terraces where breakfast is served in warm weather. A glassed-in porch, framed by giant iron filigree panels from New Orleans, is a cheery spot for afternoon tea in the winter sun. Much of the decoration in this 24 room house is authentic colonial American with the addition of typical turn-of-the-century bathroom fixtures.   The walls of the study are covered with 19th Century wooden bedsteads imported from Brittany. Many of the house's twelve working fireplaces are in the bedrooms. There is a flock of chickens that lay fresh eggs for your breakfast, gardens that produce fresh fruit for your cereal and an apiary (that the innkeeper tends) oozing with golden honey for your toast. Hamilton and nearby communities offer opportunities for those who wish to hike, bike, birdwatch, bathe on pristine ocean beaches, canoeing, sailing or x-country ski.   One can antique, golf, whale watch on special cruises and see world-class horse events, such as carriage driving competitions, polo matches and pre-olympic Three Phase Eventing.   A full complimentary breakfast, high tea and evening snacks are included. **RESERVATIONS:** One night deposit to guarantee reservation **PERMITTED:** Children, limited drinking **BROCHURE:** Yes **CONFERENCES:** Yes, for groups of 16-18 person **LANGUAGES:** Spanish, French, some

German **DISCOUNTS:** Extended stays **AIRPORT:** Boston Logan-25 mi [I07FPMA1-16718]

---

*House of Coffey	**Hanover MA**
Don & Faith Coffey	95 Broadway 02339
617-826-3141	

Rates:	**Shared Bath** 5	**Payment Terms:**
Single	$ 40-60.00	Check
Double	$ 50-95.00	

Lovely colonial residence located in the historic district of Hanover is filled with antique furnishings and includes twin and king size beds. Ten miles from the Atlantic Ocean you can visit the sights including Plymouth Rock, Twenty-five miles from Cape Cod and Boston. Continental breakfast included. **BROCHURE:** Yes **PERMITTED:** Children, limited pets, limited smoking [C11ACMA-1-733]

Cape Cod Sunny Pines Inn	**Harwich MA**
Jack & Eileen Connell	77 Main St 02671
800-356-9628 508-432-9628	**Res Times** 9am-9pm

Rates:	**Pvt Bath** 8	**Payment Terms:**
Single	$ 75-95.00*	Check
Double	$ 85-100.00*	AE/MC/V

Irish hospitality is featured in this beautiful Victorian residence which offers guests a warm, friendly stopping place that's like visiting old friends. Reminiscent of a small Irish manor, furnishings include antiques, oriental rugs, lace doilies, a/c, refrigerators and color TV. The present Captain Jack has sailed the world for twenty years research-

ing the ocean floor with a famous oceanographic institute located on the Cape. Your hostess, Eileen, is a registered nurse and now enjoys making sure all of her guests enjoy their stay. Centered on Cape Cod's south side, guests can walk to a warm beach, excellent area restaurants and the quaint village of Dennisport. A full complimentary Irish breakfast is served by candlelight on fine china and crystal! You'll dine on mixed grilled meats, eggs, juice, beverages, Irish soda bread made from an old family recipe served with Irish jams and jellies. Omelettes are a specialty along with hot Irish oatmeal with cranberry conserve in cool weather. Relax in the living room by the fireside or on the wrap around porch which overlooks the gardens, jacuzzi and pool. There's excellent golf, antiquing, arts and crafts, fishing, whale watching and trips to the islands. Fully licensed, inspected by *ABBA*. *Claddagh Tavern* offers refreshments to further enhance your visit to *Sunny Pines*, serving light fair and beverages in the authentic Irish Pub! *Rooms are all suites. **DISCOUNTS:** Off-rack rate $100.00 **PACKAGES:** Whale watch coupons and picnic lunches available **AIRPORT:** 80 mi to Logan & Green airports **RESERVATIONS:** Full payment in advance if less than one week; 50% if longer **SEASONAL:** No **BROCHURE:** Yes **PERMITTED:** Drinking, limited smoking, children 12-up **CONFERENCES:** Yes, groups of 20-30 persons [I04FPMA1-3712]

Coach House	Harwich Port MA
Mrs Calvin Ayer	74 Sission Rd 02646
508-432-9542	

Rates:	**Pvt Bath** 4	**Payment Terms:**
Single	$ 75.00	Check
Double	$ 75.00	MC/V

Perfect location for touring the New England Coast and excellent spot for whale watching!! Attractive New England colonial home with king and queen beds in a quiet and natural setting. Bike trails, nature walks, and island hopping are all possible here. Continental breakfast included. **RESERVATIONS:** Deposit at res time with refund if canceled 10 days prior to arrival date **SEASONAL:** Open 5/1-10/15 **BROCHURE:** Yes **PERMITTED:** Limited smoking [C11ACMA-1736]

Harbor Walk Guest House	Harwich Port MA
Marilyn & Preston Barry	6 Freeman St 02646
508-432-1675	**Res Times** 7am-10pm

Rates: **Pvt Bath** 4   **Shared Bath** 2   **Payment Terms:**

Single	$ 60.00	$ 40.00	Check
Double	$ 60.00	$ 45.00	

An enjoyable Victorian Summer Guest home c1880, built by Ensign Rogers in the beautiful and picturesque Wychmere Harbor area of Harwich Port. The *Harbor* is just a few steps away offering a spectacular view and fine beaches of Nantucket Sound. *Harbor Walk* offers the discriminating traveler an opportunity to relax in quiet comfort in a quaint Cape Cod with eclectic furnishings of handmade quilts, antiques with twin and king size beds in the rooms. Choose the Bayberry Room on the first floor that's heated and bath ensuite or one of the other rooms on the second floor, including the Beach Plum Room and the Cranberry Room. An attractive garden area and porch are perfect for sitting, lounging and reading. A continental breakfast is included and usually includes your host's specialty of home baked kuchen. Activities include a 22 mile bike path sure to introduce you to all of Harwich. There's excellent bird watching, two golf courses, three harbors for boating, fishing, sand beaches & tennis. Mother's Day weekend includes the Chamber's amateur golf tournament on Cranberry Valley Course **RESERVATIONS:** One night deposit at res time **SEASONAL:** May - October **BROCHURE:** Yes **PERMITTED:** Drinking, children 4-up, limited smoking **LANGUAGES:** French [Z10CPMA-1739]

Inn On Bank Street	**Harwich Port MA**
Arky & Janet Silverio	88 Bank St 02646
508-432-3206	**Res Times** 8am-10pm

Rates: **Pvt Bath** 5   **Shared Bath** 1   **Payment Terms:**

Single	$ 60-100.00	$ 55.00	Check
Double	$ 60-110.00		MC/V

A sprawling Cape Cod contemporary with library and guest rooms furnished in country style/modern touches. Close to sights, ocean is just 5 minutes walk, and restaurants, theater, & art galleries too. Full breakfast includes special cranberry crisp, French toast, and fresh homemade breads. **BROCHURE:** Yes **PERMITTED:** Children 8-up, smoking, drinking **SEASONAL:** No **LANGUAGES:** Italian, Spanish [C11ACMA-1740]

Captain Ezra Nye House — Hyannis MA
Elaine & Harry Dickson
800-388-2278 508-888-6142 **Res Times** 9am-9pm

Rates:	**Pvt Bath** 5	**Shared Bath** 2	**Payment Terms:**
Single	$ 70-90.00	$ 55-70.00	Check
Double	$ 70-90.00	$ 55-70.00	AE/MC/V

Refer to the same listing name under Sandwich, Cape Cod, Massachusetts for a complete description. [M11BPMA-9376]

Captain Sylvester Baxter House — Hyannis MA
N Krojewski/R Arenstrup 156 Main St 02061
508-775-5611 **Res Times** 9am-6pm

Rates:	**Pvt Bath** 4	**Payment Terms:**
Single	$ 69-89.00	Check
Double	$ 69-89.00	MC/V

Built in 1855 as the homestead of a deep water sailor, state senator and community leader, you'll be in the center of all the activities in this lovely setting. Historically the oldest settlement in Hyannis, the east end of Main Street retains the charm of another era. The setting is of a small village with granite curbs, flagstone walks and Colonial-styled lanterns in a comfortable and charming atmosphere. Enjoy the high ceilinged rooms in the main house or choose one of the cottages or efficiencies available. You're just a short stroll from the Cape Cod shores, the harbor area, ferries to the islands, and the town of Hyannis itself. All modern amenities are here including a/c, color TV, and an inground pool, picnic tables, barbecue, lawn chairs, and laundry facilities. A continental breakfast is included. **RESERVATIONS:** 25% of total rental required within 7 days of making reservation, 14 day cancel notice for full refund. **SEASONAL:** Season 5/26-10/09; Off-Season rates are 30% lower **BROCHURE:** Yes **PERMITTED:** Children, drinking [A10APMA-1746]

Elegance-by-the-Sea — Hyannis MA
Clark & Mary Boydston 162 Sea Street 02601
508-775-3595 **Res Times** 9am-8pm

Rates:	**Pvt Bath** 6	**Payment Terms:**

Single	$ 85.00	Check
Double	$ 85.00	AE/MC/V

This 1880 Queen Anne home offers hearty gourmet breakfasts, intimate ambiance, antique furnished guest rooms with private baths and one special two-room suite with a working fireplace. Bed arrangements vary with choices of pineapple post twin beds, 19th Century Louis XV & XVI beds, with queen-size beds in two other rooms. Furnished with crystal, lace and Victorian antiques, guests step into another period of time while here. You are within walking distance of beaches, fine restaurants, island boats, golf, trains and most major sights. A perfect setting for your vacation, romantic get-away or executive retreat. Centrally located on Cape Cod, you'll taste the flavor of the whole Cape and islands without frequent lodging changes or a lot of driving. Reservations highly recommended. Hearty, full breakfast in the dining room or outdoors on the lovely porch, weather permitting. **RESERVATIONS:** 1-3 nights, full deposit at res time; 4 or more, 50% deposit; cancellation policy, refund by rain check or gift certificate **SEASONAL:** No **BROCHURE:** Yes **PERMITTED:** Children 16-up **LANGUAGES:** French, English [R01BCMA-6091]

Sea Breeze By The Beach	**Hyannis Port MA**
Martin & Patricia Battle	397 Sea Street 02601
508-771-7231	

Rates:	Pvt Bath 3	Shared Bath 3	Payment Terms:
Single	$ 65.00	$ 55.00	Check
Double	$ 70.00	$ 60.00	

Perfect New England shingle Cape Codder, you'll enjoy the atmosphere in this quaint Inn close to all activities & ocean beaches in this famous resort area. Continental breakfast included. **SEASONAL:** No **BROCHURE:** Yes **PERMITTED:** Children, smoking, drinking. [C11ACMA-1750]

**Simmons Homestead Inn*	**Hyannis Port MA**
Bill Putman	288 Scudder Ave 02647
508-778-4999	**Res Times** 8am-10pm
	Fax 508-790-1342

Rates:	Pvt Bath 10	Payment Terms:
Single	$ 80.00*	Check

Double $ 130.00   AE/MC/V*

The *Simmons Homestead* is an 1820 Sea Captain's estate that has been lovingly transformed into the nicest Bed & Breakfast Inn on Cape Cod. Ten wonderful bedrooms all with their own bathrooms. Rates include a full breakfast in the morning and complimentary wines in the evening. The only Inn in Hyannis Port, yet only 2 minutes from the beach, downtown Hyannis and the Harbor with ferries to the Islands. We are in the center of the Cape and convenient to everything. All rooms are uniquely furnished with antiques, canopy beds, fireplaces, huge common rooms. Grand porches surround the Inn and overlook the spacious grounds and pond. We can help plan your vacation, go whale watching, beaching, antiquing, day trips to Nantucket & Martha's Vineyard, biking or shopping. We'll steer you to the right restaurants, shops, beaches and craftspeople. The Inn is traditional New England, full of charm, artworks and pleasant company. This is the nicest Inn on Cape Cod. Simply wonderful with knowledgeable host, Bill Putman, Innkeepers. **RESERVATIONS:** Full deposit if less than 3 days, 3 or more days, 50% deposit; 14 day cancel policy less 10%. *Credit card for deposit only, payment required in cash or check. **DISCOUNTS:** Special off-season rates **BROCHURE:** Yes **PERMITTED:** Drinking, limited smoking **CONFERENCES:** Yes, off-season (11/1-4/30) for entire house at special package rates call for details [Z06GPMA2-8475]

Birchwood Inn	**Lenox MA**
Joan, Dick & Dan Toner	7 Hubbard St 01240
800-524-1646 413-637-2600	**Res Times** 7am-9pm

Rates:	**Pvt Bath** 10	**Shared Bath** 2	**Payment Terms:**
Single	$ 125-190.00	$ 85-95.00	Check
Double	$ 125-190.00	$ 85-95.00	MC/V

Drive through the quaint village of Lenox and at the top of Main Street, across from the Old Church on the Hill, you'll find *The Birchwood Inn* -- a 200 year old home. Cozy fireplaces welcome guests in all of the public rooms and a parlor beckons you to read or browse while the den offers color TV for "must-see" events. Guest rooms are lavishly furnished and decorated including canopy beds and fireplaces, all with private baths. Two economical dormer rooms are available with shared baths. Guests can leisurely enjoy a complimentary breakfast offering a buffet laden with juice, coffee, tea, cereals, fruit and homemade muffins. For a real experience let our chef prepare one of his daily hot entrees where you can savor one of his specialties of Tarte d'Alsace, Eggs au Chasseur or Huevos Albuquerque! Summer evenings bring wine and cheese and wonderful breezes while relaxing outdoors on the large porch. Lenox hosts  a variety of cultural events each summer including the Boston Symphony at Tanglewood, dance and Shakespeare theaters. The area also boasts museums, golf, tennis, fishing, swimming and factory outlet shopping. The unmatched beauty of autumn is a perfect time for hiking and biking. Winter offers x-country and downhill skiing. Your innkeepers, who attended the prestigious La Varenne School in Paris, host getaway weekends in winter featuring Saturday night adventures in dining with regional specialties from around the world. **DISCOUNTS:** 10% for weekly stays. **AIRPORT:** Albany 1 hr, Hartford-Springfield 1-1/2 hrs **PACKAGES:** *Winter "Getaway Weekends", Skiing, Hiking & Mountain Biking* **RESERVATIONS:** One night's deposit bal due 10 days prior to arrival, 7 day cancel policy for refund; 3-day min during Tanglewood Festival; 2-day min Autumn and holiday weekends. **BROCHURE:** Yes **PERMITTED:** Drinking, limited children, limited smoking **CONFERENCES:** Yes; ideal for off-site business meetings, seminars and retreats [I09DPMA-1759]

Brook Farm Inn	**Lenox MA**
Bob Jacob	15 Hawthorne St 01240
413-637-3013	

Rates:	Pvt Bath 12	Payment Terms:
Single	$ 65.00-Up	Check
Double	$ 76-130.00	MC/V

Quaint 100-year-old Inn for those seeking solace with a pool, English Tea, Shaded Glen, fall foliage, fireplaces, and over 500 volumes of poetry with over 60 poets on tapes to enjoy during your stay. Close to Tanglewood & museums. Full breakfast included. Library, swimming pool, sitting rooms **SEASONAL:** No **BROCHURE:** Yes **PERMITTED:** Children 16-up [C11ACMA-1761]

Gables Inn	Lenox MA
Frank & Mary Newton	103 Walker St 01240
413-637-3416	**Res Times** 8am-8pm

Rates:	**Pvt Bath** 17	**Payment Terms:**
Single	$ 60-140.0	Check
Double	$ 60-140.00	AE/MC/V

This former home of author Edith Wharton has been fully restored to its original turn-of-the-century appearance. Edith's upstairs bedroom is one of the most attractive and includes a four-poster canopy bed in pink & white and a deep plum sofa next to the fireplace. Guests can visit the unusual eight-sided library where the author wrote some of her short stories. All of the guest rooms include private bath and each guest room has a unique theme. The *"Jockey Club Suite"* has a brass bed and an ample sitting area which includes a big-screen TV and two sofas. A private entrance from the backyard assures privacy. Another room, the *"Show Business Room"*, is filled with autographed photos of movie stars along with a library of showbiz volumes which guests can enjoy reading during their stay. A complimentary continental breakfast includes goodies such as banana bread or sour-cream cake. Your hosts enjoy socializing with their guests and often become a willing partner for tennis in the back yard. An enclosed solar-heated swimming pool, jacuzzi are available for the guests year-round enjoyment. **RESERVATIONS:** Deposit required at res time, 3 night min stay in season (July-August) **SEASONAL:** Rates vary **BRO-CHURE:** Yes **PERMITTED:** Children 12-up, drinking, smoking [S07GPMA2-14820]

Garden Gables Inn	Lenox MA
Mario & Lynn Mekinda	141 Main St 01240
413-637-0193	**Res Times** 8am-10pm
	Fax 413-637-4556

Rates:	**Pvt Bath** 18	**Payment Terms:**
Single	$ 65-175.00	Check
Double	$ 70-200.00	AE/DISC/MC/V

Garden Gables, a 220-year-old gabled Inn, was built originally as a private estate. Located in the historic district of Lenox, the Inn is well back from the main road on five wooded acres, dotted with gardens, maples and fruit trees. It's a perfect place for guests looking for a peaceful and relaxing atmosphere. The common rooms, with an abundance of books, magazines and board games, have several fireplaces and are beautifully furnished with antiques and 18th Century Dutch oil paintings. Guests are served a full breakfast in the beautiful dining room which overlooks the front and side gardens. Tanglewood is one mile away and summer brings guests outdoors to enjoy the large 72 foot swimming pool! Operated as an Inn since 1947, *Garden Gables* has eighteen cozy bedrooms - all with private baths. All bedrooms are uniquely decorated with choices between twin, double, queen and king-size beds, phones, fireplaces, porches and a/c in some rooms. **DISCOUNTS:** Weekly and monthly stays. **RESERVATIONS:** Full deposit at res time **BROCHURE:** Yes **PERMITTED:** Drinking, limited smoking **LANGUAGES:** German, French [S05FPMA2-1767]

Walker House	Lenox MA
Richard & Peggy Houdek	74 Walker St 01240
413-637-1271	

Rates:	Pvt Bath 8	Payment Terms:
Single	$ 55-75.00	Check
Double	$ 65-130.00	

Become pampered in this country setting on three acres within walking distance of all points of interest. Bikes, piano, and sitting rooms are available. Continental breakfast included. Complimentary sherry/wine. **SEASONAL:** No **BROCHURE:** Yes **PERMITTED:** Children 8-up, limited smoking, limited drinking. [C11ACMA-1772]

**Harborside House*	Marblehead MA
Susan Livingston	23 Gregory St 01945
617-631-1032	**Res Times** 8am-8pm

Rates:	Shared Bath 2	Payment Terms:
Single	$ 60-65.00	Check
Double	$ 70-75.00	

This 1850 Colonial overlooks the picturesque harbor in the historic district of Marblehead, yachting capital of America. Guests enjoy waterviews from the wood panelled and beamed living room, the period dining room, sunny breakfast porch and the 3rd story deck. Antique furnishings and reproduction wallpapers enhance the charm of this comfortable quiet home. Generous breakfast

includes juice, fresh fruit, homebaked breads and muffins, choice of cereals. Bedside Harbor Sweets candy at bedtime. Large twin bed guest room views the harbor. Romantic double bed guest room with antique mirrored dressing table looks out on flower gardens & deck. Quaint shops, gourmet restaurants and the historic sites of Old Town are just a pleasant stroll away. Marblehead also offers beaches, Audubon Bird Sanctuary, wind-surfing and sailing lessons. Whale-watching excursions and harbor cruises are available nearby. Half-hour travel time to Logan Airport; 45 mins to Boston. Hostess/owner is a thirty-year resident, Historical Society member, professional dressmaker and nationally-ranked competitive Master swimmer. *Harborside House* offers warmth and hospitality in gracious surroundings. Special events include: Marblehead Arts Festival (July 4th wknd), Race Week (mid-July) Halloween Celebration in Salem and Christmas Walk (early Dec). **DISCOUNTS:** Extended stays, travel agents. **RESERVATIONS:** Full deposit if 2 nights or less, if more, 50%; 10 day cancel policy less 15% service fee; 2pm check-in, 11am check-out **BROCHURE:** Yes **PERMITTED:** Children over 10, limited drinking **LANGUAGES:** French [I07FPMA2-1782]

**Spray Cliff On The Ocean	**Marblehead MA**
Dick & Diane Pabich	25 Spray Ave 01945
800-626-1530 508-744-8924	

Rates:	**Pvt Bath** 7	**Payment Terms:**
Single	$ 139-179.00	AE/DC/MC/V
Double	$ 139-179.00	

This old English Tudor mansion is set high above the Atlantic providing guests with an unsurpassed view for relaxation and viewing. Guests can enjoy the gulls, black cormorants and ducks serenade indoors or outside on a patio surrounded by beautiful flower gardens. All of the guest rooms reflect a homey attitude with antique furnishings and touches of flowers and wicker. A continental plus breakfast of breads, pastries, fresh seasonal fruit and hot beverages gets everyone started again - ready for exploring the sights or just relaxing. Guests can enjoy Preston Beach, one of the finest in Marblehead which is just a minute away! This Atlantic setting is a year-round attraction for all the water activities with the finest fish and lobster dining anywhere! Just 15 miles north of Boston, guests can enjoy the serenity of this oceanside setting and all of the activities of Boston. **DISCOUNTS:** *AAA* **AIRPORT:** Boston Logan-15 mi **RESERVATIONS:** One night's deposit within one week of reservation. Bal due on arrival for full period, 7 day cancel notice for refund less $15 service fee **BROCHURE:** Yes **PERMITTED:** Drinking, children, limited smoking **CONFERENCES:** Excellent conference facilities for groups to 20 persons [Z07GPMA2--1781]

Arbor   **Marthas Vineyard MA
Peggy Hall
508-627-8137   **Res Times** 8am-8pm

Rates:	Pvt Bath 8	Shared Bath 2	Payment Terms:
Single	$ 90-135.00	$ 75-95.00	Check
Double	$ 90-135.00	$ 75-95.00	MC/V

Refer to the same listing name under Edgartown, Massachusetts for a complete description. [M12DPMA-9462]

Thorncroft Inn   **Marthas Vineyard MA
Karl & Lynn Buder   278 Main St 02568
800-332-1236 508-693-3333   **Res Times** 9am-9pm

Rates:	Pvt Bath 19	Payment Terms:
Single	$ 129-299.00*	Check
Double	$ 129-299.00*	AE/MC/V

Thorncroft Inn is a nineteen room antique appointed, romantic and intimate Bed & Breakfast Country Inn comprised of four restored homes in two locations all on the enchanting island of Martha's Vineyard, seven miles off the coast of Mass. Each building has a distinct non-commercial atmosphere enhanced by authentic restoration & architectural integrity. Each room decor is unique. Many rooms have four poster canopied beds, balconies and working wood-burning fireplace for off-season enjoyment and all rooms are fully a/c. There are suites that include color TV, phones, a jacuzzi for two or a private hot tub. Room prices include afternoon tea, evening turndown service and the morning paper! *AAA* ♦♦♦♦

Rating, it is the only lodging establishment on the Island to achieve this award. A full breakfast is served at both locations. The storybook island of Martha's Vineyard is a vacationer's delight. With miles of unspoiled beaches and lack of new building & development, a throwback to simpler times. There are many fine restaurants, out-of-the-way shops, galleries and boutiques. The Vineyard is considered as a final point of destination for vacationers and not an overnight trip because of it's remote and charming location. **RESERVATIONS:** Deposit: 100% for 1-2 nights, 50% for longer periods, due prior to arrival, two week cancel policy for refund. **SEASONAL:** *Off season rates are $129-219.00 **BROCHURE:** Yes **PERMITTED:** Limited children, drinking, smoking [Z06EPMA-1785]

Centerboard Guest House	**Nantucket MA**
Ms Marcia Wasserman	8 Chester St 02554
508-228-9696	**Res Times** 7am-9pm

Rates:	**Pvt Bath** 7	**Payment Terms:**
Single		Check
Double	$ 145-245.00	AE/MC/V

The *Centerboard* is a charming Victorian home lovingly renovated and restored in 1986, located on the quiet perimeter of the Historic District just a few blocks from the cobblestoned shopping streets, white sand beaches, museums, galleries, and fine restaurants. You can choose from seven beautifully appointed guest rooms designed expressly for luxury and guest comfort. Individually decorated, each room provides a queen bed or two double beds, telephone, refrigerator, color TV, all within a gentle romantic ambiance. Choose the two room suite with white-on-white bedroom decor, huge four poster canopied bed, green marble bath complete with an oversized shower, jacuzzi bath and extra-ordinary accessories. A continental buffet breakfast is offered guests and includes breads and muffins, cereal, fresh fruits and a fine selection of morning beverages served in the softly lit dining room. Each Season is special here with plenty to do year round! **RESERVATIONS:** Rates based on double occupancy, $25.00 for add'l persons, deposit of first and last night or 50% entire stay, which ever is greater, 21 day cancel notice for refund **SEASONAL DISCOUNTS:** Off-season $85-125.00 **BROCHURE:** Yes **PERMITTED:** Children 12-up **CONFERENCES:** Yes, full house rental for 11-20 persons [A03FPMA2-1795]

Century House   Nantucket MA
Jean & Gerry Heron Connick   10 Cliff Rd 02554
508-228-0530

Rates: **Pvt Bath** 2   **Shared Bath** 3   **Payment Terms:**
Single $ 80.00 $ 70.00   Check
Double $ 90-135.00 $ 80.00

Serving weary travelers since the mid-1880's and still offering antique period furnishings, Laura Ashley print wallcoverings and fabrics, you'll be close to the ocean and all activities in this resort setting. Continental breakfast included. **BROCHURE:** Yes **PERMITTED:** Children, limited smoking, limited drinking **SEASONAL:** Rates vary [E11ACMA-2981]

Grieder Guest House   Nantucket MA
Mrs Ruth Grieder   43 Orange St 02554
508-228-1399

Rates: **Pvt Bath** 4   **Payment Terms:**
Single   Check
Double $ 60-80.00

Circa 1700's picturesque New Englander operated for the past 35 years by the present hostess, you can expect plenty of hospitality and warmth in these spacious guest rooms complete with antique furnishings, four poster beds, braided rugs, and sea chests. Close to all points of interest. Continental breakfast included. **BROCHURE:** Yes **PERMITTED:** Children limited smoking, limited drinking **SEASONAL:** No [C11ACMA-1803]

Lynda Watts B&B   Nantucket MA
Mrs Lynda Watts   10 Upper Vestal St 02554
508-228-3828

Rates: **Pvt Bath** 1   **Shared Bath** 1   **Payment Terms:**
Single $ 60.00 $ 60.00   Check
Double $ 68.00

Contemporary home offering a great family stop-over with king beds, TV, sunny patio, and a gracious hostess. Walking distance to all sights in town center. Plenty of the outdoor activities, swimming, tennis, golf, and sightseeing. Continental breakfast included. **PERMITTED:** Children, limited smoking **SEASONAL:** No [C11ACMA-1814]

Phillips House			Nantucket MA

Mary Phillips
508-228-9217

54 Fair St 02554

Rates:	**Pvt Bath** 1	**Shared Bath** 2	**Payment Terms:**
Single	$ 60.00	$ 55.00	Check
Double	$ 75.00	$ 65.00	

Quaint 200 year old whaler's residence just minutes from the village green and within walking distance of all sights. Providing New England hospitality to frequently guests, all activities are included with golf, tennis, swimming nearby. Continental breakfast included. **BROCHURE:** Yes **PERMITTED:** Limited children and smoking. [E11ACMA-2982]

Quaint Cape Victorian Inn			Nantucket MA

Bob Pickle
508-322-0123

688 S Main St 02554
Res Times 8am-5pm

Rates:	**Pvt Bath** 4	**Shared Bath** 2	**Payment Terms:**
Single	$ 65.00	$ 45.00	Check
Double	$ 70.00	$ 60.00	AE/MC/V

Beautiful Victorian with breath-taking views of the Cape and ocean takes guests back in time and elegance to the Victorian era! Perfectly furnished with period antiques and family heirlooms - with all the important details, such as original gas lights, marble mantels, stained glass windows, spiral stairwell, carved oak woodwork and fine examples of oriental rugs covering the highly polished original oak floors. Guest rooms include king-size beds with either four-poster or canopy details and all modern amenities. Full New England breakfast is served in the formal dining room or "in-bed" if you like and includes fresh home-baked family recipes for muffins, breads and waffles. You're within easy strolling distance of all the Cape's sights, so you can park your car on the premises. **RESERVATIONS:** 50% deposit for entire stay within 5 days of booking; check-in by 6pm; 5-day cancellation policy for refund **SEASONAL:** No **BROCHURE:** Yes **PERMITTED:** Limited children, limited drinking [GO2BFMA-6576]

Seven Sea Street	Nantucket Island MA
Matt & Mary Parker	7 Sea St 02554
508-228-3577	**Res Times** 8am-10pm

Rates:	**Pvt Bath** 8	**Payment Terms:**
Single	$ 85-155.00	Check
Double	$ 95-165.00	AE/MC/V

Featured in *The New York Times Travel Section - Seven Sea Street Inn* offers travelers a chance to make their time special - a trip that they will fondly remember for a long time after. Your hosts pride themselves on attentive service and elegant accommodations to make your stay on the island - unforgettable. Travelers to Nantucket Island will relive the "Early American Spirit" while staying in this newly constructed red oak post & beam cozy Country Inn, reminiscent of a bygone period. Colonial furnishings combined with modern comforts and conveniences in each of our guest rooms and suites, provide a cozy respite on this romantic island, thirty miles at sea. Amenities include queen size canopy bed, cable TV, small refrigerator and private bath. Spectacular views of Nantucket Harbor abound from the rooftop "widow's walk". The cozy common rooms provide a perfect fireside visiting, reading and letter writing area - while the full-size heated Jacuzzi is enjoyable any time of the day. The Inn is centrally located, just a block from Nantucket Yacht Club and only a five minute walk to Main Street, Children's Beach and the Steamship Ferry Terminal. An elegant continental breakfast consisting of fresh fruit and juices, home-baked bread and muffins with coffee, tea and milk, is served in the common area or in your room, if you like. Our rates are neither the lowest nor the highest to be found on Nantucket Island, but they represent an excellent value for travelers and fond memories upon your return home. **DISCOUNTS:** Yes, off-season (Oct 13 to June 25) 15% for weekly stays and 10% for 3 or more weekdays, Sun to Thur. **AIRPORT:** Island airport-3 mi **RESERVATIONS:** Full payment for two days or less, 50% deposit if longer, 14 day cancel policy less 10% service fee **SEASONAL:** No **BROCHURE:** Yes **PERMITTED:** Drinking and limited children **CONFERENCES:** Special events, meetings, parties, wedding groups. Full dinners and authentic New England Clambakes. Full A/V **LANGUAGES:** French [J02EPMA-7153]

**1810 House B&B	**Norwell MA**
Susanne & Harold Tuttle	147 Old Oaken Bucket 02061
617-659-1810	**Res Times** 8am-9pm

Rates:	**Pvt Bath** 2	**Shared Bath** 1	**Payment Terms:**
Single	$ 55-65.00	$ 50-55.00	Check
Double	$ 65-75.00	$ 55-65.00	

The *1810 House* is a comfortable bed and breakfast home lovingly restored and added to by the owners, Harold and Susanne Tuttle. The antique half-cape with it's original beamed ceilings, three working fireplaces, wide pine floors and hand-stenciled walls was recently featured on the *Christmas Tour* of Norwell homes. The house is furnished with antiques, beautiful oriental carpets and interesting accessories collected over a period of many years. Harold is a woodworker and refinisher who has done extensive restoration in the house, while Susanne is a seamstress who has created the custom window treatments. Three bright, cheery rooms, one with a canopy bed, one with twin beds and one with an antique spool bed share two full baths. The two rooms on the second floor are ideal for two couples traveling together or families. A full New England breakfast is served by the kitchen fireplace or on the screened porch. Norwell, a beautiful historic town, is located half-way between Plymouth and Boston on Massachusetts South Shore. It is an ideal spot for day trips to Cape Cod, Newport RI, Concord, Lexington, Salem and Rockport - all a short drive away. Public transportation to Boston via a subway or commuter boat is close-by. A tour of the area in Harold's restored 1915 Model T Depot hack adds to the feeling of a bygone era and is part of fun staying at the *1810 House B&B*. Featured in *Country Magazine*, Aug/Sept 1993. **RESERVATIONS:** One night's deposit to guarantee reservation, 7 day cancel policy for refund **SEASONAL:** No **PERMITTED:** Children 6-up **BROCHURE:** Yes **AIRPORT:** Boston Logan-25 mi [K08GPMA2-13172]

**Oak House	**Oak Bluffs MA**
Betsi Convery-Luce	Seaview & Pequot Aves 02557
508-693-4187	

Rates:	**Pvt Bath** 10	**Payment Terms:**
Single	$ 85-175.00*	Check
Double	$ 85-175.00*	MC/V

Enter the romance of a yesteryear seaside holiday at our Victorian Bed & Breakfast Inn, the richly restored 1872 beachfront summer home of Governor Claflin. Elegant oak paneled interior, authentic antiques, leaded glass windows, wide wrap around porches and balconies, offer sweeping views of the ocean & nearby beach, complement our charming ten guest rooms, all uniquely furnished in various themes. Just perfect for relaxing away the day. *Closed late Fall & Winter. **RESERVATIONS:** 50% deposit required, balance upon arrival (3 days or less full deposit) with 14 day cancel policy for refund less 10%. Rates subject to tax and gratuities. **SEASONAL:** *25% discount 5/15-6/20 & 9/20-10/14. **BROCHURE:** Yes **PERMITTED:** Drinking, smoking, limited children [Z11CPMA-1857]

**Onset Pointe Inn	**Onset MA**
Toni & Carl Larrabee	9 Eagle Way 02558-1450
800-35-ONSET 508-295-8442	**Res Times** 8am-8pm

Rates:	**Pvt Bath** 14	**Payment Terms:**
Single	$ 85-140.00	Check
Double	$ 85-140.00	AE/MC/V

Situated on its own sandy point jutting into Buzzard's Bay, *The Onset Pointe Inn* is an elegant accommodation operated in a casual manner that delights its many returning guests. The Inn caters to a discerning clientele seeking excellent facilities and amenities and offers fourteen waterview rooms in three buildings; an 1880 restored mansion, a cottage (which was the mansion's original carriage house), and a renovated Cape Cod home. The beach surrounding the property is clean, the waters are clear and wave-free for swimmers. A beachside gazebo provides a wonderful spot for relaxing, an evening refreshment or even the exchange of wedding vows! The mansion with seven accommodations has a variety of rooms, each furnished with a combination of tastefully selected and placed furnishings. Two poster-bedded rooms have outside balconies and two larger rooms enjoy lovely sunset views of the bay. Breakfast during the week is served in the dining room or spacious sun parlor and is the Innkeeper's choice of the day; croissant French toast, blueberry pancakes, cheddar omelettes .... and always with fresh fruit. On weekends a buffet service permits guests to take breakfast to the sun parlor, the wide verandas or to the gazebo. Within walking distance are several restaurants offering a variety of fare and even an alternative music dance club is nearby. Guests may enjoy tee or court-time privileges at the neighboring country club which boasts an 18-hole championship course, or enjoy a cruise on the Cape Cod Canal. **RESERVATIONS:** Stays to 3 nights, full payment, 50% for longer periods at reservation time to guarantee rooms, 14 day cancel policy less $15 service fee **SEASONAL:** Closed March **PERMITTED:** Limited children, drinking **BROCHURE:** Yes **CONFERENCES:** Social gatherings, weddings and parties on the grounds **DISCOUNTS:** 10% midweek, seniors, corporate **AIRPORT:** New Bedford-20 min; Providence-1 hr; Hyannis-30 min [I08FPMA2-17974]

**The Farm House	**Orleans MA**
Dot Standish	163 Beach Rd 02653
617-255-6654	**Res Times** 9am-10pm

Rates:	Pvt Bath 4	Shared Bath 4	Payment Terms:

Single	$ 60-95.00	$ 32-65.00	Check
Double	$ 60-95.00	$ 32-65.00	MC/V

Come and enjoy this nineteenth century farmhouse that has been carefully restored and furnished to provide a unique blend of country life in a seashore setting. An outside deck is used for breakfast of freshly baked coffee cake with steaming coffee as well as for guests activities while enjoying a peeking view of the ocean. A short walk (1/2 mi) to beautiful Nauset Beach. Guests are close to sailing, golf, tennis, fine restaurants, shops, museums, beach strolling and surfing!! Guests can experience the best lobsters, quahogs, chowders and an always fresh "catch of the day" in one the many fine nearby restaurants - which your hostess will kindly recommend if needed. The guest rooms offer twin, double or king size beds finished with handmade quilts, afghan and bed ensembles. Some rooms provide ocean views. The Farmhouse is a licensed Bed and Breakfast awaiting guests who would like to enjoy Cape Cod to the fullest. *"Be Our Guests"*. **RESERVATIONS:** Deposit required and advanced reservations are advised. **PERMITTED:** Children (6-up), drinking, limited smoking **BROCHURE:** Yes **DISCOUNTS:** Yes, inquire at res time **AIRPORT:** Boston Logan-2 hrs [Z07GPMA2-1859]

Boggastowe Farm			**Pepperell MA**
John & Shirley Ritichie			Shattuck St 01463
508-433-9987			**Res Times** 8am-8pm

Rates:	**Pvt Bath** 2	**Shared bath** 2	**Payment Terms:**
Single	$ 55.00	$ 45.00	Check
Double	$ 65.00	$ 55.00	

Hideaway in this charming c1790 country farm home and experience New England at it's best - just 60 minutes from Boston, on the Mass and New Hampshire border. This 200 year old farmhouse sits atop a grassy knoll and is surrounded by giant maple trees and beautiful meadows. Guests enjoy watching the sheep and horses graze or feeding the ducks around the large farm pond. In March, guests can help make maple syrup. Two large bedrooms have adjoining baths and two bedrooms have private baths. Two bedrooms, a guest living room, dining room and kitchen have working fireplaces. Antique furnishings. Your hosts, a retired engineer and teacher, prepare a hearty full breakfast with farm-fresh eggs from the hen-house -- maple syrup made in their own sugarhouse. The scenery is beautiful year-round and the quaint country towns nearby have plenty of antiquing, shopping and national historic parks for outdoor activities and sports. Guests are conveniently located to Lowell & Concord MA (30 mins) and Nashua NH (20 mins). **RESERVATIONS:** One night's deposit with 7 day cancel policy less 10% service fee **SEASONAL:** No **BROCHURE:** Yes **PERMITTED:** Children, pets, limited drinking, limited smoking. [S09CPMA-11288]

**Winterwood At Petersham	**Petersham MA**
Robert Day	N Main St 01336
617-724-8885	

Rates:	**Pvt Bath** 5	**Payment Terms:**
Single	$ 75.00	Check
Double	$ 85.00	

Greek Revival mansion in the center of town and listed on *National Register of Historic Places* offering guests the warmth of antique furnishings and fireplaces in all rooms.   Continental breakfast included. **BROCHURE:** Yes **PERMITTED:** Children, limited smoking, drinking **SEASONAL:** No **CONFERENCES:** Yes, including dining and social hours [E11ACMA-1863]

**Allen House	**Plymouth MA**
Christine Gilmour	
617-545-8221	**Res Times** 8am-10:30am

Rates:	**Pvt Bath** 2	**Shared Bath** 2	**Payment Terms:**
Single	$ 89-119.00	$ 79-99.00	Check
Double	$ 89-119.00	$ 79-99.00	AE/MC/V

Refer to the same listing name under Scituate, Massachusetts for a complete description. [M01FPMA2-16687]

**Morton Park Place	**Plymouth MA**
James & Janine Smith	1 Morton Park Rd 02360
800-736-3276 508-747-1730	**Res Times** 9am-5pm

Rates:	**Pvt Bath** 2	**Shared Bath** 2	**Payment Terms:**
Single	$ 55-65.00		Check

Double $ 90-110.00   MC/V

Lovely New England Colonial situated at the entrance to Little Pond, you're just a short walk to fresh water ponds for swimming, boating, fishing while visiting "America's Hometown". Situated on a large lot that provides secluded areas for privacy, lawn games, and cookout if you like while here. This home has been completely restored and furnished with Victorian and 20th Century antiques with guest rooms offering Red Maple Colonial and oak veneer Art Deco pieces. Location is everything here!! You're just a 15 minute walk from the center of Plymouth, the Mayflower, and Plymouth Rock. Plenty of antique shopping, fine restaurants and unique boutiques & unusual shops. Continental breakfast included. Baby-sitting & limo services are available at extra cost. **RESERVATIONS:** 25% deposit, two weeks in advance of res date, 7 day cancellation for full refund, add 9.7 tax, 4pm check-in **SEASONAL:** Rates vary **BROCHURE:** Yes **PERMITTED:** Children, drinking & smoking all limited [A11CPMA-1867]

Bradford Gardens Inn	**Provincetown MA**
Susan Culligan	178 Bradford St 02657
508-487-1616	**Res Times** 9am-9pm

Rates:	**Pvt Bath** 8	**Payment Terms:**
Single	$ 84-102.00*	Check
Double	$ 84-102.00	

Built in 1820, Provincetown's historic *Bradford Gardens Inn* brings true hospitality with all the comfort and convenience of a gracious country home. All the rooms are different in character combining charm (working fireplaces in most rooms) with period and modern conveniences. The Morning Room with its fireplace and large bay window is a delightful setting for guests to mingle and enjoy the full comp country breakfast. Guests can enjoy the year-round scenery (Spring & Summer flowering cherry & fruit trees) and the fabulous Fall for enjoying the unhurried shopping and natures brightest colors. *Guests can choose one of the cottage rentals ($82-118) with maid service, firewood, parking and a full breakfast included. Add 8% Mass tax to rates. Activities include biking, exquisite walking trails, boating, fishing and neighboring towns of Truro and Wellfleet. **RESERVATIONS:** One night's deposit (or 50% if longer) with reservation; 14 day cancel policy for refund; add $25 per day in high season (6/24-Memorial Day and $10 per day 9/6-10/31

DISCOUNTS: Off-season and mid-week rates **SEASONAL:** Rates vary **BROCHURE:** Yes **PERMITTED:** Limited children, smoking, drinking [E06BCMA-1874]

Lamplighter Guest House	**Provincetown MA**
Mike Novik/Joe Czarnecki	26 Bradford St 02657
508-487-2529	**Res Times** 8:30am-11pm
	Fax 508-487-0079

Rates:	**Pvt Bath** 8	**Shared Bath** 2	**Payment Terms:**
Single	$ 95.00	$ 55.00	Check*
Double	$ 95.00	$ 55.00	AE/MC/V

Our charming Sea Captain's home, built in 1853, offers panoramic views of Provincetown, the Bay and all of Cape Cod. The *Mayflower* anchored right in front of our Inn and the Pilgrims came ashore nearby. Activities abound such as whale watching, unique shopping, biking, sightseeing, swimming or strolling our numerous beaches. Our Inn provides two suites, rooms with private or semi-private baths, plus a separate cottage which is fully equipped to sleep four. The grounds surrounding the Inn are groomed daily and called the loveliest in Provincetown. Maid service, a continental breakfast and parking are provided. Reservations are required and free pick-up at the local airport, ferry or bus depot is provided with advance arrangements. **DISCOUNTS:** Off-season **AIRPORT:** Provincetown Airport-2 mi; Boston's Logan-2 hrs **PACKAGES:** Off-season, inquire at res time **RESERVATIONS:** 50% deposit required; *check accepted for deposit **BROCHURE:** Yes **PERMITTED:** Drinking, smoking **CONFERENCES:** Seasonal roof deck provides a unique setting [R10EPMA2-1879]

Land's End Inn	**Provincetown MA**
David Schoolman	22 Commercial St 02657
508-487-0706	**Res Times** 9am-10pm

Rates:	**Pvt Bath** 16	**Payment Terms:**
Single	$ 98-240.00	Check/Tvlrs Check
Double	$ 98-240.00	

Land's End Inn commands a splendid wind-swept and breath-taking site with a high view of Provincetown and the entire Cape Cod Bay! Built in the shingled-bungalow style of the late Victorian

Period by Charles Higgins, a Boston merchant, *Lands End* still houses part of his extensive collection of oriental wood carvings and stained glass. The Inn's large and airy living room is comfortably and informally furnished for relaxation, contemplation and quiet socializing before a large stone fireplace. The guest rooms are filled with antique furnishings and period decor providing a homey, comfortable and lived-in feeling; where books abound - and the modern world doesn't intrude. The large front porch offers wonderful views of the town, Bay and picturesque sunrises & sunsets you won't forget! Situated in the quiet residential West End of Provincetown, *Land's End* is close to the surrounding National Seashore beaches and numerous quaint New England towns for **fine restaurants and great seafood!** Continental breakfast is included. **AIRPORT:** Boston Logan-130 mi; Provincetown Municipal 3 mi **RESERVATIONS:** 50% deposit at res time to hold room; min 2 day weekends, 3 day holidays and 7 day summer periods **BROCHURE:** Yes **PERMITTED:** Smoking, drinking, limited children **CONFERENCES:** Yes, for small groups [Z07GPMA2-1880]

Allen House   **Quincy MA
Christine Gilmour
617-545-8221   **Res Times** 8am-10:30am

Rates:	**Pvt Bath** 2	**Shared Bath** 2	**Payment Terms:**
Single	$ 89-119.00	$ 79-99.00	Check
Double	$ 89-119.00	$ 79-99.00	AE/MC/V

Refer to the same listing name under Scituate, Massachusetts for a complete description. [M01FPMA2-16686]

---

*Gilberts B&B   **Rehoboth MA**
Jeanne & Martin Gilbert   30 Spring St 02769
617-252-6416

Rates:	**Pvt Bath** 3	**Shared Bath** 4	**Payment Terms:**
Single	$ 50.00	$ 42.00	Check
Double	$ 57.00	$ 50.00	

c1840s farmhouse nestled on seventy acres of pastoral and wooded fields just outside of Providence furnished with period antiques and family heirlooms. Pleasant hosts offer inground pool, pony rides for children and a full country breakfast with farm-fresh eggs you'll gather yourself. **RESERVATIONS:** One night's deposit to guarantee room. **BROCHURE:** Yes **SEASONAL:** No **PERMITTED:** Children, limited smoking, limited pets [E11ACMA-1891]

Inn On Cove Hill	Rockport MA
John & Marjorie Pratt	37 Mt Pleasant St 01966
508-546-2701	

Rates:	Pvt Bath 9	Shared Bath 2	Payment Terms:
Single	$ 60-74.00	$ 55.00	Check
Double	$ 70-85.00	$ 65.00	

Overlook the historic harbor area of Rockport from this delightful 200 year old Inn furnished in period decor with antique and canopy beds in some of the guest rooms. Continental breakfast is served on antique china indoors or, weather permitting, outdoors. Activities include golf, tennis and plenty of sight-seeing. **RESERVATIONS:** Deposit to hold room, 10 day cancel policy **SEASONAL:** Open 4/1-10/15 **BROCHURE:** Yes **SEASONAL:** No **PERMITTED:** Children 15-up, [E11ACMA-1899]

Seafarer Inn	Rockport MA
	86 Marmion Way 01966
508-546-6248	**Res Times** 9am-9pm

Rates:	Pvt Bath 8	Payment Terms:
Single	$ 50-70.00	Check
Double	$ 60-80.00	MC/V

A distinctive Inn built in 1890s rests directly on Gap Cove at the end of a quiet residential coastal road in one of Rockport's most desirable areas. Guests can fully relax in this peaceful waterfront setting with its invigorating salt air, fragrant wild roses combined with bright sunshine while gulls cry overhead, lobstermen tend their traps and sailboats catch quick ocean breezes. All the guest rooms are bright and airy for watching perfect sunrises and sunsets over the ocean. Guest rooms are comfortably furnished with two lovely large rooms on the third floor which include kitchenettes & charming breakfast nooks. There's a small cottage-like efficiency apartment with a private entrance available too - all suitable for a weekly or seasonal use. A continental breakfast is included. Favorite sights include the second largest artists colony in the USA with over one hundred galleries and studios and favorite activities include nature trails, bird watching, jogging and rock sitting, capturing the refreshing ocean sprays. **RESERVATIONS:** One night's deposit or credit card to guarantee res, 14 day cancel policy for refund **SEASONAL:** No **BROCHURE:** Yes **PERMITTED:** No pets, children, smoking. **LANGUAGES:** French [R07BCMA-2630]

Yankee Clipper Inn	**Rockport MA**
Robert & Barbara Ellis	96 Granite St 01966
800-545-3699 508-546-3407	**Res Times** 24 Hrs

Rates:	**Pvt Bath** 27	**Payment Terms:**
Single	$ 65-155.00 MAP	Check
Double	$ 85-165.00 MAP	

Ocean-front estate setting gorgeous landscaped grounds with three facilities nestled into a hilltop location overlooking the ocean. Great views from most guest rooms and the enclosed porch and dining room on the premises. Full facility including salt water pool and local fare in the dining room . . lobster! Guest rooms are unique and furnished with antiques. **RESERVATIONS:** Deposit required at res time, 10 day cancel policy for refund **SEASONAL:** Closed Christmas **BROCHURE:** Yes **PERMITTED:** Children 16-up, smoking, drinking [E11ACMA-3633]

****Harborside House*	**Salem MA**
Susan Livingston	
617-631-1032	**Res Times** 8am-8pm

Rates:	**Shared Bath** 2	**Payment Terms:**
Single	$ 60-65.00	Check
Double	$ 70-75.00	

Refer to the same listing name under Marblehead MA for a complete description. [M07GPMA2-14782]

****Salem Inn*	**Salem MA**
Richard & Diane Pabich	7 Summer St 01970
800-446-2995 508-741-0680	

Rates:	**Pvt Bath** 31	**Payment Terms:**

Single	$ 89-169.00	Check
Double	$ 89-169.00	AE/DC/MC/V

Relive Salem's history in the heart of the Historic District at this lovely restored Inn, dating back to Revolutionary times. Originally owned by Capt West, a sailing captain, the Inn reflects all the detail and craftsmanship of early American sailing vessels. Each of the 31 spacious guest rooms are uniquely different with a blend of period decor, antique furnishings and homey touches. Your hosts take pride in the old-fashioned New England ambiance and hospitality of their Inn. A restaurant on the premises, Massachusetts, offers informal settings like the secluded brick patio that's perfect on warm summer days. The *Salem Inn* has an uncommon place in history and is the perfect place for relaxing and enjoying the nearby sights including Marblehead's sailing and Old Town where interesting shops offer antiques to boutiques. Boston is just a sort walk to the nearby train station and within 35 minutes you'll arrive at Boston's North Station - certainly the *"best way"* to get to town! The Inn, located on the *Heritage Walking Trail*, is convenient to the National Maritime Site, Waterfront, museums and shops. **RESERVATIONS:** One night's deposit, 7 day cancel policy for refund less a $15 service fee **BROCHURE:** Yes **PERMITTED:** Children, drinking, limited smoking, limited pets **DISCOUNTS:** *AAA* **AIRPORT:** Boston Logan-15 mi [Z07GPMA2-3637]

**Capt Ezra Nye House	**Sandwich MA**
Elaine & Harry Dickson	152 Main St 02563
800-388-2278 508-888-6142	**Res Times** 9am-9pm

Rates:	**Pvt Bath** 5	**Shared Bath** 2	**Payment Terms:**
Single	$ 70-90.00	$ 55-70.00	Check
Double	$ 70-90.00	$ 55-70.00	AE/DC/MC/V

Selected as *one of the Top Fifty Inns in America* by *The Inn Times* and winner, ***Best Bed & Breakfast, Upper Cape***, *Cape Cod Life* magazine, 1993 and 1994, also featured in *Glamour, Innsider, and Cape Cod Life* magazines, this 1829 Inn is a classic example of the stately Federal period homes built by sea captains of yore. The seven guest rooms are furnished with antiques. Three have queen canopy beds, another a queen four-poster, with a working fireplace. A suite with private entrances, has a queen bed in one room and a small sitting room with a single sofa bed. Common rooms are the parlor with piano, a cozy den with fireplace, library and cable TV, and a large dining room where either an 8 or 9 am breakfast is served. The *Captain Ezra Nye House* is within walking distance of the Thornton Burgess, Doll and Glass Museums, Heritage Plantation, Hoxie House, tennis courts, shops and restaurants. Cape Cod Bay and the canal bike trail are one mile. **DISCOUNTS:** 10% for five or more days or three midweek day stay. **AIRPORT:** Boston Logan-60 miles. **RESERVATIONS:** Guaranteed with credit card number, 8 hr cancel policy for refund, late arrival with advance notice **BROCHURE:** Yes **PERMITTED:** Children 6-up, drinking **LANGUAGES:** Spanish [Z07GPMA2-6543]

Six Water Street	Sandwich MA
Linda & Mike Levitt	Water St 02563
508-888-6808	

Rates: **Pvt Bath** 2   **Payment Terms:**
Single $ 60.00   Check
Double $ 100.00

Romantic setting on Shawnee Pond, this elegant residence offers romantic candlelight breakfast, rowing on pond, and a decanter of sherry in each guest room. Continental breakfast included. Complimentary tennis, sitting room, rowboats. **BROCHURE:** Yes **PERMITTED:** Children 16-up **SEASONAL:** No [E11ACMA-3644]

Summer House	Sandwich MA
David & Kay Merrell	158 Main St 02563
508-888-4991	**Res Times** 9am-10pm

Rates: **Pvt Bath** 1   **Shared Bath** 4   **Payment Terms:**
Single $ 55-65.00 $ 40-50.00   Check
Double $ 65-75.00 $ 50-60.00   AE/DC/MC/V

Twice featured in *Country Living* magazine, this residence is an exquisite example of c1835 Cape Cod Greek Revival architecture in a setting of equally stunning historically significant homes and public buildings. Centrally located in the heart of historic Sandwich, a quintessential New England village (settled in 1637) and with strolling distance of restaurants, museums, shops, pond and gristmill and boardwalk to the beach. Antique furnishings, hand-stitched quilts, spacious airy rooms, original woodwork, latch hardware, wavy hand-fashioned glass window panes and seven

fireplaces evoke a gracious homelife. Full breakfast of freshly ground coffee, English or herbal teas, fruit juice, fresh seasonal fruit, entree of stuffed French toast, strata, Belgian waffles, quiche, garden fritatta, eggs benedict and two homebaked items (scones, muffins, yeast breads, fruit cobbler) are elegantly served in the sunny breakfast room (on cloudy days by candlelight). Special diets happily accommodated with advance notice. Complimentary English-style afternoon tea, brewed in antique silver pots, or iced, is served at an umbrella table in the garden or on the wicker furnished sunporch overlooking antique roses seldom seen today. Secluded hammocks beckon guests to daydream in the sun or shade. Small library, board games, local newspapers, restaurant menus and color TV are available in the guest parlor. Tranquil Sandwich village makes an excellent "base" from which to explore all of the Cape. **DISCOUNTS:** Travel agents **AIRPORT:** Boston or Providence RI-60 mi. **RESERVATIONS:** Credit card or check deposit of 50% of stay, 10 day cancel refund policy; less than 10 day notice only if rebooked **SEASONAL:** No **BROCHURE:** Yes **PERMITTED:** Drinking [I04EPMA-3645]

**Allen House	**Scituate MA**
Christine Gilmour	18 Allen Place 02066
617-545-8221	**Res Times** 8am-10:30am

Rates:	**Pvt Bath** 4	**Shared Bath** 2	**Payment Terms:**
Single	$ 89-149.00	$ 79-119.00	Check
Double	$ 89-149.00	$ 79-119.00	AE/DISC/MC/V

Don't pay in stress and dollars to stay, drive and park in Boston when you can stay 30 miles south in a quiet unspoilt fishing town, sleep peacefully and enjoy a fabulous gourmet breakfast before driving comfortably to a commuter boat and going to the city center in 35 minutes of civilized, stylish and comfortable sightseeing across Boston Harbor. Scituate is a beautiful small historic town on the South Shore where the Gilmours, gourmet caterer Christine and former journalist and corporate writer Ian, opened the *Allen House* primarily to provide engaging hospitality and a warm

English welcome for visitors and friends of local families and businesses. Just six rooms, four with private baths, overlook the town center, harbor and ocean beyond. Working fireplaces in the parlor and dining room make winter visits almost as wonderful as eating a summer breakfast on their sun-filled porch. Restaurants, shops and most of the town's services are within a three minute walk. Reservations of three or more nights (excluding Fridays and Saturdays) enjoy discount rates. **DISCOUNTS:** Winter Season, midweek year round **AIRPORT:** Boston Logan-30 miles **RESERVATIONS:** Deposit required (check ok, minimum one week prior to arrival) or credit cards **SEASONAL:** Closed March **BROCHURE:** Yes **PERMITTED:** Children 14-up, social drinking, Smoking is not permitted **LANGUAGES:** Little French, German, Spanish [Z08GPM-A2-12510]

**Race Brook Lodge			**Sheffield MA**

*Eve Van Syckle   864 Undermountain Rd   01257
413-229-2916

Fax 413-229-6629

Rates:	**Pvt Bath** 16	**Shared Bath** 2	**Payment Terms:**
Single	$ 70.00	$ 60.00	Check
Double	$ 75.00	$ 65.00	AE/MC/V

Rustic and elegant . . . . *Race Brook Lodge* is a place you can rest your feet and feel reborn. This 19th Century Berkshire barn has been beautifully restored offering guest rooms furnished in warm country-style with textured fabrics, quilts, rugs, handhewn beams, original artwork and stenciling. The owner-architect, Dave Rothstein, retained the hand hewn beams, thick plank floors, hideaway corners - creating rooms and suites designed especially for the 90's family reunions, small group retreats and quiet getaways. The *Barn Suite, Hayloft Suite* and *Harness Barn* offer a range of two to  four room bed room suites, perfect for extended families, friends or groups. A hearty breakfast buffet is featured daily and includes fruits, juices, granola, bagels, homemade muffins, great tea and our own special blend coffee while Sundays frequently feature lively jazz sessions accompanied by Sunday papers and interesting refreshments. Located on scenic Undermountain Road between Salisbury, Connecticut and South Egermont, Massachusetts - the old custom of changing stagecoach horses every seven miles explains our wonderful location. Hikers can cross the foot bridge from the lodge and hike to Race Brook Falls on the Appalachian Trail; skiers are 15 mins from Catamount or Butternut and just 20 miles from Tanglewood - and close to many great town and country restaurants offering gourmet to family style meals. *Race Brook Lodge* with its whispering brook and old maples invites you to renew and refresh by finding your cozy corner, put your feet up and recharge - while being pampered in this rural wonderland. **RESERVATIONS:** Flexible **PERMITTED:** Children, limited pets, limited smoking **CONFERENCES:** Extensive facilities for small and large workshops, seminars, executive retreats - featuring intimate setting for full privacy **BROCHURE:** Yes **AIRPORT:** Albany-45 min; Hartford's Bradley-1 hr **LANGUAGES:** Spanish, French, Czech **PACKAGES:** *Ski, Hunting, Antique Shopping* Meals available for groups upon request and prior notice [I03GPMA2-18782]

Wyndemere House			**Sippewissett MA**
			718 Palmer Ave 02540
508-540-7069			

Rates:	**Pvt Bath** 1	**Shared Bath** 2	**Payment Terms:**
			Check
Single	$ 65.00	$ 45.00	
Double	$ 75.00	$ 65.00	

Completely restored in 1980, this Paul Revere colonial built c1790's offers guests a true New England feeling with fine antique furnishings, and English pieces accenting the rooms. You might relax on the patio or in the library or TV room, with complimentary tea, coffee, sangria. Full breakfasts include host's specialty of Eggs Benedict if you like. Close to beaches and sights. **RESERVATIONS:** Reduced weekly rates **BROCHURE:** Yes **PERMITTED:** Children 13-up, smoking, drinking. Airport pick-up with prior notice. [E05ACMA-3657]

Bull Frog B&B	**South Ashfield MA**
Lucille & Moses Thibault	01330
413-628-4493	

Rates:	**Shared Bath** 2	**Payment Terms:**

Single	$ 55.00	Check
Double	$ 65.00	

Exciting 225 year farmhouse offering guests all the comfort of home with king size beds and plenty of New England hospitality. Furnished with a collection of country antiques and warmth, you'll enjoy visiting with the hosts who tend to all your interests. Full hearty New England breakfast is prepared by Lucille. Close to five colleges in Northhampton and Amherst with great outdoor activities nearby. **RESERVATIONS:** Deposit for 50% of stay within ten days of reservation **SEASONAL:** Closed Christmas and January **PERMITTED:** Limited children. [E11ACMA-3658]

Ye Olde Nantucket House	**South Chatham MA**
Norm Anderton	2641 Main St 02659
508-432-5641	**Res Times** 9am-9pm

Rates:	**Pvt Bath** 5	**Payment Terms:**
Single	$ 70-82.00	Check
Double	$ 70-82.00	MC/V

Midway between Cape Cod and Provincetown is an ideal location especially when guests can stay in this classic Greek Revival traditional Cape home moved to its present location in 1867 from Nantucket. Located in a designated Historic District, the atmosphere is friendly, informal and delightful. The stenciled walls, wide-pine plank floors, antique furnishings and attractive window and wall coverings combine into a unique Victorian flavor, fitting for a traditional stay on The Cape! Just a short walk to Nantucket Sound beach and the conveniently located areas for dining, shopping, golfing and fishing. An ideal location for visiting all the Capes attractions, there are plenty of fine shops, restaurants, summer band concerts, picturesque lighthouses, concerts & plays, church suppers and great summer festivals, surfing and sailing, craft and nautical antique shops, as well as ordinary antiques. Plymouth & Boston are within easy driving range and daily ferry trips will bring guests to Martha's Vineyard and Nantucket. A complimentary continental breakfast includes seasonal fresh fruit and juice, home-baked goods and hot beverages. Off-season rates are $10 less, special winter rates are available. **RESERVATIONS:** One night's full deposit or 50% if longer to confirm res; 2 day min on high season weekends & 3 day min on major holidays, 7 day cancel policy for full refund, early departures subject to no refund

SEASONAL: No **BROCHURE:** Yes **PERMITTED:** Children 8-up, drinking, limited smoking [R06BCMA-3659]

**Little Red House	**South Darmouth MA**
Meryl Amoroso	631 Elm St 02748
508-996-4554	**Res Times** 9am-9pm

Rates:	**Shared Bath** 2	**Payment Terms:**
Single	$ 55.00	Check
Double	$ 65.00	

Charming New England red gambrel colonial home overlooking a horse and cow pasture is located in the lovely coastal village of Padanaram. This home is beautifully furnished with many country accents, antiques, a lovely living room with corner fireplace, luxuriously comfortable four-poster or brass and iron beds. A gazebo in the backyard offers a perfect setting for relaxing moments. A full homemade breakfast served in the candlelit dining room satiates the appetite. Each morning you'll awake to the aroma of freshly brewed coffee and a surprise treat of sausage and biscuits with a special sauce, french toast, mushroom and spinach quiche, egg and sausage strata, buttermilk pancakes or apple fritters accompanied by juices, fresh fruit dishes and Meryl's special raisin bran muffins, cranberry bread, scones and homemade preserves. Close to the harbor and superb restaurants, beaches, historic sites, and just a short distance to major tourist areas such as New Bedford, Newport, Plymouth, Boston and Cape Cod. The ferry to Martha's Vineyard is just 10 mins away. Centrally located for many a day's excursion, your friendly hospitable hosts will welcome you back with late afternoon tea and cookies or a refreshing cool drink. **AIRPORT:** Providence RI Green Airport-45 mins **RESERVATIONS:** One night's deposit or 50% of length of stay; 14 day cancel policy for refund less 10% service fee, 11 am check-out **BROCHURE:** Yes **PERMITTED:** Limited drinking, children 16-up [Z07GPMA2-10932]

---

*Federal House Inn	**South Lee MA**
Robin Slocum & Ken Almgren	Rt 102 01260
617-350-6657	

Rates:	**Pvt Bath** 7	**Payment Terms:**
Single	$ 55.00-Up	Check

Double $ 65-145.00

Early 19th Century brick Federal building furnished with bright and cheerful touches including wallcoverings and family heirloom antiques such as Robin's great grandfather's sleigh bed.   Full gourmet country breakfast prepared by Ken, a professional chef, offering delightful entrees and appetizers on their complete luncheon and dinner menu.   Close to x-country skiing, Shakespeare and other sights. **BROCHURE:** Yes **PERMITTED:** Limited smoking, limited drinking [E11ACMA-3664]

Captain Farris House B&B	**South Yarmouth MA**
Scott Toney	3098 Old Main St 02664
800-350-9477 508-760-2818	**Fax** 508-398-1515

Rates:	**Pvt Bath** 10	**Payment Terms:**
Single	$ 85-175.00	Check
Double	$ 115-225.00	AE/MC/V

Built in 1845 by a sea captain, this Greek Revival and French Second Empire home offers luxurious guest rooms with beautiful antique furnishings reflecting the international travels of a world-travelled sea captain of the mid-1800's. Guest will find furnishings with a myriad of styles, countries of origins and periods prior to the 1850s. The many uses and additions to the original houses have been brilliantly incorporated to create a unique and special place for guests.   The two houses offer ten guest rooms, including one and two bedroom suites, with a variety of amenities which include Jacuzzi bathtubs with fine soaps and bath salts for luxurious soaking, canopy beds, private terraces, while all rooms offer private and semi-private entrances, cable TV and phones. A complimentary gourmet breakfast is served in the dining room or the open-air courtyard in season. A wrap around veranda offers relaxation anytime of the day - while the beautiful nearby sights offer plenty of shopping, museums and dining. Great location for travel, guests are only forty-five minutes from both Plymouth and Provincetown; twenty minutes to Hyannis and Nantucket Sound. Within a few minutes are nearby ferries, Bass River offering classic Cape Cod scenery and great fishing and complimentary bikes bring the beaches within a ten minute ride - while golf, canoeing, birdwatching, beach hiking and antiquing are within an easy drive. *The Captain Farris House* is an exceptionally appointed bed and breakfast for escapes, vacations, tours, special occasions, weekends, honeymoons or whatever you desire. **RESERVATIONS:** One night non-refundable deposit, two night min weekends, three night min holidays **SEASONAL:** No **BROCHURE:** Yes **PERMITTED:** Drinking **AIRPORT:** Boston Logan-80 mi [R03GPMA2-18181]

**Amerscot House	**Stow MA**
Doreen & Jerry Gibson	61 W Acton Rd 01775
508-897-0666	**Res Times** 9am-6pm

Rates:	**Pvt Bath** 3	**Payment Terms:**
Single	$ 75-90.00	Check
Double	$ 80-95.00	AE/MC/V

Amerscot House is a beautiful early American farmhouse built in 1734. Come home from a day of business or vacationing and enjoy the ambiance and warmth of the past. Linger over a glass of sherry or tea and scones by the fire. Antiques, handmade quilts and fresh flowers reflect *Amerscot's* personal touch. Each guest room has a fireplace, full private bath, phone and cable TV. The Lindsay suite has a sitting room and bath with jacuzzi. The Barn Room will accommodate up to 60 people for conferences or private parties. Visit historic sites, shop in the select stores of Concord and Boston, golf on any of the four top-flight courses, canoe, hike and enjoy fresh-picked apples from the nearby orchards. Stow is only five minutes from Rt 495 and Rt 2. Business services available include conference facilities, secretarial, copier and fax. A full breakfast is included with fresh fruit, homemade granola, bread, muffins and an entree. **RESERVATIONS:** Reservations must be guaranteed with deposit, 7 day cancel policy for refund **SEASONAL:** No **DIS-COUNTS:** Corporate & extended-stay special rates Check-in 4-9pm, check-out by 11am **BROCHURE:** Yes **PERMITTED:** Children **CONFERENCES:** The Barn Room is perfect for business or social parties for groups to 60 persons [R03CPMA-10637]

**Captain Samuel Eddy House Inn	**Sturbridge MA**
John & Carilyn O'Toole	
508-832-5282	**Res Times** After 4pm

Rates:	**Pvt Bath** 5	**Payment Terms:**
Single	$ 52.00	Check
Double	$ 67-90.00	AE/MC/V

Refer to the same listing name under Auburn, Massachusetts for a complete description. [M02BCMA-6569]

Col E Crafts Publik House   Sturbridge MA
Noel Hennebery   Fiske Hill Rd   01566
508-347-3313

Rates:	Pvt Bath 8	Payment Terms:
Single	$ 85.00	Check
Double	$ 95.00	AE/MC/V

Spectacular views from atop Fiske Hill are offered in this 1786 restored country farmhouse with deluxe accommodations, swimming pool, piano, and continental plus breakfast. **BROCHURE:** Yes **PERMITTED:** Children, smoking, drinking **SEASONAL:** No **LANGUAGES:** French [E11ACMA-3675]

Captain Parkers Inn At Quinebaug   Sturbridge MA
David Parker/Cynthia Miller
800-707-7303   203-935-5219   **Res Times** 24 Hrs

Rates:	Pvt Bath 4	Shared Bath 2	Payment Terms:
Single	$ 95.00	$ 55.00	Check
Double	$ 95.00	$ 55.00	MC/V

Refer to the same listing name under Thompson, Connecticut for a complete description. [M08GPCT2]

**Sturbridge Country Inn*   Sturbridge MA
Kevin MacConnell   530 Main St   01566
508-347-5503   **Res Times** 7am-11pm

Rates:	Pvt Bath 9	Payment Terms:
Single	$ 69.00	Check
Double	$ 149.00	AE/DC/MC/V

Close to Old Sturbridge Village, on the old "Boston Post Road" (530 Main St), lies this mid-19th Century Country Inn offering gracious surroundings. This grand structure is now known as the *Sturbridge Country Inn*. We welcome you to enjoy a respite in our luxurious accommodations where we have preserved the charm of the

---

past while providing all of the fine comforts of today. All rooms are tastefully decorated with period colonial furnishings, a private fireplace, vaulted ceilings and whirlpool tubs. For the more discriminating guest, the Corner rooms offer a large whirlpool tub, sun porch and breakfast ensuite if desired. The Loft Suite with its king-size bed, skylights, sitting room, wet bar and breakfast ensuite provides elegance beyond your expectations. We encourage your special occasion, whether it is a wedding, anniversary, birthday, executive retreat or a weekend getaway. Complimentary champagne greets each guest upon their arrival and your hosts can look after any details ranging from limousine and airport service, VCR rentals, Old Sturbridge Village tickets to fresh flowers. The perfect location for your afford able weekend getaway or special occasion. **AIRPORT** Bradley or Logan - 60 mi. **RESERVATIONS:** 50% deposit at res time with 14 day cancel policy for refund. **BROCHURE:** Yes **PERMITTED:** Children, drinking, smoking [I07GPMA2-8242]

**_Longfellow's Wayside Inn_	**Sudbury MA**
Robert Purrington	Wayside Inn Rd 01776
508-443-1776	

Rates:	**Pvt Bath** 10	**Payment Terms:**
Single	$ 75.00	AE/DC/MC/V
Double	$ 85.00	

Longfellow's Wayside Inn, immortalized in 1863 by Longfellow in his *Tales of A Wayside Inn*, is located off US Rt 20, on Wayside Inn Rd. Next to the Inn, there's a working gristmill (open April-November) and the red school house of *Mary Had A Little Lamb* fame (open in seasonal weather). The Martha Mary Chapel is available for weddings and special functions. The *Wayside Inn* offers facilities for small meetings and functions. Reservations for lodging or dining should be made well in advance. Our entire staff looks forward to welcoming you and showing you the hospitality that has made the *Wayside Inn* a special place for nearly three hundred years. **RESERVATIONS:** Deposit required **PERMITTED:** Children, drinking, smoking **BROCHURES:** Yes **SEASONAL:** No

CONFERENCES: Meeting and conference rooms available **AIR-PORT:** Boston Logan-25 mi [R11EPMA2-3679]

**The Hanover House	**Vineyard Haven MA**
Kay & Ron Nelson	#10 Edgartown Rd 02568
508-693-1066	**Res Times** 8am-10pm

Rates:	**Pvt Bath** 15	**Payment Terms:**
Single	$ 95-158.00	Check
Double	$ 95-158.00	AE/MC/V

Recommended by The New York Times, *The Hanover House* is a large old Inn that has been fully renovated offering guests modern convenience with the quaintness and personalized hospitality of the lovely old inns of yesteryear. All rooms include private baths, color cable TV, a queen size bed or two double beds, a/c and individual heat controls. Vineyard Haven is a quaint and unspoiled island/town which is reached by the Woods Hole Ferry. The town is filled with craft shops, fine restaurants and theaters. *The Hanover House* is within walking distance of the ferry, island tours and shuttle buses to Oak Bluffs and Edgartown. Activities include sailing, windsurfing, swimming, fishing, biking, tennis, golf and horseback riding. Fully-equipped housekeeping units including kitchens are available for longer stays. **RESERVATIONS:** Full deposit 1 to 3 days, 50% for 4 days or longer and must be received within 7 days of booking; 14 day written cancel notice for refund less 10% ($20 min). No refunds for early departure **BROCHURE:** Yes **PERMITTED:** Children, limited drinking, non-smoking. A homemade continental breakfast is included [Z07GPMA2-3690]

**Lothrop Merry House			**Vineyard Haven MA**
Mary & John Clarke			Owen Park 02568
508-693-1646			

Rates:	**Pvt Bath** 2	**Shared Bath** 1	**Payment Terms:**
Single			Check
Double	$ 85-120.00	$ 70.00	AE/MC/V

18th Century guest house nestled right on a hilltop setting with its own private beach and overlooking the harbor. All rooms offer guests lovely views, fireplaces, and quaint furnishings. Continental breakfast includes homemade breads. **PERMITTED:** Children, limited smoking, drinking **SEASONAL:** No [C11ACMA-3691]

**Honeysuckle Hill	**West Barnstable MA**
Barbara Rosenthal	591 Main St 02668
508-362-8418	

Rates:	**Pvt Bath** 3	**Payment Terms:**
Single	$ 90-105.00	Check
Double	$ 90-105.00	AE/DC/MC/V

"Country Elegance at its Best" - Honeysuckle Hill was originally built in the early 1800s as a farm house near the great salt marshes of Cape Cod. Completely restored, the Inn is a comfortable, rambling place, decorated in a Cape Cod version of English Country: chintz, antiques, cushions, comfortable chairs, feather beds and down comforters and includes two shaggy dogs named *Fred* and *Annie*. Theme guest rooms are named Peter Rabbit (filled with antique furnishings and Peter Rabbit memorabilia); Rose Room featuring a working fireplace perfect for a romantic weekend; the very private Cape Cod Room tucked away on the second floor. In-addition to fluffy terry robes, each private bath includes a basket of English toiletries, fresh flowers in each guest room when in season, a carafe of ice water and *a bedside tin of homemade cookies*. Complimentary beach towels, beach chairs, umbrellas are always on the porch along with a bulletin board of area events. Hearty country breakfasts featuring memorable entrees such as sausage souffles or blueberry pancakes and traditional afternoon tea are served in the dining room. A wrap-around screen porch filled with wicker furniture provides summer relaxation while winter has everyone gathering in comfortable chairs around the fireplace in the Great Room with its game table and large screen TV. Located in Old Kings Hwy historic district on Rt 6A, guests are still close to the dunes of Sandy Neck Beach, Hyannis, historic Sandwich Village while Boston and Provincetown are just and hour's drive. A perfect starting point for all of the Cape's excitement of whale watching, antiquing, beaches, golf, tennis and country auctions. **RESERVATIONS:** One night's deposit to confirm reservation **PERMITTED:** Limited children, limited pets, limited smoking **BROCHURE:** Yes **CONFERENCES:** Facility for small groups in a large great room setting **SEASONAL:** No **LANGUAGES:** Some French, Italian **DISCOUNTS:** Off-season **AIRPORT:** Boston Logan-65 mi; Providence-75 mi [R10EPMA2-3699]

Lions Head Inn   **West Harwich MA**

The Dentons

800-321-3155 508-432-7766

186 Belmont Rd 02671

Res Times 9am-9pm

Rates:	**Pvt Bath** 6	**Payment Terms:**
Single	$ 60-100.00	Check
Double	$ 70-110.00	AE/MC/V

The *Lion's Head Inn* is a delightfully romantic Inn with a sense of history . . . blended with the quiet elegance and updated amenities of a tastefully decorated country manor. Built in the 1800's as a Cape Half House, it was the home of Thomas L Snow, a sea captain of Orient-bound schooners. The architectural characteristics of the early 1800's are evident throughout the Inn. Adding to the original flavor are the furnishings, some of which are period antiques, and the tastefully decorated guest suites and common areas. A warm atmosphere awaits each guest at the Lion's Head Inn. Each morning a bountiful breakfast is served. Since *Lion's Head Inn* is centrally located on the Cape, one's choice of pastime is close at hand. Whether in the warm waters of Nantucket Sound, a half mile from the Inn, enjoying a dip in the Inn's swimming pool, riding nearby bicycle paths, fishing or sailing in the Cape Cod Bay or the Sound waters, whale watching, enjoying a round of golf, shopping or antiquing, enjoying local theatre or dining at the area's superb restaurants, visitors will find their stay relaxing or full as they wish it to be. *Rated 3 Crowns-Excellent* by *ABBA* **AIRPORT:** Boston Logan-70 mi **RESERVATIONS:** 50% deposit at time of reservation **SEASONAL:** No **BROCHURE:** Yes **PERMITTED:** Children 4-up, drinking, limited smoking [R11EPMA2-3711]

Card Lake Inn & Restaurant   **West Stockbridge MA**

Ed & Lisa Robbins

413-232-0272

29 Main St 01266

Rates:	**Pvt Bath** 4	**Shared Bath** 4	**Payment Terms:**
Single	$ 95-125.00	$ 70-80.00	Check
Double	$ 95-125.00	$ 70-80.00	DC/MC/V

The *Card Lake Restaurant and Country Inn*, in beautiful West Stockbridge, offers guests fine food and lodging in the Berkshires. Your innkeepers at *Card Lake* provide guests with charming, clean, comfortable guest rooms (most have brass beds and antique furnishings) and a delicious continental breakfast. The restaurant, open daily from 11am until 9pm, Wednesday through Monday, offer hearty country cuisine and tempting desserts along with a fine selection of liquors, wines, beer and plenty of good company and cheer. Just minutes away from attractions such as Tanglewood, Jackob's Pillow, Berkshire Theatre Festival and major ski areas. **AIRPORT:** Albany-1 hr **RESERVATIONS:** First night deposit, min two night stay on weekends in season (May-Oct), one week cancel policy for refund **SEASONAL:** Rates vary **BROCHURE:** Yes **PERMITTED:** Children, drinking, limited smoking [Z07GPMA2-7213]

Victorian	Whitinsville MA
Martha Flint	583 Linwood Ave 01588
508-234-2500	

Rates:	**Pvt Bath** 8	**Payment Terms:**
Single	$ 95.00-Up	Check
Double	$ 100-125.00	AE/MC/V

Elegant Victorian mansion with twenty-three rooms, sumptuous grounds offers marble fireplaces, twelve foot ceilings and furnished with beautiful antiques and family heirlooms from the period. Continental breakfast included. **BROCHURE:** Yes **PERMITTED:** Limited children, smoking, limited pets **SEASONAL:** No [E11ACMA-5872]

Worthington/Four Corners	Worthington MA
Debi & Joe Shaw	Old North Rd 01098
413-238-4441	

Rates:	**Pvt Bath** 4	**Payment Terms:**
Single	$ 80.00	Check
Double	$ 80.00	AE/MC/V

Nestled on fifteen acres where the Hampshire hills meet the Berkshires, the *Worthington Inn* is central to this quaint New England town and accessible to Springfield, Williamstown & Pittsfield and the five college area of Amherst & Northampton. Dating from 1780 and fully restored, it is listed on the Massachusetts *Register of Historic Sites.* You'll enjoy the picture-postcard setting that offers guests billowy European down comforters and delicious homemade gourmet breakfasts being served in the fireplaced dining room. There's plenty to do: x-country skiing, canoeing, swimming and hiking, as well as plenty of antiquing. **RESERVATIONS:** One night's deposit at res time. **BROCHURE:** Yes **PERMITTED:** Limited children, limited smoking, drinking okay **SEASONAL:** No **LANGUAGES:** German [E01BCMA-3733]

**Liberty Hill Inn On Cape Cod	**Yarmouth Port MA**
Jack & Beth Flanagan	77 Main St 02675
800-821-3977 508-362-3976	**Res Times** 8am-10pm

Rates:	**Pvt Bath** 5	**Payment Terms:**
Single	$ 50-70.00	Check
Double	$ 70-125.00	AE/MC/V

Elegant, historic and romantic ... this Bed & Breakfast Inn offers distinctive accommodations for the most discriminating traveler. Featured in many guidebooks such as *Fodor* and in magazines such as *Colonial Homes*. *"Best Bed & Breakfast"*, *Insiders Guide to Cape Cod*. AAA **Approved, Mobil ★★★**. The Greek Revival style, mini-mansion has

high ceilings, modern private baths and spacious rooms filled with early American antiques. History is celebrated everywhere on Cape Cod but especially on the Old Kings Highway in the village of Yarmouth Port. The Inn stands on a little rise with a view of the bay on the site of the Liberty Pole, a gathering place for patriots during the Revolutionary War. Nearby are historic restorations, conservation areas, golf courses, fine beaches, whale watching, professional theatre, restaurants and gift shops. A full complimentary breakfast is included while lunches are available at added cost. You'll find cable TV in the Common Room, attraction brochures, maps of the area and menus from local restaurants. Guest telephone available, plenty of off-street parking. **RESERVATIONS:** One night's deposit if less than 4 days, 50% deposit if longer; 14 day cancel policy for refund **PERMITTED:** Children, drinking, limited smoking **BROCHURE:** Yes **CONFERENCES:** Yes, for groups to twelve with fax and copy machine nearby. Guest phone available **AIRPORT:** Boston Logan-77 mi; Barnstable County Airport-3 mi. Free airport pick-up, prior arrangement **PACKAGES:** Sun-Thursday, 5 nights for the price of 4; *Golf, Theatre* [I06FPMA1-3739]

Wedgewood Inn   Yarmouth Port MA

Milt & Gerrie Graham   83 Main St 02675
508-362-5157   **Res Times** 24 Hrs

Rates: **Pvt Bath** 6   **Payment Terms:**
Single $ *105-150.00   Check
Double $ *105-150.00   AE/DC/MC/V

The *Wedgewood Inn* is a handsome Greek Revival built in 1812 on the historic north side of Cape Cod and is listed in the *National Registry of Historic Places.* This romantic Inn has 2+ beautifully landscaped acres of lawn and gardens, with a gazebo for the guest's enjoyment. There are six rooms, all with private baths. Most of the rooms have working fireplaces, wide board floors, and pencil post or canopy beds. Two full suites and a junior suite offer private porches and private sitting rooms. The decor is formal Country with antiques and oriental rugs. Fresh fruit is placed in each room, as is an Afternoon Tea tray. A sunny dining room with a large bay window provides a pleasant setting for a multi-course full breakfast. Homebaked goods, fresh fruit and a choice of entrees such as Belgian waffles with strawberries and whipped cream are featured. Nearby area activities include antique shops, fine restaurants, art galleries and of course, water sports and whale watching. Nature trails, bird watching and bicycle trails are also popular attractions. **DISCOUNTS:** *Off-season rates $90-135.00, travel industry, extended stays over 5 nights **SEASONAL:** Rates vary **AIRPORT:** Boston Logan-70 mi; Hyannis-3 mi. **RESERVATIONS:** On night's deposit to 3 night stay, over 3 nights, 50% deposit **BROCHURE:** Yes **PERMITTED:** Children 10-up, drinking, limited smoking. **CONFERENCES:** Yes for small groups [I07GPMA2-3744]

Adams
BUTTERNUT INN

Agawam
HARTLEYS GUEST
HOUSE

Amherst
ALLEN HOUSE INN
413-253-5000

AMITY HOUSE
413-549-6446

Andover
ANDOVER INN
508-475-5903

Ashfield
*ASHFIELD INN
413-628-4571

GOLD LEAF INN
413-628-3392

Attleboro
COL BLACKINTON
617-222-6022

EMMA C'S B&B
508-226-6365

Auburn
**CAPT SAMUEL
EDDY HOUSE INN**
508-832-5282

Barnstable
*ASHLEY MANOR
508-362-8044

B&B ON
BEAUTIFUL CAPE
COD

508-362-6556

BACON BARN INN
508-362-5518

BEECHWOOD INN
508-362-6618

CHAS HINKLEY
HOUSE
508-362-9924

COBBS COVE
508-362-9356

GOSS HOUSE B&B
508-362-8555

**HONEYSUCKLE
HILL**
508-362-8418

LAMB & LION
508-326-6823

THOMAS HUCKINS
HOUSE
508-362-6379

Barre
OLDE JENKINS
GUEST HOUSE
508-355-6444

Bass River
ANCHORAGE
617-398-8265

*BELVEDERE B&B
617-398-6674

*CAPTAIN ISAIAHS
HOUSE
617-394-1739

OLD CAPE HOUSE
617-398-1068

Becket
CANTERBURY
FARM
413-623-8765

LONG HOUSE

Belchertown
MCFADYENS

Berlin
STONEHEDGE
617-838-2574

Billerica
BILLERICA B&B
617-667-7317

Boston
**1810 HOUSE
B&B**
617-659-1810

ALLEN HOUSE
617-545-8221

BALLEYS II
BOSTON HOUSE
617-262-4534

**BEACON HILL
B&B**
617-523-7376

BOSTONIAN
HOTEL

**CAPE COD
SUNNY PINES INN**
508-432-9628

CHANDLER INN
800-842-3450

*EMMA JAMES
HOUSE
617-288-8867

FARRINGTON INN
800-767-5337

**HARBORSIDE
HOUSE**
617-631-1032

LAFAYETTE HOTEL

LAND'S END INN
508-487-0706

LENOX HOTEL
800-225-7676

**MANOR ON
GOLDEN POND**
800-545-2141

**OASIS GUEST
HOUSE**
617-267-2262

OMIN PARKER
HOUSE

TERRACE
TOWNHOUSE
617-350-6520

THISTLE HILL
703-987-9142

VICTORIAN B&B
617-247-1599

YORK HARBOR

INN
207-363-5119

Brewster
BEECHCROFT INN
508-896-9534

BRAMBLE INN
508-896-7644

BREWSTER
FARMHOUSE INN

CANDLEBERRY INN
508-896-3300

*CAPTAIN
FREEMAN INN
508-896-7481

HIGH BREWSTER
INN
508-896-3636

**ISAIAH CLARK
HOUSE**
508-896-2223

*OCEAN GOLD B&B
617-255-7045

OLD MANSE INN
508-896-3149

OLD SEA PINES INN
508-896-6114

Brookline
*BEACON INNS
617-566-0088

BEACON PLAZA
617-232-6550

BEECH TREE INN
800-544-9660

BROOKLINE
MANOR HOUSE
617-232-0003

Buckland
1797 HOUSE
413-625-2697

SCOTT HOUSE
413-625-6624

Cambridge
BETTINAS B&B

*CAMBRIDGE
HOUSE
800-232-9989

Cape Cod
*SALTY DOG
508-428-5228

Castleton
BLUE KNOLL FARM
703-937-5234

Centerville
CARVER HOUSE
617-775-9414

COPPER BEECH
INN
617-771-5488

*INN AT
FERNBROOK
508-775-4334

OLD HUNDRED
HOUSE
508-775-6166

TERRACE
GARDENS
508-775-4707

Charlemont
*FOREST WAY
FARM
413-337-8321

INN AT
CHARLEMONT
413-339-5796

Chatham
BOW ROOF HOUSE
508-945-1346

CAPTAINS HOUSE
INN
508-945-0127

CHATHAM BARS
INN
508-945-0096

CHATHAM TOWN
HOUSE INN
508-945-2180

CRANBERRY INN AT
CHATHAM
800-332-4667

CYRUS KENT
HOUSE
800-338-5368

INN AMONG
FRIENDS
508-945-0792

INN AT THE DOLPIN
508-945-0070

OLD HARBOR INN
508-945-4434

QUEEN ANNE INN
508-945-0394

SHIPS INN AT
CHATHAM
508-945-5859

WEQUASSETT INN

Chatham Center
*BRADFORD INN
800-562-4667

Chelmsford
WESTVIEW
LANDING
508-256-0074

Chestnut Hill
PLEASANT
PHEASANT
617-566-4178

Chilmark
BREAKFAST AT
TIASQUAM
508-645-3685

Colrain
GRANDMOTHERS
HOUSE
416-624-3771

Concord
*ANDERSON
WHEELER
HOMESTEAD
508-369-3756

*COL ROGER
BROWN HOUSE

508-369-9119

COLONIAL INN
508-369-9200

GARFIELD HOUSE

*HAWTHORNE INN
508-369-5610

Conway
POUNDSWORTH
B&B
413-369-4420

THE MERRIAMS
413-369-4052

Cummington
CUMWORTH FARM
413-634-5529

HILL GALLERY
413-238-5914

INN AT
CUMMINGTON
FARM
800-562-9666

**SWIFT RIVER
INN**
800-532-8022

WINDFIELDS FARM
413-684-3786

Cuttyhunk
ALLEN HOUSE INN
617-996-9292

Dalton
DALTON HOUSE
413-684-3854

Danvers
APPLETON INN
KING'S GRANT INN

SALEM VILLAGE
B&B
617-774-7851

Deerfield
DEERFIELD INN
800-926-3865

YELLOW GABLED
HOUSE
413-665-4922

Dennis
****FOUR
CHIMNEYS**
508-385-6317

****ISAIAH HALL
B&B INN**
800-736-0160

SOFT BREEZES INN
508-385-5246

Dennisport
BY THE SEA
GUESTS
508-398-8685

****ROSE PETAL
B&B**
508-398-8470

Duxbury
CAMPBELLS
COUNTRY
617-934-0862

WINDSOR HOUSE
INN

617-934-0991

East Falmouth
PETERSONS B&B
508-540-2962

East Orleans
NAUSET HOUSE
INN
508-255-2195

*PARSONAGE
508-255-8217

SHEPHERDS INN
508-823-8777

****SHIP'S KNEES
INN**
508-255-1312

East Sandwich
*WINGSCORTON
FARM

Eastham
**OVERLOOK INN
800-356-1121

*WHALEWALK INN
508-255-0617

Edgartown
**ARBOR
508-627-8137

ASHLEY INN
508-627-9655

****CAPT DEXTER
HOUSE**
508-627-7289

CHADWICK HOUSE

508-627-4435

CHARLOTTE INN
508-627-4751

**COLONIAL INN
800-627-4701

DAGGETT HOUSE
508-627-4600

EDGARTOWN
HERITAGE HOTEL
508-627-5161

*EDGARTOWN INN
508-627-4794

GOVERNOR
BRADFORD INN
508-627-9150

HARBORSIDE INN
508-627-4321

KATAMA GUEST
HOUSE
508-627-5158

KELLY HOUSE
508-627-4394

MEETING HOUSE
INN
508-627-8626

**POINT WAY INN
508-627-8633

SHIRETOWN INN
800-541-0090

SHIVERICK INN
508-627-3797

VICTORIAN INN
508-627-4784

Essex
*GEORGE FULLER
HOUSE
508-768-7766

Fairhaven
**EDGEWATER
B&B**
508-997-5512

Falmouth
AMHERST
508-548-2781

**CAPT TOM
LAWRENCE HOUSE**
508-540-1445

COONAMESSETT
INN
617-548-2300

ELM ARCH INN
508-548-0133

GLADSTONE INN
508-548-9851

GRAFTON INN
800-642-4069

HASTINGS BY THE
SEA
508-548-1628

MOORINGS LODGE
508-540-2370

MOSTLY HALL B&B
508-548-3786

PALMER HOUSE
INN
800-4RB-ANDB

**PEACOCKS INN
ON THE SOUND**
508-457-9666

VILLAGE GREEN
INN
508-548-5621

WOODS HOLE
PASSAGE
508-548-9575

WORCESTER
HOUSE

Gloucester
BLUE SHUTTERS
INN
617-281-2706

GRAY MANOR
617-283-5409

RIVERVIEW B&B
617-281-1826

WILLIAMS GUEST
HOUSE
617-283-4931

Goshen
WHALE INN
413-268-7246

Great Barrington
BREAD & ROSES
413-528-1099

COFFING-
BOSTWICK HOUSE

413-528-4511

ELLINGS GUEST
HOUSE

LITTLEJOHN
MANOR
413-528-2882

RED BIRD INN
413-229-2433

**ROUND HILL
FARM
NON-SMOKERS
B&B**
413-528-3366

*SEEKONK PINES
INN**
800-292-4192

THORNEWOOD INN
413-528-3828

TURNING POINT
INN
413-528-4777

WINDFLOWER INN
413-528-2720

Greenfield
BRANDT HOUSE
B&B
413-773-8184

HITCHCOCK
HOUSE
413-774-7452

Groton
GREENVIEW

Hamilton
MILES RIVER COUNTRY INN
508-468-7206

Hancock
MILL HOUSE INN
518-733-5606

Hanover
HOUSE OF COFFEY
617-826-3141

Harwich
BIDE A WEE

CAPE COD SUNNY PINES INN
800-356-9628

THE WINSTEAD
508-432-4586

Harwich Center
VICTORIAN INN AT HARWICH
617-432-8335

Harwich Port
#10 B&B
508-432-9313

AUGUSTUS SNOW HOUSE
508-430-0528

CAPTAINS QUARTERS
800-992-6550

BAYBERRY SHORES
800-992-6550

BEACH HOUSE INN
508-432-4444

CAPTAINS QUARTERS
800-992-6550

COACH HOUSE
508-432-9542

COUNTRY INN ACRES
508-432-2769

DRANGEA HOUSE

DUNSCROFT INN
800-432-4345

HARBOR BREEZE INN
800-992-6550

HARBOR WALK GUEST HOUSE
508-432-1675

INN ON BANK STREET
508-432-3206

SHOALS GUEST HOUSE
508-432-3837

Holyoke
*YANKEE PEDDLER
413-532-9494

Huntington
PAULSON B&B
413-667-3208

Hyannis

CAPT EZRA NYE HOUSE
800-388-2278

CAPTAIN SYLVESTER BAXTER HOUSE
508-775-5611

CRANBERRY COVE
508-775-7049

ELEGANCE BY-THE-SEA
508-775-3595

FAIRBANKS INN
508-487-0386

INN ON SEA STREET
508-775-8030

SEA BREEZE BY THE BEACH
508-771-7231

Hyannis Port
SIMMONS HOMESTEAD INN
508-778-4999

Kingston
BLACK POODLE

Lancaster
CARTER-WASHBURN HOUSE

Lanesboro
AMC-BASCOM LODGE
413-743-1591

TUCKERED
TURKEY
413-442-0260

Lanesborough
TOWNRY FARM

Lee
DONAHOES
413-243-1496

HAUS ANDREAS
413-243-3298

MORGAN HOUSE
413-243-0181

RAMSEY HOUSE
413-243-1598

WHITE HORSE INN
413-443-0961

Lenox
AMITY HOUSE
413-637-0005

APPLE TREE INN
413-637-1477

BIRCHWOOD INN
800-524-1646

BLANTYRE
413-637-3556

*BROOK FARM INN
413-637-3013

CANDLELIGHT INN
413-637-1555

CARON B&B
800-666-3076

CLIFFWOOD INN
413-637-3330

CORNELL HOUSE
413-637-0562

GABLES INN
413-637-3416

**GARDEN GABLES
INN**
413-637-0193

GATEWAYS INN
413-637-2532

ROCKWOOD INN
413-637-9750

STRAWBERRY HILL
413-637-3381

UNDERLEDGE INN
413-637-0236

VILLAGE INN
413-637-0020

*WALKER HOUSE
413-637-1271

WHEATLEIGH
413-637-0610

WHISTLERS INN
413-637-0975

Lexington
ASHLEYS B&B
617-862-6488

HALEWOOD
HOUSE
617-862-5404

INNVAL HILL

Lowell
SHERMAN BERRY
HOUSE
617-459-4760

Lunenberg
COACH HOUSE
INN
508-582-9921

Lynn
BAYSIDE INN

Manchester
OLD CORNER INN
617-526-4996

Marblehead
10 MUGFORD
STREET
617-631-5642

HARBOR LIGHT
INN
617-631-2186

**HARBORSIDE
HOUSE**
617-631-1032

LINDSEYS
GARRETT
617-631-2653

SEA STREET B&B
617-631-1890

**SPRAY CLIFF ON
THE OCEAN**
800-626-1530

STILLPOINT

617-631-2653

Marion
PEREGRINE B&B

Marstons Mills
PRINCE HOUSE

Marthas Vineyard
**ARBOR
508-627-8137

FARMHOUSE
508-693-5354

****THORNCROFT
INN**
800-332-1236

Melrose
WINDSLOW HOUSE

Mendon
ARNOLD TAFT
HOUSE
508-634-8159

Menemsha
BEACH PLUM INN
617-645-9454

Merrimac
BENJAMIN CHOATE
HOUSE
617-462-4786

Middlefield
STRAWBERRY
BANKE FARM
413-623-6481

Monument Beach
BAY BREEZE
GUEST HOUSE

Nantucket
76 MAIN STREET
508-228-2533

ANCHOR INN
508-228-0072

BEACHSIDE
508-228-2241

BRANT POINT INN
508-228-5442

BRASS LANTERN
INN
508-228-4064

CARLISLE HOUSE
508-228-0720

CARRIAGE HOUSE
508-228-0326

****CENTERBOARD
GUEST HOUSE**
508-228-9696

*CENTURY HOUSE
508-228-0530

CLIFFSIDE BEACH
CLUB
508-228-0618

CORNER HOUSE
508-228-1530

DOLPHIN GUEST
HOUSE
617-228-4028

EIGHTEEN
GARDNER STREET
508-228-1155

FOUR CHIMNEYS
INN
508-228-1912

***GRIEDER GUEST
HOUSE**
508-228-1399

HALLIDAYS
NANTUCKET
HOUSE
508-228-9450

HARBOR HOUSE
508-228-1500

HAWTHORNE
HOUSE
508-228-1468

HOUSE AT TEN
GAY STREET
508-228-4425

HOUSE OF SEVEN
GABLES
508-228-4706

HUNGRY WHALE
508-228-4206

HUSSEY
HOUSE-1795
508-228-0747

INDIA HOUSE
508-228-9043

IVY LODGE
508-228-0305

JARED COFFIN
HOUSE
508-228-2405

LE LANGUEDOC
INN
508-228-2552

***LYNDA WATTS
B&B**
508-228-3828

MARTINS GUEST
HOUSE
508-228-0678

NANTUCKET
LANDFALL
508-228-0500

NESBITT INN
617-228-0156

PARKER GUEST
HOUSE
508-228-4625

PERIWINKLE
GUEST HOUSE
508-228-9267

*PHILLIPS HOUSE
508-228-9217

***QUAINT CAPE
VICTORIAN INN**
508-322-0123

QUAKER HOUSE
INN
508-228-9156

ROBERTS HOUSE
508-228-9009

SAFE HARBOR
GUEST HOUSE
508-228-3222

SHIPS INN
508-228-0400

STUMBLE INNE
508-228-4482

TEN HUSSEY
508-228-9552

TEN LYON STREET
508-228-5040

TUCKERNUCK INN
800-228-4886

WAKE UP ON
PLEASANT STREET
508-228-0673

WEST MOOR INN
508-228-0877

WHARF COTTAGES

WHITE ELEPHANT
INN

WHITE HOUSE
508-228-4677

WOODBOX
508-228-0587

Nantucket Island
BEACHWAY GUEST
HOUSE
508-228-1324

CHESTNUT HOUSE
508-228-0049

CLIFF LODGE
508-228-9480

COBBLESTONE
INN
508-228-1987

FAIR GARDENS
508-228-4258

LE PETITE MAISON
508-228-9242

****SEVEN SEA
STREET**
508-228-3577

WAUWINET
800-426-8718

**Nantucket-
Siasconset**
SUMMER HOUSE
508-257-9976

Needham
BROCKS B&B
617-444-6573

New Bedford
DURANT SAIL LOFT
508-999-2700

MELVILLE HOUSE
B&B
508-990-1566

New Marlborough
GEDNEY FARM
413-229-3131

OLD INN ON THE
GREEN
800-752-1896

New Seabury
NEW SEABURY

Newburyport
ESSEX STREET INN
508-465-3145

GARRISON INN
617-327-6929

MORRILL PLACE
INN
508-462-2808

*WINDSOR HOUSE
508-462-3778

Newtonville
SAGE & THYME
617-332-0695

North Eastham
*PENNY HOUSE
508-255-6632

North Falmouth
WINGATE
CROSSING
617-540-8723

North Scituate
WRIGHT PLACE

Northampton
AUTUMN INN
413-584-7660

*KNOLL
413-584-8164

Northfield
CENTENNIAL
HOUSE
413-498-5921

NORTHFIELD
COUNTRY HOUSE

413-498-2692

Norwell
**1810 HOUSE B&B
617-659-1810

Oak Bluffs
ATTLEBORO
HOUSE
508-693-4346

CIRCUIT HOUSE
508-693-2966

DOCKSIDE INN
508-693-2966

NARRAGANSET
HOUSE
508-693-3627

NASHUA HOUSE
508-693-0043

OAK BLUFFS INN
508-693-7171

**OAK HOUSE
508-693-4187

SHIPS INN
508-693-2760

Onset
****ONSET POINTE
INN**
800-35-ONSET

Orleans
EDGARS B&B

THE FARM HOUSE
617-255-6654

Osterville
EAST BAY LODGE
617-428-6961

Pepperell
**BOGGASTOWE
FARM**
508-433-9987

Peru
CHALET D'ALICIA
413-655-8292

Petersham
***WINTERWOOD AT
PETERSHAM**
617-724-8885

Pittsfield
GREER B&B
413-443-3669

Plymouth
**ALLEN HOUSE
617-545-8221

ANOTHER PLACE
INN
508-746-0126

COLONIAL HOUSE
617-746-2087

HALLS B&B

HAWTHORNE HILL
508-746-5244

LITCHFIELD
HOUSE

****MORTON PARK
PLACE**
800-736-3276

Princeton
HARRINGTON
FARM
800-736-3276

HILL HOUSE
617-464-2061

Provincetown
1807 HOUSE

ADMIRALS LAND-
ING GUEST HOUSE
508-487-9663

AMPERSAND
GUEST HOUSE

ASHETON HOUSE
508-487-9966

BED N BREAKFAST
508-487-9555

***BRADFORD
GARDENS INN**
508-487-1616

CAPE CODDER
GUEST HOUSE
508-487-0131

CAPTAIN
LYSANDER
508-487-2253

ELEPHANT WALK

GABRIELS
508-487-3232

HARGOOD HOUSE

**LAMPLIGHTER

GUEST HOUSE
508-487-2529

**LAND'S END INN
508-487-0706

OCEANS INN

RED INN
508-487-0050

ROSE & CROWNS
GUEST HOUSE
508-487-3322

SOMERSET HOUSE
508-487-0383

SUNSET INN
508-487-9810

TWELVE CENTER
INN
508-487-0381

VICTORIA HOUSE
508-487-1319

WATERSHIP INN

WESTWINDS
ON GULL ST

WHITE WIND INN
508-487-1526

WINDJAMMER
HOUSE
508-487-0599

Quincy
**ALLEN HOUSE
617-545-8221

Rehoboth
*GILBERTS B&B
617-252-6416

PERRYVILLE INN
617-252-9239

Richmond
COGSWELL GUEST
HOUSE
413-698-2750

WESTGATE

Rockport
*ADDISON CHOATE
INN
508-546-7543

CABLE HOUSE
508-546-3895

EDEN PINES INN
508-546-2505

INN AT SEVEN
SOUTH STREET
617-546-6708

***INN ON COVE
HILL**
508-546-2701

LINDEN TREE INN
508-546-2494

MOORINGSTONE
for
NONSMOKERS
508-546-2479

OLD FARM INN
508-546-3237

PEG LEG INN

PLEASANT STREET
508-546-3915

RALPH WALDO
EMERSON INN

ROCKY SHORES
INN
508-546-2823

SEACREAST
MANOR
508-546-2211

*SEAFARER INN
508-546-6248

SEAWARD INN
508-546-3471

***YANKEE CLIPPER
INN**
800-545-3699

Rutland
GENERAL RUFUS
PUTNAM HOUSE
508-886-4256

Sagamore Beach
BED & BREAKFAST
617-888-1559

Salem
AMELIA PAYSON
GUEST HOUSE
617-744-8304

CLIPPER SHIP INN

COACH HOUSE INN
800-688-8689

****HARBORSIDE
HOUSE**
617-631-1032

INN AT
SEVEN WINTER ST
617-745-9520

NATHANIEL
BOWDITCH GUEST
HOUSE

**SALEM INN
800-446-2995

STEPHEN DANIELS
HOUSE
617-744-5709

STEPPING STONE
INN
617-741-8900

SUZANNAH FLINT
HOUSE
617-744-5281

Sandisfield
NEW BOSTON INN
413-258-4477

Sandwich
*BAY BEACH B&B
508-888-8813

****CAPT EZRA NYE
HOUSE**
800-388-2278

DANIEL WEBSTER
INN
800-444-3566

HAWTHORN HILL

508-888-3333

*ISAIAH JONES
HOMESTEAD
800-526-1625

QUINCE TREE
508-888-1371

SETH POPE HOUSE
508-888-5916

***SIX WATER
STREET**
508-888-6808

**SUMMER HOUSE
508-888-4991

VILLAGE INN AT
SANDWICH
800-922-9989

WIND SONG B&B
508-888-3567

Scituate
**ALLEN HOUSE
617-545-8221

RASPBERRY INN
508-545-6629

Seekonk
SIMEONS
MANSION
617-336-6674

Sheffield
CENTURYHURST
GUEST HOUSE
413-229-8131

COLONEL ASHLEY

413-229-2929

IVANHOE
COUNTRY HOUSE
413-229-2143

**RACE BROOK
LODGE**
413-229-2916

STAGECOACH HILL
413-229-8585

STAVELEIGH
HOUSE
413-229-2129

*UNIQUE B&B
413-229-3363

Shelburne Centre
PARSON HUBBARD
HOUSE
413-625-9730

Shelburne Falls
COUNTRY
COMFORT
413-625-9877

Sippewissett
*WYNDEMERE
HOUSE*
508-540-7069

South Ashfield
BULL FROG B&B
413-628-4493

South Chatham
*YE OLDE
NANTUCKET
HOUSE*
508-432-5641

South Darmouth
**LITTLE RED
HOUSE**
508-996-4554

South Deerfield
ORCHARD
TERRACE
413-665-3829

SUNNYSIDE FARM
B&B

YELLOW GABLED
HOUSE
413-665-4922

South Dennis
COUNTRY
PINEAPPLE
617-760-3211

South Egremont
1780 EGREMONT
413-528-2111

WEATHERVANE INN
413-528-9580

WINDFLOWER INN
800-992-1993

South Harwich
HOUSE ON THE
HILL
617-432-4321

South Lancaster
DEERSHORN
MANOR B&B
508-365-9022

South Lee
FEDERAL HOUSE

INN
617-350-6657

*HISTORIC
MERRELL
TAVERN INN
413-243-1794

South Orleans
HILLBOURNE
HOUSE
617-255-0780

South Sudbury
WAYSIDE INN
617-443-8846

South Yarmouth
**CAPTAIN FARRIS
HOUSE**
800-350-9477

FOUR WINDS B&B
617-394-4182

RIVER STREET
GUEST HOUSE
617-398-8946

Southfield
LANGHAAR HOUSE
413-229-2007

Springfield
*OLD MILL INN
203-763-1473

Sterling
STERLING INN
508-422-6592

Stockbridge
ARBOR ROSE
413-298-4744

Massachusetts

BERKSHIRE
THISTLE
413-298-3188

BROAD MEADOWS

INN AT
STOCKBRIDGE
413-298-3337

OLDE
LAMPLIGHTER
413-298-3053

RED LION INN
413-298-5545

STIRLING MOFFAT
GUEST HOUSE

WOODSIDE B&B
413-298-4977

Stow
**AMERSCOT
HOUSE**
508-897-0666

Sturbridge
**CAPTAIN PARKERS
INN AT
QUINEBAUG**
800-707-7303

**CAPT SAMUEL
EDDY HOUSE INN**
508-832-5282

CHAMBERLAIN
HOUSE
508-347-3313

*COL E CRAFTS
PUBLIK HOUSE

508-347-3313

LAKESHORE B&B
508-347-9495

**STURBRIDGE
COUNTRY INN**
508-347-5503

Sudbury
CHECKERBERRY
CORNER
508-443-8660

COACH HOUSE INN
508-443-2223

**LONGFELLOW'S
WAYSIDE INN**
508-443-1776

SUDBURY B&B
508-443-2860

Swampscott
CAP'N JACKS
WATERFRONT INN
617-595-7910

MARSHALL HOUSE
617-595-6544

OAK SHORES
617-599-2677

Taunton
*INN AT CEDAR
STREET
508-823-8966

Townsend
WOOD FARM
617-597-5019

Truro
B&B IN TRURO

PARKER HOUSE
B&B
617-349-3358

SOUTH SLOPE B&B
617-487-3498

Tyringham
GOLDEN GOOSE
413-243-3008

Uxbridge
CAPRON HOUSE
617-278-2214

Vineyard Haven
ALDWORTH
MANOR
508-693-3203

CAPTAIN DEXTER
HOUSE
508-693-6564

CROCKER HOUSE
INN
508-693-1151

GAZEBO B&B
508-693-6955

**HANOVER
HOUSE**
508-693-1066

HIGH HAVEN
HOUSE
508-693-9204

*LOTHROP MERRY
HOUSE**

508-693-1646

OCEAN SIDE INN
508-693-1296

*THORNCROFT INN
508-693-3333

TISBURY INN
508-693-2200

*TUCKERMAN
HOUSE
508-693-0417

Ware
WILDWOOD INN
800-999-3416

Wareham
LITTLE HARBOR
GUEST HOUSE
617-295-6329

MULBERRY B&B
508-295-0684

Wellfleet
HOLDEN INN
617-349-3450

INN AT DUCK
CREEKE
617-349-9333

West Barnstable
**HONEYSUCKLE
HILL**
508-362-8418

West Boyleston
ROSE COTTAGE
617-835-4034

West Brookfield
DEER MEADOW
FARM

West Dennis
BEACH HOUSE
617-398-8321

CHRISTIAN HILL

LIGHTHOUSE INN
508-398-2244

West Falmouth
INN AT WEST
FALMOUTH
508-540-7696

OLD SILVER
BEACH B&B
508-540-5446

West Falmouth CC
ELMS
617-540-7232

SJOHOLM INN
508-540-5706

West Gouldsboro
SUNSET HOUSE
207-963-7156

West Harpswell
VICARAGE EAST
LTD

West Harwich
BARNABY INN
617-432-6789

LIONS HEAD INN
800-321-3155

TERN INN
508-432-3714

West Hawley
STUMP SPROUTS
LODGE
413-339-4265

West Newton
WITHINGTON
HOUSE
617-332-8422

West Stockbridge
**CARD LAKE INN
& RESTAURANT**
413-232-0272

SHAKER MILL
TAVERN
800-322-8565

WILLIAMSVILLE INN
413-274-6118

West Tisbury
LAMBERTS COVE
508-693-2298

OLD PARSONAGE
B&B

West Yarmouth
MANOR HOUSE
B&B
617-771-9211

Westminster
WESTMINSTER
VILLAGE INN
617-874-5911

Weston
WEBB BIGELOW

PLACE

Whatley
SUNNYSIDE FARM
413-665-3113

Whitinsville
*VICTORIAN
508-234-2500

Wilbraham
B&B BOB & BARB
413-228-7283

Williamsburg
TWIN MAPLES B&B
413-268-7925

Williamstown
FIELD FARM
GUEST HOUSE
413-458-3135

HOUSE ON MAIN
STREET
413-458-3031

LE JARDIN
413-458-8032

RIVERBEND FARM
413-458-5504

STEEP ACRES
FARM
413-458-3772

Winchester
INN OF THE SEVEN
SEAS

Woburn
APPLETON INN

Woods Hole
MARLBOROUGH
508-548-6218

Worthington
COUNTRY CRICKET
VILLAGE INN
413-238-5356

Worthington
FRANKLIN BURRS
413-238-5826

INN YESTERDAY
413-238-5529

*WORTHINGTON
INN/FOUR
CORNERS
413-238-4441

Yarmouth
COLONIAL HOUSE
800-999-3416

DOCKSIDE GUEST
QUARTERS

OLD YARMOUTH
INN

Yarmouth Port
CROOK JAW INN
508-362-6111

JOSHUA SEARS
MANOR
508-362-5000

LANES END
COTTAGE
508-362-5298

**LIBERTY HILL

INN ON CAPE COD
800-821-3977

OLDE CAPTAINS
INN
508-362-4496

ONE CENTRE
STREET
508-362-8910

VILLAGE INN
508-362-3182

**WEDGEWOOD
INN**
508-362-5157

New Hampshire

---

*Stone Rest B&B | **Alexandria NH**

Richard Clarke
603-744-6066

652 Fowler River Rd 03222

Rates: | **Shared Bath** 4 | **Payment Terms:**
Single | $ 50.00 | Check
Double | $ 50.00 |

Quiet country setting with picturesque view of Mount Cardigan with queen-size beds and a bunkroom. Fly fishing in the backyard, cross-country trails is nearby and beautiful year-round New England scenery. The Fall Foliage season is spectacular and brings travelers from around the world. Full delicious home made breakfast included with fresh baked muffins and other breakfast breads. Dinner available, at added cost. **BROCHURE:** Yes **SEASONAL:** No **PERMITTED:** Children 10-up [E11ACNH-2259]

Glynn House Inn | **Ashland NH

Betsy & Karol Paterman
800-637-9599 603-968-3775

43 Highland St 03217

Rates: | **Pvt Bath** 4 | **Shared Bath** 2 | **Payment Terms:**
Single | $ 75.00 | $ 55.00 | Check
Double | $ 85.00 | $ 60.00 | MC/V

Enjoy the gracious elegance of the 1890s in a beautifully restored Victorian Inn tucked away in the quaint New England village of Ashland *the heart of the White Mountains* - just minutes from year-round activities - and Squam Lake, of *On Golden Pond* fame. A picture-perfect example of the Victorian era, guests marvel at the Inn's cupola towers and gingerbread wrap-around porch. Upon arrival, guests are greeted by a magnificent foyer accented with carved oak woodwork and pocket doors. The inn is beautifully furnished with Queen Anne furniture offering guests the warmth and hospitality of being "home" in the 1890s! Each bedroom has its own mood, distinguished by unique interior decor, period furnishings and amenities. A full gourmet breakfast is included

---

and served in an elegant sunny dining room. Year-round activities include world-class downhill and x-country skiing, swimming, fishing, biking & hiking nature trails, gorgeous fall foliage, tennis golf and plenty of antiquing. Guests are centrally located between the Lakes and White Mountains and just two hours from Boston, four hours from Hartford or Montreal and six hours from NYC I-93 exit 24. Come discover and share the Victorian Love Affair your hosts have preserved! **RESERVATIONS:** 50% deposit to confirm reservation, 14 day cancel policy for refund, 3pm check-in, 11am check-out **SEASONAL:** No **BROCHURE:** Yes **PERMITTED:** Children, drinking, limited smoking (in living room only - not bedrooms) **LANGUAGES:** Polish, Russian [Z04FPNH1-11476]

**Bradford Inn	**Bradford NH**
Connie & Tom Mazol	RR 1 Box 40 Main St 03221
800-669-5309 603-938-5309	**Res Times** 9am-11pm

Rates:		**Payment Terms:**
	Pvt Bath 12	
Single	$ 55-75.00	Check
Double	$ 59-79.00	AE/DC/MC/V

The *Bradford Inn* is a rural country hotel that was opened in May 1898.It offers guests a choice of twelve guest rooms (all with private bath) each tastefully decorated to reflect the charm and character of its turn-of-the-century beginning. Most of the guest rooms are on the second and third floor and vary in size from rooms with bath to parlor (mini) suites. The first floor is dedicated to the guests enjoyment and relaxation in either of the two large parlors which includes a fireplace and fine old antique and casual country furnishings. Wicker furniture beckons guests outdoors on sunny days. J Alberts restaurant serves a continental cuisine with an emphasis on cuisines of Eastern Europe. The full Breakfast is never a disappointment. Fresh juices, breads and pastries, cereals, egg and meat dishes and delicious coffee are just some of the items guests might find on the morning menu. Enjoy New England's finest natural display year round here with strolls along country lanes, antique shop browsing, driving the gentle rolling hills & mountains offers breath-taking vistas and the seasonal colors! There's swimming, sailing, golf, summer theater, lake cruises with great x-country or downhill skiing in winter. **MEALS:** Dinner and other meals available. **DISCOUNTS:** Yes, for multiple night stays **PACKAGES:** Ski with maps available. **RESERVATIONS:** One night deposit to guarantee room, 14 day cancel policy less $10 service fee; less that 14 day notice, refund only if room is rented. **BRO-CHURE:** Yes **PERMITTED:** Children, drinking, smoking **CONFER-ENCES:** Yes for groups to 75 persons **LANGUAGES:** Arabic. [Z07GPNH2-2272]

Mountain Fare Inn	**Campton NH**
Susan & Nick Preston	Mad River Rd 03223
603-726-4283	**Res Times** 8am-10pm

Rates:	Pvt Bath 5	Shared Bath 3	Payment Terms:
Single	$ 40.00	$ 30.00	Check
Double	$ 56-64.00	$ 48-56.00	

Your professional skier/hosts invite guests to share their year-round village farm house c1840's. Typical of the white clapboard New England style, with black shutters, multi-gabled roof line and a long open porch. Nestled on six acres at the edge of Campton Village, a charming town that grew up in the days of logging and steam engines. The decor is purely country, simple, cheerful, clean and full of handicrafts, with woodstoves and fireplaces to keep everyone toasty in winter! The guest rooms vary in size (with some accommodating 4-5 persons), and are well furnished with attractive & homey touches of lovely fabrics, country antiques and crafts. Hearty New England breakfasts are included and start-off your day right with a treat of fresh fruit garnished with herbs and flowers in the summer; carbo-high for skiers in winter. During ski season, dinner is served on Sat nights. Perfect locale for outdoor activities year-round. In the winter you have a lodge for active alpine or x-country. In the spring, fall and summer, the White Mountains offer a peaceful retreat for hiking, biking, fishing, golfing, canoeing, horseback riding and plenty of wildflowers and gardening on the inn's grounds. Your hosts keep busy teaching the Freestyle Skiing program for Waterville Valley Ski Club and keep active year-round with all the other outdoor activities. We specialize in family re-unions year-round for up to 20 persons and offer guided hiking week-ends May-October. We'll pack trail lunches for you and your friends and offer candlelight dining including garden-fresh vegetables Summer and Fall. **RESERVATIONS:** $10 per night deposit, 10-day cancel policy for refund **SEASONAL:** No **BROCHURE:** Yes **PERMITTED:** Children, drinking **CONFERENCES:** Yes, to 20 persons including dining [I07DPNH2277]

Farmhouse B&B	Chocorua NH
Kathie & John Dyrenforth	Page Hill Rd 03817
603-323-8707	

Rates:	**Shared Bath** 4	**Payment Terms:**
Single	$ 50.00	Check
Double	$ 60.00	

Pre-Civil War homestead in country setting of lakes and mountains with hiking, canoeing, fishing, and skiing nearby.   Farm fresh breakfast includes pancakes and maple syrup fresh from the farm **SEASONAL:** No **BROCHURE:** Yes **PERMITTED:** Children, smoking, drinking [E11ACNH-2284]

Bradford Inn	Concord NH
Connie Mazol	
800-669-5309 603-938-5309	**Res Times** 9am-11pm

Rates:	**Pvt Bath** 12	**Payment Terms:**
Single	$ 55-75.00	Check
Double	$ 59-79.00	AE/DC/MC/V

Refer to the same listing name located under Bradford, NH for complete description. [M07GPNH2-8254]

Kancamagus Swift River Inn	Conway NH
The Beckenbach's	PO Box 1650 03018
800-255-4236 603-447-2332	**Res Times** 24 Hrs

Rates:	**Pvt Bath** 10	**Payment Terms:**
Single	$ 65.00	Check
Double	$ 65.00	

A newly constructed Inn located in the scenic White Mountain National Forest offers travelers quality lodging in a stress-free environment for enjoying the beauty of New Hampshire year-round.

This Mount Washington Valley location offers fishing, bathing, nature trails, x-country skiing, exciting picnic areas, spectacular views, artist studios, antique shops and convenience while located along the Kancamagus Hwy, claimed to be the most beautiful highway in all of New Hampshire. Nearby are five major ski areas, bargain factory outlet stores and many picturesque covered bridges. Accommodations offer new large rooms, each with a private bath and shower, two full size beds, TV, individual heat and a complimentary continental breakfast served in the Inn's dining room. **RESERVATIONS:** One night's deposit to confirm room, 5 day cancel policy for refund, less than 5 day's notice, refund only if room is rebooked **SEASONAL:** No **BROCHURE:** Yes **PERMITTED:** Children and smoking, limited drinking **LANGUAGES:** Polish [Z05FPNH2-7372]

Village House   Conway NH

Robin Crocker
800-972-8343 603-383-6666

Fax 603-383-6464

Rates:	Pvt Bath 13	Shared Bath 2	Payment Terms:
Single	$ 40-125.00	$ 40-125.00	Check
Double	$ 40-125.00	$ 40-125.00	MC/V

Refer to the same listing name under Jackson, New Hampshire for a complete description. [M08GPNH2-15321]

Chase House B&B   Cornish NH

Hal & Marilyn Wallace   Rt 12A 03745
603-675-5391   **Res Times** 8am-8pm

Rates:	Pvt Bath 4	Payment Terms:
Single	$ 75.00	Check
Double	$ 95.00	MC/V

History buffs will love this darling Inn built 1766!! Listed on the *National Register of Historic Places*, the Chase family tree includes the Governor of Ohio, Sec of Treasury for Lincoln, the Chase from Chase Manhattan Bank, and a Chief Justice of the Supreme Court. Perfectly furnished for recalling our past, you'll enjoy making a trip just to stay here. **SEASONAL:** No **RESERVATIONS:** Deposit required at time of reservation. **BROCHURE:** Yes **PERMITTED:** Limited children. [E11ACNH-2290]

Inn At Danbury   Danbury NH

Joan & George Issa   Rt 104   03230
603-768-3318

Rates:	**Shared Bath** 8	**Payment Terms:**
Single	$ 37.00	Check
Double	$ 45.00	

Tranquil town setting for this turn-of-the-century farmhouse offering pleasant and comfortable surroundings and hospitality. Outdoor activities include skiing, fishing, swimming, canoeing, nature trails, biking, and hiking.   Great home-cooked meals available including full breakfast, all served family style. **SEASONAL:** No **BROCHURE:** Yes **PERMITTED:** Children, smoking, drinking [E11ACNH-2292]

Highland Lake Inn   East Andover NH

The Petras Family   Maple Street   03231
603-735-6426   **Fax** 603-735-5355

Rates:	**Pvt Bath** 10	**Payment Terms:**
Single	$ 85-100.00	Check
Double	$ 85-100.00	AE/MC/V

Built in 1767 and expanded in 1805, this classic building, set atop twelve acres, overlooks Highland Lake, Kearsarge, Tucker and Ragged Mountains.   Beautifully decorated, the Inn has been recently renovated to include private baths in each of our ten spacious guest rooms.   Rooms are furnished with king, queen or two twin beds; several rooms have four-poster beds.   Extra rollaways are available.   A sumptuous and different breakfast is served each morning.   Cross country ski or hike trails on our twenty-one acre nature conservancy, sit in front of our large hearth fireplace or enjoy one in your room, and in summer, frolic on the beach.   Bring your boat and your fishing gear, the Highland Lake boat ramp is close-by.   The area boasts two first-class 18 hole golf courses and is central to several fine ski areas and less than an hour from the major slopes of the White Mountains. Antique, craft fairs and outlet shopping are nearby.   Located just twenty-three miles northwest of Concord, we are easy to reach from Rts 89, 91 and 93, yet we are tucked away in a rich, rural landscape surrounded by fields, barns and century-old farmhouses. Enjoy the perfect New England getaway. A full breakfast is included. **RESER-**

VATIONS: One night's stay or 50% deposit within 7 days of booking required to guarantee reservation, 14 day cancel policy less $10 service fee, $20 per additional person in room **SEASONAL:** No **PERMITTED:** Children 8-up, drinking **BROCHURE:** Yes **AIRPORT:** Manchester-50 mi **LANGUAGES:** Greek [R08GPNH2-18981]

Moose Mountain Lodge   **Etna NH**

Peter & Kay Shumway   Moose Mountain 03750
603-643-3529

Rates:	Shared Bath 12	Payment Terms:
Single	$ 40.00/Person	Cash
Double		

Splendid views of Green Mountains and Connecticut River Valley from this wood and stone lodge built from materials on the property in 1938. Fireplaces, log beds, and great meals make for a memorable visit. All outdoor activities are available year-round. Near Hanover and Dartmouth Colleges. American Plan and MAP option available for all meals. **SEASON:** No **BROCHURE:** Yes **PERMITTED:** Children 5-up, limited smoking **LANGUAGES:** Spanish, Swedish, French [E11ACNH-2300]

Bungay Jar B&B   **Franconia NH**

Lee Strimbeck & Kate Kerivan   Easton Valley Rd 03580
603-823-7775   **Res Times** Anytime
                              Fax 603-444-0100

Rates:	Pvt Bath 2	Shared Bath 2	Payment Terms:
Single	$ 75-85.00	$ 55.00	Check
Double	$ 75-85.00	$ 65.00	AE

Built in 1969 from a century-old barn of post and beam construction and nestled among eight acres of woodlands, bounded by the Franconia Range of the White Mountain National Forest. You'll be treated to spectacular views of the rivers, forests and mountains! Choose from one of the unique guest rooms with antiques, four poster beds or the shared bathrooms. Relax before a roaring fire with the aroma of mulled cider in the two-story living room reminiscent of a hayloft, or find an antique that interests you, because many are for sale. Your hosts are avid hikers & skiers, so you'll benefit from their expert knowledge of the local AMC trails, wildlife and woodlands. Full breakfast included, with dinner by prior arrangement. **RESERVATIONS:** 50% deposit; 7-day cancellation policy; 2 night min weekends/holidays & foliage season **SEASONAL:** No **BROCHURE:** Yes **PERMITTED:** Limited children, drinking okay [E02BCNH-2307]

**Franconia Inn	**Franconia NH**
Richard & Alec Morris	Easton Valley Rd 03580
800-473-5299 603-823-5542	**Res Times** 24 Hrs

Rates:	Pvt Bath 30	Shared Bath 4	Payment Terms:
Single	$ 65-up	$ 55.00	Check
Double	$ 75-up	$ 65.00	AE/MC/V

The *Franconia Inn* has been welcoming guests since 1886. Today, the *Franconia Inn* is operated by Alec and Richard Morris, third generation innkeepers. Nestled on 107 acres in the Easton Valley just below the White Mountain's famed Franconia Notch, home of the *Old Man of the Mountain.* White clapboards and green shutters; three stories, thirty rooms and three suites . . Living room, Library, Dining Room, Rathskeller, Lounge and two spacious verandas with spectacular mountain views. Guests enjoy Elegant American Cuisine, Bach, Classic Wines and attentive, friendly service - all part of the *Franconia Inn's* unpretentious dining experience. Guests are encouraged to partake from the wealth of recreational activities on the property. Summer brings tennis, horseback riding, swimming, fishing, soaring (gliding), croquet, badminton, bicycles and lots of hiking. Winter offers x-country Ski Tour Center with 60km of groomed trails, horse-drawn sleigh rides, ice skate and snow shoe rentals, hot tub, hot buttered rums and of course roaring fireplaces in each common room. Honeymoon suites and extended stay packages are available. *AAA* ♦♦♦ *Rated, Guide To Recommended Country Inns of New England, Inn Spots and Special Places, Family Inns of America.* The Inn is located 2-1/2 hours north of Boston and 3-1/2 hours south of Montreal. **RESERVATIONS:** One night's deposit at res time, 14 day cancel policy for refund **SEASONAL:** Rates vary **BROCHURE:** Yes **PERMITTED:** Children, drinking limited smoking **CONFERENCES:** Yes for groups to 65 persons including spectacular mountain views. **LANGUAGES:** French [I07GPNH2-2309]

Horse & Hound Inn	**Franconia NH**
The Larson Family	Off Rt 18 Cannon Mtn 03580
603-823-5501	

Rates:	Pvt Bath	6	Shared Bath	5	Payment Terms:
Single	$ 60.00		$ 55.00		Check
Double	$ 75.00		$ 65.00		MC/V

Natural setting close to ski lifts and other activities including hand gliding, water sports on nearby lake, and a cable car for spectacular viewing. Robert Frost's home is just a short distance. **RESERVATIONS:** Deposit for one night required at res time **SEASONAL:** No **BROCHURE:** Yes **PERMITTED:** Smoking [E11ACNH-2311]

Maria W Atwood Inn	**Franklin NH**
Andy LaBrie	RFD 2 Rt 3A 03235
603-934-3666	

Rates:	Pvt Bath	8	Payment Terms:
Single	$ 62.00		Check
Double	$ 69.00		AE/MC/V

Large brick Federal residence c1880 fully restored and furnished with antique pieces and family heirlooms, fireplaces, two formal gardens, sitting rooms, library. Close to skiing & antiquing, swimming, boating. Full breakfast included. **SEASONAL:** No **BROCHURE:** Yes **PERMITTED:** Children [E11ACNH-2315]

Cartway House	**Gilford NH**
Shortway Family	Old Lake Shore Rd 03246
603-528-1172	

Rates:	Pvt Bath	5	Shared Bath	5	Payment Terms:
Single	$ 60.00		$ 52.00		Check
Double	$ 70.00		$ 58.00		MC/V

Great skiing Inn that's been renovated since its original 1771 beginning with a French Country kitchen just added. Some guest rooms have bunk beds for groups of skiers or larger family groups with the private beaches, and plenty of mountains for skiing in winter. Full breakfast includes specialties such as Eggs Benedict, with afternoon comp tea. **RESERVATIONS:** Deposit of 50% of stay **BROCHURE:** Yes **PERMITTED:** Children, smoking, drinking [E11ACNH-2319]

Gables			Gorham NH
John & Coleen Guinen			139 Main St 03581
603-466-2876			

Rates:	Pvt Bath 2	Shared Bath 2	Payment Terms:
Single	$ 35.00	$ 35.00	Check
Double	$ 35.00	$ 50.00	AE

Clapboard New England farmhouse furnished in country antiques and family heirlooms. Plenty of hospitality and entertaining conversation. Full New England homemade breakfast included. Close to antiques and Mount Washington. **SEASONAL:** No **BROCHURE:** Yes **PERMITTED:** Children, smoking, drinking [E11ACNH-2325]

**Greenfield Inn*			Greenfield NH
Barbara & Vic Mangini			Forest Lane Rt 31 03047-0156
603-547-6327			

Rates:	Pvt Bath 4	Shared Bath 4	Payment Terms:
Single			Check
Double	$ 79-100.00	$ 59-69.00	MC/V

Beautifully restored Victorian mansion situated on three acres of lawn in the lovely Valley of Monadnock Mountains (Crotched, Temple, & Monadnock). Relax while viewing the mountain country from the spacious veranda with white wicker chairs & rockers. Peaceful retreat for the first and second honeymooners. Visited twice by Bob and Dolores Hope!! Beautiful Victorian setting offering a quiet togetherness, comfort, and good dining. Large rooms, some with king size beds and all with modern amenities. TV in some. Street level bedrooms & suites available. Guests are encouraged to enjoy social room. Very close to skiing, swimming, hiking, tennis, golf, biking, and antique shopping at bargain prices. Manchester, Keene, Peterborough & Nashua nearby. Eighty minutes to Boston, five hours plus to NYC. Delightful full breakfast included with excellent dining nearby. **RESERVATIONS:** $25.00 per nite stay deposit at res time, 4pm check-in, after 9pm by arrangement **SEASONAL:** No **BROCHURE:** Yes **PERMITTED:** Limited children, limited smoking, limited drinking **CONFERENCES:** Groups to 12 indoor or open veranda and lawn with gourmet catering available **LANGUAGES:** Stock Market and antiques! [A11DPNH-2329]

Stonecrest Farm B&B   **Hanover NH

Gail Sanderson
802-295-2600

Rates:	Pvt Bath 3	Shared Bath 2	Payment Terms:
Single	$ 90.00	$ 80.00	Check
Double	$ 100.00	$ 90.00	MC/V

Refer to the same listing name under Wilder, Vermont for a complete description. [M07FPVT2-17775]

Inn On Golden Pond   **Holderness NH

Bill & Bonnie Webb   PO Box 680 Rt 3 03245
603-968-7269   **Res Times** 8am-10pm

Rates:	Pvt Bath 9	Payment Terms:
Single	$ 65.00	Check
Double	$ 95-105.00	AE/MC/V

A gracious home built in 1879 and nestled on fifty wooded acres offering guests a traditional New England setting where you can escape and enjoy warm hospitality and personal service of the resident hosts. Each room is individually decorated for your comfort and pleasure. Common rooms include a game room, sitting room with a roaring fire  during the winter months, and a sixty foot screened porch to enjoy the outdoors during the summer. Close to Squam Lake setting for *On Golden Pond*, you can enjoy all the outdoor sporting activities year-round. You're only 15 minutes from Tenney Mountain Ski area and 30 minutes from the best skiing in New Hampshire. Squam Mountain Range and the White Mountain National Forest are close by for any water or land sports year-round, including ice fishing and x-country skiing. Hearty New England breakfast includes homemade breads, muffins, jams, and farm fresh eggs. **AIRPORT:** Boston Logan-2 hrs **RESERVATIONS:** One night's deposit, refunded if canceled 14 days prior to arrival **BROCHURE:** Yes **PERMITTED:** Drinking. Not permitted: smoking, children and pets [I07GPNH2-2346]

Manor On Golden Pond	**Holderness NH**
David & Bambi Arnold	Rt 3 Box T 03245
800-545-2141 603-968-3348	**Res Times** 9am-9pm

Rates:	**Pvt Bath** 27	**Payment Terms:**
Single	$ 110-175.00 MAP	Check
Double	$ 155-220.00 MAP	AE/MC/V

Nestled on the gentle slopes of Shepard Hill, rising above the western shore of pristine Squam Lake (site of the movie *On Golden Pond*), the estate commands a panoramic 65-mile view of the lake and surrounding mountains. Built as a private home in 1903 by wealthy Englishman Isaac Van Horn, this stately old mansion embodies the elegant yet casual charm of a typical English country estate. The Manor House offers seventeen invitingly decorated guest rooms and common rooms with magnificently carved moldings, rich wood paneling and grand fireplaces - an ambience and heritage from the past which cannot be duplicated today. Spacious grounds (13 acres) provide a tranquil, dramatic setting for the mansion's outdoor pool and clay tennis court set among ancient pines. A separate lakefront cottage and boathouse complement the private sandy beach. Whatever season, you'll find the Manor a Country Inn of uncommon quality. Summer activities include all water sports, golf, horseback riding, hiking, biking, browsing antique shops, while winter brings downhill and x-country skiing, ice skating, sleigh rides and a relaxed pres ski atmosphere. Since its completion, the estate has passed though many hands and the present owners, David and Bambi Arnold have dedicated themselves to restoring the traditional grace and beauty of the original home. They hope you will visit *The Manor* and invite you to establish your own tradition of returning each season. They look forward to meeting you and providing a truly memorable experience. **AIRPORT:** Manchester NH-1 hr; Boston Logan-2 hrs. **PACKAGES:** *Holidays* and some *Special Events* **RESERVATIONS:** One night's deposit, 50% deposit for longer stays **SEASONAL:** No **BROCHURE:** Yes **PERMITTED:** Limited children, drinking, limited smoking **CONFERENCES:** Available for groups to twenty [I10EPNH2-2347]

**Inn At Jackson	**Jackson NH**
Lori & KR Tradewell	Main St At Thorn Hill 03846
800-289-8600 603-383-4321	**Res Times** 9am-9pm

Rates:	**Pvt Bath** 12	**Payment Terms:**
Single	$ 49-129.00	Check
Double	$ 59-129.00	AE/DC/DISC/MC/V

This Stanford White Mansion c1902 has been renovated into a quaint Country Inn snuggled in the White Mountains and offers New England country atmosphere, decor and great hospitality. The spacious guest rooms, all with private bath and public rooms, offer fireplaces, a/c and vistas at every turn. Offering year-round activities, guests can choose skiing at one of the four challenging downhill areas or x-country right at the doorstep or the outdoor hot tub jacuzzi. A horsedrawn sleigh ride brings unforgettable memories of the snow covered mountains. Spring blossoms brings out the nature lover in everyone and shopping Specials at the nearby outlet malls! Summer provides outdoor sporting and nature watching events. And the Fall shouldn't be missed! A full New England breakfast is served fireside in the dining room or in summer in the glassed-in porch with picturesque views. *AAA* ♦♦♦ **DISCOUNTS:** Yes, inquire at res time **AIRPORT:** Portland-1-1/2 hrs **PACKAGES:** Yes, inquire at res time **RESERVATIONS:** 50% deposit by check or credit card to guarantee, 14 day cancel policy for refund **SEASONAL:** Rates vary **BROCHURE:** Yes **PERMITTED:** Children, drinking, limited smoking **PACKAGES:** *Extended stays, 3 nights-up* [Z08FPNH2-2355]

Village House   Jackson NH

Robin Crocker   PO Box 359 Rt 16A 03846
800-972-8343 603-383-6666

Fax 603-383-6464

Rates:	**Pvt Bath** 13	**Shared Bath** 2	**Payment Terms:**
Single	$ 40-125.00	$ 40-125.00	Check
Double	$ 40-125.00	$ 40-125.00	MC/V

When you cross the red covered bridge and enter into Jackson Village, you are at *The Village House*. We have been serving guests here for over 100 years. Our Inn offers the amenities of a large resort but with the warmth and friendliness of a small Country Inn. Thirteen of our guest rooms have private baths and include queen and king size beds. Five new rooms include a combination of the following: family suites with kitchenettes, doubles with kitchenettes and doubles with jacuzzi tub. We offer a delightful living room area with a guest refrigerator, cable TV and warm fire in winter. Enjoy breakfast in our sunroom or out on the front porch. Winter breakfast is a traditional full country meal, while summer breakfast offers more flexibility with a continental-style array of fresh fruits, homemade cereals, breads and home baked pastries. In the summer you can enjoy our swimming pool, tennis court and jacuzzi. Nearby are many local Mount Washington Valley attractions, as well as hiking, biking, canoeing and scenic drives. In winter, x-country skiing begins right at your front door and nearby are four major mountains offering excellent downhill skiing. Don't miss out on the excitement of sleigh rides, ice skating, warming-up in the outdoor jacuzzi or peaceful evenings at the local pubs all right here in our Village. **AIRPORT:** Portland-1-1/2 Hrs; Boston-2-1/2 Hrs. **PACKAGES:** Yes, inquire at res time **DISCOUNTS:** Groups **RESERVATIONS:** 50% deposit of length of stay required by credit card or check prior to arrival, two week cancellation policy for refund **BROCHURE:** Yes **PERMITTED:** Drinking, smoking, limited children **CONFERENCES:** Yes, for small groups [Z08GPNH-2-2358]

**Benjamin Prescott Inn   Jaffrey NH

Barry & Jan Miller   Rt 124 E 03452
603-532-6637   **Res Times** 8am-9pm

Rates:	**Pvt Bath** 10	**Payment Terms:**
Single	$ 60-80.00	Check
Double	$ 60-130.00	AE/MC/V

Fashioned in the Greek Revival style, this family home of Colonel Benjamin Prescott of Revolutionary War fame, stands shaded by maples. Enter by the front steps, graced with Old Glory stirring in the breeze and travel back into America's infancy. Inside, careful attention has been taken to see that the early American atmosphere has been preserved

Built in 1853

through use of color and design. All guest rooms in the Inn have private bath, complete with classic toiletries the discerning traveler has come to expect. Each room is decorated and furnished to bring out the individuality and charm. Antiques abound and lend credence to the ever-present feeling one has stepped back in time. Suites are available for those wanting to feel even more at home. After a hearty New England breakfast with home made fruit breads, enjoy the quiet countryside surrounding the Inn. For the adventurous, there is Mount Monadmock, the most climbed mountain in America, the most beautiful and challenging golf course in New Hampshire and x-country skiing. For those seeking quiet reflection, a leisurely stroll up Witt Hill Road provides spectacular views of the mountains and the century-old operating dairy farm. For those seeking culture, enjoy the Amos Fortune Forum, Monadnock Music, Petersborough Players, Sharon Art Center and Cathedral of the Pines. Antiques and local artisans abound. **RESERVATIONS:** One night's deposit, 10-day cancellation policy for refund; two night minimum some weekends **SEASONAL:** No **BROCHURE:** Yes **PERMITTED:** Children 10-up, limited smoking [I11DPNH-2360]

Lilac Hill Acres   Jaffrey NH

Frank & Ellen McNeil   5 Ingalls Rd   03452
603-532-7278

Rates:	Pvt Bath 1	Shared Bath 5	Payment Terms:
Single	$ 65.00	$ 50.00	Check
Double		$ 70.00	

Farm life at its best in this five star location at the base of Mount Monadnock. Furnished with family heirlooms and antiques. Year-round activities. Full breakfast included. **SEASONAL:** No **BROCHURE:** Yes **PERMITTED:** Children, smoking, social drinking

[E11ACNH-2364]

Mill Pond Inn   **Jaffrey NH**
S Fitzgerald/E A Woodruff   50 Prescott Rd   03452
603-532-7687

Rates:	**Shared Bath** 5	**Payment Terms:**
Single	$ 55.00	Check
Double	$ 65.00	

Overlook this scenic mill pond from an 1825 homestead nestled on a five acre setting bordering Mount Monadnock and Annett State Park for year-round beauty. Gracious hosts make your stay enjoyable and they are prepared for helping you find "your thing" whether it's skiing, boating, nature trails or whatever. Fireplaces abound with several in guest rooms with as-well-as antique furnishings, plants, and family treasures in many rooms. Full home made breakfast including quiche. **RESERVATIONS:** Two night min 9/1-10/30 & holidays, deposit for one night at res time **SEASONAL:** No **BROCHURE:** Yes **PERMITTED:** Children, limited drinking [E11ACNH-2365]

Applebrook B&B   **Jefferson NH**
Sandra Conley/Martin Kelly   Rt 115A   03583
800-545-6504   603-586-7713   **Res Times** 7am-10pm

Rates:	**Pvt Bath** 3	**Shared Bath** 9	**Payment Terms:**
Single	$ 50.00	$ 20-40.00	Check
Double	$ 60.00	$ 40-50.00	MC/V

Bring the children if you like . . . the more the merrier", for an unforgettable experience this large Victorian farmhouse where casual comfort (put-your-feet-up) reigns. In-addition to individuals rooms, a great dormitory brings kids together and provides an economical choice for biking, hiking and ski groups. A spacious sunny living room with stained glass windows, beautiful sunset views of Mt Washington, plenty of books and magazines and an evening fire becomes the favorite gathering place for socializing. Located on acres of meadows and woods in the Northern White Mountains, this is truly a four-season vacation area. Winter provides three major downhill and x-country ski areas within thirty minutes (Bretton Woods, Wildcat, Cannon Mountain) - snowmobiles with direct access to the roads; moonlight toboggan rides and ice skating in the village center. Warm weather brings streams for trout fishing, swimming, canoeing or kayaking and mountain trails for hiking, biking and delicious mid-summer wild raspberries. Fall foliage in the White Mountains is spectacular - and shouldn't be missed! Still adding improvements, your hosts recently completed a x-country ski trail on their property, a campfire area and a hot tub for your pleasure. Nearby activities include golf, antiquing, theater and for children, Six Gun City and Santa's Village. A complimentary hearty New England breakfast served each morning usually includes French Toast, eggs or pancakes with home fries, hot or cold cereal, fresh fruit, muffins, coffee, juice and assorted teas. Home cooked family style dinners are available at additional costs with advance notice. We hope you will consider us when planning your next ski trip, reunion, bike trip or quiet weekend getaway in the mountains. **RESERVATIONS:** 50% deposit appreciated **SEASONAL:** No **PERMITTED:** Children, well-mannered pets, drinking **BROCHURE:** Yes **DISCOUNTS:** Group rates **AIRPORT:** Boston Logan-165 mi **PACKAGES:** Biking, hiking and skiing groups, including gourmet dinner [I09EPNH2-15540]

*Tin Whistle	Laconia NH
Maurine Blazok	1047 Union Ave 03246
603-528-4185	

Rates:	Shared Bath 4	Payment Terms:
Single	$ 55.00	Check
Double	$ 65.00	MC/V

Elegantly restored Victorian residence in the center of the Lake Region, overlooking Paugus Bay on Lake Winnipesaukee. Large verandas to enjoy your full breakfast. Furnished with loving care for your comfort. Homemade breakfasts!! **BROCHURE:** Yes **SEASONAL:** No **PERMITTED:** Children, limited smoking [E11ACN-H-5863]

****Ammonoosuc Inn**   **Lisbon NH**

Steve & Laura Bromley   Bishop Rd 03585
603-838-6118

Rates:	**Pvt Bath** 9	**Payment Terms:**
Single	$ 40-69.00	Check
Double	$ 55-79.00	AE/MC/V

Nestled in a quaint valley among the scenic White Mountains of New Hampshire is this charming Country Inn. A 100 year old farmhouse, newly renovated, overlooks the Ammonoosuc River. Each guest room is individually decorated and includes a private bath. Stepping outside, guests find a challenging golf course, designed by Ralph M Bartin, because located at the Inn, is the Lisbon Village Country Club, complete with all facilities. Try the spectacular course, outdoor tennis, fine fishing, game rooms and in winter, x-country skiing right at the door! Within minutes are The Old Man & The Mountain, The Tramway at Cannon Mountain, Mount Washington and Franconia Notch State Park for picturesque nature trails, climbing, hiking, swimming, horseback riding, canoeing and sailplane rides. In winter, skiers are just 15 mins to Cannon Mountain and 35 mins to Loon and Bretton Woods. Part time and full-time relaxing is encouraged on the spacious porch, filled with plenty of wooden rockers. A continental breakfast with coffee cake, danish and plenty of fresh coffee is served while the Cobbler, an on-premises restaurant specializes in fine New England fare, including homemade breads & deserts to complement your mouth-watering dinner. Top all this off with warmth, hospitality and attentive service and you'll agree this is the perfect getaway. **DISCOUNTS:** Yes, inquire at res time **AIRPORT:** Boston Logan-3 hrs **PACKAGES:** *Golf* & *Meal Plans* **RESERVATIONS:** 50% deposit for one night's stay or credit card to guarantee res **SEASONAL:** No **BROCHURE:** Yes **PERMITTED:** Children, drinking, limited smoking, limited pets [O07FPNH2-2376]

**Beal House Inn			**Littleton NH**

Catherine & John Fisher-Motheu   247 W Main St   03561
603-444-2661   **Res Times** 7am-11pm

Rates:	**Pvt Bath** 9	**Shared Bath** 4	**Payment Terms:**
Single	$ 50.00	$ 40.00	Check
Double	$ 55-80.00	$ 50-60.00	MC/V

Live the White Mountains with us in our 1833 Federal Renaissance farmhouse! Relaxation and quiet elegance are balanced with a zest for adventure and the charm of this lovely little village. In our thirteen guest rooms, you will find antique furnishings, canopy beds, down comforters and special touches that will encourage you to feel right at home here. Tradition at the *Beal House*, an Inn since 1938, allows you to purchase many of the furnishings and native artwork that may catch your fancy as they decorate the Inn. Our parlor, game room and enclosed porch invite you to unwind, visit with other travelers and enjoy our treasures and collections. Breakfast gatherings by fire and candlelight feature Belgian waffles made fresh by your Belgian host, in addition to a bountiful buffet. Evening dining in our jazzy little dining room celebrates robust European fare, with very special classic French creations and a wine list of over 300 wines. So close to so much in the White Mountains, revitalize yourself with fresh air while hiking, skiing, biking, fishing, playing golf, antiquing and visiting the many sites and attractions. Three hours by car from both Montreal and Boston. **DISCOUNTS:** Yes, groups and extended stays **AIRPORT:** Manchester NH-2 hrs **RESERVATIONS:** 50% deposit of stay at res time to guarantee, 15 day cancel policy for refund, less than 15 days, 50% refund **BROCHURE:** Yes **PERMITTED:** Children, drinking **CONFERENCES:** Business gatherings to 24 persons with meetings in dining room **LANGUAGES:** French [Z07GPNH2-2378]

---

*Lyme Inn			**Lyme NH**

Fred & Judy Siemons   Rt 10   03768
603-795-2222

Rates:	**Pvt Bath** 10	**Shared Bath** 5	**Payment Terms:**
Single	$ 58.00	$ 48.00	Check
Double	$ 65.00	$ 55.00	AE/CB/DC/MC/V

Quaint Country Inn in small New England town offering traditional style furnishings in guest rooms. Full breakfast included. Dinner available on premises. **SEASONAL:** No **BROCHURE:** Yes **PERMITTED:** Children 8-up, smoking, drinking [E11ACNH-2382]

Olde Orchard Inn			**Moultonboro NH**
Pat Knoche			RR Box 256 Lee Road 03245
603-476-5004			

Rates:	**Pvt Bath** 5		**Payment Terms:**
Single	$ 60-70.00		Check
Double	$ 70-80.00		AE

Restored 1810 farmhouse on twelve acres near Lake Winnispesaukee & Squam offering x-country skiing at door. Full breakfast included. Swimming, tennis, and golf nearby. **SEASONAL:** No **BROCHURE:** Yes **PERMITTED:** Children, limited smoking, limited drinking [E11ACNH-2391]

Blue Goose Inn			**Mount Sunapee NH**
Meryl & Ron Caldwell			24 103 B Box 117 03772
603-763-5519			

Rates:	**Pvt Bath** 4	**Shared Bath** 1	**Payment Terms:**
Single	$ 43.20	$ 40.00	Check
Double	$ 55.00	$ 50.00	MC/V

The ideal location of the *Blue Goose Inn* is only one of the many reasons to stay here during your next visit to the Lake Sunapee Area. Situated on a private 3.5 acres, this early 19th Century farmhouse provides the perfect setting for a fun and relaxing get away. The five guest rooms, three of which have private baths, are furnished in a quaint country-style and are cozy and comfortable. No matter what season, your stay at *The Blue Goose Inn* will be highlighted by a hearty old-time breakfast of pancakes, scrambled eggs, Canadian-style bacon, coffee, tea and juice with lighter fare such as granola, fresh fruit and yogurt available too. Guests can snuggle-up with a book before the fire or ski Mount Sunapee in winter to enjoying games on the spacious lawn or walk to the nearby beach, barbecue and picnics in summer. In addition, the area offers golf, tennis, antiquing, summer theatre, dinner cruises, auctions and gourmet dining. With so many reasons to stay, it's hard to decide which is the best - but travelers in the "know" appreciate the affordable rates too! **AIRPORT:** Manchester Lebanon NH-30 mi **PACKAGES:** *Murder Mystery Weekends* **RESERVATIONS:** 50% deposit or credit card number to guarantee reservation. Handicap accessible **BROCHURE:** Yes **PERMITTED:** Children, drinking, limited smoking **PACKAGES:** *Ski One Stay* [Z07GPNH2-12913]

**Inn At New Ipswich	**New Ipswich NH**
Steve & Ginny Bankuti	Porter Hill Rd 03071
603-878-3711	**Res Times** 7am-10pm

Rates:	**Pvt Bath** 6	**Payment Terms:**
Single	$ 45.00	Check
Double	$ 65.00	MC/V

This gracious 1790 farmhouse, with classic red barn, instantly welcomes you. Rolling grounds are bordered by stone walls, gardens, and fruit trees. Its six guest rooms are comfortably furnished with firm beds and cozy, country-style antiques. (Two guest rooms have working fireplaces) Play chess or scrabble by the parlor fire. Choose a book from the well-stocked shelves. In summer, enjoy the sun on the front porch rockers or evening breezes on the screened porch. If peaceful getaways are your pleasure, *The Inn at New Ipswich* is the perfect place to relax. The Inn is located a short distance from myriad activities in the Monadnock Region, including golf, antiques, Summer Theater, concerts, arts & crafts, and auctions. Mount Monadnock (the most-climbed mountain in North America) offers fine hiking trails. Fall foliage is unsurpassed and in winter, x-country and downhill skiing is nearby. Guests awaken to aromas of fresh-baked muffins or breads and superb coffee. To quote guests, *"Breakfast alone is worth the trip"*. Tea, coffee and snacks are offered upon your arrival. **AIRPORT** Manchester NH-30 mi; Boston Logan Intl-65 mi **DISCOUNTS:** 15% weekday business rate, 15% preferred rate for travel agents **RESERVATIONS:** First night's deposit in full within 7 days to hold room; 10 day cancel policy less $5 service charge **SEASONAL:** No **BROCHURE:** Yes **PERMITTED:** Children over 8, limited drinking **LANGUAGES:** Hungarian [Z05FPNH1-12914]

**Inn At Coit Mountain	**Newport NH**
Dick & Judi Tatem	HCR 63 Box 3 03773

800-367-2364 603-863-3583

Rates:	Pvt Bath 2	Shared Bath 5	Payment Terms:
Single	$ 100-120.00	$ 70-100.00	Check
Double	$ 120-140.00	$ 85-115.00	AE/MC/V

The Inn was the summer home of Cheronnet-Champollion family, well-known in France for deciphering the Rosetta Stone and in the United States for Austin Corbin and the Long Island Railroad, Coney Island and Corbin Park. This classic Georgian Inn is elegant yet comfortable with five guest rooms. The Library has fifteen foot ceilings, is panelled in oak and has a granite fireplace. Some bedrooms have fireplaces. A full hearty gourmet breakfast is included. Located in the Sunapee Region, year round activities are many. Lunch and dinner are available with prior notice and additional cost. **DISCOUNTS:** Mid-week ski; extended stays, stay one week, the 7th night is free. **AIRPORT:** Manchester NH-1 hr. **PACKAGES:** Ski packages begin at $55.00 pppd **RESERVATIONS:** One night deposit applied to last day of stay; 10 day cancel policy for refund **SEASONAL:** No **BROCHURE:** Yes **PERMITTED:** Children, drinking, limited smoking [R12EPNH2-2396]

**Cranmore Inn	**North Conway NH**
Chris & Virginia Kanzler	Kearsarge St 03860
800-526-5502 603-356-5502	**Res Times** 9am-9pm

Rates:	Pvt Bath 14	Shared Bath 4	Payment Terms:
Single	$ 39-69.00	$ 39-52.00	Check
Double	$ 49-79.00	$ 39-52.00	MC/V

There is a uniqueness about this authentic Inn that surrounds you with a tradition of warm New England hospitality that has kept guests returning since the Inn opened in 1863. Centrally located in North Conway Village, in the heart of New Hampshire's spectacular White Mountains, guests can walk to village shops, restaurants, theatres, golf, playground and attractions. Find hiking, rock climbing, canoeing and boating just minutes away. In winter, x-country ski right from the Inn - or access four major downhill ski areas in minutes, including Mount Cranmore just 1/3 of a mile away. The Inn operates as a Bed and Breakfast, serving a hearty country breakfast to begin your day right. Dinners or luncheons are available to groups with advance notice. The Inn has retained much of its historic charm through period furnishings, dating from the 1800's through the 1940's. There are no televisions or telephones in the guest rooms, however these amenities are available to guests in our public sitting rooms. There is an outdoor pool where you can relax with iced tea or lemonade in summer, or relax by the fireplace with hot coffee or cocoa in winter, from our afternoon tea service. You will find New England charm with Yankee hospitality. **DISCOUNTS:** Groups **AIRPORT:** Portland Jetport-50 mi **RESERVATIONS:** Deposit or credit card number at res time to guarantee **SEASONAL:** Closed Christmas **BROCHURE:** Yes **PERMITTED:** Children limited drinking (BYOB) **CONFERENCES:** Public sitting areas for small groups [R05FPNH2-2402]

**Peacock Inn	**North Conway NH**
Claire J Jackson	PO Box 1012 03860
800-328 9041 603-356-9041	**Res Times** 9am-9pm

Rates:	Pvt Bath 14	Shared Bath 4	Payment Terms:
Single	$ 74-118.00*	$ 74-118.00*	Check
Double	$ 84-118.00	$ 74-118.00	AE/DIS/MC/V

A Classic Country Victorian Inn dating from 1775 (the guest book dates from 1875) offers relaxing New England Hospitality! This charming Inn is nestled in the heart of Mount Washington Valley near the quaint village of North Conway which offers spectacular year-round scenery and activities. Most of the guest rooms of this 215 year old period mansion have been lovingly restored and furnished with a variety of brass or canopy beds, antique rockers or skylights! Your hosts have created a warm, romantic and intimate atmosphere for their guests. They enjoy celebrations too, so if you have a special occasion, let them know and they'll have cake or champagne ready! There are breath-taking views of the sunsets over the Moat Mtns from within the Inn and if you like, splash in the babbling brook across the road! A hearty New England full breakfast begins each day and comp beverages, cheese & crackers are served each afternoon next to the large fireplace in the common room. Nearby activities include passes to Mount Cranmore Recreation Center for indoor swimming, racquet-ball or tennis, sauna and whirlpool. On your departure - don't be surprised if you find a package of cookies or fresh fruit packed by your hosts for you to enjoy on your trip home! *Special Package Rates*: stay 2 nights receive a 3rd night *free*; stay 3 nights and receive the next 2 nights *free*! **RESERVATIONS:** Full payment in advance; 20 day cancel notice for credit refund less $20 service fee **SEASONAL:**

Rates vary **BROCHURE:** Yes **PERMITTED:** Children, drinking, limited smoking **CONFERENCES:** Yes, for groups to 30 persons [R12CPNH-3749]

Stonehurst Manor	**North Conway NH**
Peter Rattay	PO Box 1937 Off Rt 16 03860
800-525-9100 603-356-3271	**Res Times** 24 Hrs

Rates:	**Pvt Bath** 24	**Payment Terms:**
Single	$ 75.00	Check
Double	$ 75-Up	AE/MC/V

Stonehurst Manor: **A Landmark in Lodging, Food and Spirits for over 46 years offering traditional hospitality in the Grand Manor!** The Staff of *Stonehurst Manor* invite you to enjoy the luxury of their elegant, turn-of-the-century mansion. Originally part of carpet baron Erastus Bigelow's summer estate, guests are surrounded with beautiful stain and leaded glass, hand-carved oak woodwork, a multitude of stone fireplaces - created by European craftsmen at the turn-of-the-century. Set on 33 secluded acres of pine forest, the Manor offers a truly unique and unforgettable White Mountain's vacation. From our exceptional mountain views to the peace and quiet of the fireplaced Library Lounge, you'll be surrounded by beauty and comfort. (Seven of the guest rooms also have working fireplaces). Chef Brian Coffey has created a wonderful approach to eating out here at the Manor. It's elegant yet casual, combining delicious tradition with inventive taste discoveries, and presented in a relaxing atmosphere of timeless ease enhanced by superb service and style. Watch as we make our famous wood-fired gourmet pizza in our outdoor patio oven in summer and in our indoor brick oven in winter. Enjoy the pleasures of our large outdoor pool, hot tub, tennis court and walking trails leading from our door ... in winter, you'll x-country ski these trails for 65 scenic kilometers. At the Manor we also offer one to five day guided walking and hiking vacations, through beautiful countryside and the unspoiled wilderness of the White Mountains. *Discover what it's like to live in royal-style without paying a king's ransom.* We promise it's an experience you won't soon forget! The *Sonehurst Manor has been recommended* by *Bon Appetite and Country Inn of New England.* **DISCOUNTS:** Yes, inquire at res time **AIRPORT:** Portland ME-60 mi; Boston-125 mi **PACKAGES:** Yes, $48.00 per night includes breakfast and dinner off regular menu. Walking and Hiking Tours. **RESERVATIONS:** One night's deposit, 14 day cancel policy for refund **BROCHURE:** Yes **PERMITTED:** Children, drinking, smoking **CONFERENCES:** Perfect setting for weddings and private parties to 200; conferences and meetings to 75 persons **LANGUAGES:** French, German [J07GPNH2-2409]

Follansbee Inn			**North Sutton NH**
Sandy & Dick Reilein			Keyer Rd 03260
603-927-4221			

Rates:	**Pvt Bath** 11	**Shared Bath** 12	**Payment Terms:**
Single			Check
Double	$ 70.00	$ 60.00	MC/V

New England farmhouse c1840 on Kezar Lake, with old fashioned porch & charming bedrooms for true Yankee hospitality. Off I-89 at exit 10, close to Dartmouth, skiing, antiques and Mount Sunapee State Park. Full breakfast included. **SEASONAL:** No **BROCHURE:** Yes **PERMITTED:** Children 8-up [E11ACNH-2411]

Wilderness Inn B&B			**North Woodstock NH**
Michael/Rosanna Yarnell			Rt 3 & Courtney Rd 03262
800-200-WILD 603-745-3890			**Res Times** 7am-10pm

Rates:	**Pvt Bath** 6	**Shared Bath** 2	**Payment Terms:**
Single	$ 50-85.00	$ 40-55.00	Check
Double	$ 50-85.00	$ 40-55.00	AE/MC/V

A year-round retreat snuggled within the White Mountain National Forest offers guests a true New England Experience while staying in *"turn-of-the-century elegance".* The 80-year old *Wilderness Inn* has seven uniquely decorated guest rooms, family suites and cottage with private baths and views of the Inn's gardens or nearby mountains. Lost River flows through the backyard and offers guests swimming or a pleasant afternoon picnic spot. In winter, ski downhill at Loon Mountain (3 miles) or Cannon Mtn (8 miles) or x-country ski nearby. Enjoy tea or hot mulled cider fireside upon your return. A complimentary full breakfast is served of freshly ground coffee, muffins, omelettes or cranberry-walnut pancakes, with pure maple syrup. Just 2-1/2 hrs from Boston, 3 hrs from Portland & Providence, 6-1/2 hrs from NYC and 3-1/2 hrs from Montreal **RESERVATIONS:** One night's deposit at res time; 14 day cancel policy for refund **SEASONAL:** Rates vary **BROCHURE:** Yes **PERMITTED:** Children welcomed **CONFERENCES:** Yes, groups to 15 persons **LANGUAGES:** French, Italian, Bengali, Amharic [Z07GPNH2-7341]

Meadow Farm B&B	Northwood NH
Doug & Janet Briggs	Jenness Pond Rd 03261
603-942-8619	

Rates:	**Pvt Bath** 20	**Shared Bath** 8	**Payment Terms:**
Single	$ 50.00	$ 45.00	Check
Double	$ 62.00	$ 57.00	

Traditional New England farm house c1770, set on 50 acres of pasture and woods, built with beamed ceilings, fireplaces, and wide plank floors. Relax in this natural setting offering private beach on lake and x-country skiing in winter. **BROCHURE:** Yes **PERMITTED:** Children, limited pets, smoking, drinking [C11ACNH-2414]

Home Hill Country Inn	Plainfield NH
Roger Nicolas	River Road 03781
603-675-6165	**Res Times** 24 Hrs

Rates:	**Pvt Bath** 9	**Payment Terms:**
Single	$ 105-120.00	Check
Double	$ 105-120.00	MC/V

Home Hill Country Inn and French Restaurant is a meticulously restored circa 1800 mansion on the banks of the Connecticut River. Nestled on twenty-five secluded acres, the Inn is a perfect getaway for those seeking an escape to the tranquility of a picture postcard perfect New England countryside. Each of the nine guest rooms are beautifully appointed with antiques and collectibles and includes a private bath. A two room suite, separate guest house and a pool house are also available. Ideally located for enjoying four season activities, *Home Hill* has a pool, clay tennis court and in winter, x-country ski trails on the grounds with downhill skiing minutes away. Nearby is canoeing, fishing, hiking and golf. Guests are invited to enjoy the complimentary continental breakfast in the Inn's country-style kitchen. Evening's offer the widely acclaimed French cuisine in one of three intimate dining rooms, where guests savor fine wines from the discriminating wine cellar or enjoy spirits from the fully licensed library bar. **PACKAGES:** Yes, inquire at res time **RESERVATIONS:** Prepayment to 2 nights, if longer 1st and last night's deposit, 14 day cancel policy less $15 service fee; less than 14 days, refund only if rebooked **SEASONAL:** No **BROCHURE:** Yes **PERMITTED:** Limited children, drinking, limited smoking **CONFERENCES:** Perfect for intimate, secluded events featuring excellent dining **LANGUAGES:** French [R10EPNH2-2291]

**Colonel Spencer Inn	**Plymouth NH**
Carolyn & Alan Hill	RR 1 Box 206 03264
603-536-3438	**Res Times** 8am-10pm

Rates:	**Pvt Bath** 7	**Payment Terms:**
Single	$ 30-40.00	Check
Double	$ 45-65.00	

This historic 1764 colonial home was built by Colonel Joseph Spencer, an early settler to the Pemigewasset River Valley, who fought at Bunker Hill with Gen Washington and at the battle of Cambridge during the Revolution. Rurally located in the White Mountain Region, a short drive from Franconia Notch, major mountain and lake attractions, and three miles from Plymouth State College and the Holderness School, the *Colonel Spencer* is an ideal location for downhill and x-country skiing, skating, hiking, climbing, tennis, swimming, boating, cycling and leaf-peaking. Within view of the Pemigewasset River and the mountains, the Inn is a cozy retreat furnished with period antiques and country decorations. Guests may enjoy a full country breakfast served in a fireplaced dining room overlooking a country pond. Afternoon tea and evening coffee are also served. Tastefully restored architectural features include hewn post and beam construction, Indian shutters, wainscoting, paneling, gunstock corners, wide pine floors, Christian doors and secret passageways. Seven bedrooms, two with fireplaces and one suite with a kitchenette, welcome guests with New England warmth and charm. Whether you plan to spend a night or stay a week, you'll find the *Colonel Spencer* a relaxing and inviting refuge. **DISCOUNTS:** Two nights or longer **AIRPORT:** Manchester-60 mi; Boston Logan-110 mi **PACKAGES:** *Skiing* **RESERVATIONS:** $25 deposit required prior to arrival **BROCHURE:** Yes **PERMITTED:** Children, drinking [Z07GPNH2-13946]

**Governor's House B&B	**Portsmouth NH**
Nancy & John Grossman	32 Miller Ave 03801
603-431-6546	**Res Times** 7am-10pm
	Fax 603-427-0803
Rates: **Pvt Bath** 4	**Payment Terms:**
Single $ 65-130.00	AE/MC/V
Double $ 75-140.00	

Walk into John & Nancy Grossman's stately Georgian Colonial Revival home and enjoy the relaxed elegance shared by all. Its quiet location is a short walk from virtually everything there is to do in Portsmouth. The gracious dining room has a *"bottomless"* cookie jar and afternoon tea or lemonade. The cozy living room, with its fireplace, beckons with welcoming warmth and the library is a wonderful place to curl up and read, savor early morning coffee and meet others. Each bedroom, decorated with antiques, has a different motif, with queen-sized beds and unique private baths, one with a jacuzzi, proclaiming bold ceramic designs created by Nancy, a professional tile painter and artist. Nestled amidst pines and cedars is a tennis court, hammock and a quiet sitting area. After a delicious full New England breakfast, walk into historic Portsmouth to enjoy antiquing, Strawbery Banke Museum, historical tours, harbor cruising, a horse-drawn carriage ride, shopping, theatre and many fine restaurants. Close by is the breathtaking Wentworth By The Sea

Golf Course and Kittery shopping outlets. **RESERVATIONS:** One night's deposit, 14 day cancel policy for refund **PERMITTED:** Children 14+, drinking **BROCHURE:** Yes **DISCOUNTS:** Groups **AIRPORT:** Boston Logan-1-1/4 hr; Portsmouth-10 min [I08GPNH2-18203]

Hilltop Inn	**Sugar Hill NH**
Mike & Meri Hern	Sugar Hill Rd 03585
603-823-5695	**Res Times** 9am-10pm

Rates:	**Pvt Bath** 6	**Payment Terms:**
Single	$ 50-75.00	Check
Double	$ 60-110.00	AE/DIS/MC/V

This charming Victorian Country Inn, built circa 1895, is furnished throughout with turn-of-the-century antiques making each of the six guest rooms unique and the common rooms comfortable and inviting. The Inn is close to all activities, including alpine and nordic skiing, swimming, canoeing, fishing, biking, hiking, horseback riding, wind surfing, glider rides, Cannon Mountain, the Tramway, the Old Man of the Mountain and the flume. Evening brings friendly conversation beside the cozy fireplace or fine candle-light dinner in the intimate dining room. All room rates include a large country breakfast each morning. Your hosts are professional caterers so there are always delicious surprises. **AIRPORT:** Boston-3 Hrs; Burlington-1-1/2 Hrs **PACKAGES:** *Ski discount tickets* **RESERVATIONS:** Deposit required, 8 day cancel policy, check-in 2-5:30 pm **SEASONAL:** Closed 4/1-5/15 **BROCHURE:** Yes **PERMITTED:** Children 4-up, drinking, limited pets, limited smoking [R03EPNH-2439]

Loma Lodge	**Sunapee NH**
	RFD 1 Box 592 03782
603-763-4849	

Rates:	**Shared Bath** 7	**Payment Terms:**
Single	$ 50.00	Check
Double	$ 60.00	

Perfect setting for the outdoors from this 200 year old home with atmosphere from the beamed ceiling and granite fireplace. Close to harbor and mountains with x-country and alpine skiing in winter. Full hearty breakfast included **SEASONAL:** No **BROCHURE:** Yes **PERMITTED:** Children, smoking, drinking. [E11ACNH-3009]

Village House/Sutton Mills		**Sutton Mills NH**
Peggy & Norm Forand		Grist Mill Rd 03221
603-927-4765		**Res Times** 9am-9pm

Rates:	**Shared Bath** 3	**Payment Terms:**
Single	$ 35.00	Check
Double	$ 50.00	

Our 1857 Country Victorian Guest House overlooking a quaint New England village affords our guests privacy, charm and the opportunity to be pampered. The guest rooms are tastefully decorated with antiques with everyone enjoying a selection from our antique quilt collection. Guests can enjoy yard games on our private four acres in summer, while winter offers x-country skiing, snowshoeing and snowmobiling right from the front door. Excellent downhill and x-country skiing establishments are just minutes away. A **Skiers Delight Package** offers three nights for the price of two, Sunday through Thursday, in season. Choose from among the many restaurants offering excellent dining while enjoying the great antiquing, shopping and strolling through yesteryear at the many old mill streams, water falls, mill ponds and miles of old stone walls. Outdoor activities include biking, boating, swimming and fishing. Room rates include a memorable full country breakfast with home baked bread and muffins along with maple syrup made right in the backyard. Dinner is available at a nominal added cost and with prior arrangements. Treat yourself to a memorable and comfortable retreat! **DISCOUNTS:** Yes, inquire at res time **PACKAGES:** **Ski Season** (Sunday-Thursday, stay three nights for the price of two) **RESERVATIONS:** One night's deposit, two week cancel notice for refund less $10 service fee **SEASONAL:** No **BROCHURE:** Yes **PERMITTED:** Limited children, limited drinking [R10EPNH2-2451]

Hilltop Acres		**Wentworth NH**
Marie A Kauk		East Side & Buffalo Rd 03282
603-764-5896		

Rates:	**Pvt Bath** 5	**Cottages**	**Payment Terms:**

Single	$ 65.00	$ 80.00	Check
Double	$ 65.00		MC/V

Hilltop Acres is a peaceful country retreat located in picturesque Wentworth, snuggled in the White Mountains. The home was built in 1806 and was one of the first settlements in town and offers easy access to the many tourist attractions in the Lakes and Mountains Regions. Located on 20 acres of field and pine forest, the surroundings are relaxing and inspirational. All of the guest rooms are comfortably furnished and offer beautiful views of the surrounding landscape. There is an extensive library, a large pine-panelled recreation room with fireplace, antique piano, games and cable TV. Outdoors, there's a spacious lawn area which is well-tended and surrounded by a beautiful pine forest and brook. A continental plus breakfast begins each morning. Your hostess is pleased to help with directions to all of the year-round activities which include swimming, hiking, boating, mountain biking, fishing, snowmobiling, skiing, antiquing and fine dining. And, guests won't find a shortage of peaceful relaxing spots outdoors under the shade of a shady maple tree either. Your hostess can arrange special guided tours of the area and points of interest. *Cozy housekeeping cottages are available and offer a pine-panelled room with a kitchen unit, fireplace, full separate bathroom, bedroom and a screened-in porch. **AIRPORT:** Manchester or Lebanon-1 hr and 15 mins **PACKAGES:** *Ski* **RESERVATIONS:** Deposit required to hold reservation with a 7 day cancel policy for refund, less than 7 day notice is received, deposit will not be refunded unless room is resold for that evening **SEASONAL:** May-October **BROCHURE:** Yes **PERMITTED:** Children, drinking **CONFERENCES:** Yes **LANGUAGES:** German, French [I05FPNH4-12525]

Wentworth Inn & Gallery	**Wentworth NH**
Barbara & Jim Moffat	Off Rt 25 03282
800-542-2331 603-764-9923	**Res Times** 6pm-9pm

Rates:	**Pvt Bath** 3	**Shared Bath** 4	**Payment Terms:**
Single	$ 75.00	$ 65.00	Check

Double	$ 75.00	$ 65.00	AE/DC/MC/V

In the foothills of the White Mountains and the beautiful Baker River Valley, where the pace is a little slower and life is more serene, is this stately old white colonial Inn and art gallery. Surrounded by the scenic beauty of the mountains and the babbling streams nearby, you can taste the true New England flavors year-round. The Federal-design home offers guests comfort and time to converse with the hosts who are local artists, that display the works of other artists and craftsmen. Full country breakfast starts off your day with other gourmet choices for Inn guests only with a table d'haute menu to select. Other meals available. **RESERVATIONS:** One night's deposit at booking for guarantee; 10-day cancellation notice, less 10% service fee **SEASONAL:** No **BROCHURE:** Yes **PERMITTED:** Limited children **CONFERENCES:** Yes, groups to 40 persons [E02BCNH-3758]

**Tall Pines Inn	**Winnesquam NH**
Kent & Kate Kern	752 Old Rt 3 03289
800-722-6870 603-528-3632	**Res Times** 10am-10pm

Rates:	**Pvt Bath** 1	**Shared Bath** 2	**Payment Terms:**
Single	$ 60.00	$ 50.00	Check
Double	$ 65.00	$ 55.00	DC/MC/V

Tall Pines Inn is a homestay Bed & Breakfast Country Inn located in the heart of New Hampshire's Lakes Region. The Inn is situated on the southern shore of Lake Winnisquam and features and outstanding view of the lake and mountains to the north. The Inn has three guest rooms and your innkeepers (Kent & Kate) have taken great care to create an atmosphere reflecting their hospitality and interest in having guests feel welcomed and at home. The guest rooms are bright, clean and comfortable with handmade quilts and "all you can eat" full country breakfasts. Guest rooms are designed for adult couples or single travelers. Special dinners are available with advance reservation and business travelers can join the innkeepers for dinner "du jour" at a nominal additional charge. The Lakes Region is a four-seasons destination area for recreational visitors with something for everyone. Additionally, the Inn is centrally located for business or recreational day trip travel ranging from Boston MA to Concord, Manchester and Portsmouth New Hampshire, Portland Maine or White River Vermont. Reservations are recommended and a phone call with your credit card number will confirm your reservation. Prepayment of full rental guarantees your reservation. Toll-free reservation phone: 800-722-6870 **DISCOUNTS:** Weekly rates and min-week business rates are available **AIRPORT** Manchester NH-50 mi; Portland ME-90 mi; Boston's Logan-90 mi **RESERVATIONS:** Full payment two week cancel policy for refund, two night min holidays and foliage season **SEASONAL:** No **BROCHURE:** Yes **PERMITTED:** Drinking, limited smoking, children [Z05FPNH1-13953]

Tuc' Me Inn	Wolfeboro NH
Irma Limberger	68 N Main St 03894
603-569-5702	

Rates:	Pvt Bath 2	Shared Bath 4	Payment Terms:
Single	$ 65.00		Check
Double	$ 72.00	$ 59.00	MC/V

Oldest summer resort town in USA ... offers this beautiful early 1800's colonial, tastefully decorated for comfort and warmth. Beautiful year-round area with water and snow sporting activities. Two blocks from scenic Lake Winnipesaukee. Full breakfast each day. **SEASONAL:** No **BROCHURE:** Yes **PERMITTED:** Children 12-up, drinking [E11ACNH-5873]

Alexandria
MOUNT CARDIGAN
603-744-5803

*STONE REST B&B
603-744-6066

Alstead
DARBY BROOK
FARM
603-835-6624

Alton Bay
OAK BIRCH INN

Andover
ANDOVER ARMS
GUEST HOUSE
603-735-5953

ENGLISH HOUSE
603-735-5987

Antrim
ANTRIM INN
603-588-8000

BREEZY POINT INN
603-478-5201

STEELE
HOMESTEAD
603-588-2407

UPLANDS INN
603-588-6349

Ashland
CHENEY HOUSE
603-968-7968

COUNTRY OPTIONS
603-968-7958

CYNTHIA WILLEY
HOUSE

****GLYNN HOUSE
INN**
800-637-9599

Bartlett
*COUNTRY INN AT
BARTLETT
603-374-2353

NOTCHLAND INN
603-374-6131

Bedford
BEDFORD VILLAGE
603-472-2001

Bennington
*DAVIDS INN
603-588-2458

Bethlehem
HIGHLANDS INN
603-869-3978

MULBERRY INN
603-869-3389

MULBRUN INN
603-869-2647

WAYSIDE INN
800-448-9557

Bradford
**BRADFORD INN
800-669-5309

MASSASECUM
LODGE

MOUNTAIN LAKE

INN
800-662-6005

Bretton Woods
LODGE AT
BRETTON WOODS

Bridgewater
PASQUANEY INN
603-744-2712

Bristol
BRISTOL GUEST
HOUSE

VICTORIAN
603-744-6157

Campton
CAMPTON INN
603-726-4449

***MOUNTAIN FARE
INN**
603-726-4283

OSGOOD INN
603-726-3543

Campton Village
VILLAGE GUEST
HOUSE
603-726-0444

Canaan
INN ON CANAAN
STREET
603-523-7310

TOWERHOUSE INN
603-523-7244

Canterbury
SLEEPY HOLLOW

B&B
603-267-6055

Center Conway
LAVENDER
FLOWER
800-729-0106

Center Harbor
DEARBORN PLACE
603-253-4900

KONA MANSION
INN
603-253-4900

RED HILL INN
603-279-7001

Center Ossipee
HITCHING POST
VILLAGE INN
603-539-4482

Center Sandwich
CORNER HOUSE
INN
603-284-6219

Charlestown
MAPLEHEDGE B&B
603-798-4951

Chichester
HITCHING POST
B&B
603-798-4951

Chocorua
*FARMHOUSE B&B
603-323-8707

STAFFORDS IN THE
FIELD

800-332-0355

Claremont
GODDARD
MANSION
603-543-0603

POPLARS
603-543-0858

Colebrook
MA & PA
CORMIER'S

MONADNOCK B&B
603-237-8216

Concord
**BRADFORD INN
800-669-5309

HITCHING POST
B&B
603-798-4951

WYMAN FARM
603-783-4467

Conway
DARBY FIELD INN
800-426-4147

EASTMAN INN
800-562-1300

FOOTHILLS FARM
B&B
207-935-3799

**KANCAMAGUS
SWIFT RIVER INN
800-255-4236

MERRILL FARM

RESORT
800-445-1017

VILLAGE HOUSE
800-972-8343

Cornish
*CHASE HOUSE
B&B
603-675-5391

Danbury
*INN AT DANBURY
603-768-3318

Dover
SILVER STREET
INN
603-743-3000

East Andover
**HIGHLAND LAKE
INN B&B
603-735-6462

East Sullivan
DELFORD INN
603-847-9778

Easton
BLANCHES B&B
603-823-7061

Eaton Center
INN AT CRYSTAL
LAKE
800-343-7336

PALMER HOUSE
INN
603-447-2120

ROCKHOUSE
MOUNTAIN FARM

603-447-2880

Elkins
LIMNER HAUS
603-526-6451

Enfield
KLUGES SUNSET
HILL INN

Epping
HALEY HOUSE
FARM
603-679-8713

Etna
*MOOSE
MOUNTAIN LODGE
603-643-3529

Exeter
EXETER INN
603-772-5901

Fitzwilliam
AMOS A PARKER
HOUSE
603-585-6540

BARNTIQUE

FERN HILL

FITZWILLIAM INN
603-585-9000

HANNAH DAVIS
HOUSE
603-585-3344

Francestown
FRANCESTOWN
B&B
603-547-6333

INN AT CROTCHED
MOUNTAIN
603-588-6840

Franconia
*BUNGAY JAR B&B
603-823-7775

CANNON MT INN &
COTTAGE
603-823-9574

**FRANCONIA INN
800-473-5299

*HORSE & HOUND
INN
603-823-5501

LOVETTS BY
LAFAYETTE BROOK
603-823-7761

PINESTEAD FARM
LODGE
603-823-5601

SUGAR HILL INN
603-823-5621

Franconia Village
INN AT FOREST
HILLS

Franklin
*MARIA W
ATWOOD INN
603-934-3666

WEBSTER LAKE
INN
603-934-4050

Freedom

FREEDOM HOUSE
603-539-4815

Freedom Hill
KNOB HILL B&B
603-539-6576

Gilford
*CARTWAY HOUSE
603-528-1172

GUNSTOCK INN
603-527-1086

KINGS GRANT INN
603-293-4431

Gilmanton
HISTORIC TAVERN
603-267-7349

Glen
BERNERHOF INN
800-548-8007

Gorham
*GABLES
603-466-2876

GORHAM HOUSE
INN
603-466-2271

PINKHAM NOTCH
CAMP
603-466-2727

Goshen
CUTTERS LOFT
603-863-5306

Grafton
GRAFTON INN

Greenfield
GREENFIELD INN
603-547-6327

Greenland
THOMAS AYERS
HOUSE
603-436-5992

Hampton
BLUE HERON INN
603-926-9666

INN AT ELMWOOD
CORNERS
603-929-0443

JAFFREY MANOR
INN
603-532-8069

Hampton Beach
BOARS HEAD
603-926-3911

CENTURY HOUSE

GRAYHURST

*OCEANSIDE
603-926-3542

Hancock
JOHN HANCOCK
INN
603-525-3318

Hanover
HANOVER INN

*SILVER MAPLE
LODGE-COTTAGES
800-666-1946

**STONECREST
FARM B&B**
802-295-2600

Harrisville
HARRISVILLE
SQUIRES
603-827-3925

Haverhill
HAVERHILL INN
603-989-5961

Hebron
SIX CHIMNEYS
603-744-2029

Henniker
COLBY HILL INN
603-428-3281

HANSCOM HOUSE

MEETING HOUSE
INN
603-428-3228

Hillsborough
STONEBRIDGE INN
603-464-3155

STONEWALL FARM

Holderness
**INN ON GOLDEN
POND**
603-968-7269

**MANOR ON
GOLDEN POND**
800-545-2141

Intervale
FOREST A

COUNTRY INN
800-448-3544

MOUNTAIN VALE
INN
800-545-6033

NEW ENGLAND INN
603-356-5541

*OLD FIELD
HOUSE
603-356-5478

RIVERSIDE
COUNTRY INN
603-356-9060

*WILDFLOWERS
GUEST HOUSE
603-356-2224

Jackson
BLAKE HOUSE
603-383-9057

CHRISTMAS FARM
INN
800-HI ELVES

*DANA PLACE
800-537-9276

ELLIS RIVER
HOUSE
800-233-8309

INN AT JACKSON
800-289-8600

*INN AT THORN
HILL
800-289-8990

JACKSON HOUSE
B&B
800-338-1268

NESTLENOOK INN
603-383-9443

PAISLEY &
PARSLEY
603-383-0859

VILLAGE HOUSE
800-972-8343

WHITNEYS
VILLAGE
800-252-5622

WILDCAT INN
& TAVERN
603-383-4245

Jaffrey
**BENJAMIN
PRESCOTT INN**
603-532-6637

GALWAY HOUSE
603-532-8083

GOULD FARM
603-532-6996

*LILAC HILL
ACRES**
603-532-7278

*MILL POND INN**
603-532-7687

WOODBOUND INN
800-252-3033

Jaffrey Center

MONADNOCK INN
603-532-7001

Jefferson
APPLEBROOK
603-586-7713

**APPLEBROOK
B&B**
800-545-6504

DAVENPORT INN
603-586-4320

JEFFERSON INN
800-729-7908

STAG HOLLOW
INN/LLAMA KEEP
603-586-4598

Keene
289 COURT
603-357-3195

CARRIAGE BARN
GUESTHOUSE
603-357-3812

GOOSE POND
GUEST HOUSE
603-352-2828

Laconia
FERRY POINT
HOUSE
603-524-0087

HICKORY STICK
FARM
603-524-3333

LARAN FARM
ROY FAMILY B&B

TIN WHISTLE
603-528-4185

Lancaster
A TOUCH OF
HOME

Lebanon
B&B OF BANK
STREET
603-448-2041

Lincoln
MILL HOUSE INN
800-654-6183

Lisbon
**AMMONOOSUC
INN**
603-838-6118

Littleton
1895 HOUSE
603-444-5200

**BEAL HOUSE
INN**
603-444-2661

THAYERS INN
800-634-8179

Loudon
INN AT LOUDON
RIDGE
603-267-8952

Lyme
DOWD'S COUNTRY
INN
603-795-4712

LOCH LYME
LODGE

603-795-2141

*LYME INN
603-795-2222

MARJORIES
HOUSE

Madison
MADISON
CARRIAGE HOUSE
800-851-1088

Marlborough
PEEP WILLOW
FARM
603-876-3807

THATCHER HILL
INN
603-876-3361

TOLMAN POND

Meredith
HATHAWAY INN
603-279-5521

INN AT MILL FALLS

NUTMEG INN
800-642-9229

Milford
RAM IN THE
THICKET
603-654-6440

VICTORIA PLACE

Mirror Lake
HARDIE HOUSE
B&B
603-569-5714

Monroe
SILVER BIRCHES
B&B

Moultonboro
***OLDE ORCHARD
INN**
603-476-5004

Mount Sunapee
**BLUE GOOSE INN
603-763-5519

Munsonville
OLD MILL HOUSE
603-847-3224

Nashua
HOME AWAY FROM
HOME B&B
800-345-2127

New Ipswich
****INN AT NEW
IPSWICH**
603-878-3711

New London
HIDE-WAY LODGE
603-526-4861

MAPLE HILL FARM
603-526-2248

NEW LONDON INN
603-526-2791

PLEASANT LAKE
INN
603-526-6271

Newbury
ANDREW BROOK
LODGE

603-938-2920

Newmarket
HELGAS B&B
603-659-6856

Newport
BACK SIDE INN
603-863-5161

****INN AT COIT
MOUNTAIN**
800-367-2364

North Charleston
*INDIAN
SHUTTERS
603-826-4445

North Conway
1785 INN
800-421-1785

*BUTTONWOOD
INN
800-258-2625

CENTER CHIMNEY
603-356-6788

**CRANMORE INN
800-526-5502

CRANMORE INN
800-882-9928

CRANMORE
MOUNTAIN LODGE
800-356-3596

EASTERN SLOPE
INN

*NERELEDGE INN

603-356-2831

NEW ENGLAND INN
800-82-NEINN

OLD RED INN &
COTTAGES
603-356-2642

**PEACOCK INN
800-328 9041

SCOTTISH LION INN
603-356-6381

**STONEHURST
MANOR**
800-525-9100

*VICTORIAN
HARVEST
603-356-3548

*VILLAGE HOUSE
603-383-6666

WYATT HOUSE
ENGLISH INN
603-356-7977

**North Sutton
*FOLLANSBEE INN**
603-927-4221

North Woodstock
BIRCH HILL
COTTAGES

BIRCHES B&B
603-745-6603

CASCADE LODGE
603-745-2722

LEDGELAND
603-745-3951

****WILDERNESS INN
B&B**
800-200-WILD

WOODSTOCK INN
603-745-3951

Northwood
AVIARY
603-942-7755

LAKE SHORE FARM
603-942-5921

***MEADOW FARM
B&B**
603-942-8619

NOSTALGIA B&B
603-942-7748

RESORT AT LAKE
SHORE FARM
603-942-5921

Orford
WHITE GOOSE INN
603-353-4812

Ossipee
*ACORN LODGE
603-539-2151

Peterborough
SALZBURG INN

WILLOWS INN

Plainfield
**HOME HILL
COUNTRY INN**

603-675-6165

Plymouth
****COLONEL
SPENCER INN**
603-536-3438

CRAB APPLE INN
603-536-4476

NORTHWAY
HOUSE
603-536-2838

Portsmouth
BOW STREET INN
603-431-7760

G CLEF B&B
603-772-8850

****GOVERNORS
HOUSE B&B**
603-431-6546

INN AT CHRISTIAN
SHORE
603-431-6770

INN AT GOODWIN
PARK

INN AT
STRAWBERRY
BANKE
603-436-7242

MARTIN HILL INN
603-436-2287

SHEAFE STREET
INN
603-436-9104

SISE INN
603-433-1200

THEATRE INN
603-431-5846

Rindge
GRASSY POND
HOUSE
603-899-5166

TOKFARM INN
603-899-6646

Rye
CABLEHOUSE
603-964-5000

ROCK LEDGE
MANOR
603-431-1413

Seabrook Beach
BELLINGHAM BY
THE BAY B&B

Shelburne
PHILBROOK FARM
INN
603-466-3831

Snowville
SNOWVILLE INN
603-447-2818

Stafford
PROVINCE INN
603-664-2457

Stratham
MAPLE LODGE B&B
603-778-9833

Sugar Hill

CANNON VIEW INN
603-823-8039

HILLTOP INN
603-823-5695

HOMESTEAD
603-823-5564

INN AT SKUNK
HOLLOW
800-551-3084

LEDGELAND
603-823-5341

SOUTHWORTHS
B&B
603-823-5344

SUGAR HILL
603-823-5654

SUNSET HILL
HOUSE
603-823-5522

Sunapee
DEXTERS INN
800-232-5571

HAUS EDELWEISS
B&B
603-763-2100

INN AT SUNAPEE
603-763-4444

*LOMA LODGE
603-763-4849

OLD GOVERNORS
HOUSE
603-763-9918

SEVEN HEARTHS
INN
800-237-2464

TIMES TEN INN
603-763-5120

Suncook
SUNCOOK HOUSE
603-485-8141

Sutton Mills
****VILLAGE HOUSE
SUTTON MILLS**
603-927-4765

Tamworth
EDGEHILL INN

*TAMWORTH INN
800-933-3902

Tamworth Village
GILMAN TAVERN
603-323-8940

Temple
BIRCHWOOD INN
603-878-3285

Tilton
COUNTRY PLACE
603-386-8551

TILTON MANOR
603-286-3457

Troy
INN AT EAST HILL
FARM
603-242-6495

Twin Mountain
CARLSON'S LODGE

NORTHERN
ZERMATT
800-535-3214

PARTRIDGE HOUSE
603-846-2277

Wakefield
JONATHAN GILMAN
HOMESTEAD
603-522-3102

WAKEFIELD INN
603-522-8272

Walpole
1801 HOUSE

GREAT BROOK
HOUSE
603-756-4721

Warren
BLACK IRIS B&B
603-764-9366

BLUE SPRUCE B&B
603-764-5756

Waterville
VALLEY INN
& TAVERN

Waterville Valley
SILVER SQUIRREL
INN
603-236-8325

SNOWY OWL INN
603-236-8383

Wentworth
HILLTOP ACRES
603-764-5896

HOBSON HOUSE
603-764-9460

***WENTWORTH INN
& ART GALLERY**
800-542-2331

West Canaan
CHALET AT GOOSE
POND
603-632-4966

West Chesterfield
CHESTERFIELD
INN
800-365-5515

West Ossippee
WEST OSSIPPEE
COUNTRY INN
603-539-2874

Whitefield
1875 MOUNTAIN
INN
603-837-2220

KIMBALL HILL INN
603-837-2284

SPALDING INN &
CLUB

Wilson Mills
BOSEBUCK
MOUNTAIN CAMP

Wilton Center
STEPPING STONES
603-654-9048

Winnesquam
TALL PINES INN
800-722-6870

Wolfeboro
INN OF NEW
DURHAM

ISAAC
SPRINGFIELD
HOUSE
603-569-3529

LAKEVIEW INN
603-569-1335

*TUC' ME INN
603-569-5702

WOLFEBORO INN
800-451-2389

Woodsville
GREEN PASTURES

Rhode Island

Blue Dory Inn   **Block Island RI

Ann Loedy   Dodge Street 02807
800-992-7290 401-466-5891

Rates:	**Pvt Bath** 15	**Payment Terms:**
Single	$ 65-170.00	Check
Double	$ 65-170.00	AE/MC/V

Crescent Beach - where miles of white sand meet clear blue water - at the head of this famous beach, within a few feet of the sea is the charming *Blue Dory Inn*, a Victorian Inn dating from the turn-of-the-century. Newly renovated and furnished with antiques, fixtures and decorations, guests easily become enchanted by the Victorian charm within - evoking a time gone by. Spacious guest rooms provide town or ocean views, plush antique decor, private baths, wall-to-wall carpeting and all modern comforts. The eat-in kitchen welcomes guests each morning to a continental breakfast of fresh brewed coffee, breakfast rolls, fresh fruits, assorted juices, herbal teas and a bottomless pot of coffee. Located in the historical district, there are many fine shops, restaurants and sights within easy walking distance. Your hosts will arrange everything from Island Tours to bike rentals and can make numerous recommendations on sights to see and places to visit. Block Island has something for everyone. As a sportsman's paradise with unexcelled sailing and deep-sea fishing, or the beachcomber's delight with dunes and beaches to explore - its the perfect place to unwind during the day. Unwinding in the evening means trying one of the excellent restaurants where specialties include lobster, swordfish and quahogs. **AIRPORT:** Providence-1 hr **DISCOUNTS:** Inquire at res time **PACKAGES:** Inquire at res time. **RESERVATIONS:** 50% deposit within 7 days of booking **SEASONAL:** Rates vary **BROCHURE:** Yes **PERMITTED:** Children, pets, drinking, smoking **CONFERENCES:** Yes, for small groups [R12EPRI2-4634]

Gables Inn & Gables II   **Block Island RI**

Barbara & Stan Nyzio   Box 516 Dodge St 02807

©Bed & Breakfast Guest Houses & Inns of America, Memphis TN   209

401-466-2213 401-466-7721   **Res Times** 9am-6pm

Rates:	Pvt Bath 10	Shared Bath 15	Payment Terms:
Single	$ 75-115.00	$ 40-60.00	Check
Double	$ 75-115.00	$ 65-85.00	MC/V

A wonderful summer vacation - perfect for families, this spot has been a summer retreat for the past twenty five years - your hosts provide guests with all the essentials for enjoying the Island. A variety of accommodations meet every need, ranging from single rooms to cottages - all guaranteed to provide a memorable experience. Each room or cottage is located on the ground floor and has its own outside entrance and porch. The beach and water are nearby and all of the activities of Block Island. **RESERVATIONS:** Full deposit to two nights, 3 nights or more required 50% deposit within 5 days of booking, bal due upon check-in, 15 day cancel policy less $20 service fee **SEASONAL:** Open 5/1-11/15 **PERMITTED:** Smoking, drinking, children **BROCHURE:** Yes **DISCOUNTS:** Yes, off-season and week days in-season **AIRPORT:** Block Island State Airport-1 mi [S03GPRI2-4636]

Seacrest Inn	**Block Island RI**
	207 High St 02807

401-466-2882

Rates:	Pvt Bath 18	Payment Terms:
Single	$ 68-80.00	Check
Double	$ 68-80.00	

Old Harbor section in the historic district offers picturesque views and strolling distance to all the sights. Victorian gazebo for relaxing outdoors in the ocean breezes. A continental breakfast is included. Comp bikes for guests use. **SEASONAL:** Open May-Oct **BROCHURE:** Yes [E11ACRI-4647]

Sheffield House	**Block Island RI**
The McQueenys	High St 02807
401-466-2494	**Res Times** 9am-9pm
	Fax 401-466-5067

Rates:	Pvt Bath 5	Shared Bath 2	Payment Terms:
Single	$ 50-140.00	$ 50-100.00	Check
Double	$ 50-140.00	$ 50-100.00	AE/DC/MC/V

The *Sheffield House* is an 1888 Queen Anne Victorian quietly set among perennial gardens within the Historic District of Block Island. It's seven guest rooms and country kitchen are furnished with antiques and family heirlooms along with a collection of local artists' works. Your hosts, Steve and Claire McQueeny, are knowledgeable and willing to help guests plan their relaxation or exploration. From the *Sheffield House* it is a five minute walk to the quaint village, ferry dock, many fine restaurants, interesting shops and galleries and the island's fine bathing beaches. Before setting out for your day, guests are invited to enjoy a generous complimentary continental breakfast in our country kitchen. The Irish sideboard provides an overflowing buffet-style breakfast of homebaked pastries, exquisite jams, fresh fruit, juices, herbal teas and freshly brewed coffee. Following a day of pursuing your favorite activities, guests can relax and enjoy pleasant conversation and a cool beverage on the wrap-around porch or in the private garden. While summer is the main season, don't forget the off-season. Not only are costs lower and the island less crowded, you'll soon learn why Native Americans called Block Island *"The Island of the Little God"*. **DISCOUNTS:** Senior citizens **RESERVATIONS:** Full deposit, 3 nights or longer 50% deposit to guarantee reservation, 14 day cancel notice for refund less $25 service fee **BROCHURE:** Yes **PERMITTED:** Drinking, limited smoking [Z07GP-RI2-4648]

*Joseph Reynolds House	**Bristol RI**
Richard & Wendy Anderson	956 Hope St 02809
401-254-0230	

Rates:	**Pvt Bath** 4	**Payment Terms:**
Single	$ 55-90.00	Check
Double	$ 55-90.00	

A *National Historic Landmark* that served are the headquarters of General Lafayette in 1778 and is the oldest three-story structure, c1693, in New England. Beautiful antique furnishing with active hosts in historical preservation. Continental breakfast included **BROCHURE:** Yes **PERMITTED:** Children **SEASONAL:** No [E11ACRI-4650]

**Fairfield By The Sea	**Greenhill RI**
Jeanne Ayers Lewis	527 Green Hill Beach Rd 02879

401-789-4717   **Res Times** 24 Hrs

Rates:	**Shared Bath** 2	**Payment Terms:**
Single	$ 55.00	Check
Double	$ 60.00	AE

This artist's contemporary home in an intimate country setting offers beauty and seclusion just south of US Rt 1 between Westerly and Wakefield Rhode Island, 20 mi east of Mystic, 25 mi west of Newport. Filled with an eclectic collection of art and an interesting library - stress reduction is the order of the day here in this relaxed atmosphere. Complimentary full breakfasts feature homemade hot breads, elegant fruit, farm fresh eggs along with many local Vermont items (your host, Jeanne, was raised on a Vermont farm and is a retired home economist). A perfect location for sightseeing, guests can visit Green Hill Beach on Block Island Sound, the Theatre-By-The-Sea in Matunuck just down the road, Martha's Vineyard, Cape Cod, Boston, Newport, Plymouth and Mystic Seaport. Activities include golf, tennis, sailing, nature trails, historical sights, numerous museums, shops featuring local craftsmen, antiquing galore, bird watching (be sure to bring binoculars) fresh and saltwater fishing, blue crabs, harvesting mussels and numerous fine restaurants with excellent dining. Fall colors and apple picking reach their height the last two weeks of October while winter offers skiing at Yawgoo Mtn. Come and relax with a walk in the rolling mist or winter snow - to find a roaring fire and good book waiting for you upon your return. **AIRPORT:** Providence-25 mi **DISCOUNTS:** Off-season **RESERVATIONS:** One night deposit within 5 days of booking; 14 day cancel policy less $10 service fee, bal due upon arrival, call to advise arrival times **BROCHURE:** Yes **PERMITTED:** Children, drinking, limited smoking **CONFERENCES:** Small conference facility [R10EPRI2-4654]

**Country Goose B&B	**Middletown RI**
Paula Kelley	563 Greenend Ave 02840
401-846-6308	**Res Times** 24 Hrs

Rates:	**Pvt Bath** 1	**Shared Bath** 3	**Payment Terms:**
Single	$ 65-95.00	$ 65-95.00	Check
Double	$ 65-95.000	$ 65-95.00	MC/V

The *Country Goose* is a charming country farmhouse, built in 1898, which is the original farmhouse that was used to farm this land for three generations. Nestled in a quiet country setting trimmed with its original gingerbread trim and old fashioned front porch, furnished with wicker and surrounded by flowers and trees. A distant view of the beach allows our guests to relax after a busy day in a comfortable setting and receive a quiet night's rest. The quaint country rooms are fur-

nished with family heirlooms and antiques with the large shared bathrooms making our guests feel "right at home". The Country Goose is located only minutes from the beaches, mansions, shopping, Tennis Hall of Fame, Norman Bird Sanctuary, yachting center and all other attractions on the island. Complimentary wine and cheese awaits your arrival, with a continental breakfast served each morning in surroundings of traditional country decor. **RESERVATIONS:** Full payment for weekends, one night deposit weekdays and weekends if late booking; five day cancel policy for refund, less than five day cancel notice, refund only if rebooked, rates do not include state taxes **SEASONAL:** No **PERMITTED:** Children, social drinking, smoking in designated areas only **BROCHURE:** Yes **DISCOUNTS:** Yes, 10/15 to 6/1 **AIRPORT:** Green-30 mins **PACKAGES:** *Weekdays*, Two days or more, less 15% with coupons to mansions and other Newport attractions [I09FPRI1-12553]

Lindseys Guest House	**Middletown RI**
Anne & David Lindsey	6 James St 02840
401-846-9386	

Rates:	Pvt Bath 1	Shared Bath 2	Payment Terms:
Single	$ 65.00	$ 55.00	Check
Double	$ 75.00	$ 65.00	MC/V

Enjoy a charming split level home in a residential setting with off-street parking and a large yard. Close to the famous sights in Newport and the famous Bellevue Avenue with its mansions, wharfs, boat tour operators, shops and well-known restaurants. The charming host/couple raised their seven children here and enjoy visiting with guests. Complimentary breakfast includes juice, cereals, muffins, jams (often homemade) coffee cake, Danish and a choice of hot beverages. **RESERVATIONS:** One night's deposit, 14

ancel policy less 10% **SEASONAL:** No **BROCHURE:** Yes
ITTED: Children, limited drinking, smoking [E09BCRI-4661]

Ilverthorpe Cottage   Narragansett RI
Chris & Rich Raggio   41 Robinson St 02882
401-789-2392

Rates:	**Pvt Bath** 3	**Shared Bath** 3	**Payment Terms:**
Single	$ 65.00	$ 50.00	Check
Double	$ 70.00	$ 60.00	

Restored Victorian residence c1886 just three blocks from the
beach offering guests stenciled walls, fresh flowers, beautiful
antique furnishings with lacy touches. Close to restaurants and
the finest mansions. A full breakfast is included. **SEASONAL:**
Open 5/15-10/15 **BROCHURE:** Yes **PERMITTED:** Children,
drinking and limited smoking [E11ACRI-4671]

Brinley Victorian Inn   Newport RI
Peter Carlisle/Claire Boslem   23 Brinley St 02840
800-999-8523 401-849-7645   **Res Times** 9am-9pm

Rates:	**Pvt Bath** 5	**Shared Bath** 4	**Payment Terms:**
Single	$ 85-95.00	$ 75-85.00	Check
Double	$ 95-105.00	$ 75-85.00	

Turn-of-the-century picture-perfect restoration for this Victorian
residence where the host/owners haven't overlooked anything,
including beautiful Victorian period gardens. The inside has been
perfectly decorated with antiques reminiscent of its former elegance
including lace and satin window treatments. Amenities include
evening mints, fresh flowers and champagne and wine for your
special occasions (added cost). Continental plus breakfast is
included. **RESERVATIONS:** One night's deposit at res time, 10 day
cancel policy for refund **SEASONAL:** No **BROCHURE:** Yes **PER-
MITTED:** Children 12-up, limited drinking [E11ACRI-4690]

Cliff Walk Manor   Newport RI
Bryan Babcock   82 Memorial Blvd 02840
401-847-1300   **Res Times** 24 Hrs

Rates:	**Pvt Bath** 25	**Payment Terms:**
Single	$ 85.00 EP	Check
Double	$ 95.00 EP	AE/DC/MC/V

Spectacular 1855 Mansion setting on five acres of grounds atop the world-famous Cliff Walk where you can enjoy watching the water see and Newport's famous mansions everywhere. A full-service resort including full gourmet dining on the premises, hot tub, and entertainment. **RESERVATIONS:** Deposit to hold room 48 hr cancel policy **SEASONAL:** Open 3/1-11/30 **BROCHURE:** Yes **PERMITTED:** Children, drinking, limited smoking **LANGUAGES:** Italian [E11ACRI-4694]

***Cliffside Inn**	**Newport RI**
Norbert & Annette Mede	2 Seaview Blvd 02840
800-845-1811 401-847-1811	**Res Times** 8am-8pm

Rates:	**Pvt Bath** 12	**Payment Terms:**
Single	$ 125-205.00	Check
Double	$ 125-205.00	AE/DC/MC/V

The *Cliffside Inn* was built in 1880 by the Governor of Maryland as a summer home. Later, it became the permanent residence of Beatrice Turner, an eccentric artist who painted over 1000 self-portraits during her lifetime. Today, *Cliffside* has been transformed into a beautiful Victorian Inn with fabulous period antiques and exquisite draperies. The parlor is a comfortable gathering place where the guest meet for afternoon appetizers and for the full gourmet breakfast in the morning. Some of the guest rooms feature such amenities as whirlpool tubs, fireplaces, skylights, clawfoot tubs, canopy beds and televisions. The *Cliffside Inn* is located on a quiet residential street near the beach and the famous Cliff Walk. Experience the grace, charm, beauty and elegance which is the *Cliffside Inn.* **AIRPORT:** TF Green Airport-45 mi. **PACKAGES:** *Winter,* inquire at res time **RESERVATIONS:** One night's deposit or 50% if staying longer than two nights to guarantee room; cancellation policy: deposits non-refundable but can be applied to future reservation within 12 months **SEASONAL:** No **BROCHURE:** Yes **PERMITTED:** Children (13-up), limited drinking **CONFERENCES:** Yes, The Governor's Suite hosts executive meetings and is a fully equipped conference facility **LANGUAGES:** German, French [R09EPRI2-15545]

Hydrangea House Inn   Newport RI

Grant Edmonton/Dennis Blair		16 Bellevue Ave 02840
800-945-4667 401-846-4435		**Res Times** 9am-10pm
		Fax 401-846-4435

Rates:	**Pvt Bath** 6	**Payment Terms:**
Single	$ 55-139.00	Check
Double	$ 55-139.00	MC/V

Located at the top of the Historic Hill, the *Hydrangea House Inn* is at the center of Newport's "Walking District", with some 80% of its sights and attractions accessible by foot, right from our front door. This Victorian townhouse, built in 1876, has been carefully restored. Its six guest rooms, all with private baths, are elegantly decorated each with its own sumptuous personality. Plush carpeting, thick cozy towels, crystal water glasses, long-stemmed goblets for your wine set-up and complimentary refreshments are some of the amenities for you to enjoy. The quiet sophistication and uniqueness of the Inn's decor reflects the careers of its innkeepers, who are art and antique dealers. The non-smoking policy assures each guest a fresh, clean atmosphere. Your day will start with our gratifying hot buffet breakfast served in the contemporary fine art gallery. For your enjoyment, we will serve you our own blend of fresh-ground *Hydrangea House Coffee*, fresh-squeezed orange juice, home baked bread and granola - as well as our incredible raspberry pancakes, perhaps, or seasoned scrambled eggs. The gallery also serves as a unique setting for small conferences and business meetings. We know you'll love it here, because we do. The *Boston Globe* said of the Inn, "*. . . in a city renowned for its lodging, the Hydrangea House Inn is not to be missed!*" *AAA Inspected and Approved, 1994.* RESERVATIONS: One night deposit, 50% deposit for stays longer than 3 days, 14 day cancel policy for refund, check-in 2 to not later than 8pm, check-out 11am, min stays of two days on weekends and three days on holidays and event weekends SEASONAL: No PERMITTED: Children, drinking BROCHURE: Yes AIRPORT: Providence RI-45 min [R08GPRI2-14030]

Inn Of Jonathan Bowen   Newport RI

Paul Brandis		29 Pelham St 02840
401-846-3324		

Rates:	**Pvt Bath** 8	**Shared Bath** 3	**Payment Terms:**
Single	$ 130-155.00	$ 95.00	Check

Double $ 130-155.00 $ 95.00   MC/V

Registered on the *National Historic Register* following its faithful restoration in 1987, this twelve room home has been divided into six private suites that include woodburning fireplace and/or stove, plenty of period decor including brass beds in some rooms and antique furnishings. This is an Inn with comfortable, tastefully furnished rooms with armories, chests, brass beds, tiled baths and a myriad of antiques. A gourmet buffet breakfast is included in the Common Room. You'll enjoy all of the beautiful mansions and sights in Newport while staying here. Special off-season packages are available. **RESERVATIONS:** Deposit required at res time, 14 day cancel policy, check-out 11am **SEASONAL:** Rates vary **BROCHURE:** Yes **PERMITTED:** Children, drinking **CONFERENCES:** Yes for small seminars and meetings. [R02BCRI-4702]

**Melville House			**Newport RI**
Vince De Rico/David Horan			39 Clarke St 02940
401-847-0640			**Res Times** 7:30am-10pm
			Fax 401-847-0956
Rates:	**Pvt Bath** 5	**Shared Bath** 2	**Payment Terms:**
Single	$ 60-125.00	$ 50-100.00	Check
Double	$ 60-125.00	$ 50-100.00	AE/MC/V

Staying at the *Melville House* is like a step back into the past. *The Melville House*, built c. 1750, is listed on the *National Register of Historic Places*. We are located in the heart of the Historic Hill section of Newport, the streets of which are still lit by gas. The French General Rochambeau quartered some of his troops here when they fought in the Revolutionary War under President George Washington. The Vernon House, where Washington, Rochambeau and Major General Marqis de Lafayette met, is across the street. Just down the block is the building that still houses America's oldest military unit in continuous service under its original charter in 1741, the Newport Artillery Company. Although *The Melville House* is situated on one of the quietest streets in Newport, it is only one block away from Thames Street and the harborfront where many of the city's finest restaurants, antique shops and galleries can be found. We are also within walking distance to Newport's many places of worship such as Touro Synagogue (the oldest in the U.S.), Trinity Church (built in 1726) and St Mary's Church (where President John F. Kennedy married Jacqueline). The Tennis Hall of Fame, the famous and lavish mansions of the Vanderbilts, Astors and the Belmonts, The Naval War College and Newport's finest ocean beaches are just a very short drive. The seven rooms of the *Melville House* are furnished in traditional Colonial style. Off-street parking is available. Breakfast features homemade granola, muffins and various other baked items such as buttermilk biscuits, bagels, scones, stuffed French toast, Portuguese quiche, Yankee cornbread and Rhode Island Johnnycakes. An afternoon "tea" is served every day. Guests can enjoy refreshments or a glass of sherry and biscotti, as we discuss the days' activities and our favorite places for dinner. **RESERVATIONS:** One night's deposit, check-in by 8pm **PERMITTED:** Children 13+, drinking **SEASONAL:** Rates vary **BROCHURE:** Yes **DISCOUNTS:** Weekdays, off-season, long term stays **CONFERENCES:** Yes, call for information **AIR-PORT:** Providence TF Green-25 mi [R07GPRI2-4707]

**On The Point B&B	**Newport RI**
Sheila & George Perry	102 Third St 02840
401-846-8377	

Rates:	**Pvt Bath** 2	**Shared Bath** 2	**Payment Terms:**
Single	$ 90-110.00	$ 70-90.00	Check
Double	$ 95-125.00	$ 75-95.00	MC/V

On The Point Bed & Breakfast is conveniently located just one and one half blocks from Narragansett Bay and a very short walk to downtown Newport. This one hundred year old Victorian is in one of Newport's most historic districts. The *"Point Area"* was subdivided by the Quakers in the early 1700's and has more restored homes of the era than any other area. *On The Point Bed & Breakfast* has relaxing, beautifully furnished accommodations with either king size or twin beds in all rooms. Breakfast, which includes a fresh fruit salad and wonderful pastries, is served in antique wicker surroundings. There are nearby public tennis courts and Newport's best gourmet and seafood restaurants are a short walk. Your hosts are local history buffs and love to share their extensive collection of early Newport prints and turn-of-the-century photographs. Guests are also invited to enjoy the collection of Newport inspired books in the Victorian ambiance of this charming home. **RESERVATIONS:** First night's deposit or credit card number to guarantee reservation, bal due upon arrival **PERMITTED:** Children, drinking **BROCHURE:** Yes **DISCOUNTS:** 40% off-season (Nov-April), extended stays of one week and longer **AIRPORT:** Providence-40 min **PACKAGES:** *Dinner Package*, off-season [R07GPRI2-16934]

**Rhode Island House	**Newport RI**
John Rich/Michael Dupre	77 Rhode Island Ave 02840
401-848-7787	**Res Times** 8am-8pm

Rates:	**Pvt Bath** 5	**Payment Terms:**
Single	$ 105-225.00	Check
Double	$ 105-225.00	AE/MC/V

Dating from 1882, this was the summer home for Thomas R Hunter and his family and today guests can enjoy a traditional stay in this Grand Victorian residence while vacationing at beautiful Newport - *"America's first resort"*. Large and spacious, your hosts have recently decorated the entire home to make guests comfortable in this elegant residence with large bay windows that filter sunlight into the light and airy rooms with wide open porches for relaxing during the day and early evenings. The fine linens, tasteful details and fireplaces of each private guest room echo themes of Newport's past. All rooms have a private bath, some including the option of jacuzzi, private deck or suites. This residence is just blocks from Easton Pond, near First Beach on Historic Hill. Historic Newport offers guests a chance to tour many of the fine mansions, the Tennis Hall of Fame, Newport Art Museum and experience traditional New England seafood cuisine at it's finest. A full breakfast is included. **RESERVATIONS:** One night's deposit or 50% of entire stay within 7 days of booking to guarantee reservation, bal due upon check-in, 15 day cancel policy (30 days for multiple-room bookings) for refund less 10% service fee, minimum stay weekends, maximum two persons per room **SEASONAL:** Rates vary **AIRPORT:** Providence-30 mi **DISCOUNTS:** Off-season **LANGUAGES:** French, Spanish **BROCHURE:** Yes **PERMITTED:** Children 13-up, drinking [Z08GPRI2-8412]

**State House Inn	**Providence RI**
Frank & Monica Hopton	43 Jewett St 02908
401-785-1235	**Res Times** 9am-10pm
	Fax 401-351-4261

Rates:	**Pvt Bath** 10	**Payment Terms:**
Single	$ 65-95.00	Check
Double	$ 65-95.00	AE/MC/V

Enjoy your stay in the capitol city of Rhode Island in this conveniently located 100 year old inn. The State House Neighborhood is currently being considered for a *Historic Neighborhood Designation*. Your hosts have completely restored and renovated this historic location into a charming Bed & Breakfast Inn offering king and queen beds, Colonial and Shaker reproduction furnishings with fireplaces and canopy beds in some of the guest rooms. This perfect location is convenient to all of the state offices and sights in downtown Providence. A hearty and healthy full breakfast is included in the rate. **AIRPORT:** Providence (Green Airport) just 5 miles. **RESERVATIONS:** 50% deposit, check-in by 10 pm **BROCHURE:** Yes **PERMITTED:** Children, drinking and limited smoking. [Z07GPRI2-11948]

**The Villa	**Westerly RI**
Jerry Maiorano	190 Shore Rd 02841
800-722-9240 401-596-1054	**Res Times** 9am-9pm
	Fax 401-596-6268
Rates: **Pvt Bath** 5	**Payment Terms:**
Single $ 70-170.00	Check
Double $ 75-175.00	AE/MC/V

From the moment you arrive at *The Villa*, you will fall in love with this *"wonderful land of Amore"*. Escape to this perfect romantic hideaway of flower gardens, Italian porticos and verandas, where you can swim in a sparkling, sapphire pool, surrounded by lush green plants and spectacular sunshine. Where soothing, hot waters calm and massage you while you relax in the outdoor jacuzzi spa. Open year-round, *The Villa* is the ideal setting for weddings, honeymoons and rekindling romance. Imagine yourself in a cozy, private suite in the middle of winter, gazing at the hypnotic flames of a sensuous, crackling fire. Summers here are warm and golden with cool ocean breezes and festive nights of music and Italian cuisine. Of *The Villa's* five attractive suites, some offer fireplaces and jacuzzi and all have cable TV, a/c and private baths. A pleasing complimentary buffet breakfast is served at the pool house, at poolside or in your private room. The romance of Italy awaits you. Experience the magic yourself! *The Villa* is located at the crossroads of historic Westerly and Watch Hill and is close to Mystic, Misquamicut Beach and Foxwoods Resort and Casino. **RESERVATIONS:** Deposit required to guarantee reservation **SEASONAL:** No **PERMITTED:** Limited children, limited pets, limited drinking, limited smoking **BRO-CHURE:** Yes **LANGUAGES:** Italian **DISCOUNTS:** *AAA*, Weekly stays, corporate, travel agents **PACKAGES:** *Romantic Rendezvous* (Two nights stay, champagne and dinner for two [I04GPRI2-14035]

Cookie Jar B&B	**Wyoming RI**
Dick & Madelein Sohl	64 Kingstown Rd 02898
800-767-4262 401-539-2680	**Res Times** 10am-9pm

Rates:	Pvt Bath 1	Shared Bath 2	Payment Terms:
Single	$ 58.50	$ 54.00	Check
Double	$ 65.00	$ 60.00	

The heart of our home, the living room, was built in 1732 and served as a blacksmith's shop for many years. Later, the forge was removed and a large granite fireplace was built by an American Indian stone-mason. The original wood ceiling, handhewn beams and granite walls remain today. Initially, the property was called *The Perry Plantation* and yes, they had two slaves who lived above the blacksmith shop. Over the generations, rooms were added to the smithy and some 65 years ago this building was used as a restaurant and called *The Cookie Jar Tea Room*; therefore, we thought it appropriate to call our Bed and Breakfast *The Cookie Jar*. There are only some three acres left of the original plantation. On the property we have two homes, a barn, swimming pool, fifty plus fruit trees, grape vines, berry bushes, a flower garden and an acre of grass. A perfect environment for rest and relaxation. Nearby are many beautiful white sand beaches, scenic drives, shoreline attractions and historical sights. Take day trips to see the Newport Mansions, Mystic Seaport or Cape Cod. Visit the fishing villages of Gaulee or Stonington, take a ferry to Block Island or go deep sea fishing. **RESERVATIONS:** 50% deposit required within 5 days of booking to guarantee reservation **SEASONAL:** No **PERMITTED:** Children, drinking **BROCHURES:** Yes **DISCOUNTS:** 10% off for 4 nights or longer, 7th night free **AIRPORT:** TF Green-25 min [R09FPRI2-18171]

Block Island

1661 INN
401-466-2421

ADRIAN
401-466-2693

ART
CONSTRUCTION
STUDIO
401-466-2924

ATLANTIC INN
401-466-5883

BALLARDS INN
401-466-2231

BARRINGTON
401-466-5510

BAYBERRY HEATH
401-466-2838

BELLEVUE
401-466-2389

BELLEVUE HOUSE
401-466-2912

**BLUE DORY INN
800-992-7290

CABLES INN
401-466-2213

CAPT WILLIS
HOUSE
401-466-5883

CONTINENTAL B&B
401-466-5136

CORNER HOUSE

401-466-2624

DRIFTWIND
GUESTS
401-466-5548

F CASEY INN
401-466-5502

GABLES INN
401-466-2213

GOTHIC COTTAGE
OCEAN VILLA
401-466-2918

GUEST HOUSE
401-466-2676

HARBOR VIEW
GUEST HOUSE
401-466-2807

HARDY SMITH
HOUSE
401-466-2466

HIGHVIEW
COUNTRY INN
401-466-5912

HOTEL MANISSES
401-466-2063

INN AT OLD
HARBOR
401-466-2212

ISLAND HOME
401-466-5944

ISLAND MANOR
RESORT
401-466-5567

LEWIS FARM
GUEST HOUSE
401-466-2113

LILAC COTTAGE
401-466-5954

MILL POND
COTTAGES
401-466-2423

MITCHELL
COTTAGE
401-446-5053

NATIONAL HOTEL
800-252-2449

NEPTUNE HOUSE
401-466-2988

NEW SHOREHAM
HOUSE INN
800-272-2601

OLD TOWN INN
401-466-5958

POND VIEW B&B
401-466-2927

ROSE FARM INN
401-466-2021

SAMUEL PECKHAM
INN
401-466-2439

SASAFRASH
401-466-5486

SEA BREEZE INN
401-466-2275

*SEACREST INN
401-466-2882

**SHEFFIELD
HOUSE
401-466-2494

SMUGGLERS COVE
401-466-2828

SPRING HOUSE
800-234-9263

STAR COTTAGE
401-466-2842

WATER STREET
INN
800-825-6254

WHITE HOUSE
401-466-2653

WILLOW GROVE
401-466-2896

Bristol
*JOSEPH
REYNOLDS HOUSE
401-254-0230

ROCKWELL HOUSE
401-254-0230

WILLIAM GRANT
INN
401-253-4222

Carolina
BRENDAS B&B
401-364-3608

Charlestown
GENERAL STANTON

401-364-8888

INN THE MEADOW
401-789-1473

NORDIC LODGE
401-783-4515

ONE WILLOW BY
THE SEA B&B
401-364-0802

WINDSWEPT FARM
401-364-6292

Exeter
DOVECREST
401-539-7795

Glocester
FREEMAN FARM
B&B
401-568-6561

Greenhill
**FARIFIELD BY
THE SEA
401-789-4717

Hopkinton City
GEN THURSTON
HOUSE-1763
401-377-9049

Jamestown
BAY VOYAGE INN
401-423-2100

CANDLEWICK
401-423-2692

JAMESTOWN B&B
410-423-1338

LIONEL CHAMPLIN
HOUSE
401-423-2782

MARY W MURPHY
401-423-1338

Kingston
ADMIRAL DEWEY
INN
401-783-2090

HEDGEROW B&B
401-783-2671

Lincoln
WHIPPLE-CULLEN
FARMSTEAD
401-333-1899

Little Compton
BALLYVOREEN
401-655-4396

Middletown
ATLANTIC HOUSE
401-847-7259

B&B N'MORE
401-846-3646

BARTRAMS B&B
401-846-2259

BLISS MINE ROAD
HOUSE
401-846-2979

**COUNTRY
GOOSE B&B
401-846-6308

FINNEGANS INN
SHADOW LAWN

401-847-0902

HEDGEGATE
401-846-3906

***LINDSEYS GUEST
HOUSE**
401-846-9386

MAUDE KERRS
B&B
401-847-5997

PICKHAMS GUEST
HOME
401-846-2382

POLLYS PLACE
401-847-2160

SEA BREEZE
401-847-5628

STONE TOWERS
401-846-3227

STONEYARD
401-847-0494

WOLCOTT HOUSE
BY THE SEA
401-846-9376

Misquamicut
ANDREA HOTEL
401-348-8788

*Misquamicut
Beach*
OCEAN VIEW
401-596-7170

Narragansett
1900 HOUSE

401-789-7971

23 PERKINS
401-783-9158

CASA MARABELE
401-782-6852

CHESTNUT HOUSE
401-789-5335

DUCK HARBOR
401-783-3495

EDWARD EARLE
HOUSE
401-789-4363

ENDLESS SUMMER
401-789-0615

FOUR GABLES
401-789-6948

GRINNELL INN

HISTORIC HOME
401-789-7746

*HOUSE OF SNEE
401-783-9494

***ILVERTHORPE
COTTAGE**
401-789-2392

KENYON FARMS
401-783-7123

LINDEMERE
401-783-2798

LOUIS SHERRY
COTTAGE

401-783-8626

MAISON
BIENVENUE
401-783-1190

MON REVE
401-783-2846

MURPHYS B&B
401-789-1824

NANSEA BY THE
BAY
401-783-4045

OLD CLERK
HOUSE
401-783-8008

PHOENIX INN
401-783-1918

PIER HOUSE
401-783-4704

PLEASANT
COTTAGE
401-783-6895

REGINA COTTAGE
401-783-1875

RHYNERS GUEST
HOUSE
401-783-6001

RICHARD/JOYCE
SAINT ONGE
401-789-7695

ROCKPORT
COTTAGE
401-783-2647

SEA GULL GUEST
HOUSE
401-783-4636

SEAFIELD
COTTAGE
401-783-2432

SOUTHWEST WIND
ACRES
401-783-5860

STARR COTTAGE
INN
401-783-2411

STEPHEN FARMER
401-789-0763

SWAN COTTAGE
B&B
401-783-4391

VICTORIAN LADY
401-789-6222

WHITE ROSE
401-789-0181

Newport
1812 HOUSE
401-847-1188

1855 MARSHALL
SLOCUM HOUSE
401-847-3787

503 SPRING
401-847-3132

ADMIRAL BENBOW
800-343-2863

ADMIRAL

FARRAGUT
800-343-2863

ADMIRAL FITZROY
800-343-2863

AILINAS
401-847-3903

ALEXANDER JACK
JR HOUSE

ANCESTRAL
WOODBINE MANOR

BELLE REVE INN
401-846-4262

BELLEVUE HOUSE
401-847-1828

BETHSHAN B&B
401-846-1777

BITTERSWEET
GUEST HOUSE
401-849-7567

BLISS COTTAGE
401-846-6932

BLUE STONE B&B
401-846-8250

*BRINLEY
VICTORIAN INN
800-999-8523

BURBANK ROSE
401-849-9457

CASTLE KEEP
401-846-0362

CLIFF VIEW GUEST
HOUSE
401-846-0885

**CLIFF WALK
MANOR**
401-847-1300

****CLIFFSIDE INN**
800-845-1811

CLOVER HILL
GUEST HOUSE
401-847-7094

COMMODORE
PERRY
800-343-2863

COVELL GUEST
HOUSE
401-847-8872

EASTONS INN ON
THE BEACH
401-846-0310

ELLERY PARK
HOUSE
401-847-6320

ELLIOTT ROSS
HOUSE
401-849-9425

ELM STREET INN
401-849-7397

ELM TREE
COTTAGE
800-882-3ELM

FG HANSON
401-846-6932

FLAG QUARTERS
401-849-4543

FLOWER GARDEN
GUESTS
401-846-3119

FRANCIS MALBONE
HOUSE
401-846-0392

HALIDON HILL
GUEST HOUSE
401-847-8318

HAMMETT HOUSE
800-548-9417

HARRIS B&B
401-847-5626

HARBORSIDE INN
401-846-6600

HOSPITALITY
HOUSE
401-849-9439

**HYDRANGEA
HOUSE**
800-945-4667

INN AT CASTLE
HILL
401-849-3800

*INN OF
JONATHAN BOWEN*
401-846-3324

INN ON LONG
ROOF
800-225-3522

INNTOWNE
800-457-7803

IRISH DANDELION

IVY LODGE
401-849-6865

JAILHOUSE INN
401-847-4638

JENKINS GUEST
HOUSE
401-847-6801

JOHN BANISTER
HOUSE
401-846-0050

JOHN EASTON
HOUSE
401-849-6246

LA FORGE
COTTAGE
401-847-4400

LOWELL MANOR
401-849-8155

MA GALLAGHERS
401-849-3975

MARIONS GUEST
HOUSE
401-847-6938

MARTINS B&B
401-847-5630

**MELVILLE
HOUSE**
401-847-0640

MERRITT HOUSE
GUESTS
401-847-4289

MILL STREET INN
401-849-9500

MOULTON
WEAVER HOUSE
401-847-0133

MOUNT VERNON
INN
401-846-6314

NELSONS B&B
401-849-2982

NEW
FOUNDLANDER
401-846-2483

OCEANCLIFF
401-849-9000

OLD DENNIS
HOUSE
401-846-1324

**ON THE POINT
B&B**
401-846-8377

ONE BLISS
401-846-5329

OSBORN HOUSE
401-847-4199

PILGRIM HOUSE
800-525-8373

POPLAR STREET
GUEST HOUSE

800-537-1430

QUEEN ANNE INN
401-846-5676

RHODE ISLAND HOUSE
401-848-7787

RICKY'S PLACE
401-846-2114

ROSE ISLAND LIGHTHOUSE
401-847-4242

SAMUEL HONEY HOUSE
401-847-2669

SANFORD-COVELL VILLA MARIA
401-847-0206

SARAH KENDAL HOUSE
401-846-7976

SPRING STREET INN
401-847-4767

STELLA MARIS INN
401-849-2862

SUNNYSIDE MANSION
401-849-3114

THAMES STREET INN
401-847-4459

TURN-OF-CENTURY

401-846-6113

VICTORIAN LADIES
401-849-9960

VILLA LIBERTE
401-846-7444

*WATERVIEW
401-847-4425

WAYSIDE
401-847-0302

*WILLOWS OF NEWPORT
401-846-5486

WM FLUDDER HOUSE
800-225-5087

YANKEE PEDDLER
401-846-1323

YELLOW COTTAGE
401-847-6568

North Kingstown
BITTERSWEET FARM
401-885-0053

JOHN COZZENS HOUSE
401-295-1369

MEADOWLAND
401-294-4168

MORANS
401-294-3497

WILLIAM

HOLLOWAY HOUSE
401-295-1528

Peacedale
GOING MY WAY
401-789-3479

Portsmouth
2108 HOUSE
401-683-0849

BROWNS BAYVIEW GUEST HOUSE
401-683-0155

HOLIDAYS B&B
401-683-2416

MILLSTONES
401-683-9225

TWIN SPRUCE TOURIST
401-683-0673

Providence
HELEN MEIER B&B
401-751-5914

LANSING HOUSE
401-421-7194

LAST RESORT BY THE BAY
401-433-1577

OLD COURT B&B
401-757-2002

STATE HOUSE INN
401-785-1235

Richmond

COOKIE JAR B&B
401-539-2680

COUNTRY ACRES
B&B
401-364-9134

Saunderstown
QUARRY HOUSE
B&B
401-295-2805

Smithfield
PAST THYMES
401-231-2173

South Kingstown
ALMOST HEAVEN
401-789-9272

NARROW RIVER
COTTAGE
401-783-9751

Tiverton
BONNIEBIELD
COTTAGE
401-624-6364

SQUIRE CHASE
HOUSE
401-624-9873

Wakefield
BB HIGHLAND
401-783-2408

GARDNER HOUSE
401-789-1250

LARCHWOOD INN
401-783-5454

ROADS END

401-783-7547

SHANAMAR
401-789-8059

WHIPPOORWILL
FARM
401-789-8331

Warren
NATHANIEL
PORTER INN
401-245-6622

Warwick
DEMASI LODGING
401-781-8433

ENCHANTED
COTTAGE
401-732-0439

OPEN GATE INN
401-884-4490

PAWTUXET B&B
401-941-4011

Watch Hill
HARTLEY'S GUEST
HOUSE
401-348-8253

INN AT WATCH
HILL
401-596-0665

NARRAGANSETT
INN
401-596-0665

OCEAN HOUSE

WATCH HILL INN

800-356-9314

Weekapaug
WEEKAPAUG INN
401-322-0301

West Kingston
STONE COTTAGE
401-789-0039

West Warwick
Westerly
CORNERSTONE
INN
401-322-3020

GRANDVIEW B&B
INN
401-596-6384

HARBOUR HOUSE
401-348-8998

J LIVINGSTONS
INN
401-322-0249

LONGVUE GUEST
HOUSE
401-322-0465

SEVEN GRANITE
ST 800-441-6384

*SHELTER
HARBOR
401-322-8883

SHORE INN
401-348-8637

THIRTY SEVEN
ELM
401-596-6849

**VILLA MALORANO
800-722-9240

WOODY HILL
GUEST HOUSE
401-322-0452

Wickford
JOHN UPDIKE
HOUSE
401-294-4905

MEADOWLAND
401-294-4168

SPARROWS NEST
401-295-1142

Wyoming
****COOKIE JAR
B&B**
800-767-4262

WAY STOP
401-539-7233

Vermont

Inn At Highview | **Andover VT
Greg Bohan | RR 1 Box 201   05143
802-875-2724 |

Rates:	**Pvt Bath** 8	**Payment Terms:**
Single	$ 80-115.00	Check
Double	$ 90-125.00	MC/V

High on East Hill, with panoramic views of the surrounding mountains, sits *The Inn at Highview*, an immaculately restored 18th Century farmhouse filled with antique furnishings, but relaxingly unpretentious and comfortable. *Highview* is truly a step back in time to a Vermont you thought only existed in your dreams and in Hollywood movies, at the same time being convenient to all of the modern reasons for visiting Vermont ... Okemo Mountain Ski Area, the Villages of Weston (home to the Weston Playhouse, Weston Priory and Vermont Country Store), and Chester are all within a fifteen minute drive. Winding through the Inn's seventy-two acres is a network of breath-taking hiking and x-country ski trails which connect with others for an uninterrupted network comprising 15km. After you've had your exercise, put your feet up and relax by the fire, enjoy our sauna, or, in summer, have a dip in our rock garden swimming pool overlooking the valley below. Our country dining room has become well-known for its excellent Italian cuisine available only to Inn guests to guarantee attentive service. For small retreats and business meetings, we offer an excellent conference facility with full conference support services. A full complimentary breakfast is included. **RESERVATIONS:** One night's deposit or credit card number; 10 day cancel policy for refund, less than 10 day notice, refund only if room is rebooked **SEASONAL:** No **PERMITTED:** Limited children, limited pets, drinking **BROCHURE:** Yes **CONFERENCES:** Full conference facility; complete audio, video, fax, copier and services (word processing, chart and graph making) **LANGUAGES:** Italian, Spanish **DISCOUNTS:** Yes, inquire at res time **AIRPORT:** Hartford CT-100 mi/2 hrs **PACKAGES:** *Meeting, Summer Week, Holiday Weekend* [R07GPVT2-16520]

Arlington Inn   **Arlington VT**

Mark & Deborah Gagnon   Historic Rt 7A 05250
800-443-9442 802-375-6532   **Res Times** 9am-5pm

Rates: **Pvt Bath** 13   **Payment Terms:**
Single $ 70-180.00   AE/CB/DISC/MC/V
Double $ 70-180.00

THE ARLINGTON INN
ARLINGTON, VERMONT

This beautiful Greek Revival Mansion is the perfect place to step back in time and relive yesteryear. Once you enter the Inn with its gleaming wood floors and splendid Victorian antique furnishings, you begin to imagine yourself as part of a bygone era. Your hosts have taken care of every detail for a memorable stay - including beautifully furnishing and decorating each guest room in its own special way - including private baths for all rooms. The Inn boasts an *award winning (Travel Holiday) dining room* where your chef uses only fresh provisions to create his sumptuous fare. In Spring, Summer and Fall, the beautiful grounds surrounding the Inn offer tennis on the grounds as well as nearby hiking, biking, golf, swimming, canoeing and fishing. Winter brings the magic of snow with world-class cross country and downhill skiing nearby. Although the Town of Arlington has remained the picture of *"small town America"* that lives in all of our thoughts, its close proximity to Manchester and Bennington provide a myriad of activities including exciting antique-hunting. A full breakfast begins your day. **RESERVATIONS:** One night's deposit, 14 day cancel policy for refund **PERMITTED:** Children, drinking **BROCHURE:** Yes **AIRPORT:** Albany-1 hr **DISCOUNTS:** Repeat guests **LANGUAGES:** French [I08GPVT2-2797]

Blue Haven Christian B&B   **Bellows Falls VT**

Helene Champagne   Rt 1 Box 328 05101
802-463-9008

Rates: **Pvt Bath** 4   **Shared Bath** 2   **Payment Terms:**
Single $ 58.00 $ 48.00   Check
Double $ 78.00 $ 68.00   AE/MC/V

Innkeeper/artist, Helene, warmly welcomes guests to her creatively decorated and furnished Inn - a former country school. The lovingly restored series of clapboard buildings retain the hardy aura of the 1830 school house. Your charming hostess has personalized every corner with personalized touches to insure the guests comfort and enjoyment. The country feeling begins with original wide-plank flooring in the common rooms and a working, massive stone fireplace that boasts stones from travels here and abroad. Special touches of goose-down comforters, coverlets, bed canopies of wonderful fabrics, Helene's art and hand-painted furniture appear throughout the Inn as she tried to make each guest room a "little jewel". A festive breakfast is set with colorful antique dishes and includes special recipes for homemade granola, pancakes or French toast, Apple-Cranberry-Pecan muffins - and in season, wild blackberries and raspberries picked fresh from nearby - all served with plenty of conversation in a beautiful rambling, wood warm country kitchen. Daytime activities nearby include art shows, canoeing, cycling, fishing, flea markets, hiking, historical walking tours, Christmas shops, antiquing, swimming, theater, skiing, x-country and downhill, or simply getting comfortable. Sip mulled cider and put-up your feet and browse a broad art library, play a tune on the mellow upright piano, watching TV and games, whatever you please. **DISCOUNTS:** *AARP, AAA*, mid-week, off-season **AIRPORT** Hartford's Bradly-1.5 hrs; Boston-2 hrs; Keene-NH 20 min **PACKAGES:** Yes, please inquire at res time **RESERVATIONS:** One night's deposit **SEASONAL:** No **BROCHURE:** Yes **PERMITTED:** Children; drinking. **CONFERENCES:** Yes for 12-30 persons. **LANGUAGES:** French [I10DPVT-14498]

Eastwood House			**Bethel VT**
Christine & Ron Diamond			River Street 05032
802-234-9686			

Rates:	**Pvt Bath** 5	**Shared Bath** 2	**Payment Terms:**
Single	$ 40-65.00	$ 45-60.00	Check
Double	$ 40-65.00	$ 45-60.00	AE/MC/V

Beautiful Federal-style architecture in this 1816 residence built as a stagecoach stop-over and still serving travelers today! Five working fireplaces (four are in bedrooms), original floors, hardware and hand-stenciled walls reminds guest of another era. You'll be surrounded by beautiful scenery including mountains just in the distance. A full Yankee breakfast gets everyone off to a fresh start each day. **RESERVATIONS:** Deposit required to hold room **SEASONAL:** No **BROCHURE:** Yes **PERMITTED:** Children, limited smoking [E11ACVT-2809]

Aplenrose Inn	**Bondville VT**
Rosemarie Strine	Winhall Hollow Rd 05340
802-297-2750	

Rates:		**Payment Terms:**
Pvt Bath 9		Check
Single	$ 45-65.00	MC/V
Double	$ 45-65.00	

Cozy atmosphere in this hideaway that's convenient and within minutes of the Volvo Tennis Tournament and ski slopes. Full breakfast included, MAP winters. Fireplace in dining room and lounge. Tennis and swimming are nearby. **BROCHURE:** Yes **PERMITTED:** Children and limited smoking **SEASONAL:** No **LANGUAGES:** German [E11ACVT-2813]

Hugging Bear Inn & Shoppe	**Chester VT**
Georgette Thomas	Main St 05143
800-325-0519 802-875-2412	**Res Times** 9am-10pm

Rates:		**Payment Terms:**
Pvt Bath 6		Check
Single	$ 55-65.00	AE/DC/MC/V
Double	$ 75-95.00	

Bed, Breakfast & Bears! This lovely Victorian Inn, built in 1850, is located on the green and is set in the heart of Chester's historic district. It is difficult to miss as there are bears on the lawn, bears on the porch, bears peering out of the windows and bears in every nook and cranny of the Inn. The six bedrooms have private baths and are simply furnished with various teddy bear motifs, including a teddy bear in every bed. There are three family rooms for guests with TV, toys, games and a fireplace. Sun streams in the bay window of the dining room where a hearty Vermont breakfast is served. Some of the favorite entrees are apple pancakes and French toast. The attached shop has four rooms with over 4000 different types of teddy bears and **bearaphernalia**. It is a collector's paradise, as well as fun for the playful at heart. Nearby guests can enjoy skiing, sledding, swimming, antiquing and delightful shopping. The *Hugging Bear* will be a part of the pleasant memories of childhood for those fortunate enough to spend some magical nights in bear country, Vermont style. Children of all ages are welcomed. **AIRPORT:** Boston Logan-3 hrs; Albany-2 hrs; Hartford-2 hrs **RESERVATIONS:** 50% non-refundable deposit required within 7 days of booking, two day min on holidays and high season weekends **SEASONAL:** Closed Thanksgiving and Christmas **BROCHURE:** Yes **PERMITTED:** Children, drinking, limited pets [R10EPVT2-2832]

Inn At Highview Chester VT
Greg Bohan
802-875-2724

Rates:	Pvt Bath 8	Payment Terms:
Single	$ 80-115.00	Check
Double	$ 90-125.00	MC/V

Refer to the same listing name under Andover VT for a complete description. [M07GPVT2-17784]

Inn Victoria Chester VT
KC & Tom Lanagan   On The Green   05143
800-732-4288 802-875-4288

Rates:	Pvt Bath 7	Payment Terms:
Single	$ 65-150.00	Check
Double	$ 65-150.00	MC/V

"The most romantic Inn in Southern Vermont", *Vermont Green Mountain Guide*. *Inn Victoria*, the perfect getaway, where upon arrival you can relax with afternoon tea, sit on the front porch in antique wicker and watch the world go by, take a nap in a queen size bed laden with embroidered pillows, or soak in the rose-scented bubbles in a sunken tub for two. A perfect start to the first day on your stay is a sumptuous breakfast served on antique china. From our "on the green" location in picturesque Chester, you can

walk to shops and restaurants. In the surrounding area, go antiquing, golfing, boating, swimming, biking or hiking on the Appalachian or the Long Trail. Attend an auction, summer theatre or polo, or drive the short distance to three major ski areas. There are many interesting things to add to your enjoyment while at the *Inn Victoria*. On

Saturday evening, your hosts, KC and Tom, open the *Inn Victoria*, by reservation only, to a very elegant dinner party where the menu might include Vermont Smokehouse specialties, Maple Apple Pie and always Champagne and Chocolate. We also host special weekends throughout the year - *Overture to Christmas, Murder Mysteries, Country Fairs, Beer Brewing* and a *Quilt Festival, Victorian Tea Party* and *Vintage Fashion Show*. Each is a special opportunity to getaway, relax and have some interesting activities scheduled. *Inn Victoria's* own *Teapot Shop* is just next door and features teapots for collectors and drinkers from local artists, as well as from artisans from around the world. **RESERVATIONS:** Credit card number for one night's deposit to guarantee reservation, two week cancel policy for refund **PERMITTED:** Children, drinking, smoking **BROCHURE:** Yes **CONFERENCES:** Large rooms with fireplace, conversation table, comfortable seating with a kitchen perfect for cooking class **DISCOUNTS:** Yes, inquire at res time **AIRPORT:** Albany NY-2 hrs; Bradley-1-1/2 hr; Boston-3 hrs [I07FPVT1-14063]

**Stone Hearth Inn	**Chester VT**
Don & Janet Strohmeyer	Rt 11 West 05143
802-875-2525	**Res Times** 8am-10pm

Rates:	**Pvt Bath** 10	**Payment Terms:**
Single	$ 45-60.00	DIS/MC/V
Double	$ 60-100.00	

Relax and leave stress, problems and the phone behind and visit this lovely, informal 1810 Country Inn known for its traditional Vermont Hospitality! All the rooms have been lovingly restored while retaining the original features including beams, fireplaces and wide-pine floors. An attached barn has been converted into a comfortable common room providing guests with a perfect New England atmosphere including a fieldstone fireplace for chilly evenings. Guest can relax or enjoy some of the many activities such as table tennis, pool or one of the many board games. Every room invites guests to relax and enjoy your home away from home. An inviting library awaits your choice for curling up with before the original "Stone Hearth". Outdoor activities abound year-round for everyone's taste. Bike tours, walking tours, x-country & alpine skiing, sledding, snowmobiling and for that perfect experience, an evening candlelight sleigh ride that's superb! To sooth those aches guests can choose one of the private whirlpool spas, available at a modest added cost. A full country breakfast is included with other meals available in the English Pub or a candlelight dining room for dinner (advanced res required). Guests won't forget the "Nutcracker Suite" featuring German nutcrackers, cuckoo clocks and a collection of fine beer steins. **RESERVATIONS:** One night's deposit in advance, 14 day cancel policy for refund **SEASONAL:** No **BROCHURE:** Yes **PERMITTED:** Children, drinking, limited smoking **CONFERENCES:** Yes for groups to 20 persons **LANGUAGES:** German, French, Dutch [Z04FPVT1-2834]

Inn On The Common	Craftsbury VT
Michael & Penny Schmitt	Main St 05827
800-521-2233 802-586-9619	**Res Times** 24 hrs

Rates:	**Pvt Bath** 18	**Payment Terms:**
Single	$ 95.00	Check
Double	$ 100-135.00	MC/V

Enjoy New England in this quaint Inn that pampers guests with beautiful antique furnishings, elegant decor and gourmet dining located on the premises. Delightful and gracious accommodations for those looking for the best. Swimming, tennis, library, sauna, white water rafting and golf nearby. A full breakfast is included with other meals available. **RESERVATIONS:** One night's deposit or credit card number, 48 hr cancel policy for refund **SEASONAL:** No **BROCHURE:** Yes **PERMITTED:** Children 12-up, smoking, drinking [E11ACVT-2839]

Waybury Inn	East Middlebury VT
Jim & Betty Riley	Rt 125 05740
802-388-4015	**Res Times** 7am-11pm

Rates:	**Pvt Bath** 14	**Payment Terms:**
Single	$ 80-up	Check
Double	$ 90-135.00	AE/MC/V

Traditional New England Inn c1810 that had it's beginning as a stagecoach stop located at the foot of the Green Mountains that still carries on its tradition of fine service. Beautiful interior decor includes original wood beams with antique furnishings in all the rooms. Close to all the sights, guests will find tennis, golf, excellent fishing, mountain hiking, nature walks, antiquing, skiing, and exciting Fall foliage that's perfect for picnicking. A full breakfast includes scrumptious blueberry pancakes prepared from a wonderful family recipe. **RESERVATIONS:** One night's deposit required **SEASONAL:** No **BROCHURE:** Yes **PERMITTED:** Limited children, smoking, drinking [E11ACVT-2856]

**Berkson Farms	**Enosberg Falls VT**
Susan & Terry Spoonire	RFD 1 05450
802-933-2522	

Rates:	**Pvt Bath** 1	**Shared Bath** 3	**Payment Terms:**
Single	$ 45.00	$ 40.00	Check
Double	$ 65.00	$ 55.00	

Relax in our 150 year-old farmhouse on a working dairy farm located on 600 acres of meadowland surrounded by a variety of animals, nature and warm hospitality. Guests can help out with the chores or just enjoy the friendly atmosphere, picnic, hike through the fields, bike in the warmer months, x-country ski and sled in the winter. We serve a hearty home-style full breakfast using our maple syrup and farm fresh dairy products. We are located just a few miles from the Canadian border. Swimming, golf and major ski areas are nearby. Reservations are suggested. We are open year round. **DISCOUNTS:** Weekly rates **AIRPORT:** Burlington-1 hr **RESERVATIONS:** Deposit required **BROCHURE:** Yes **PERMITTED:** Children, pets, drinking [Z07GPVT2-2857]

**Maplewood Inn & Antiques	**Fair Haven VT**
Cindy Baird	Rt 22A S 05743
800-253-7729 802-265-8039	**Res Times** 9am-9pm

Rates:	**Pvt Bath** 5	**Payment Terms:**
Single	$ 65-100.00	Check
Double	$ 70-105.00	AE/CB/DC/MC/V

Rediscover romance in this exquisite 1843 Greek Revival-style Inn which is listed on the Vermont *Register of Historic Places*. Once part of a prosperous dairy, *Maplewood* was transformed into a warm and inviting Inn in 1986 after remaining in one family for over 100 years. Experience panoramic country views, spectacular sunsets and a romantic and intimate atmosphere amid many fine antiques. Conveniently located in Central Vermont's Lakes Region near many recreational attractions such as Lakes Bomoseen, St Catherine and Champlain, Killington and Pico ski areas, historical sites, museums, shopping and great restaurants. Close to many New York State destinations, such as Lake George and Fort Ticonderoga. Our first class accommodations are expertly decorated in outstanding period decor. Doubles feature 4-poster and brass beds, private baths, seating areas and most have working fireplaces. Suites feature a full living room, large bedroom, bath and fireplace. All accommodations have a/c, fans, radios, color TV and in-room phone available on request. Fine touches such as evening turn-down, mints, custom toiletries, bicycles and a canoe are our standard. Several lovely common rooms include Keeping Room with fireplace; Gathering Room with library; Parlor with Complimentary Cordial Bar and games and BYOB Tavern area. Our bountiful Breakfast Buffet will begin your morning. A wonderful antique shop is filled with country antiques. Featured in *Country, New England Getaways, Americana, Innsider* magazines, many fine guidebooks, **_Mobil_** ★★★, **_AAA_** ◆◆◆. **DISCOUNTS:** Groups, extended stays **AIRPORT:** Burlington VT-70 mi; Albany NY-85 mi **PACKAGES:** Off-season between Nov-April (except holidays), inquire at res time **RESERVATIONS:** 50% deposit within 7 days of booking or credit card number, 14 day cancel policy for refund less $15 service fee. Less than 14 days refund only if rebooked **BROCHURE:** Yes **PERMITTED:** Limited children, limited smoking, drinking **CONFERENCES:** Yes, common rooms available for groups of 10-12 [I07GPVT2-13623]

**Inn At Buck Hollow Farm   Fairfax VT

Dody Young/Bradley Schwartz   RR 1 Box 680 05454
802-849-2400   **Res Times** 24 Hrs

Rates:	Shared Bath 4	Payment Terms:
Single	$ 45.00	Check
Double	$ 55.00	MC/V

We are an intimate New England Country Inn. Nestled on 400 spectacular acres just 30 miles from Burlington, the Inn is truly a four-season retreat. Whether you walk our wooded trails, cuddle a spring lamb, listen to a brook or sit by the heated pool and watch the birds, you will appreciate our special country atmosphere. Come fall, foliage is awe-inspiring, especially on country roads. After hiking, biking or walking, you may decide to sit before the fire, browse through the antique shop or simply enjoy the sounds of migrating geese. Winter offers x-country skiing on our property with major ski areas close by. Watch the production of maple syrup in our sugar house and taste the results on your pancakes the next morning. A glass of wine, a crackling fire and a friendly cat welcome you at the end of the day. The Inn occupies a 1790's carriage house with the original beams left exposed. The guest rooms are decorated with antiques, queen-size canopy beds, quilts and color Tvs. Guests can relax in the two-person jacuzzi. Children are welcome and love both the fenced-in play area and complimentary pony rides. A full complimentary breakfast is included. The *Inn at Buck Hollow Farm -- **A Special Place*. **DIS-COUNTS:** Yes, inquire at res time. **AIRPORT:** Burlington Intl-30 mins **RESERVATIONS:** One night's deposit or 50% of stay, which ever is greater; 14 day cancel policy, less than 14 days, refund if rebooked or deposit held for future booking **SEASONAL:** No **BROCHURE:** Yes **PERMITTED:** Children, drinking, limited smoking [R05EPVT-15466]

*Hillside View Farm   Fairfield VT

Jacqueline Tretreault   South Rd 05455
802-827-4480

Rates:	Shared Bath 2	Payment Terms:
Single	$ 50.00	Check
Double	$ 50.00	

Your chance to experience the excitement of "rolling hills" of a

Vermont farm with beautiful year-round New England scenery. This charming home and hostess offers warmth and hospitality to all guests while visiting their working dairy farm. Just minutes from St Albans in a quiet village setting, you'll relish the peace and tranquility of this picturesque setting. Interesting and helpful hosts welcome you to New England and their farming life-style. And they'll make sure you see all the sights while here. A continental breakfast is included. Close to Stowe (an hour drive) and Montreal Quebec (two hour drive). **SEASONAL:** No **BROCHURE:** Yes **PERMITTED:** Children [A05ACVT-2860]

Silver Maple Lodge & Cottages	**Fairlee VT**
Scott & Sharon Wright	S Main St 05045
800-666-1946 802-333-4326	**Res Times** 7am-10pm

Rates:	**Pvt Bath** 12	**Shared Bath** 2	**Payment Terms:**
Single	$ 48-58.00	$ 38.00	Check
Double	$ 52-62.00	$ 42-44.00	AE/MC/V

Historic Bed & Breakfast Country Inn located in scenic four-season resort area in the Upper Connecticut River Valley between the Green Mountains & the White Mountains, built in the late 1700s. Choose one of the freshly renovated rooms in a quaint antique farmhouse or one of the knotty pine cottages with wide-plank floors made from lumber cut on the property. Guests can lounge on a wrap-around porch or picnic among the apple trees. All outdoor activities are here including lawn games of badminton, croquet, horseshoes and water sports at nearby Lake Morey & Lake Fairlee. (1 & 4 miles). Appalachian Trail, gliding & flying lessons and great x-country skiing are just a mile away and its just ten miles to a full downhill ski area. Plenty of fine restaurants make your time well-spent too. Vermont hospitality flourishes with these special hosts. A continental breakfast is included. *AAA Approved.* **PACKAGES:** *Hot Air Balloon, Inn to Inn Walking, Bicycle and Canoe, Summer Specials, Golf* **DISCOUNTS:** Senior Citizens, AAA, travel agents **AIRPORT:** Burlington VT-80 mi **RESERVATIONS:** One night's deposit 1-4 days, 50% deposit if longer, 14 day cancel policy for refund less $2 service fee **SEASONAL:** No **BROCHURE:** Yes **PERMITTED:** Children, drinking with limited smoking **CONFERENCES:** Three common rooms are available for meetings up to 15 persons [A11DPVT-2865]

**Blueberry Hill Inn	**Goshen VT**
Tony Clark	RD3 05733
800-448-0707 802-247-6735	**Res Times** 8am-10pm
	Fax 802-247-3983
Rates: **Pvt Bath** 12	**Payment Terms:**
Single $ 84-150.00 MAP	Check
Double $ 168-210.00 MAP	MC/V

Located in the tranquility of the Green Mountain National Forest, our twelve rooms are artistically fashioned with antiques, warm quilts and private baths. The greenhouse is just off the kitchen, with brick walkway and every-blooming plants, bringing the outdoors inside. It is a favorite gathering place in winter with a cup of tea, a chocolate chip cookie and the warmth of the woodstove. With 75km of groomed and tracked trails, a full service ski shop and complimentary hot homemade soup offered each day, the Inn is a cross country skier's paradise. The activities are endless - with the famous New Years Eve night ski and bonfire on Hogback Mountain, to the American Ski Marathon entering its eighteenth year. In summer, the ski trails are used for hiking, walking, running and mountain biking. In October, *Blueberry Hill* will host the 4th Annual Knobby Rock, a cross country mountain bike race. And in July, the 17th Annual Goshen Gallop, a 10km cross country run through some of the most scenic trails in Vermont. Dinner is served in our cozy dining room which boasts a large fieldstone fireplace and the imaginative upside-down garden of straw flowers and herbs hanging from the ceiling beams. There are four creative courses served in an unhurried pace, always using as many local producers as possible, including the *Blueberry Hill* gardens. Herbs, lettuces, vegetables and edible flowers all will grace the cuisine. Breakfast is an event also, served in courses beginning with juice, fruit, followed by homemade granola, a pastry and main course. As you exit the dining room, be sure to stop at the ever-full chocolate chip cookie jar, taking one to savor later on your walk or hike. Visit the blacksmith's shop next door for various *Blueberry Hill* items you can purchase. Including the handcrafted coffee mugs, dried herbs and prints. In summer, step out the back door and pick blueberries to your heart's content or relax by the pond and take a swim. ***Come to Blueberry Hill Inn and share our special way of life.*** **RESERVATIONS:** $45 per night per person deposit required at res time, refund only if rooms are re-rented **SEASONAL:** Rates vary **PERMITTED:** Children, drinking (BYOB) **BROCHURE:** Yes **DISCOUNTS:** Groups, Corporate rates **AIRPORT:** Burlington-55 mi **CONFERENCES:** Groups to forty persons **LANGUAGES:**

Vermont

French, Czech, German **PACKAGES:** *Cross Country Ski* [R08GPVT2]

Tyler Place			**Highgate Springs VT**
Tyler Family			PO Box 45 05460
802-868-3301			**Res Times** 8am-9pm

Rates:	**Pvt Bath** 8	**Shared Bath** 3	**Payment Terms:**
Single	$ 78.00	$ 48.00	Check
Double	$ 82-92.00	$ 52-70.00	

Built over 160 years ago, this restored sea captain's home invites guests to an old-style New England lodging surrounded by the charm of yesteryear while offering the convenience of today. This intimate setting, just a short stroll to scenic Nauset Beach on Cape Cod offers lantern-lit door-ways to nineteen rooms, each individually appointed in special colonial colors and authentic antiques. There are beamed ceilings, quilts, and old four poster beds. Several rooms include beautiful ocean views and fireplaces. In addition, overlooking the Orleans Cove, is the *Cove House* with three rooms and a one-bedroom apartment, and two housekeeping cottages offering the escape. Seclusion and serenity await the less adventuresome vacationer at Nauset Beach. Swimming pool on the premises is available to guests, with golf, horseback riding, tennis, lovely Cape Cod shopping and sightseeing nearby. Continental Breakfast is included. **RESERVATIONS:** One night's deposit at res time, balance upon arrival cancel notice of 14 days for refund **SEASONAL:** *Season 5/2-10/30, Off-season rates 25% lower **BROCHURE:** Yes **PERMITTED:** Children 12-up, drinking & smoking. [C12CCVT-2878]

Fitch Hill Inn			**Hyde Park VT**
Richard A Pugliese			Fitch Hill Rd 05655
800-639-2903 802-888-3834			

Rates:	**Pvt Bath** 1	**Shared Bath** 6	**Payment Terms:**
Single	$ 95.00	$ 50-63.00	Check
Double	$ 105.00	$ 59-73.00	MC/V

Historic elegance - at affordable rates! Charles Kuralt, on one of his much publicized tours, described Hyde Park as one of several villages in which he would be happy to live. Situated in the lovely

Lamoille River Valley, on a hill overlooking the magnificent Green Mountains, *Fitch Hill Inn* offers a special opportunity to enjoy the true Vermont experience. Set in four acres of woodland and central to Vermont's all-season vacation country, you can choose from any number of activities. You can ski, fish, hike, bike, canoe, play tennis or golf, visit a country auction or browse the many barn sales and antique shops. Six tastefully decorated guest rooms, a colonial dining room, a federalist-style living room and a comfortable library full of video tapes and books for your viewing and reading. A hearty complimentary breakfast is provided while gourmet dinners, prepared by your innkeeper, are available at an additional charge. Whether for a night, weekend or an extended stay - you will find *Fitch Hill Inn* to be a very special place in a very special world. **AIRPORT:** Burlington Intl-38 mi **DISCOUNTS:** Weekdays, extended stays **PACKAGES:** *Ski, Canoeing* **RESERVATIONS:** One night's deposit, 14 day cancel policy for refund, late arrival only by prior arrangement **SEASONAL:** Rates vary **BROCHURE:** Yes **PERMITTED:** Limited children, drinking, no smoking **CONFERENCES:** For groups to ten persons **LANGUAGES:** Spanish, French [Z07GPVT2-2879]

Henry M Field House B&B	Jericho VT
Mary & Terrence Horan	Rt 2 Box 395 05465
802-899-3984	**Res Times** See below

Rates:	**Pvt Bath** 3	**Payment Terms:**
Single	$ 60-70.00	Check
Double	$ 65-75.00	MC/V

The picturesque New England village of Jericho is the setting for this beautiful Victorian Italianate circa 1875 offering guests all of the ambience of the Victorian era. The interior features tall ceilings, ornamental plaster, etched glass, curved windows, large paneled doors and mouldings of mahogany and chestnut. Gleaming wood floors set-off the beautiful colors chosen for the rooms, each filled with period furnishings and lighting. From original sinks to sunlit entry foyer - you'll relax in wicker and palm-filled surroundings. The guest rooms offer queen size beds and period furnishings while the two parlours and library provide for relaxation and socializing with other guests. The dining room is large and family-style full breakfasts are served here or the outdoor porch in summer. Gardens and 3-1/2 acres of woods and meadow surround the home which is adjacent to the Brown's River. Year-round activities at Mt Mansfield and nearby Lake Champlain include golf, cycling, swimming, hiking, skiing, boating with excellent antiquing and shopping. Nearby schools include Univ of Vermont, Champlain College, Trinity College, Vermont College, St Michaels College and many others. Burlington is twelve miles. Your hosts enjoy meeting people and have flexible schedules to assure your comfort. **RESERVATIONS:** 50% deposit of stay required, 14 day cancel policy less $5 service fee, minimum stay holidays and peak season. Check-in after 10pm only with prior arrangement **PERMITTED:** Limited children, drinking **BROCHURE:** Yes **DISCOUNTS:** Extended stays; $5 deduct if breakfast is not desired **AIRPORT:** Burlington Intl **PACKAGES:** Group rentals longer than two nights, *Reservation Times: 7/1-8/30, 24 Hrs; 9/1-6/30 after 5pm **SEASONAL:** Closed 12/23-1/3; 8/1-8/10 [I07GP-VT2-10861]

**_Inn At Long Trail_	**Killington VT**
The McGrath Family	Rt 4 Box 267 05715
800-325-2540 802-775-7181	**Res Times** 8am-11pm

Rates:	**Pvt Bath** 20	**Payment Terms:**
Single	$ 46-98.00*	Check
Double	$ 56-98.00*	AE/MC/V

Situated high in the Green Mountains of Vermont alongside the famous Appalachian & Long Trails which meet just a few hundred yards into the woods, from the Inn. Spectacular Fall foliage is everywhere at this elevation and in Winter, you're fortunate because you're right between Pico (1/4 mi) and Killington (1 mi) ski resort areas. This 1938 ski lodge setting was the first in Vermont! Everything is here for your leisure, including wood-panelled common rooms, candlelight dining areas, an Irish Pub, hot tub, wonderful year-round mountain views and fireplaces are in some of the guest rooms. New England specialties are offered at the restaurant on the premises and a full breakfast is included with your room. Owned and operated by the McGraths since 1977, this lovely Country Inn is perfect for travelers who love the natural setting at 2200 ft elevation. Immaculate rooms are sure to satisfy everyone. Nearby activities include antiquing and Vermont postcard scenery. **SEASONAL:** Closed: 4/15-6/20; 10/25-11/20. *Mid-week rates $46-98.00 and $294-384.00 MAP packages for winter weekends. **AIRPORT:** Burlington Intl-1-1/2 hrs; Albany-2--1/2 hrs **RESERVATIONS:** One night's deposit, 50% if more than one night, 14 day cancel policy, less $15 service fee. **BROCHURE:** Yes **PERMITTED:** Children, drinking, limited smoking **CONFERENCES:** Yes for groups to 30 persons [A07GCVT2-2889]

**The Vermont Inn			**Killington VT**
Susan & Judd Levy			Rt 4 05751
800-541-7795 802-775-0708			**Res Times** 8am-10pm

Rates:	**Pvt Bath** 15	**Shared Bath**	**Payment Terms:**
Single	$ 70-130.00	$ 70-90.00	Check
Double	$ 80-150.00	$ 80-150.00	AE/MC/V

The Vermont Inn is a small Country Inn located on six acres in the mountains of Killington. Originally a farmhouse built in 1840, the Inn provides country charm, a warm atmosphere and gourmet dining in a beautiful mountain setting. The parlor, lounge and dining room have fireplaces or wood-burning stoves. The dining room has spectacular views and

a ♦♦♦ *Award* from *AAA*. The restaurant also won *first place in Killington/Korbel Champagne Dine-Around Contest in 1990 and 1991*. The Inn's own herb garden provides fresh flavorings for many of the award-winning dishes. Specialties include fresh fish, veal and duckling. Everything is homemade including the herb rolls and desserts. An extensive wine list is available. Complimentary tea and warm cookies are offered every afternoon. This family operated Inn offers excellent year-round facilities including a sauna, hot tub, tennis court and swimming pool. The game room has bumper pool and a collection of board games. Winter brings downhill skiing at Pico (2 mi) or Killington (8 mi). Two excellent x-country ski touring centers are just ten minutes away. In summer and fall, guests enjoy lawn games, a PGA Championship Golf Course, summer theatre, ballet, farmer's market, Norman Rockwell Museum, great discount shopping and many other attractions. The Inn is centrally located in Vermont so guests can stay several days and easily tour the countryside with trips to nearby Woodstock, Manchester and Burlington. This is one of the few Inns in Vermont offering a handicap accessible room. **DISCOUNTS:** Yes, for 3 & 5 days stays **AIRPORT:** Rutland-18 mi **PACKAGES:** 3 & 5 day available. **RESERVATIONS:** 50% deposit at res time, 14 day cancel policy for refund less $25 service fee **SEASONAL:** Closed 4/15-5/15 **BROCHURE:** Yes **PERMITTED:** Children 6-up, drinking and limited smoking. **CONFERENCES:** Yes for small group meetings including dining [I06EPVT-4842]

Inn At Highview   Ludlow VT
Greg Bohan
802-875-2724

Rates:	Pvt Bath 8	Payment Terms:
Single	$ 80-115.00	Check
Double	$ 90-125.00	MC/V

Refer to the same listing name under Andover VT for a complete description. [M07GPVT2-17783]

Echo Lake Inn   Ludlow VT
John & Yvonne Pardieu/Chip Connelly   PO Box 154 05149
800-356-6844 802-228-8602   **Res Times** 7am-10pm
                                                          Fax 802-228-3075

Rates:	Pvt Bath 11	Shared Bath 14	Payment Terms:
Single	$ 72-113.00*	$ 62- 95.00*	Check
Double	$ 120-188.00*	$ 104-158.00*	AE/DISC/MC/V

An historic 1840's Country Inn with four stories and a gabled roof on a scenic route near Echo Lake and surrounded by spacious lawns, a tennis court and swimming pool. The twenty five guest rooms range from suites to shared family units and have been individually decorated, some with antiques. Sit by the fire and read a book, enjoy a cocktail in the intimate lounge, or relax in one of the antique red rocking chairs on the front porch and watch the birds feeding in the evening. Stroll through the fall foliage, play a game of tennis, relax in the jacuzzi or take a steam bath before dinner. Take a picnic to Echo Lake Island in a complimentary canoe or hike, jog, or bike through the woods. The full service dining room offers cocktails and a full wine list and features gourmet cuisine served by candlelight with porch dining during the summer. Sample culinary delights such as fresh *Lobster Ravioli, Rainbow Trout* sauteed with artichoke hearts and sundried tomatoes, or our famous *Roast Country Duckling.* In the morning, enjoy a full breakfast with an omelette du jour, Vermont buttermilk pancakes, or waffles with sauteed fresh fruits. **RESERVATIONS:** Deposit required *MAP, plus tax and service **SEASONAL:** Closed 4/1-5/1 and November 1st to Thanksgiving **PERMITTED:** Limited children, drinking, limited smoking **BROCHURE:** Yes **CONFERENCES:** Yes, groups to 12 **AIRPORT:** Rutland-20 mi; Lebanon, NH-30 mi **PACKAGES:** *Fly Fishing* [R08GPVT2]

**Inn At Manchester	**Manchester VT**
Stan & Harriet Rosenberg	Rt 7A PO Box 41 05254
802-362-1793	**Res Times** 7am-11pm

Rates:	**Pvt Bath** 14	**Shared Bath** 6	**Payment Terms:**
Single	$ 90-125.00	$ 70-80.00	Check
Double	$ 90-125.00	$ 70-80.00	AE/MC/V

Welcome to this historic Inn which was built in 1880 as a summer home and in succeeding years served as a private residence and as an Inn. This Victorian gem, listed on the *National Register of Historic Places,* was meticulously restored in 1978 by Stan and Harriet with over 450 rolls of wallpaper, countless gallons of paint and hundreds' of

hours of work and elbow grease. Their efforts turned the proud Inn to its former glory and elegance while adding the modern amenities guests expect when staying in a fine lodging. The Carriage House, built in 1867, was also renovated in 1985 under the auspices of the Vermont Dept of Historic Preservation adding more guest rooms. Today, each guest room has a unique personality named for wildflowers growing in the meadow surrounding the Inn. Guests can choose the Blackeyed Susan, Blue Phlox, Sunflower, Primrose and others. A five-window view of the Green Mountains is seen from the Primrose Suite. Guests staying in the Carriage House and Inn will find original antique furnishings throughout - with a romantic star-gazing window set in the soaring ceilings of the Sweet William room. A Village House, about a mile from the Inn, is another lodging choice providing unique decor and furnishings. A full and hardy New England complimentary breakfast brings guests together each morning for fresh juice, home-made granola, old fashioned oatmeal, apple buttermilk pancakes with original Vermont Maple Syrup, sausage patty and plenty of hot beverages. Daily activities are unhurried and frequently include swimming in the pool, the nearby abandoned marble quarry or Emerald Lake with sand beaches, boating and picnic areas. Bike enthusiasts will find complete packages and routes already prepared by your hosts that include exciting plans for lunch stops and dinner along the wayt. Winter brings excellent downhill and cross country skiing at Bromley Mountain and Stratton areas. There's plenty of money-saving shopping at the local factory outlets, auctions, estate sales and craft shows. Robert Todd Lincoln's estate of Hildene is open for touring while local entertainment provides evening enjoyment. **AIRPORT:** 70 miles **DISCOUNTS:** Yes, inquire **PACKAGES:** *Ski, Golf, Tennis, Theatre, Mix & Match*. **RESERVATIONS:** Two night's deposit is required to guarantee reservation, except special occasions when full payment in advance is required; 14 day cancel policy less $5 service fee per room per night **BROCHURE:** Yes **PERMITTED:** Drinking, children over 8, limited smoking **CONFERENCES:** Yes, perfect for Corporate Retreats and small conferences that particpants will remember for years to come; all meals available for seminars and business events. [I03FPVT2-4859]

Manchester Highlands Inn	**Manchester VT**
Patricia & Robert Eichorn	Highland Ave 05255
800-743-4565 802-362-4565	
	Fax 802-362-4028

Rates:	**Pvt Bath** 15	**Payment Terms:**
Single	$ 60-95.00	Check
Double	$ 85-125.00	AE/MC/V

Welcome to Manchester's best kept secret! Perched on a hill overlooking the town, away from the crowds, the *Manchester Highlands Inn* is unforgettable. Upon entering this lovely Victorian, you feel the special atmosphere with classical music in the background; Humphrey, the cat, curled up on the sofa and the aroma of something delicious baking in the oven. The Inn and Carriage House guest rooms have been recently refurbished with such amenities as feather beds, down comforters and lace curtains. The living room, sun-filled wicker room, game room and pub are comfortable spots for relaxing, snoozing or meeting fellow guests. In summer, you can laze by the pool, try croquet on the lawn or rock the evening away on the porch while enjoying the sunset over Mount Equinox. A full breakfast includes your host's selection of an entree such as Morning Glory Muffins, Banana Oat Bran Pancakes, Cheddar Souffles - all with plenty of Vermont syrup . . while afternoon brings delicious homemade snacks. Dinner available for parties of eight or more, with prior arrangements. As a year-round vacation destination, the famous Battenkill offers excellent fishing, canoeing, hiking and biking along beautiful back roads. Swimming, golf, tennis, craft fairs, antique car shows, polo, flea markets, country auctions and summer theatre and concerts make for a full day. Autumn brings brilliant sugar maple red and gold mantles - slowly turning winter's white with the first snow fall. Stratton and Bromley ski areas, just minutes away, offer miles of downhill and x-country skiing. Manchester's fine restaurants, shops and galleries await you - as does our warm and gracious hospitality. Sharing our home is what we like best - so please come and discover us - we won't be a secret for long! **DISCOUNTS:** Corporate, off-season, mid-week **PACKAGES:** *Mid-week, Ski, Christmas Prelude Weekends* and others, inquire at res time. **RESERVATIONS:** One night or 50% of length of stay to guarantee reservation, deposit applied to last night of stay; 14 day cancel policy for refund less $10 service fee **BROCHURE:** Yes **PERMITTED:** Children, drinking, limited smoking **CONFERENCES:** Small groups ten to fifteen persons, making our location perfect for family reunions, special celebrations, seminars, special events and memorable business meetings **LANGUAGES:** French, German [I07GPVT2-4860]

Brookside Meadows	Middlebury VT
Linda & Roger Cole	RD 3 Box 2460 05753
802-388-6429	**Res Times** 7am-9:30pm

Rates:	**Pvt Bath** 5	**Payment Terms:**
Single	$ 65-79.00	Check
Double	$ 65-110.00	

Picturesque 19th Century farmhouse built in 1979 is nestled in a storybook setting on twenty acres. Enjoy a peaceful country atmosphere before a wood-burning stove while enjoying the beautiful views of nearby Green Mountains. Outdoor activities abound with water sports, golf, exceptional hiking, winter sports in the center of world-famous Killington and Sugarbush. Middlebury College Snow

Bowl offers family skiing without crowds, a friendly atmosphere at moderate cost. Cross country skiing from the door, sleigh rides in winter and carriage rides in summer. Middlebury College, Shelburne Museum, antique shops and over 20 fine restaurants nearby. A full breakfast (described as a banquet by one guest) will include 100% Vermont Maple Syrup. **RESERVATIONS:** One night's deposit, 14 day cancel policy less $15 fee. Min two night stay during high season and weekends **SEASONAL:** No **BROCHURE:** Yes **PERMITTED:** Children 10-up, limited smoking, limited drinking [Z11BPVT-4870]

Middletown Springs Inn		**Middletown Springs VT**
Eugene & Jayne Ashley		On The Green 05757
802-235-2198		

Rates:	Pvt Bath 8	Shared Bath 2	Payment Terms:
Single	$ 60-80.00	$ 50-55.00	Check
Double	$ 80-120.00	$ 60-70.00	MC/V

A Victorian mansion built in 1879 and located on the village green in the historic town of Middletown Springs, Vermont, once a fashionable spa. Listed on the *National Register of Historic Places*, it was converted to an Inn in 1971. Most of the Inn's original architectural features have been preserved, contributing to a delightful atmosphere of period elegance which is complemented by antique furnishings. The Inn contains five public rooms for the use of guests on the first floor centered around a gracious entrance hall with curved staircase. The second floor has seven guest bedrooms, each with a private bath. Adjacent to the main house is an 1840's vintage carriage house (once the village blacksmith shop) which has been tastefully renovated to provide additional three bedrooms and two baths. *Middletown Springs* is conveniently located 27 miles north of Manchester Center with its wide selection of restaurants and designer factory outlet stores, and 19 miles southwest of Rutland. Golf, horseback riding, fishing, boating and alpine skiing are a convenient drive away. Cycling, hiking and x-country skiing are available at your doorstep. A full breakfast is included and dinner is available with prior notice prepared only with fresh ingredients and imaginative vegetarian dishes are available. Your hosts, Eugene, a New England native and Jayne, a native of Old England have combined the charm of a New England Country Inn with the graciousness of an English Country House Hotel - an experience guests won't forget! **RESERVATIONS:** One night's deposit at res time, 7 day cancel policy for refund less 10% **SEASONAL:** No **BROCHURE:** Yes **PERMITTED:** Limited drinking, limited smoking, limited children **CONFERENCES:** Yes for groups to 20 persons [I12DPVT-4873]

**Northfield Inn	**Montpelier VT**

Aglaia & Alan Stalb
802-485-8558

Rates:	**Pvt Bath** 8	**Payment Terms:**
Single	$ 55-225.00	Check
Double	$ 85-225.00	MC/V

Refer to the same listing name under Northfield, Vermont for a complete description [M07FPVT1-17770]

**Newtons 1824 House	**Northfield VT**

Nicholas & Joyuce Newton
802-496-7555

Rates:	**Pvt Bath** 6	**Payment Terms:**
Single	$ 65-115.00	AE/MC/V
Double	$ 75-125.00	

Refer to the same listing name under Waistfield, Vermont for a complete description [Mo8GPVT2]

**Northfield Inn	**Northfield VT**

Aglaia & Alan Stalb   27 Highland Ave 05663
802-485-8558

Rates:	**Pvt Bath** 8	**Payment Terms:**
Single	$ 55-225.00	Check
Double	$ 85-225.00	MC/V

Restored to its original grand style, this lovely turn-of-the-century Victorian offers guests elegance and luxurious period furnishings and decor that includes private baths, antiques and brass or carved

27 Highland Avenue
In Northfield, Vermont

THE NORTHFIELD INN

wood beds with European feather bedding. Nestled in the heart of the Green Mountains, the *Northfield Inn* is just minutes from Montpelier, the state capital and Barre, the granite capital of the world. Framed by scenic mountains, the Inn is nestled on a hillside overlooking the village of Northfield and the historic campus of Norwich University, America's first private military college with its famous on-campus alpine skiing. Guests step back to an era of **Comfort & Congeniality** when people had time for afternoon tea and pleasant conversation. Our Library, parlors, game room and formal dining room with fine music and a cozy fire, will warm your heart and spirit on those chilly evenings. A complimentary full, hearty, old-fashioned multi-course breakfast begins your day of panoramic views of scenic valleys, wildflower meadows and lovely gardens, birds and the outdoors which can be enjoyed from the front porch rockers. Northfield's historic district and charming village offers shopping and sights and there's a full offering of lawn games, sledding on the lawn, sleigh rides, mountain trails to explore, hiking, fishing, tennis, golf and an old swimming hole. Winter brings world-class skiing at nearby Sugarbush, Mad River Glen or Stowe. **RESERVATIONS:** First and last night deposit required, late arrival only with prior arrangement. Two suites are available **SEASONAL:** No **PERMITTED:** Children 15-up, BYOB social drinking, smoking outdoors, nearby kennel boarding can be arranged for pets **BROCHURE:** Yes **CONFERENCES:** Yes, groups to thirty persons **LANGUAGES:** Greek **DISCOUNTS:** Groups and extended stays **AIRPORT:** Burlington-37 mi **PACKAGES:** *Four Nights*, breakfast, queen size bedroom $169.00 per person; Stay seven nights - 7th night free [O08GPVT2-13626]

**Brookside Farms	**Orwell VT**
Joan & Murray Korda	Hwy 22A 05760
802-948-2727	**Res Times** 24 hrs

Rates:	**Pvt Bath** 4	**Shared Bath** 3	**Payment Terms:**
Single	$ 75-150.00	$ 50.00	Check
Double	$ 85-150.00	$ 85.00	

This stately neo-classical Greek Revival mansion rests proudly with its shimmering white Ionic columns on a 300-acre working farm having celebrated its ***200th Anniversary in 1989***! - dating from 1789! Listed on the *National Register of Historic Places*, it has been meticulously restored and maintained as a fabulous showplace of yesterday's elegance while including today's conveniences. The main house and an adjacent guest house are furnished with classical antiques from its history. The guest house is part of the antique shop and everything is for sale - including the bed you sleep in! You can even try your hand at the first Bosendorfer piano brought into the USA before the war! Or browse through the extensive 10,000 volume library for a favorite novel. The full breakfast is a real treat offering farm-fresh eggs, maple syrup from the trees on the 300 acres and the tastiest bacon you've ever eaten - all prepared just to each guest's taste. Spend the day strolling the well manicured grounds with spectacular views and lush countryside. Boating & fishing are nearby, swimming, horseback riding, skiing, ice skating and your own x-country trails right on the property. Sights include Morgan Horse Farm, Vermont Marble Exhibit, Frog Hollow Craft Center, Lake Champlain, Mount Independence and Fort Ticongeroga. **MEALS:** Lunch and dinner available, all home prepared by your hostess **DISCOUNTS:** 10% to travel agents **AIRPORT:** Burlington Intl **PACKAGES:** Yes, inquire at res time **RESERVATIONS:** One night deposit to hold room **SEASONAL:** No **BROCHURE:** Yes **PERMITTED:** Children, drinking, limited smoking **CONFERENCES:** Yes for groups to fifty persons **LANGUAGES:** French, Spanish, Italian, Hungarian, Russian, Greek, Hebrew [I08GPVT2-7533]

Gwendolyns B&B	**Perkinsville VT**
Laurie, Win & Gwen	Rt 106 PO Box 225 05151
802-263-5248	**Res Times** 7am-12am

Rates:	**Pvt Bath** 4	**Shared Bath** 2	**Payment Terms:**
Single	$ 65.00	$ 60.00	Check
Double	$ 92.00	$ 82.00	DC/MC/V

"We came to admire. We leave enchanted", Lynn Jordan, writer, Seattle Washington. Our 1872 Victorian, graced with veranda and grand curved stairway, opens it's doors, enter a romantic era, recapturing the charm and elegance of it's day. Fine linens and antiques enhance the ambiance of this stately mansion. Each guest room has been given individual attention, adorned with canopy and timeless cherished treasures, patiently collected by Laurie over many years, with her dream of one day opening a Bed & Breakfast Inn, expressly in mind. Our Country Water Gardens lend a certain charm. Take in the scent of our lovely flowers while relaxing by our fish pond, the perfect respite for the weary traveler, just what the doctor ordered! The aroma of home baking complements a distinctive breakfast always served on our finest antique china, silver and lovely linens. The attention and special service we offer is incomparable, evidence of the love and care we relish, welcoming travelers, our friends. Our warm-welcoming atmosphere *Welcomes you home.* Picnic lunches, BBQ, private dining room service available upon request and advance notice. Year-round activities include antiquing, art galleries, hiking, swimming, biking, downhill and x-country skiing and great New England dining within moments. By car: Albany or Hartford, 2-1/4 hrs; Boston, 2-1/2 hrs; Providence, 3 hrs; New

York 4-3/4 hrs; Philadelphia 6-1/2 hrs. Pick-ups by bus in Springfield VT, by train at Bellows Falls VT, by plane into Lebanon or Burlington VT and by private plane at Hartness Airport, just 2 miles from the Inn. **DISCOUNTS:** Check at res time for seasonal, promotional and mid-week rates. **PACKAGES:** *Ski, Honeymoon, Equestrian* **RESERVATIONS:** 50% deposit required with 7 days of booking. Train, bus and plane pick-up available with advance notice **SEASONAL:** No **BROCHURE:** Yes **PERMITTED:** Children, drinking, limited smoking **CONFERENCES:** Yes, perfect for groups to 16 for weddings, social and business functions. Phones, fax and copier available. **LANGUAGES:** Limited French [I02EPVT-14502]

**Inn At Weathersfield	**Perkinsville VT**
Mary Louise & Ron Thorburn	Rt 106 PO Box 165 05151
800-477-4828 802-263-9217	**Res Times** 8am-11pm
	Fax 802-263-9219

Rates:	**Pvt Bath** 12	**Payment Terms:**
Single	$120-130.00 MAP	Check
Double	$175-190.00 MAP	AE/CB/DC/MC/V

Built in 1795, the Inn is a re-creation in architecture and spirit of the 1790's to the 1860's with exposed beams, period antiques and a functional cooking hearth with beehive bake oven. Here, Mary Louise master-minds complete meals using period recipes on winter holidays. High English tea, five-course Nouvelle Cuisine dinners, and four-course grand  buffet breakfasts, included in your room rate, are served near one of the twelve working fireplaces. The Inn's own farm-raised pheasants and partridges are featured, along with fresh salmon, rack of lamb, filet mignon and a vegetarian stir fry, for example. Nestled at the base of Hawks Mountain on twenty-one acres, there are hiking trails, a pond for fishing and swimming and horses for sleigh and carriage rides. Nearby recreational activities abound with hiking on Ascutney Mountain, Alpine and x-country skiing, two highly acclaimed golf courses, and tennis courts. Historic places to visit include the home and studio of America's most famous sculptor, Augustus St Gaudens; Robert Todd Lincoln's home and gardens; Billings Farm, a museum and farm depicting life in Vermont around 1890; Pres Coolidge's birthplace and summer White House; and Weston Priory's Benedictine Monks. The Inn's library of several thousand volumes keeps guests busy. The fitness center features aerobic equipment and a Finnish sauna. A fully licensed tavern, extensive wine cellar and two grand pianos providing nightly entertainment, round out **the ultimate Country Inn experience. DISCOUNTS:** Weekdays, multiple night stay, corporate **AIRPORT:** Boston Logan; Hartford Bradley Field, Lebanon NH. **PACKAGES: Five Day Stay** beginning Sunday depart Friday, stay five nights, pay or four **RESERVATIONS:** One night deposit on all reservations **SEASONAL:** Rates lower April-June **BROCHURE:** Yes **PERMITTED:** Limited children, limited pets, drinking, limited smoking **CONFERENCES:** Two meeting rooms for groups to forty, including AV (projector, easel, boards, screens etc) **LANGUAGES:** German [I08GPVT2-4978]

Allens Inn of Proctorsville	Proctorsville VT
Charles & Joan Racicot	Depot St 05153
802-226-7970	

Rates:	Pvt Bath 3	Shared Bath 5	Payment Terms:
Single	$ 95.00 MAP	$ 85.00 MAP	Check
Double	$ 95.00 MAP	$ 85.00 MAP	MC/V

Gingerbread Victorian Inn with country antiques, furnishings, flowers and plenty of home atmosphere with charming hosts. Relax and enjoy that "at home feeling" while visiting with Chuck and Joan. Full breakfast is prepared by Joan and will start-off your day on the right foot. **RESERVATIONS:** 50% deposit at res time **SEASONAL:** Closed April **BROCHURE:** Yes **PERMITTED:** Children 10-up, limited smoking [E11ACVT-4906]

**Inn At Buck Hollow Farm*	Saint Albans VT
Dody Young/Brad Schwartz	
802-849-2400	**Res Times** 24 Hrs

Rates:	Shared Bath 4	Payment:
Single	$ 45.00	Check
Double	$ 55.00	MC/V

Refer to the same listing name under Fairfax, Vermont for a complete description. [M05EPVT-15509]

1860 House	**Stowe VT**
Rick Hubbard	School St 05672
800-248-1860 802-253-7351	**Res Times** 7am-11pm

Rates:	**Pvt Bath** 5	**Payment Terms:**
Single	$ 65-115.00	Check
Double	$ 85-115.00	MC/V

Enjoy year-round activities in this Center Village residence, charmingly restored and listed on the *National Historic Register*. There are five beautifully furnished and a/c guest bedrooms, with private bath and a choice of king, queen and twin beds with firm mattresses and Vermont handmade quilts. All rooms are furnished with antiques or reproductions and silver accent pieces. A wonderful romantic retreat for couples. Guests enjoy friendly conversation in the sunny dining room or the spacious plant-filled living room or outside, on the patio surrounded by lovely flower gardens. There's a quiet reading nook in the living room, an antique writing or game table, an excellent upright piano, stereo with classical choices and a large comfy couch to relax before a crackling fire. Enjoy the nearby health club & pool at no additional cost, a six mile walking path and four tennis courts close-by for guests use. Just strolling distance to all the Stowe Village shops, restaurants and sights. A light breakfast includes fresh fruit, orange juice, fresh baked breads and pastries, whole grain cereals and hot beverages. Kitchen privileges, daily housekeeping services, along with plenty of parking, washer/dryer and a workroom for bikes on the premises included. **RESERVATIONS:** 50% of total due at booking time, balance due 30 days prior to arrival; 30 day cancel policy for refund less 10% service fee **SEASONAL:** No **BROCHURE:** Yes **PERMITTED:** Children, drinking, limited pets, No smoking **CONFERENCES:** Yes, when entire home is rented by one group **LANGUAGES:** German [Z01DPVT-4936]

Edson Hill Manor		**Stowe VT**
Anita Heath		1303 Edson Hill Rd 05672
800-621-0284 802-253-7371		
		Fax 802-653-2694
Rates:	**Pvt Bath** 21 **Shared Bath** 6	**Payment Terms:**
Single	$ 83-99.00 EP $ 83-99.00 EP	Check

Double $ 69-109 MAP $ 69-99.00 EP   AE/MC/V

A romantic Country Inn on a 300-acre private estate that was used in the filming of Alan Alda's wonderful movie, **The Four Seasons**. Beautifully furnished guest rooms include private bath, fireplaces and picture windows filled with dramatic mountain views, many of which appear in the movie. Take advantage of the swimming pool, the stocked stream, hiking trails and riding stable that make this Inn a year-round resort. There's tennis and golf nearby. Winter brings horseback riding, sleigh rides, x-country touring (rentals and lessons are available). Excellent cuisine - **AAA and Mobil Rated**. Secluded location but close to all of Stowe's attractions. **MEALS:** Meals available on the premises when on EP or MAP rate. **SEASONAL:** No **BROCHURE:** Yes **PERMITTED:** Children, smoking, drinking **CONFERENCES:** Yes [A11CPVT-4940]

Fitch Hill Inn   **Stowe VT**
Richard A Pugliese
800-639-2903 802-888-3834

Rates:	**Pvt Bath** 1	**Shared Bath** 6	**Payment Terms:**
Single	$ 95.00	$ 50-63.00	Check
Double	$ 105.00	$ 59-73.00	MC/V

Refer to the same listing name under Hyde Park VT for a complete description. [M07GPVT2-16413]

Brass Lantern Inn   **Stowe VT
Andy Aldrich   717 Maple St 05672
800-729-2980 802-253-2229   **Res Times** 8am-9:30pm

Rates:	**Pvt Bath** 9	**Payment Terms:**
Single	$ 65-150.00	Check
Double	$ 65-150.00	AE/MC/V

Enjoy a traditional Bed & Breakfast Inn surrounded by the Green Mountains. The Inn is an **award-winning AAA** ♦ ♦ ♦, restoration of an early 1800's farmhouse and carriage barn. There are nine guest rooms. Each room has a private bath, planked floors, antiques and handmade quilts; fireplaces are available in three guest rooms. The Inn is fully air-conditioned and rooms are individually heated. A full traditional Vermont breakfast awaits each guest, made with fresh Vermont products and produce. There are spectacular views of Mount Mansfield from the Inn. The Inn is located 1/2 mile from the village center of Stowe. Guests may engage in many activities, including skiing, biking, hiking, shopping, antiquing, golf, tennis, horseback riding and sightseeing. In the late afternoon, guests relax  by the fireplace in the living room or watch the sunset over Mount Mansfield from the patio, while enjoying complimentary coffee, tea, hot chocolate and fresh-baked goods. In the evening, guests can sample one of the over forty restaurants in Stowe, the great nightlife and night skiing. Try one of our packages. Amenities include gym privileges for stays of two or more days; a check-out day guest bathroom and shower. **AIRPORT:** Burlington Intl-30 mi **RESERVATIONS:** Deposit required, refundable if canceled 15 days prior to arrival, 30 days for Christmas season; arrival after 9pm only with prior arrangements **SEASONAL:** Rates vary **DISCOUNTS:** Multiple nights and packages **BROCHURE:** Yes **PERMITTED:** Children (adult environment normally), drinking **CONFERENCES:** Yes, for groups to twenty-four **PACKAGES:** *Honeymoon, Golf, Ski, Summertime, Theater* [I07GPVT2-11172]

<u>*Logwood Inn*</u>	<u>**Stowe VT**</u>
Melanie & Sam Kerr	199 Edison Hill Rd 05672
800-426-6697 802-253-7354	

Rates:	**Pvt Bath** 25	**Shared Bath** 4	**Payment Terms:**
Single	$ 70-90.00	$ 55-65.00	Check
Double	$ 70-90.00	$ 55-65.00	MC/V

Lovely year-round resort in beautiful a New England Country Lodge secluded on five acres of lawn with mature trees and beautiful country gardens. Babbling mountain brook in your "own backyard" along with super year-round activities including World-Class alpine and x-country ski areas at Mount Mansfield (highest mountain in Vermont). Summer offers Championship 18-hole golf, riding, hiking, bike-touring, (with rentals available) canoeing and clay tennis courts. You can choose to relax in the heated pool or in front of the fieldstone fireplace in the handsome main lodge that still includes the original wide-plank floors, with open & comfortable sitting areas, separate TV lounge with cable, game room and a bar area (BYOB). Guest rooms are comfortably furnished and include handmade quilts for snuggling in winter! A full breakfast is included with dinner available, at added cost from 12/15-4/10. **RESERVATIONS:** One night's deposit, 14 day cancel policy for refund, late arrival notice appreciated **SEASONAL:** No **BROCHURE:** Yes **PERMITTED:** Children, drinking, smoking [A05FCVT1-4950]

**Strong House Inn	**Vergennes VT**
Mary & Hugh Barigiel	Rt 22A 05491
802-877-3337	**Res Times** 7am-10pm

Rates:	**Pvt Bath** 5	**Shared Bath** 2	**Payment Terms:**
Single	$ 80-up	$ 65-up	Check
Double	$ 80-up	$ 65-up	Ae/MC/V

Experience New England in this comfortable, elegant lodging, c1834 Federal-style home on the *National Register of Historic Places.* Built by Samuel Paddock Strong, the son of General Samuel Strong who directed the Vermont militia at the Battle of Plattsburgh during the war of 1812 and who made his mark in banking and railroads. Located in the Lake Champlain Valley on a slight ridge which commands fine views of the Green Mountains to the east and the Adirondack Range to the west, the Strong family passion for building grand houses is reflected in this elegant residence. Some of the interior details include the free-standing main staircase with curly maple railings, the formal fireplace over which hangs a portrait of Samuel Strong as a young man and the elegant mouldings and doors throughout. The residence has been tastefully decorate with antiques, family heirlooms and handcrafts to portray the feeling and spirit of Vermont. A full breakfast is included along with other meals available with prior notice. Centrally located to enjoy all of Vermont's year-round sights and pleasures, guests are just seven miles from the shores of Lake Champlain and 30 miles from Sugarbush/Mad River Valley Ski areas. The Vermont outdoors offers brisk mountain streams, canoeing, hiking Mt Philo, cycling the gently rolling hills and valleys, wandering down country lanes during Vermont's incomparable fall foliage and an unparalled variety of alpine and x-country ski trails. Cultural and heritage activities include renowned Vermont Mozart Festival, village band on the greens, Champlain Shakespeare Festival and Shelburne Museum with thirty-five historic buildings, the nation's oldest and most famous village museum. Vermont's fine restaurants offering *New England Cuisine* at its finest, art galleries and country antiques round-out an unforgettable trip bringing travelers back again and again. **RESERVATIONS:** $45 deposit per room night to confirm reservation, fourteen day cancellation policy for refund **BROCHURE:** Yes **PERMITTED:** Children, limited drinking [I07GPV-T2-4961]

**Newtons 1824 House Inn	**Waitsfield VT**

Nicholas & Joyce Newton   Rt 100 Box 159   05672
802-496-7555

Rates:	**Pvt Bath** 6	**Payment Terms:**
Single	$ 65-115.00	AE/MC/V
Double	$ 75-125.00	

Enjoy relaxed elegance. On the Mad River are fifty-two scenic acres in the heart of Vermont's best ski area. This white clapboard historical, two-story "telescope" farmhouse with ten gables offers the warm charm of yesteryear. Antiques and period furniture fill each room along with Oriental rugs gracing the floors and museum-quality art adorn-

ing the walls, all creating an atmosphere of warmth and elegance. The Inn has been featured in the *Los Angeles Times, Glamour, Skiing* and *Vermont Life* '93. Awake from behind the soft, puffy continental quilt in the morning to the smell of fresh muffins baking and see the picture-perfect views of winter's blanket of snow or the magical colors of autumn in this natural wonderland. Your hosts prepare gourmet breakfasts of souffle, blueberry pancakes with pure Vermont maple syrup and fresh squeezed orange juice served in the sunny dining room or on the porch overlooking a lovely setting. Outdoors, guests can try a dip in the Inn's swimming hole, catch a trout or two or picnic along the river bank. Year-round activities include all the sports (Sugarbush, Stowe, Mad River Glen) and sights (Ben & Jerrys, Lake Champlain & the Trapp Family Lodge) within easy driving distance. **PACKAGES:** Sun-Thur 5 weekday stay, less 20% **AIRPORT:** Burlington VT-30 mi **AAA** ♦♦♦ **Mobil** ★★ **RESERVATIONS:** 50% deposit, 14 day cancel policy for refund. Full daily rate charged on late arrivals or early departures **BROCHURE:** Yes **PERMITTED:** Limited children, limited drinking **LANGUAGES:** Spanish [I07GPVT2-8365]

**Northfield Inn	**Waitsfield/Warren VT**

Aglaia & Alan Stalb
802-485-8558

Rates:	**Pvt Bath** 8	**Payment Terms:**
Single	$ 55-225.00	Check
Double	$ 85-225.00	MC/V

Refer to the same listing name under Northfield, Vermont for a complete description. [M07FPVT1-17771]

---

*White Rocks Inn	**Wallingford VT**

June & Alfred Matthews
802-446-2077

RD 1 Box 297 05773

Rates:	**Pvt Bath** 5	**Payment Terms:**
Single	$ 70-95.00	Check
Double	$ 70-95.00	MC/V

Escape to this century old elegant farmhouse whose renovation carefully preserved the wide board floors, wainscoting, ornate moldings and high ceilings. Rooms are lovingly decorated and furnished with antiques, oriental carpeting and canopied beds with the convenience of modern private baths. Panoramic view of the White Mountains across a valley setting brings guests to nature everywhere they turn. The Appalachian Long Trail offers hiking; Otter Creek is perfect for trout, canoeing or swimming in the local ol' swimming hole! A country breakfast is served outdoors in summer overlooking the spotted cows that graze nearby and in winter guests relax in the antique furnished dining room. You'll delight to the fresh squeezed orange juice, homemade muffins or banana pancakes, raisin bread French toast all prepared from family recipes. Listed on the *National Historic Register*, guests will be able to bring their horses for boarding once the separate stall barn is complete. Meanwhile guests can enjoy wintry horse drawn sleigh rides! **RESERVATIONS:** One night's (or 50% if longer than one night), 14 day cancel policy, full deposit forfeited if canceled less than 48 hrs **SEASONAL:** Closed November **BROCHURE:** Yes **PERMITTED:** Children 10-up, BYOB drinking **LANGUAGES:** French, Spanish [E06BCVT-4972]

**Grunberg Haus	**Waterbury VT**
Mark Frohman/Christopher Sellers	RR 2 Box 1595 05676
800-800-7760 802-244-7726	**Res Times** 10am-10pm

Rates:	**Pvt Bath** 5	**Shared Bath** 10	**Payment Terms:**
Single	$ 45-85.00	$ 35-55.00	Check
Double	$ 75-135.00	$ 55-85.00	AE/DIS/MC/V

Bavaria in Vermont! This picture-postcard Tyrolian-style Bed & Breakfast is tucked on a hillside in Vermont's Green Mountains and is the perfect location to reach Stowe (six miles), Smugglers' Notch, family-style Bolton Valley, Mad River Glen and Sugarbush just down the road. Wonderful views are offered year-round from the traditional wood balcony extending around the stucco and wood-trimmed chalet while inside the giant stone fireplace is a favorite gathering place for guests. Individually decorated guest rooms include antiques, quilts, cozy comforters and collectibles - with all rooms opening onto the balcony. A morning wake-up call from the Guinea hens (they also provide the fresh eggs) announces a full gourmet breakfast with frequent selections of spiced fruit bowl, apple cheddar muffins, lemon-ricotta pancakes or grape fruit ambrosia, pancake bread or ginger cakes! Guests come back just for breakfast. The evening fire warms up the Steinway Grand, Chris (a professional vocalist) and all guests so inclined to partici- pate. Activities include spectacular autumn leaf-peaking, x-country skiing on the premises, golf, boating, bicycling, soaring, canoeing, hiking, antiquing, outlet shopping and visiting Ben & Jerry's ice cream factory. Evening home-style dinners are available with prior arrangements and additional cost. **DISCOUNTS:** Seniors, extended stays, travel industry. **AIRPORT:** Burlington Intl-23 mi; Burlington Amtrak & bus-3 mi. **PACKAGES:** *Ski Escape*: Lifts, lodging, meals & fireside entertainment; *Sweet Deal*; Lodging, meals, wine, candy, Bed & Jerry's factory tour; *Golf Getaway*: Green fees, meals, lodging **RESERVATIONS:** Deposit required, 14 day cancel policy less service fee. No-shows will be billed room rate plus tax **SEA-SONAL:** Rates vary **BROCHURE:** Yes **PERMITTED:** Limited children, limited smoking, drinking **CONFERENCES:** For groups to twenty-five [R11EPVT2-2849]

**Inn At Blush Hill	**Waterbury VT**
Pam & Gary Gosselin	Blush Hill Rd 05676
800-736-7522 802-244-7529	**Res Times** 9am-9pm

Rates:	**Pvt Bath** 4	**Shared Bath** 2	**Payment Terms:**
Single	$ 60-100.00	$ 50-80.00	Check
Double	$ 65-110.00	$ 55-85.00	AE/MC/V

The *Inn at Blush Hill* was once a stagecoach stopover between Waterbury and Stowe and now this c1790 Cape Cod is a haven for travelers seeking comfort, hospitality and a cozy atmosphere for capturing a brief moment of reflection and to enjoy time. Select a book from the library and curl-up in a comfortable chair in one of the Inn's many common rooms. The living room, with a roaring fire on chilly days, invites guests to relax on the overstuffed couches. The dining room, with antiques and wide-planked floors also has a fireplace and chairs for reading or chatting. There is a large front porch with rockers to watch the golfers on the adjacent 9-hole public course or view the manicured perennial gardens. Nearby you can swim, fish or canoe on an 880 acre reservoir. The cozy guest rooms are filled with country antiques, heirlooms, coordinating fabrics and wallpapers. There are fresh flowers in the summer and heated mattress pads in the winter. One room offers a working fireplace, another, spectacular mountain views. Located just off scenic Rt 100 at I-89, 10 miles from Stowe, Sugarbush and Bolton Valley ski areas; 25 miles from Burlington and one mile from Ben and Jerry's Ice Cream factory. A full country breakfast is included which may consist of fresh juice or local cider, fresh seasonal fruits such as strawberries, and specialties of apple pancakes or French toast ala mode (with what else but Ben and Jerry's Ice Cream) with plenty of freshly ground coffee and herb teas. **RESERVATIONS:** Advance payment or guarantee with credit card, 12 day cancel policy except 9/15-10/15 and holidays when 21 day cancel policy required for refund **SEASONAL:** No **BROCHURE:** Yes **PERMITTED:** Children over 6, drinking, limited smoking **CONFERENCES:** Yes for groups to ten persons [Z11CPVT-4976]

****Thatcher Brook Inn** — **Waterbury VT**

Pete & Kelly Varty
800-292-5911 802-244-5911

Rt 100 Rd #2 Box 62 05676-0490
Res Times 10am-11pm

Rates:	**Pvt Bath** 24
Single	$ 60-115.00
Double	$ 75-165.00

Payment Terms:
Check
DIS/MC/V

An exquisitely restored Victorian gem that's listed on Vermont's *Register of Historic Buildings* offers guests a true romantic New England experience. No expense was spared in the construction of this beautiful example of Victorian architecture including unique touches of a beautiful hand carved fireplace and stairway that remain intact today. Numerous kinds of woods are used throughout and include oak, Bird's eyed maple, spruce, Quarter-sawn maple, cherry and birch - all tastefully blended together. One of the most striking features of the Inn is the twin gazebo-type front porch which overlooked the railroad cars which use to pass the front yard on the way to Stowe. Things remain much the same today - enjoying another era and experiencing fine gourmet dining, Yankee hospitality and the pleasant year-round seasonal changes. A deluxe continental breakfast is included with each overnight stay. Rooms with fireplaces or whirlpools are available. Nearby there's skiing, biking, hiking, golf, tennis, riding, fishing, canoeing, gliding and fine antiquing. **RESERVATIONS:** 50% of length of stay must be received within 7 days of booking, 10 day cancel policy less $10 service fee. No shows will be charged the room rate; rates do not include 8% tax **SEASONAL:** No **BROCHURE:** Yes **PERMITTED:** Limited children (6-up), smoking **CONFERENCES:** Yes for groups to 75 persons for weddings, social and business retreats [I11DPVT-7040]

Weathervane Lodge — **West Dover VT**

Liz & Ernie Chabot
802-464-5426

HCR 63 57 Dorr Fitch Rd 05356

Rates:	**Pvt Bath** 4	**Shared Bath** 5	**Payment Terms:**
Single	$ 25-44.00	$ 25-32.00	Check

Double $ 50-88.00 $ 50-64.00

A true ***"year-round resort"***, the *Weathervane Lodge* is a paradise of outdoor activities as a getaway for couples and full family vacations.   Only four miles from Mount Snow Haystock and Corinthia for Alpine skiing in winter, summer offers wonderful mountain biking and over seventy miles of x-country trails throughout the valley - including trails beginning just outside of the back door! This Tyrolean-style ski lodge is decorated with authentic antiques and a warm blend of colonial and modern charm.   Guests are welcomed to make themselves at home in the lounge, dining and recreation room with a cozy fireplace, BYOB bar (complimentary set-ups are provided) and a microwave for hot snacks.   Summer brings lakeside swimming, boating, fishing, tennis, golf (three nearby courses) horseback riding, museums and the Marlboro Music Festival. The spectacular Fall Foliage shouldn't be missed. Tranquility is assured on the spacious landscaped grounds that include outdoor picnic tables and a gas grill for cooking. Your hosts are *seasoned pro's"*, hosting guests for the past thirty-two years from all over the world. **RESERVATIONS:** 50% deposit at res time, 7 day cancel policy for full refund **SEASONAL:** No **PERMITTED:** Children, drinking, limited smoking **BROCHURE:** Yes **AIRPORT:** Hartford 1-1/2 hr; Albany 1-1/2 hr [I04FPVT1-4985]

Inn At Highview   **Weston VT
Greg Bohan
802-875-2724

Rates:	**Pvt Bath** 8	**Payment Terms:**
Single	$ 80-115.00	Check
Double	$ 90-125.00	MC/V

Refer to the same listing name under Andover VT for a complete description. [M07GPVT2-17782]

Stonecrest Farm B&B **Wilder VT**

Gail Sanderson   119 Christian St 05088
802-295-2600

Rates:	Pvt Bath 3	Shared Bath 2	Payment Terms:
Single	$ 90.00	$ 80.00	Check
Double	$ 100.00	$ 90.00	MC/V

Located 3.5 miles from Dartmouth College in Hanover New Hampshire, this gracious historic 1810 country home with handsome barns was formerly a dairy farm. Here, Arthur Stone, a prominent local citizen, entertained guests such as President Coolidge and Ameila Earhart. *Stonecrest*, in a village on the Connecticut River, is convenient to many year-round recreation and cultural activities. We participate in a summer *"Inn to Inn"* two-day canoeing trip. Your well-traveled host, a former headmaster's wife and a practicing attorney, has welcomed many Dartmouth alumni and parents, and visitors from as far as China. Five graciously decorated guest rooms are furnished comfortably with antiques, down comforters and lots of reading material. Choose a king or queen bed with a private bath or a canopied doubled bed or twin beds with the shared bath. Apreś ski, bikes or hikes, snuggle-up with a book next to the fireplace, play the baby grand. Scout the antique shops. In warm weather, relax on our stone terrace, surrounded by flowers and fine old trees. Savor nearby views of New Hampshire mountains. Enjoy a continental breakfast of fresh fruit, homemade scones, muffins and such in our sunny dining room. **RESERVATIONS:** Credit card deposit to guarantee, 14 day cancel policy for refund less $10 service fee; check-in 3-9pm **SEASONAL:** No **PERMITTED:** Drinking, limited children **BROCHURE:** Yes **LANGUAGES:** German, French (understand only) **DISCOUNTS:** Week stays, last night free **AIRPORT:** Lebanon-4 mi, connects to Boston & NYC **PACKAGES:** *Inn to Inn* [R07FPVT1-16460]

Inn At Quail Run **Wilmington VT**

Tom & Marie Martin   HCR 63 Box 28 Smith Rd 05363
800-34 ESCAPE 802-464-3362 **Res Times** 8am-11pm

Rates:	Pvt Bath 14	Shared Bath 1	Payment Terms:
Single	$ 90.00	$ 90.00	Check
Double	$ 90.00	$ 90.00	MC/V

The picturesque surroundings and tranquil atmosphere of the *Inn at Quail Run* will make you remember how getaways were meant to be. Relax and lose yourself in time in the gracious and romantic accommodations. Each guest room is tastefully appointed with antique or brass beds and cozy comforters for warm nights. Make yourself at home in the comfortable living room where you'll find a crackling fire and spectacular views of the outdoors. Each morning your hosts prepare a bountiful homemade country breakfast before starting out. As a year-round resort, guests enjoy brilliant fall colors of the sugar maples; door front x-country skiing on 40km network of the Sitzmark or downhill skiing at Mount Snow and Haystack, just 4 miles away. Enjoy TV, socializing with the other guests, stroll the beautiful countryside, try the clay tennis courts or refresh in the solar heated pool. More than the beautiful surroundings - *Quail Run* **is a place to relax and unwind to just enjoy the luxury of time - - because your hosts remember how getaways were meant to be.** **AIRPORT:** Hartford CT-1.5 hrs; Albany NY 1.5 hrs **RESERVATIONS:** One night's deposit, 50% if longer, 7 day cancel policy for refund **SEASONAL:** Closed 4/15-5/15 **BROCHURE:** Yes **PERMITTED:** Children, limited drinking, limited smoking (outdoors only). Check-in 3pm, check-out 11am **CONFERENCES:** Yes, for groups to 20 persons [R11DPVT-13656]

**Charleston House	**Woodstock VT**
Bill & Barb Hough	21 Pleasant St 05091
802-457-3843	**Res Times** 8am-9pm

Rates:	**Pvt Bath** 7	**Payment Terms:**
Single	$ 90.00	Check
Double	$ 145.00	MC/V

Fine craftsmanship and beautiful surroundings combine with warmth and hospitality reminiscent of a family homecoming. This 1835 Greek Revival townhouse is listed on the *National Historic Register* and is located in the picturesque Village of Woodstock - regarded as one of the most beautiful villages in the USA by *National Geographic Magazine.* Completely restored to provide modern comfort along with maintaining historic authenticity, the Inn offers period antique furnishings, fine reproductions and an eclectic selection of art and Oriental rugs. In Woodstock, you can leave your car parked and walk throughout the town, listening to the Revere Bells ring out on the hour, sit on a river bank watching the water slide by, relax on the town Green - the site of winter yule festivals and summer social events, as well as relaxed conversation between villagers. There's Summer Stock, golf at Woodstock Country Club (course designed by Robert Trent Jones), tennis, game fishing, a Rockwellesque swimming hole, leisure country drives where you learn the old-fashioned methods of the Vermont farmers. Winter in Woodstock is unforgettable. There's excellent skiing minutes away at Suicide Six, Killington, Pico, Mount Ascutney, Okemo and Mountain Meadows and sleigh rides ending before the warmth of a winter's fire. In sum, your hosts offer a beautifully decorated room and home, a hearty full breakfast at our common table or a continental breakfast in bed and hospitality usually extended only to "kith and kin" which become cherished memories as year pass. **AIRPORT:** Lebanon NH-15 mi **DISCOUNTS:** Mid-week **PACKAGES:** Midweek in winter **RESERVATIONS:** One night's deposit to guarantee **SEASONAL:** No **BROCHURE:** Yes **PERMITTED:** Drinking, limited children [R10EPVT2-5010]

**Woodstocker B&B	**Woodstock VT**
E Deignan/Romano Formichella	Rt 4 05091
802-457-3896	**Res Times** 24 hrs

Rates:	**Pvt Bath** 9	**Payment Terms:**
Single	$ 60-110.00	Check
Double	$ 65-120.00	MC/V

Located in a historic colonial New England village, this inviting and charming Bed & Breakfast offers great New England warmth and hospitality. The nine guest rooms are comfortably furnished and spacious while reflecting New England decor. There are two suites which include a living room, kitchen and deck for the ideal setting for an intimate family vacation. Year-round activities are at your doorstep: skiing, fishing, biking, hiking, swimming and a sports center for racquetball and other indoor activities. At day's end, you can plan your evening events while refreshing in the whirlpool and enjoying your favorite beverage and snack. Common rooms include TV, a wide array of fascinating books and plenty of board games. **MEALS:** A complimentary breakfast buffet includes fresh fruit, homemade cereals, quiche, breads and muffins with plenty of fresh brewed coffee. Picnic baskets are available for your day's trip into the country. Special packages available, eg: ***Midweek Alpine Ski Trips***, includes lodging, breakfast and all day lift tickets for just $45.00 per person, double occupancy. **RESERVATIONS:** 50% deposit at res time with 14 day cancel policy **SEASONAL:** Rates vary **PACKAGES:** *Mid-week Alpine Ski Trip* includes lodging, breakfast and all day lift tickets for just $45 per person, double occupancy **BROCHURE:** Yes **PERMITTED:** Drinking, limited children **CONFERENCES:** For groups to 25 persons **LANGUAGES:** Italian [Z05FPVT1-5012]

Alburg
AUBERGE ALBURG
802-796-3169

*THOS MOTT
HOMESTEAD
802-796-3736

YE OLDE
GREYSTONE
802-796-3911

Andover
HILLSIDE
802-875-3844

****INN AT
HIGHVIEW**
802-875-2724

Arlington
****ARLINGTON INN**
800-443-9442

*EVERGREEN
802-375-2272

HILL FARM INN
800-882-2545

INN AT
SUNDERLAND
802-362-4213

INN ON COVERED
BRIDGE GREEN
802-375-9489

IRA ALLEN HOUSE
802-362-2284

*SHENANDOAH
FARM
802-375-6372

WEST MOUNTAIN
INN
802-375-6516

Barnet
OLD HOMESTEAD
INN
802-633-4100

Barre
*WOODRUFF
HOUSE
802-476-7745

Barton
BARTON INN
802-525-4721

FOX HALL B&B
802-525-6903

LAFONTS DAIRY
FARM
ESTERS

Bellows Falls
****BLUE HAVEN
CHRISTIAN B&B**
802-463-9008

HORSEFEATHERS
B&B

RIVER MIST B&B
802-463-9023

Belmont
LESLIE PLACE
802-259-2903

PARMENTER
HOUSE
802-259-2009

Bennington
BENNINGTON
HOUSE
802-447-7972

MOLLY STARK INN
802-442-9631

MT ANTHONY
GUEST HOUSE
802-447-7396

MUNRO HAWKINS
HOUSE
802-447-2286

SOUTH SHIRE INN
802-447-3839

Benson
GREEN MOUNTAIN

MEADOWBROOK
FARM

Bethel
*EASTWOOD
HOUSE
802-234-9686

GREENHURST INN
802-234-9474

POPLAR MANOR
802-234-5426

Bolton Valley
BLACK BEAR INN
800-395-6335

BOLTON VALLEY
RESORT

Bondville

*ALPENROSE INN
802-297-2750

BARN LODGE
802-297-1877

BROMLEY VIEW
INN
802-297-1459

Bradford
MERRY MEADOW
FARM
802-222-4412

VILLAGE INN OF
BRADFORD
802-222-9303

Brandon
BRANDON INN
802-247-5766

CHURCHILL HOUSE
INN
802-247-3078

COX MOUNTAIN
INN

GAZEBO INN
802-247-3235

LE RELAIS

MOFFETT HOUSE
802-247-3843

OLD MILL INN
802-247-8002

STONE MILL FARM
802-247-6137

**Bridgewater
Corners**
OCTOBER
COUNTRY INN
802-672-3412

Bristol
LONG RUN INN
802-453-3233

MAPLEWOOD FARM
802-453-2992

Brookfield
*GREEN TRAILS
COUNTRY INN
802-276-3412

Brownsville
INN AT MT
ASCUTNEY
802-484-7725

*MILL BROOK B&B
802-484-7283

Burlington
HAUS KELLEY B&B

HOWDEN
COTTAGE
802-864-7198

**THATCHER
BROOK INN
800-292-5911

TRUAX TOURIST
HOME
802-862-0809

YELLOW HOUSE

Calais

WHITE HOUSE AT
KENTS CORNER
802-229-9847

Charlotte
CHARLOTTES WEB
B&B
802-425-3341

GREEN MEADOWS
B&B
802-425-3059

INN AT
CHARLOTTE
802-425-2934

Chelsea
SHIRE INN
800-441-6908

Chester
*CHESTER HOUSE
802-875-2205

GREENLEAF INN
802-875-3171

HENRY FARM INN
802-875-2674

**HUGGING BEAR
INN & SHOPPE**
800-325-0519

****INN AT
HIGHVIEW**
802-875-2724

INN AT LONG LAST
802-875-2444

**INN VICTORIA
800-732-4288

NIGHT WITH A
NATIVE

****STONE HEARTH
INN**
802-875-2525

Chittenden
MOUNTAIN TOP INN
800-445-2100

TULIP TREE INN
802-483-6213

Colchester
ON THE LAMB B&B
802-586-2848

Craftsbury
CRAFTSBURY B&B
ON WYLIE HILL
802-586-2206

CRAFTSBURY INN
800-336-2848

GARY MEADOW
DAIRY FARM
802-586-2536

***INN ON THE
COMMON**
800-521-2233

ONE AKRE FARM

Cuttingsville
MAPLE CREST
FARM
802-492-3367

SHREWSBURY INN

Danby

QUAILS NEST B&B
802-293-5099

SILAS GRIFFIN INN
802-293-5567

Derby Line
DERBY VILLAGE
INN
802-873-3604

Dorset
BARROWS HOUSE
802-867-4455

CORNUCOPIA OF
DORSET
802-867-5751

DORSET INN
802-867-5500

DOVETAIL INN
802-867-5747

LITTLE LODGE AT
DORSET
802-867-4040

MARBLE INN
802-867-4155

VILLAGE AUBERGE
802-867-5715

Duxbury
SCHNEIDER HAUS
802-244-7726

East Barnett
INWOOD MANOR
802-633-4047

East Burke

BLUE WAX FARM
802-626-5542

BURKE GREEN
GUEST HOUSE
802-467-3472

DARION INN

GARRISON INN
802-626-8329

HOUSE IN THE
WOOD

NUTMEGGER

OLD CUTTER INN
802-626-5152

VILLAGE INN OF
EAST BURKE
802-626-3161

East Calais
LAKE HOUSE B&B

East Dorset
KILN GUEST
HOUSE
802-362-4889

East Dover
COOPER HILL
LODGE
802-348-6333

East Fairfield
WHISPERING
PINES
802-827-3827

East Hardwick
BRICK HOUSE

802-472-5512

East Middlebury
LORDS B&B

OCTOBER
PUMPKIN INN

ROBT FROST MTN
B&B

*WAYBURY INN
802-388-4015

East Poultney
EAGLE TAVERN ON
THE GREEN
802-287-9498

**East Saint
Johnsbury**
ECHO LEDGE
FARM INN
802-748-4750

Enosberg Falls
****BERKSON
FARMS**
802-933-2522

RICK LANSINGS
B&B

Essex Junction
TANDYS B&B
802-878-4729

VARNUMS
802-899-4577

Fair Haven
FAIRHAVEN INN
802-265-3833

HAVEN EST 1948
802-265-3373

****MAPLEWOOD INN
& ANTIQUES**
800-253-7729

VERMONT
MARBLE
800-535-2814

Fairfax
FOGGY HOLLOW
FARM

****INN AT BUCK
HOLLOW FARM**
802-849-2400

Fairfield
***HILLSIDE VIEW
FARM**
802-827-4480

Fairlee
ALOHA MANOR
802-333-4478

RUTLEDGE INN

****SILVER MAPLE
LODGE
COTTAGES**
800-666-1946

Ferrisburg
1810 FARMHOUSE
INN
802-877-2576

Franklin
FAIR MEADOWS
FARM
802-285-2132

Gassetts
OLD TOWN FARM
INN
802-875-2346

Gaysville
COBBLE HOUSE
INN
802-234-5458

LAOLKE LODGE
802-234-9205

Goshen
****BLUEBERRY
HILL INN**
800-448-0707

Grafton
EAGLEBROOK OF
GRAFTON

HAYES HOUSE
802-843-2461

OLD TAVERN AT
GRAFTON
802-843-2231

WOODCHUCK HILL
FARM
802-843-2398

Greensboro
HIGHLAND LODGE
802-533-2647

Guildhall
GUILDHALL INN
802-676-3720

Hancock
*KINCRAFT INN
802-767-3734

Hardwick
KAHAGON AT
NICHOLS POND
802-472-6446

Hartford
HOUSE OF SEVEN
GABLES
800-325-2540

Hero
THOMAS MOTT
B&B
802-372-5777

Highgate Springs
*TYLER PLACE
802-868-3301

Huntington
CAMELS HUMP
NORDIC CENTER

Hyde Park
**FITCH HILL INN
802-888-3834

Irasburg
IRASBURG GREEN
B&B
802-754-6012

Jamaica
THREE MOUNTAINS
INN
802-874-4140

Jay
JAY VILLAGE INN
802-988-2643

WOODSHED
LODGE
802-988-4444

Jeffersonville
JEFFERSON
HOUSE
802-644-2030

MANNSVIEW INN
800-937-MANN

SMUGGLERS
NOTCH INN
802-644-2412

WINDRIDGE INN
802-644-8281

Jericho
EATON HOUSE
B&B
802-899-2354

**HENRY M FIELD
HOUSE B&B**
802-899-3984

HOMEPLACE
802-899-4694

MILLIKENS
802-899-3993

SAXON INN
802-899-3015

Killington
CHALET
KILLINGTON
800-451-4105

GREY BONNETT
INN
800-342-2086

**INN AT LONG
TRAIL**

800-325-2540

INN OF SIX
MOUNTAINS

KILLINGTON
VILLAGE

MOUNTAIN
MEADOW LODGE
802-775-1010

MOUNTAIN
MORGANS

SHERBURNE
VALLEY INN
802-422-9888

**THE VERMONT
INN**
800-541-7795

Landgrove
NORDIC INN
802-824-6444

VILLAGE INN AT
LANDGROVE
802-824-6673

Londonderry
BLUE GENTIAN
LODGE
802-824-5908

COUNTRY HARE
802-824-3131

HIGHLAND HOUSE
802-824-3019

INN ON MAGIC
MOUNTAIN

VILLAGE INN
800-669-8466

Lower Waterford
FLOWER
COTTAGE
802-748-8441

RABBIT HILL INN
800-76-BUNNY

Ludlow
ANDRIE ROSE INN
802-228-4846

BLACK RIVER INN
802-228-5585

COMBES FAMILY
INN
802-228-8799

**ECHO LAKE INN
800-356-6844

FLETCHER MANOR
802-228-3548

GOVERNORS INN
800-GOVERNOR

****INN AT
HIGHVIEW**
802-875-2724

JEWELL BROOK
FARM

OKEMO INN
802-228-8834

Lyndonville
*WILDFLOWER INN
800-627-8310

Manchester
1811 HOUSE
802-362-1811

BIRCH HILL INN
802-362-2761

BOOK N HEARTH
INN
802-362-3604

EQUINOX
800-362-4747

****INN AT
MANCHESTER**
802-362-1793

INN AT WILLOW
POND
802-362-4733

****MANCHESTER
HIGHLANDS INN**
800-743-4565

RIVER MEADOW
FARM
802-362-3700

SKYLINE INN
802-362-1113

VILLAGE
COUNTRY INN
800-379-0300

WILBURTON INN
800-648-4944

Marlboro
LONGWOOD INN
802-257-1545

WHETSTONE INN
802-254-2500

Mendon
RED CLOVER INN
800-752-0571

Middleburg
PEACEFUL ACRES
802-388-2076

Middlebury
***BROOKSIDE
MEADOWS**
802-388-6429

MIDDLEBURY INN
800-842-4666

POINT OF VIEW

SWIFTHOUSE INN
802-388-9925

**Middletown
Springs**
****MIDDLETOWN
SPRINGS INN**
802-235-2198

Montgomery
FALLBROOK
HOUSE
802-326-4616

**Montgomery
Center**
EAGLE LODGE

INN ON TROUT
RIVER
800-338-7049

ZACKS ON THE

ROCKS

Montgomery Village
BLACK LANTERN INN
802-326-4507

Montpelier
INN AT MONTPELIER
802-223-2727

MONTPELIER B&B
802-229-0878

NORTHFIELD INN
802-485-8558

Moretown
CAMELS HUMP VIEW FARM
802-496-3614

HONEYSUCKLE INN
802-496-6200

Morgan
SEYMOUR LAKE LODGE
802-895-2752

Mount Holly
AUSTRIA HAUS
802-259-2441

HORTONVILLE INN
802-259-2587

HOUNDS FOLLY
802-259-2718

Mount Snow
SNOW LAKE

LODGE

Newbury
CENTURY PAST
802-866-3358

Newfane
FOUR COLUMNS INN
802-365-7713

INN AT SOUTH NEWFANE

OLD NEWFANE INN
802-365-4427

WEST RIVER LODGE
802-365-7745

North Ferrisburg
DUNN-INN
802-425-2902

North Hero
CHAS NORTHLAND LODGE
802-372-8822

NORTH HERO HOUSE
802-372-8237

North Thetford
STONE HOUSE INN
802-333-9124

North Troy
NORTH TROY INN
802-988-2527

ROSE APPLE ACRES FARM

802-988-4300

Northfield
NORTHFIELD INN
802-485-8558

Norwich
INN AT NORWICH
802-649-1143

Old Bennington
FOUR CHIMNEYS INN
802-447-3500

Orleans
VALLEY HOUSE INN
802-754-6665

Orwell
BROOKSIDE FARMS
802-948-2727

Perkinsville
*GWENDOLYNS B&B**
802-263-5248

INN AT WEATHERSFIELD
800-477-4828

PEREGRINES REST
802-263-5784

Peru
JOHNNY SEESAWS
802-824-5533

WILEY INN
802-824-6000

Pittsfield
PITTSFIELD INN
802-746-8943

SWISS FARM
LODGE
802-226-7744

Pittsford
FOX BROS FARM
802-483-2870

SUNNI G HILL

Plainfield
YANKEES
NORTHVIEW B&B
802-454-7191

Plymouth
HAWK INN &
MOUNTAIN
RESORT
800-685-4295

SALT ASH INN
802-672-3748

SNOWY OWL
LODGE
802-672-5018

Post Mills
LAKE HOUSE
802-333-4025

Poultney
LAKE ST
CATHERINE INN
802-287-9347

STONEBRIDGE INN
802-287-9849

TOWER HALL B&B
802-287-4004

Proctorsville
***ALLENS INN OF
PROCTORSVILLE**
802-226-7970

CASTLE INN
802-226-7222

GOLDEN STAGE
INN
802-226-7744

OKEMO LANTERN
LODGE
802-226-7770

Putney
HICKORY RIDGE
HOUSE
802-387-5709

MAPLETON FARM
B&B
802-257-5252

MISTY MEADOW
B&B
802-722-9517

PUTNEY INN
802-387-6617

Quechee
PARKER INN
FRENCH
RESTAURANT
802-295-6077

QUECHEE INN AT
MARSHLAND FARM
800-235-3133

QUECHEE LAKES

Quechee Village
ABEL BARRON
HOUSE
802-295-1337

Randolph
PLACIDIA FARM
B&B
802-728-9883

THREE STALLION
INN
802-728-5575

Rawsonville
BEAR CREEK INN

Reading
GREYSTONE B&B
802-484-7200

HAPGOOD
COTTAGE

PEEPING COW INN
802-484-5036

Readsboro
OLD COACH INN
802-423-5394

Ripton
CHIPMAN INN
802-388-2390

Rochester
HARVEYS MT VIEW
802-767-4273

KINGSBURYS
FOREST HOME
B&B

LIBERTY HILL
FARM
802-767-3926

NEW HOMESTEAD
802-767-4751

Roxbury
INN AT
JOHNNYCAKE
FLATS
802-746-8943

Royalton
FOX STAND INN
802-763-8437

Rutland
HILLCREST GUEST
HOUSE
802-775-1670

INN AT RUTLAND
802-773-0575

Saint Albans
****INN AT BUCK
HOLLOW FARM**
802-849-2400

ISLAND VIEW

Saint Johnsbury
BROADVIEW FARM
B&B
802-748-9902

ECHO LEDGE
FARM INN
802-748-4750

LOOKING GLASS
INN
802-748-3052

Saxtons
SAXTONS RIVER
INN
802-869-2110

Shelburne
HULLCREST B&B
SHELBURNE
HOUSE
802-985-8498

Shoreham
SHOREHAM INN
800-255-5081

Shrewsbury
BUCKMASTER INN
802-492-3485

Simonsville
ROWELLS INN
802-875-3658

South Burlington
LINDENWOOD A
COUNTRY INN
802-862-2144

South Londonderry
LONDONDERRY
INN
802-824-5226

South Newfane
INN AT SOUTH
NEWFANE
802-348-7191

South Strafford
*WATERCOURSE
WAY
800-562-5110

South Wallingford
GREEN MOUNTAIN
TEA ROOM
802-446-2611

South Woodstock
KEDRON VALLEY
INN
802-457-1473

Springfield
HARTNESS HOUSE
802-885-2115

Starksboro
MILLHOUSE B&B
802-453-2008

Stockbridge
SCARBOROUGH
INN
802-746-8141

STOCKBRIDGE INN
802-746-8165

WILD BERRY INN
802-746-8141

Stowe
**1860 HOUSE
800-248-1860

ANDERSEN LODGE
AUSTRIAN INN
802-253-7660

*BAAS' GASTHAUS
802-253-8376

BITTERSWEET INN
802-253-7787

BUTTERNUT INN

AT STOWE
800-3 BUTTER

COTTAGE IN
MAGICAL FOREST
802-253-9577

**EDSON HILL
MANOR**
800-621-0284

FIDDLERS GREEN
INN
802-253-8124

FITCH HILL INN
802-888-3834

FOUNTAIN B&B
802-253-9285

FOXFIRE INN
802-253-4887

GABLES INN
800-GABLES1

GOLDEN KITZ
LODGE
800-KITS LOV

GREEN MOUNTAIN
INN
800-445-6629

GREY FOX INN
802-253-8921

GUEST HOUSE
CRISTEL HORMAN
802-253-4846

HADLEIGH HOUSE
802-253-7703

HOB NOB INN
802-253-8549

**BRASS LANTERN
INN**
800-729-2980

INNSBRUCK INN
802-253-8582

LOGWOOD INN
800-426-6697

NICHOLS LODGE
802-253-7683

PLUM DOOR
802-253-9995

PUB AT STOWE
802-253-8669

RASPBERRY PATCH
B&B
802-253-4145

SCANDINAVIA INN
& CHALET
802-253-8555

*SIEBENESS
800-426-9001

SKI INN
802-253-4050

SPA AT STOWE
GREEN
MOUNTAIN INN

SPRUCE POND INN
802-253-4828

STOWE AWAY

LODGE
802-253-7547

STOWE BOUND
LODGE
800-72-STOWE

STOWEHOF INN
802-253-9722

TEN ACRES LODGE
800-327-7357

**THATCHER
BROOK INN
800-292-5911

TIMBERHOLM INN
802-253-7603

TOPNOTCH AT
STOWE

*YE OLDE
ENGLISH INNE
800-477-3771

YODLER

*Stratton
Mountain*
BIRKENHAUS
802-297-2000

Sugarbush
SUGARTREE
A COUNTRY INN
802-583-3211

WHITE HORSE INN
802-496-2476

Taftville
APPLEBUTTER INN

802-457-4158

Thetford Hill
FAHRENBRAE
802-785-4304

Tinmouth
FIVE M FARM

Townsend
TOWNSEND INN

Townshend
BOARDMAN HOUSE
802-365-4086

Underhill Center
HAUS KELLEY B&B
802-899-3905

Vergennes
EMERSONS GUEST
HOUSE
802-877-3293

****STRONG HOUSE
INN**
802-877-3337

Waitsfield
HYDE AWAY
800-777-HYDE

HONEYSUCKLE INN
802-496-6200

KNOLL FARM
COUNTRY INN
802-496-3939

*LAREAU FARM
COUNTRY INN
800-833-0766

*MAD RIVER BARN
802-496-3310

MILLBROOK INN
802-496-2405

MOUNTAIN VIEW
INN
802-496-2426

****NEWTONS 1824
HOUSE INN**
802-496-7555

ROUND BARN
FARM
802-496-2276

SNUGGERY INN
802-496-2322

*TUCKER HILL
LODGE
802-496-3983

VALLEY INN
802-496-3450

WAITSFIELD INN
802-496-3979

WEATHERTOP
LODGE
802-496-4909

Waitsfield/Warren
**NORTHFIELD INN
802-485-8558

Wallingford
VICTORIAN INN
802-446-2099

*WHITE ROCKS

INN
802-446-2077

Warren
BEAVER POND
FARM
802-583-2861

CHRISTMAS TREE
INN

RYNES B&B
802-496-6042

SGT PEPPERS
LODGE

SOUTH HOLLOW
FARM
802-496-5627

SUGARBUSH INN

Waterbury
*BLACK LOCUST
INN
802-244-7490

****GRUNBERG
HAUS**
800-800-7760

****INN AT BLUSH
HILL**
800-736-7522

****THATCHER
BROOK INN**
800-292-5911

Waterbury Center
MAY FARM LODGE
802-244-7306

West Arlington
FOUR WINDS
COUNTRY INN
802-375-6734

INN ON COVERED
BRIDGE GREEN

West Brattleboro
CAPTAIN HENRY
CHASE HOUSE
802-254-4114

West Charleston
HUNTS HIDEAWAY
802-895-4432

West Dover
AUSTIN HILL IN
800-332RELAX

DEERHILL INN
802-464-3100

DOVEBERRY INN
802-464-5652

GRAY GHOST INN
802-464-2474

INN AT SAWMILL
FARM
802-464-8131

SHIELD INN
802-464-3984

SNOW DEN INN
800-852-9240

SNOW TREE/SNOW

RESORT

**WEATHERVANE
LODGE**
802-464-5426

WEST DOVER INN
802-464-5207

West Glover
RODGERS DAIRY
FARM

West Rutland
SILVER FOX INN
802-438-5555

West Townshend
GENERAL
FLETCHER
HOMESTEAD
802-874-4853

WINDHAM HILL INN
802-874-4080

Weston
1830 INN ON THE
GREEN
802-824-6789

COLONIAL HOUSE
802-824-6286

DARLING FAMILY
INN
802-824-3223

****INN AT
HIGHVIEW**
802-875-2724

INN AT WESTON
802-824-5804

WILDER

HOMESTEAD
802-824-8172

**White River
Junction**
SERENITY HILL
FARM

Wilder
****STONECREST
FARM B&B**
802-295-2600

Williamstown
AUTUMN CREST
INN
802-433-6627

ROSE WOOD INN
802-433-5822

Williamsville
COUNTRY INN AT
WILLIAMSVILLE
802-348-7148

Williston
PARTRIDGE HILL
802-878-4741

Wilmington
BROOK BOUND
BLDG/HERMITAGE
802-464-3511

DARCROFT'S
SCHOOLHOUSE
802-464-2631

****INN AT QUAIL
RUN**
800-34ESCAPE

MISTY MOUNTAIN

802-464-3961

NORDIC HILLS
LODGE
802-464-5130

NUTMEG INN
802-464-3351

ON THE ROCKS
LODGE
802-464-8364

RED SHUTTER INN
802-464-3768

TRAILS END
LODGE
802-464-2727

WHITE HOUSE OF
WILMINGTON
802-464-2135

Windsor
JUNIPER HILL INN
800-359-2541

Wolcott
GOLDEN MAPLE
INN
802-888-6614

Woodstock
CANTERBURY
HOUSE
802-457-3077

CARRIAGE HOUSE
OF WOODSTOCK
802-457-4322

****CHARLESTON
HOUSE**

802-457-3843

DEERBROOK INN
802-672-3713

JACKSON HOUSE
802-457-2065

LINCOLN COVERED
BRIDGE INN
802-457-3312

THOMAS HILL
FARM
802-457-1067

THREE CHURCH
STREET
802-457-1925

VILLAGE INN OF
WOODSTOCK
802-457-1255

WINSLOW HOUSE
802-457-1820

WOODSTOCK
HOUSE
802-457-1758

WOODSTOCK INN &
RESORT
800-448-7900

****WOODSTOCKER
B&B**
802-457-3896

Canada

Rates:	**Pvt Bath** 30	**Suites**	**Payment Terms:**
Single	$ 100.00 CN	$ 160.00 CN	Check
Double	$ 100.00 CN	$ 160.00 CN	MC/V

Take a memory home with you - *Halliburton House Inn*! Experience the pleasure of stepping into the past by visiting this *Heritage Property,* for an overnight stay or gourmet meal. *Halliburton House* was build in 1816 as the home of Sir Brenton Halliburton, Chief Justice of the Nova Scotia Supreme Court. From 1885 to 1887, the building served as Dalhousie University Law School. Today, this registered heritage property is Halifax's finest Inn. All of the Inn's thirty comfortable guest rooms are tastefully furnished with period antiques. Each has a private bath, as well as the modern amenities expected by today's guests. Several suites are available, some with fireplaces. Sit in front of a warm crackling fire and relax before dinner in the library. Our restaurant offers a relaxed elegant setting for both lunch and dinner. The *Halliburton* menu specializes in wild game and fresh Atlantic seafood. During the summer months, relax over lunch in the outdoor garden cafe. With its central location and free parking, the Inn is ideally located in the heart of downtown Halifax. *Halliburton House Inn* is known for its high standards, relaxed ambience and excellent service. **DISCOUNTS:** Yes, inquire at res time **RESERVATIONS:** One night's deposit, 24 hr cancel policy **SEASONAL:** Rates vary **BROCHURE:** Yes **PERMITTED:** Children, drinking, limited smoking **CONFERENCES:** Yes, our boardroom seats 25 persons **LANGUAGES:** English, French [I07GPCN2-11793]

Canada

Albert House — Ottawa ON

John & Cathy Delroy
800-267-1982 613-236-4479

478 Albert St K1R 5B5
Res Times 8am-11pm

Rates: **Pvt Bath** 17
Single $ 62-85.00 CN
Double $ 72-95.00 CN

Payment Terms:
Tvlrs Check
AE/DC/MC/V

Albert House is a charming Victorian mansion built in 1875 by and for noted Canadian architect, Thomas Seaton Scott who was the Chief Architect for the Ministry of Public Works at that time. Scott oversaw many government projects including the original Customs House and Post Office in downtown Ottawa and part of the Parliament Buildings. Our seventeen guest rooms are individually decorated and all have ensuite facilities, colour cable TV, direct dial phones and air conditioning/individual heat control. Guests can enjoy our famous Albert House full, hot breakfast in the dining room or continental service is available for those who wish to breakfast in their room. A cozy lounge with fireplace provides a pleasant place to chat with other guests or read one of the many periodicals from our large selection. Complimentary tea, coffee, fruit juices are available during the day and evening. Our downtown location allows guests to park their cars and walk to most of Ottawa's attractions, both cultural and recreational. We have two very large but friendly dogs who have become quite well-known and welcome presence at *Albert House*. **DISCOUNTS:** Seasonal weekends **AIRPORT:** Ottawa Intl-7 mi **RESERVATIONS:** One night's deposit or credit card number, arrival before 11pm unless prior arrangements made **BROCHURE:** Yes **PERMITTED:** Limited children, limited pets, drinking, smoking **LANGUAGES:** English, some French [Z07GP CN2-9185]

Austrealis Guest House — Ottawa ON

Brian & Carol Waters
613-235-8461

35 Marlborough Ave K1N 8E6
Res Times 8am-10pm

Rates: **Pvt Bath** 1 | **Shared Bath** 2 | **Payment Terms:**
Single $ 88.00 CN $ 35-Up CN Check
Double $ 58.00 CN $ 45-Up CN

We are the oldest established and still operating Bed & Breakfast in the Ottawa area. Located on a quiet, tree-lined street one block from the Rideau River, with its ducks and swans and Strathcona

Park ... but just a twenty minute walk from the Parliament Buildings. This period, architecturally designed house boasts leaded windows, fireplace, oak floors and unique eight foot high stained glass windows overlooking the hall. Our spacious rooms, including a suite and private bathroom, features many of our collectibles from our time living in different parts of the world. The hearty, home-cooked delicious breakfast, with homebaked breads, pastries ensure you will start the day in just the right way. Our Australian and English heritage combined with our time in Canada provide a truly international flavor with a relaxed atmosphere. We are located downtown and have off-street parking. In-addition, we provide free pick-up and delivery from/to the bus and train stations for our guests. We speak both English and French. Multiple-winner of the **Ottawa Hospitality Award** *and* **recommended** *by Newsweek*. We are full members of the Ottawa Tourism and Convention Authority. **RESERVATIONS:** One night's deposit **PERMITTED:** Children, limited smoking **SEASONAL:** No **BROCHURE:** Yes **LANGUAGES:** English, French **DISCOUNTS:** 10% off-season 11/1-3/1 **PACKAGES:** Yes, with local restaurants [R05FPCN1-9186]

****Burken Guest House**   Toronto ON

Burke Friedrichkeit & Ken Bosher322 Palmerston Blvd M6G 2N6
416-920-7842   **Res Times** 10am-7pm
   Fax 416 960-9529

Rates:	**Shared Bath** 8	**Payment Terms:**
Single	$ 45-50.00 CN	Cash
Double	$ 60-65.00 CN	MC/V

Burken Guest House is located in a beautiful residential downtown Toronto neighborhood next to public transportation and where most attractions can be reached within 30 minutes. Our home is well-kept, quiet and accommodates only non-smokers. Four guest rooms on each floor are wonderfully furnished with antiques with European-style bath facilities (washbasins in each room) while sharing the full bath with three others on the same floor. Each room is equipped with a telephone and includes maid service. A continental breakfast is served in the breakfast room or on the outdoor deck in summer. A TV lounge provides relaxation with a generous supply of newspapers and books. Limited free parking is available on the premises. Your hosts are into their tenth successful year of pleasing guests and are members of *FOBBA, MTCVA* and the *American B&B Assoc* and many others. Their friendly and capable service will make your visit to Toronto most enjoyable. **DISCOUNTS:** Weekly rates Nov to April **AIRPORT:** Toronto Pearson Intl-15 km. **RESERVATIONS:** Deposit required to guarantee reservation, 48 hr cancel policy **BROCHURE:** Yes **PERMITTED:** Children, drinking. **LANGUAGES:** English, German, French [K07GPCN2-9199]

**Albion Guest House	**Vancouver BC**
Bill Browning	592 W Nineteenth Ave V5Z 1W6
604-873-2287	

Rates:	Pvt Bath 2	Shared Bath 2	Payment Terms:
Single	$ 110.00 CN	$ 66.00 CN	
Double	$ 110.00 CN	$ 99.00 CN	MC/V

On a quiet tree-lined residential street near city hall is the turn-of-the-century character home with five restful rooms and whose beds are covered with thick feather mattresses, fine cotton linens and down-filled duvets. Imagine yourself sitting in the beautiful sitting room with freshly cut flowers, while relaxing in front of the fireplace, sipping complimentary wine or sherry. At the *Albion Guest House*, we serve a sumptuous breakfast in the formal dining room overlooking the flower garden. Later, you may use one of the complimentary bikes to explore Vancouver on your own. Because we're near city hall, Chinatown and Gastown are just a few minutes away along with the Expo Skytrain; you're just a few minutes walk to gambling casinos, restaurants, specialty coffee shops, delicatessens, theatre and Queen Elizabeth Park. A myriad of attractions and activities are available, including boating, parasailing, windsurfing and health clubs. It's just a 30 minute drive to the famous Capilano Suspension Bridge or to Grouse Mountain, a major ski area with panoramic views of Vancouver. **RESERVATIONS:** Deposit is required to guarantee reservation, one week cancel policy for refund **SEASONAL:** No **PERMITTED:** Drinking **BROCHURE:** Yes **LANGUAGES:** French **DISCOUNTS:** Off-season **AIRPORT:** Vancouver-20 min **PACKAGES:** *Romantic* (Bubble bath, Champagne, Candies and fresh cut flowers) [R09FPCN1-17199]

**Abigails   Victoria BC

Catherine Wollner   906 Mc Clure St V8V 3E7
604-388-5363   **Res Times** 7:30am-10pm

Rates:	Pvt Bath 16	Payment Terms:
Single	$ 90-175.00 CN	Check
Double	$ 90-175.00 CN	MC/V

Following in the tradition of European-style Inns, *Abigails* has been marvelously transformed into a small luxurious hotel. Decorated with soft colours, comfortable furnishings, crystal chandeliers and fresh flowers, you will want to guiltlessly pamper yourself in this romantic ambience . . . All guest rooms have private baths and fluffy goose down comforters. Dream before your crackling fire or relax in a jacuzzi or soaking tub before retiring. Join us in the library each late afternoon for a platter of cheese, fresh fruit and a glass of port before you sample some of the best restaurants in Victoria. In the morning you'll awake to the aroma of fresh coffee and our famous Innkeepers full breakfast. Located just four blocks east of the city centre, we are within strolling distance of Victoria's specialty shops, floral parks and oceanside delights. Ours is a world of intimate charm and pleasure . . . **RESERVATIONS:** Credit card deposit at res time, 48 hr cancel policy for refund, no check-in after 10pm **SEASONAL:** No **BROCHURE:** Yes **PERMITTED:** Children and limited drinking [R08BCCN-6620]

**Beaconsfield Inn   Victoria BC

Hazel Prior   998 Humboldt St V8V 2Z8
604-384-4044   **Res Times** 7:30am-10pm

Rates:	Pvt Bath 12	Payment Terms:
Single	$ 100-196.00 CN	Check
Double	$ 100-196.00 CN	MC/V

In 1905, during the Edwardian Era, **"the height of the British Empire"**, famous architect Samuel McClure was commissioned by RP Rithet to build the *Beaconsfield* for his daughter, Gertrude, as a wedding gift. A gleaming sun room/conservatory, rich mahogany panelling, period antiques, oil paintings, a book-lined library and a cozy kitchen complete the main floor. The guest rooms have their own names, such as Rosebud, Oscar's (after Oscar Wilde), Willie's, Daisy's and Lillie's (named after Lilly Langtree), both mistresses of Edward VII. Each guest room has a private bathroom, goose down comforter and is luxuriously decorated. Some guest rooms include wood-burning fireplaces, clawfoot tubs or jacuzzi baths. Each afternoon join us in the library for a sherry hour where we serve an assortment of cheese, crackers and fresh fruit. The following morning guests awake to the aroma of our special blend coffee and the Innkeeper's famous full breakfast. Located only a few minutes walk from our specialty shops, Beacon Hill Park and the Inner Harbor. *The Beaconsfield Inn*, an experience that will linger in your memory - **RESERVATIONS:** Credit card deposit, 48 hr cancel policy, no check-in after 10pm **SEASONAL:** No **BROCHURE:** Yes **PERMITTED:** Children, limited drinking [Z11CPCN1-6619]

**Rose Cottage B&B	**Victoria BC**
Robert & Shelley Bishop	3059 Washington Ave V9A 1P7
604-381-5985	

Rates:	**Shared Bath** 4	**Payment Terms:**
Single	$ 70-80.00 CN	
Double	$ 70-80.00 CN	MC/V

Victoria's oldest Bed and Breakfast, *Rose Cottage* is a 1912 traditional Victorian home carefully restored to retain all of the **Heritage** features of the turn-of-the-century Victoria. *Rose Cottage* has high ceilinged rooms, period furniture, guest parlor in a nautical theme, a large dining room with library and quiet, well-appointed bedrooms. Your hosts, Robert and Shelley, are part of the character of the *Rose Cottage*. We have travelled extensively before settling in Victoria and know the value of a warm welcome for our visitors. Located on a quiet street close to downtown, guests are just a few blocks from the beautiful Gorge Park Water-way. A full course complimentary breakfast includes fresh fruit and muffins. We have lots of inside info about Victoria to make your visit as adventuresome or as relaxing as you wish. **RESERVA-TIONS:** First night's deposit or credit card number to guarantee reservation **PERMITTED:** Children, drinking **BROCHURE:** Yes **LANGUAGES:** Canadian and American **DISCOUNTS:** Yes **AIR-PORT:** Victoria Intl-10 mi [R07FPCN1-9114]

*Blomidon Inn	**Wolfville NS**
*Jim Laceby	127 Main St B0P 1X0
902-542-2291	

Rates:	Pvt Bath 25	Shared Bath 2	Payment Terms:
Single	$ 61-88.00 CN	$ 39.00 CN	AE/MC/V
Double	$ 72-99.00 CN	$ 49.00 CN	**Fax** 902-542-7461

Situated only an hour's drive from Halifax International Airport is this elegant mansion built in the 1870s by Capt Rufus Burgess. Capt Burgess made his fortune in the glorious days of sailing as a shipbuilder and sea captain. Today his home has been beautifully restored offering 27 elegant rooms (many with handmade quilts and four-poster beds) and two dining rooms and parlours, complete with fireplaces. Nestled near the world's highest tides in a micro-climate that enables the Valley to have a worldwide recognition for its apples and grape harvests! Nearby guests find Grande Pre National Park, the setting for Longfellow's *Evangeline*. A continental breakfast is included with other gourmet entrees offered in the restaurant on the premises. **RESERVATIONS:** Deposit required within 14 days of booking, with 48 hr cancel policy for refund **SEASONAL:** No **BROCHURE:** Yes **PERMITTED:** Children, drinking, smoking [E11BCCN-8785]

Albert NB
FLORENTINE
MANOR
506-882-2271

Allen SK
MOLDENHAUERS
B&B
306-257-3578

Alma NB
CAPTAIN'S INN
506-887-2017

Alton ON
HORSESHOE INN
519-927-5779

Amherst NS
AMHERST SHORE
INN
902-667-4800

**Annapolis Royal
NS**
BREAD & ROSES
902-532-5727

CHESHIRE CAT
902-532-2100

GARRISON HOUSE
902-532-5750

MILFORD HOUSE
902-532-2617

POPLAR B&B
902-532-7936

QUEEN ANNE INN
902-532-7850

Antigohsih NS
OLD MANSE INN
902-863-5696

**Augustine Cover
PE**
SHORE FARM B&B
902-855-2871

Baie St Paul QE
LA MAISON OTIS
418-435-2255

Bamfield BC
AGUILAR HOUSE
604-728-3323

Bayfield ON
LITTLE INN OF
BAYFIELD
519-565-2611

Belfast PE
LINDEN LODGE
902-659-2716

Beresford NB
LES PEUPLIERS
506-546-5271

Blackstock ON
LANDFALL FARM
416-986-5588

Blaine Lake SK
VERESHAGINS
COUNTRY B&B
306-497-2782

Bonshaw PE
CHURCHILL FARM
902-675-2481

Bracebridge ON
HOLIDAY HOUSE
INN
705-645-2245

Brackley Beach PE
SHAWS

COTTAGE
902-672-2022

Bradford ON
COUNTRY GUEST
HOME
416-775-3576

Braeside ON
GLENROY FARM
613-432-6248

Brentwood Bay BC
BRENTWOOD BAY
B&B
604-652-2012

Bulyea SK
HILLCREST
HOTEL
306-725-4874

Caledon East ON
CALEDON INN
416-584-2891

Campbell River BC
APRIL POINT
LODGE
604-285-2222

CAMPBELL
RIVER LODGE
800-663-7212

DOGWOODS
604-287-4213

Camrose AL
NORDBYE HOUSE
403-672-8131

Canning
1850 HOUSE
902-582-3052

Cap-a-l'Aigle QE
AUBERGE LA
PINSONNIERE
418-665-4431

Cape Breton NS
RIVERSIDE INN
902-235-2002

Carleton Place ON
OTTAWA
VALLEY B&B
613-257-7720

Centreville NB
REIDS FARM HOME
506-276-4787

CH Trudel QE
OTTER LAKE HAUS
819-687-2767

Charlevoix QE
LA PINSONNIERE
418-665-4431

Charlottetown PE
JUST FOLKS B&B
902-569-2089

Chemainns BC
GRANTS
604-246-3768

Chester NS
MCNEIL MANOR
B&B
902-275-4638

Cobourg ON
NORTHUMBER-
LAND HEIGHTS INN
416-372-7500

Coin duBacn-Perce QE
AUBERGE LE COIN

DU BANC
418-645-2907

Collingwood NS
COBEQUID HILLS
COUNTRY INN
902-686-3381

Como QE
WILLOW INN
514-458-7006

Comte de Mantane QE
AUBERGE LA
MARTRE
418-288-5533

Cookstown ON
CHESTNUT INN
705-458-9751

Cornwall PR
OBANLEA TOURIST
HOME
902-566-3067

Corwan PE
CHEZ HOUS B&B
902-566-2779

Cranmore AL
COUGAR CREEK
INN
403-678-4751

Cte Matapedia QE
GITE DU
PASSANT
418-775-5237

Darthmouth NS
MARTIN HOUSE
B&B
902-469-1896

Denman Island BC

DENMAN
ISLAND INN
604-335-2688

Digby County NS
HARBOUR VIEW
INN
902-245-5686

Downsview ON
SCHWEIZER
LODGE
514-538-2123

Duncan BC
NORTH PACIFIC
SPRINGS
604-748-3189

Duncan Island BC
FAIRBURN FARM
604-746-4637

Dunham QE
MAPLEWOOD
514-295-2519

Eagle Creek BC
BRADSHAW'S
LODGE
604-397-2416

Elora ON
PENSTOCK INNS
LTD
519-846-5356

Fergus ON
BREADELBANE INN
519-843-4770

Fort Steele BC
WILD HORSE FARM
604-426-6000

Frederickton AL
BACKPORCH B&B

506-454-6875

Gabriola Island BC
SURF LODGE
604-247-9231

Galiano Island BC
HUMMINGBIRD INN
604-539-5472

LA BERENGERIE
609-539-5392

Gaspe Peninsula QE
HOTEL LA
NORMANDIE
418-782-2112

Gaspesie QE
HENRY HOUSE
418-534-2115

Georgeville QE
GEORGEVILLE
COUNTRY INN
819-843-8683

Gores Landing ON
VICTORIA INN
416-342-3261

Grand Manan Isl NB
SHORECREST
LODGE
506-662-3216

Grand Manan NB
CROSS TREE
GUEST HOUSE
506-662-8663

FERRY WHARF INN
506-662-8588

GRAND HARBOUR
INN
506-662-8681

Granville Ferry NS
BAYBERRY HOUSE
902-532-2272

SHINING TIDES
B&B
902-532-2770

Guysborough NS
LIMBSCOMBE
LODGE
902-779-2307

Halfmoon Bay BC
LORD JIM'S HOTEL
604-885-7038

Halifax NS
APPLE BASKET
B&B
902-429-3019

****HALLIBURTON
HOUSE INN**
902-420-0658

QUEEN STREET
INN
902-422-9828

Hampstead NB
EVELEIGH
HOTEL
506-425-9993

Hartland NB
WOODSVIEW II
B&B
506-375-4637

Hebron NS
MANOR INN

902-742-2487

Hopewell Cape NB
DUTCH TREAT B&B
506-882-2552

Hornby Island BC
SEA BREEZE INN
604-335-2321

Howick QE
HAZELBRAE FARM
514-825-2390

Huntington St Anicet
LEDUC
514-264-6533

Iona NS
HIGHLAND
HEIGHTS INN

Iroquois ON
CEDARLANE FARM
613-652-4267

Jackson Point ON
BRIARS INN &
COUNTRY CLUB
800-465-2376

Kamourasha QE
GITE DU
PASSANT B&B
418-492-2921

Kelowna BC
BLAIR HOUSE
604-762-5090

GABLES
COUNTRY INN
604-768-4468

Kensington PE

Canada

BEACH POINT VIEW
INN
902-836-5260

BLAKENEYS B&B
902-836-3254

MURPHYS SEA
VIEW INN
902-836-5456

SHERWOOD ACRES
902-836-5430

WOODINGTONS
COUNTRY INN
902-836-5518

Kingston ON
PRINCE GEORGE
HOTEL
613-549-5440

Kleena Kleene BC
CHILANKO
RESORT
604-553-3625

Knowlton QE
AUBERGE
LAKETREE
514-243-6604

Ladysmith BC
MANANA LODGE
604-245-2312

YELLOW POINT
LODGE
604-245-7422

Lansdowne ON
IVYLEA INN
613-659-2329

Little York PE
DALVAY BY THE

SEA
902 672-2048

Lle d Orleans QE
CHEZ LES DUMAS
418-828-9442

MANOR DE L'ANSE
418-828-2248

London ON
ROSE B&B
519-433-9978

Lousibourg NS
GRETA CROSS B&B
902-733-2833

Lower Bedeque PE
WAUGHS B&B
902-887-2320

Mabou NS
CAPE BRETON
ISLAND FARM
902-945-2077

Mactaquac NB
MACTAQUAC B&B
506-363-3630

Marshfield PE
ROSEVALE FARM
902-894-7821

May River AL
HABOR HOUSE
403-874-2233

Mayne Isl BC
OCEANWOOD
COUNTRY INN
604-539-5074

Mayne Island BC
FERNHILL LODGE
604-539-2544

GINGERBREAD
HOUSE
604-539-3133

Maynooth ON
BEA'S B&B HOUSE
613-338-2239

McKeller ON
INN & TENNIS
CLUB/MANITOU
416-967-3466

Merrickville ON
SAM JAKES INN
613-269-3711

Mill Bay BC
PINELODGE B&B
604-743-4083

Millarville AL
MESA CREEK
RANCH
403-931-3573

Millet AL
BROADVIEW FARM
403-387-4963

Minden ON
MINDEN HOUSE
705-286-3263

Mont Tremblant QE
AUBERGE
SAUVIGNON
819-425-2658

CHATEAU
BEAUVALLON
819-425-7275

Montague PE
BRYDONS B&B
902-838-4717

Montreal East QE
LE BRETON
514-52-7273

Montreal ON
*MANOIR AMBROSE

Montreal QE
ARMOR INN
514-285-0894

Morris BC
DEERBANK FARM
204-746-8395

Murray Harbor PE
HARBOURVIEW
B&B
902-962-2565

Murray River PE
BAYBERRY CLIFF
INN
902-962-3395

**Musquodoboit
Harbor NS**
CAMELOT
902-889-2198

Nanoose Bay BC
THE LOOKOUT
604-468-9796

Nanton AL
TIMBERIDGE
HOMESTEAD
403-646-5683

Nelson BC
HERITAGE INN
604-352-5331

Nelson NB
GOVERNOR'S
MANSION

506-622-3036

New Brunswick NB
HAPPY APPLE
ACRES

New Hanburg ON
WATERLOT INN
519-662-2020

Newboro ON
STERLING LODGE
613-272-2435

**Niagara On Lake
ON**
ANGEL INN
416-468-3411

KIELY HOUSE
HERITAGE INN
416-468-4588

MOFFAT INN
416-468-4116

OBAN INN
416-468-2165

OLD BANK HOUSE

Nine Mile Creek PE
LAINE ACRES B&B
902-675-2402

Nobel ON
PAINES B&B
705-342-9266

Normandale ON
UNION HOTEL
519-426-5568

North Sydney NS
ANNFIELD
TOURIST MANOR

902-736-8770

**North Vancouver
BC**
**ALBION GUEST
HOUSE**
604-873-2287

GROUSE MTN B&B
604-986-9630

HELENS B&B
604-985-4869

LABURNUM
COTTAGE
604-988-4877

PLATTS B&B
604-987-4100

VICTORIAN B&B
604-985-1523

Norwich ON
WILLI-JOY FARM
B&B
519-424-2113

Okotoks AL
WILDFLOWER
COUNTRY

Ottawa ON
ALBERT HOUSE
800-267-1982

**AUSTRALIS
GUEST HOUSE**
613-235-8461

BEATRICE LYON
HOUSE
613-236-3904

BLUE SPRUCE B&B

613-236-8521

CARTIER HOUSE
INN
613-236-INNS

CONSTANCE
HOUSE
613-235-8888

DORAL INN
HOTEL
613-230-8055

FLORA HOUSE
613-230-2152

GASTHAUS
SWITZERLAND
613-237-0335

GWENS GUEST
HOUSE
613-737-4129

HAYDON HOUSE
613-230-2697

MCGEES INN

RIDEAU VIEW INN
613-236-9309

WESTMINSTER
GUEST HOUSE
613-729-2707

Owen Sound ON
MOSES SUNSET
B&B
519-371-4559

Parson BC
TALISIN GUEST
HOUSE
604-348-2247

Pender Island BC
CORBETT HOUSE
604-629-6305

Penticton BC
ROSE COTTAGE
B&B
604-492-3462

Pentifcton BC
TINA'S TUC INN
604-492-3366

Perth ON
PERTH MANOR
519-271-7129

Pictou NS
L'AUBERGE
902-485-6900

Plaster Rock NB
NORTHERN
WILDERNESS
LODGE
506-356-8327

Plympton NS
WESTWAY INN
902-837-4097

Pointe-Au-Oic QE
AUBERGE
DONOHUE
418-665-4377

Port Carling ON
SHERWOOD INN
705-765-3131

Port Dufferin NS
*MARQUIE
DUFFERIN
SEASIDE INN

Port Renfrerw BC
FEATHERED

PADDLE
604-647-5433

Port Severn ON
ARROWWOOD
LODGE
705-538-2354

Port Stanley ON
KETTLE CREEK INN
519-782-3388

Port Williams NS
PLANTER'S
BARRACKS
902-542-7879

Portneuf QE
EDALE PLACE
418-286-3168

FRANCE BEAULIEU
HOUSE
418-336-2724

Pugwash NS
BLUE HERON INN
902-243-2900

*Quathiaski Cove
BC*
TSA-KWA-LUTEN
LODGE
800-665-7745

Quebec City QE
AU CHATEAU
FLEUR
DE LIS
418-694-1884

AU MANOIR STE
GENEVIEVE
418-694-1666

AUBERGE DE LA
CHOUTTE

418-694-0232

CHATEAU DE LA
TERRASSE
418-694-9472

LE CHATEAU
DE PIERRE
418-694-0429

MAISON
MARIE-ROLLET
418-694-9271

Guyon QE
MEMORYLANE
FARM
819-458-2479

Regina SK
TURGEON INTL
B&B
306-522-4200

Riverside NB
CAILSWICK
BABBLING BROOK
506-882-2079

Rockport ON
AMARYLLIS
HOUSEBOAT B&B
613-659-3513

Rossland BC
RAMS HEAD INN
604-362-9577

Rothesay NB
SHADOW LAWN
COUNTRY INN
506-847-7539

Sackville NB
MARSHLANDS INN
506-536-0170

Salmon Arm BC
CINDOSA B&B INN
604-832-3342

SILVER CREEK
GUEST HOUSE
604-832-8870

Salt Spring Isl BC
HASTINGS HOUSE
800-661-9255

Seebe AL
BREWSTERS
KANANASKIS
RANCH
403-673-3737

Sooke BC
HARBOUR HOUSE
800-665-7745

Souix Narrows ON
YELLOWBIRD
LODGE
807-226-5279

St Andrews NB
PANSY PATCH B&B
506-529-3834

PUFF INN
506-529-4191

SHIRETOWN INN
506-529-8877

**St Anne De Mont
QE**
GITE DU MONT
ALBERT
800-463-0860

St Antoine Tilly QE
AUBERGE MANOIR
DE TILLY

418-886-2407

St Jacobs ON
JACOBSTETTEL
GUEST HOUSE
519-664-2208

St Laurent QE
MAISON SOUS LE
ARBRES
418-828-9442

**St Marc Richelieu
QE**
HANDFIELD INN
514-584-2226

**St Roch Aulnaies
QE**
LELLETIER HOUSE
418-354-2450

**St Sauveur des
Monts QE**
AUBERGE ST-
DENIS
514-227-4766

Stanley Bridge PE
CREEKSIDE FARM
B&B
902-886-2713

GULF BREEZE B&B
902-886-2678

Ste Petronille QE
AUBERGE LA
GOELICHE
418-828-2248

Stratford ON
BURNSIDE GUEST
HOME
519-271-7076

Canada

SHREWSBURY
MANOR
519-271-8520

STONE MAIDEN INN
519-271-7129

Summerland BC
THREE PINES
LODGE
604-494-1661

Summerside PE
SILVER FOX INN
902-436-4033

Sussex NB
ANDERSONS
HOLIDAY FARM
506-433-3786

Sutton QE
AUBERGE
SCHWEIZER
514-538-2129

Tantallon NS
SEABRIGHT B&B
902-823-2987

Tingish PE
HARBOUR LIGHTS
902-882-2479

Tisdale SK
PRAIRIE ACRES
B&B
306-873-2272

Tofino BC
CLAYOQUOT
LODGE
604-725-3284

Toronto ON
ASHLEIGH
HERITAGE INN

416-535-4000

****BURKEN GUEST
HOUSE**
416-920-7842

Treherne MA
BEULAH LAND INN
204-723-2828

Tyne Valley PE
WEST ISLAND INN
902-831-2495

Ucluelet BC
BURLEYS LODGE
604-726-4444

**Upper Stewiacke
NS**
LANDSDOWN INN
902-671-2749

Val David QE
AUBERGE DU
VIEUX FOYER
819-322-2686

PARKERS LODGE
819-322-2026

Vancouver BC
****ALBION GUEST
HOUSE**
604-873-2287

DIANA'S B&B
604-321-2855

PENNY
FARTHING INN
604-739-9002

PILLOW'N
PORRIDGE GUEST
HOUSE

ROSE GARDEN
GUEST INN
604-435-7129

VINCENTS GUEST
HOUSE
604-254-7462

WEST END GUEST
INN
604-681-2889

Vernon BC
FIVE JUNIPERS
B&B
604-549-3615

SCHROTH FARM
B&B
604-545-0010

TWIN WILLOWS
604-542-8293

WINDMILL HOUSE
B&B
604-549-2804

Victoria BC
**ABIGAILS
604-388-5363

BATTERY STREET
B&B
604-385-4623

****BEACONSFIELD
INN**
604-384-4044

CAPTAINS
PALACE INN
604-388-9191

CRAIGMYLE B&B
604-595-5411

©Bed & Breakfast Guest Houses & Inns of America, Memphis TN

ELK LAKE LODGE
604-658-8879

HIBERNIA B&B
604-658-5519

OAK BAY BEACH
HOTEL
604-598-4556

OXFORD CASTLE
INN
604-388-6431

PORTAGE INLET
B&B
604-479-4594

*PRIOR HOUSE
B&B

**ROSE
COTTAGE B&B**
604-381-5985

SUNNYMEAD
HOUSE
604-658-1414

TOP O'
TRIANGLE MTN
604-478-7853

TUCHERK'S B&B
604-658-5531

Victoria By Sea PE
VICTORIA
VILLAGE
902-658-2288

Vieux-Quebec QE
AU PETIT HOTEL
418-694-0965

W Vancouver BC

BRAMBLEWYCK BY
THE SEA
604-926-3827

Wallace NS
SENATOR GUEST
HOUSE
902-257-2417

Waterloo QE
PERRAS
514-539-2983

Wawota SK
PLEASANT VISTA
ANGUS FARM
306-739-2915

Weymouth NS
GILBERTS COVE
FARM
902-837-4505

Whistler BC
DURLACHER HOF
604-932-1924

SABEY HOUSE B&B
604-932-3498

Windermere ON
WINDERMERE
HOUSE
705-769-3611

Winnipeg MA
CHESTNUT B&B
204-772-9788

Wolfville NS
BLOMIDON INN
902-542-2291

TATTINGSTONE INN
902-542-7696

VICTORIA
HISTORIC INN
902-542-5744

York PE
AMBER LIGHTS
B&B
902-894-5868

Youngs Point ON
OLD BRIDGE INN
705-652-8507

Note Page

_____

_____

_____

_____

_____

_____

_____

_____

_____

_____

_____

_____

_____

_____

_____

_____

_____

_____

_____

_____

_____

_____

Let the innkeeper know you found them in this publication. Knowing which books are used by guests helps them to plan where to advertise. If you know of a Bed and Breakfast or Country Inn not included in this publcation, tell them about this book so they can become listed in future editions. All innkeepers meeting our general membership guidelines receive a complimentary Index Listing.

Note Page

_____

_____

_____

_____

_____

_____

_____

_____

_____

_____

_____

_____

_____

_____

_____

_____

_____

_____

_____

_____

_____

_____

Let the innkeeper know you found them in this publication. Knowing which books are used by guests helps them to plan where to advertise. If you know of a Bed and Breakfast or Country Inn not included in this publcation, tell them about this book so they can become listed in future editions. All innkeepers meeting our general membership guidelines receive a complimentary Index Listing.

Note Page

_____

_____

_____

_____

_____

_____

_____

_____

_____

_____

_____

_____

_____

_____

_____

_____

_____

_____

_____

_____

_____

_____

Let the innkeeper know you found them in this publication. Knowing which books are used by guests helps them to plan where to advertise. If you know of a Bed and Breakfast or Country Inn not included in this publcation, tell them about this book so they can become listed in future editions. All innkeepers meeting our general membership guidelines receive a complimentary Index Listing.

Note Page

_____

_____

_____

_____

_____

_____

_____

_____

_____

_____

_____

_____

_____

_____

_____

_____

_____

_____

_____

_____

_____

_____

_____

_____

Let the innkeeper know you found them in this publication. Knowing which books are used by guests helps them to plan where to advertise. If you know of a Bed and Breakfast or Country Inn not included in this publcation, tell them about this book so they can become listed in future editions. All innkeepers meeting our general membership guidelines receive a complimentary Index Listing.

Note Page

_____

_____

_____

_____

_____

_____

_____

_____

_____

_____

_____

_____

_____

_____

_____

_____

_____

_____

_____

_____

_____

_____

Let the innkeeper know you found them in this publication. Knowing which books are used by guests helps them to plan where to advertise. If you know of a Bed and Breakfast or Country Inn not included in this publcation, tell them about this book so they can become listed in future editions. All innkeepers meeting our general membership guidelines receive a complimentary Index Listing.

Note Page

_____

_____

_____

_____

_____

_____

_____

_____

_____

_____

_____

_____

_____

_____

_____

_____

_____

_____

_____

_____

_____

_____

Let the innkeeper know you found them in this publication. Knowing which books are used by guests helps them to plan where to advertise. If you know of a Bed and Breakfast or Country Inn not included in this publcation, tell them about this book so they can become listed in future editions. All innkeepers meeting our general membership guidelines receive a complimentary Index Listing.

Note Page

_____

_____

_____

_____

_____

_____

_____

_____

_____

_____

_____

_____

_____

_____

_____

_____

_____

_____

_____

_____

_____

_____

Let the innkeeper know you found them in this publication. Knowing which books are used by guests helps them to plan where to advertise. If you know of a Bed and Breakfast or Country Inn not included in this publication, tell them about this book so they can become listed in future editions. All innkeepers meeting our general membership guidelines receive a complimentary Index Listing.

Note Page

_____

_____

_____

_____

_____

_____

_____

_____

_____

_____

_____

_____

_____

_____

_____

_____

_____

_____

_____

_____

_____

_____

_____

Let the innkeeper know you found them in this publication. Knowing which books are used by guests helps them to plan where to advertise. If you know of a Bed and Breakfast or Country Inn not included in this publcation, tell them about this book so they can become listed in future editions. All innkeepers meeting our general membership guidelines receive a complimentary Index Listing.

Note Page

_____

_____

_____

_____

_____

_____

_____

_____

_____

_____

_____

_____

_____

_____

_____

_____

_____

_____

_____

_____

_____

Let the innkeeper know you found them in this publication. Knowing which books are used by guests helps them to plan where to advertise. If you know of a Bed and Breakfast or Country Inn not included in this publcation, tell them about this book so they can become listed in future editions. All innkeepers meeting our general membership guidelines receive a complimentary Index Listing.

Note Page

_____

_____

_____

_____

_____

_____

_____

_____

_____

_____

_____

_____

_____

_____

_____

_____

_____

_____

_____

_____

_____

_____

_____

_____

_____

Let the innkeeper know you found them in this publication. Knowing which books are used by guests helps them to plan where to advertise. If you know of a Bed and Breakfast or Country Inn not included in this publcation, tell them about this book so they can become listed in future editions. All innkeepers meeting our general membership guidelines receive a complimentary Index Listing.

Note Page

_____

_____

_____

_____

_____

_____

_____

_____

_____

_____

_____

_____

_____

_____

_____

_____

_____

_____

_____

_____

_____

_____

Let the innkeeper know you found them in this publication. Knowing which books are used by guests helps them to plan where to advertise. If you know of a Bed and Breakfast or Country Inn not included in this publcation, tell them about this book so they can become listed in future editions. All innkeepers meeting our general membership guidelines receive a complimentary Index Listing.

Bed & Breakfast Inn Arizona

 ## Arizona Accommodation Reservations

• Inns • Bed & Breakfasts • Hotels
• Resorts • Dude Ranches
• Vacant Apartments & Condos
Throughout Arizona

Phoenix, Scottsdale, Sedona, Prescott, Flagstaff,
Grand Canyon, Lake Powell, Mounment Valley,
Canyon de Chelly, White Mountains, Bisbee,
Tombstone, Tucson and more!

Discounts on Self-drive, Unlimited Milage Auto Rentals

Tel: 602-561-0335   Fax: 602-561-2300

Bed & Breakfast Inn Arizona
PO Box 11253 Glendale, Arizona 85318 - USA

Master Card VISA American Express Accepted

A Real Member Benefit

With the LDDS *Association Savers™ Program*, your membership in this organization qualifies you for a special discounted rate on all long distance calls - one that's even lower than our standard rates, which are already less than AT&T, MCI and Sprint.

LDDS is the nation's fourth largest long distance company, with a fiber optic network that provides access to the United States and the world. And an array of business and residential services, from outbound long distance to 800 service to world wide calling cards, all backed by superb customer service.

We'll switch you over from your current long distance service *free*! So call us today. Start saving tomorrow.

Call 800-741-1993 for savings.

InnTravel™ Club

The Bed & Breakfast Collection™ is a national association for innkeepers and guests too, with the introduction of the first frequent B&B guest travel program - the *InnTravel Club™*. Members earn free stays, gifts, trips and plane trips when staying at member Bed & Breakfast's located across the USA! In addition, members receive discounts on thousands of products and services.

Look for member B&B's - begin earning free gifts with every stay! Tell your favorite innkeeper about the program too - so they can join - helping you to earn free trips, stays and prizes with each stay. Join *InnTravel Club™* today by sending your name, address, phone number for all of the details and your membership card. Membership benefits include:

- Trip Routing
- Travel Information
- Newsletter
- Quality Assurance
- CD Rom & Online

- *InnTravel Club™*
- Gifts and Prizes
- Car Rental Discounts
- Travel Discounts
- Product Discounts

THE BED & BREAKFAST COLLECTION™
A Division of DSI Inc

PO Box 38929   Memphis, Tennessee 38183-0929